BOARDROOM SCANDAL

Boardroom Scandal

The Criminalization of Company Fraud in Nineteenth-Century Britain

JAMES TAYLOR

OXFORD
UNIVERSITY PRESS

OXFORD
UNIVERSITY PRESS

Great Clarendon Street, Oxford, OX2 6DP,
United Kingdom

Oxford University Press is a department of the University of Oxford.
It furthers the University's objective of excellence in research, scholarship,
and education by publishing worldwide. Oxford is a registered trade mark of
Oxford University Press in the UK and in certain other countries

First Edition published in 2013
Impression: 2

British Library Cataloguing in Publication Data
Data available

ISBN 978–0–19–969579–9

Printed in Great Britain
CPI Group (UK) Ltd, Croydon, CR0 4YY

For Marianne

Contents

Acknowledgements

Although I had planned to write a book on company fraud for some time, I only started serious work on it after moving to Lancaster University, and I am grateful to the History Department for granting me relief from teaching and study leave which helped me to get the book completed. I would also like to thank the British Academy for awarding me a Small Grant in 2007 (SG-46863), which paid for Peter Yeandle to research and photocopy some of the material on which this book is based. I was hugely impressed by just how much Peter managed to track down in a limited space of time.

I am grateful to Liz Fawcett and Helen Clish at Lancaster University Library, John Weedy at www.iln.org.uk, Nicholas Hiley at the British Cartoon Archive, and staff at the British Library—Euston and Colindale branches—for providing scans of the illustrations used in this book. I would like to thank the British Library for permission to reproduce their images, and also Colin Heath for permission to reproduce his grandfather's illustration, 'The Devil-fish of To-day'. Thanks also to Sarah Williams at the Museum of London for putting me in touch with Colin.

I am indebted to Martin Daunton, Paddy Ireland, and David Sugarman for reading the initial book proposal, and to Michael Lobban, Roger Ryan, David Sugarman, and John Turner for reading draft chapters; I am certain that all their suggestions improved the end result enormously. Equally, OUP's readers who commented on the original proposal and the final manuscript were very perceptive and helpful. My thanks also go to Christopher Wheeler and Stephanie Ireland at OUP for being so supportive throughout.

Above all, I would like to thank Marianne Blaauboer. As well as reading the whole manuscript and discussing its subject with me at great length, she has been generous with her love and good cheer (even though the process of writing meant fewer holidays than she would have liked). Without her, this book would probably have been published in 2023 not 2013. I dedicate it to her with love and thanks.

List of Illustrations

List of Abbreviations

DPP	Director of Public Prosecutions
ER	*English Reports*
LR	*Law Reports*
LT	*Law Times*
OBP	*Old Bailey Proceedings*
ODNB	*Oxford Dictionary of National Biography*
PP	*Parliamentary Papers*
POSB	Post Office Savings Bank
RBS	Royal Bank of Scotland
TNA	The National Archives

1

Introduction: Company Fraud in Historical Perspective

On Christmas Eve 1862, a shoemaker's apprentice named Charles Gardner strolled into his local butcher's shop in Hull to change a five-pound note for his employer. Gardner had often come into the shop on errands and the butcher, who was busy with other customers, thought little about taking the note, which he did not look at closely, and providing four sovereigns and a pound of silver. The next morning, when he took out the note, he received a nasty surprise. At first glance, he thought it was a Lloyd's Bank note, but when he put his glasses on, he was astonished to find that it was issued by the 'Lovers Banking Company', and bore the text 'I promise to pay to you on demand the entire love of the applicant who sends this'. He marched over to the shoemaker, a respectable man and a local lay preacher, and showed him the note. The shoemaker had not seen it before, and doubted that his apprentice—'a very pious lad' of 19—could have had anything to do with it. When confronted, Gardner denied all knowledge, so the butcher prosecuted him for obtaining money by false pretences. The case came to trial at Hull borough sessions the following spring. The prosecution called two witnesses who testified that they had also received 'love notes' from Gardner; one said that Gardner also manufactured notes on behalf of the 'Bank of Elegance'. Hearing this, the jury found the apprentice guilty, and he was sentenced to seven months' imprisonment.[1]

In the nineteenth century, Britain's rapidly developing economy generated many new opportunities for swindling. Some of them, like Gardner's deception, the legal system proved competent to deal with. Obtaining 'by any false Pretence... any Chattel, Money or valuable Security, with Intent to defraud' had been a crime since 1757, and the statute was sufficiently flexible to reach a variety of offences.[2] Often, the main sticking point was proving the *mens rea*, the guilty mind, but in a case such as Gardner's, where several people had been given notes which could have no conceivable monetary value, this was not so difficult. If the law recognized what Gardner did as a crime, the machinery for seeing it applied to him was also adequate. Unlike Scotland and Ireland which both had systems of public

[1] *Reg. v. Gardner* (1863), *Hull Packet*, 17 April 1863. Although criminal actions were taken in the name of the Crown (hence '*Reg. v. Gardner*'), 'they were viewed, in political ideology as well as in law, as adversarial proceedings between private individuals': Douglas Hay and Francis Snyder, 'Using the Criminal Law, 1750–1850: Policing, Private Prosecution, and the State', in Douglas Hay and Francis Snyder (eds), *Policing and Prosecution in Britain, 1750–1850* (Oxford, 1989), 35.

[2] The wording is from the 1861 Larceny Act, which was very similar to the original act of 1757.

prosecution, English law placed the onus on injured parties to prosecute.[3] Though a small number of cases, usually involving sedition or treason, were prosecuted by the Attorney General, and coining offences could be taken up by the Treasury Solicitor, the vast majority of prosecutions were private.[4] In this case, the angry butcher proved willing and able to perform this role and obtain a verdict against the youth who had defrauded him.

However, economic development also threw up more complex and multifaceted types of deception which the law dealt with less convincingly. Many of these were associated with the rise of the joint-stock company.[5] Adopted in order to finance large infrastructural projects such as canals and railways, and schemes requiring large numbers of investors to spread risk, like banks and insurance companies, the joint-stock company was a mixed blessing. Whilst it undoubtedly facilitated economic development, which contemporaries were rarely slow to acknowledge, it also presented many opportunities for abuse, due to the division of ownership and control between shareholders on one hand and managers and boards of directors on the other. Because directors were looking after other people's money rather than their own, their oversight of employees was sometimes lax, which encouraged embezzlement. Because control was vested in paid managers, these managers often pursued policies that benefited their own interests rather than their shareholders. Because company shares were usually publicly traded, maintaining confidence was essential, which created incentives for concealing losses, even insolvency, from shareholders and the wider public. This could lead boards to present false balance sheets, and to declare dividends out of capital rather than profits.[6]

These new kinds of offences were assimilated with a traditional vocabulary. Just as the term 'corruption' was used to describe a host of evils in the political sphere, from unfair tax systems and sinecures to restricted franchises and electoral malpractices, so 'fraud' served as an umbrella term in the economic sphere. Derived from the Latin word 'fraus', meaning deceit or deception, the label was applied to a range of financial misdeeds in the joint-stock economy. But linguistic assimila-

[3] Hay and Snyder, 'Criminal Law', 28–9; John McEldowney, 'Crown Prosecutions in Nineteenth-Century Ireland', in Hay and Snyder, *Policing and Prosecution.*

[4] Hay and Snyder, 'Criminal Law'; Clive Emsley, *Crime and Society in England, 1750–1900* (2nd edn, Harlow, 1996), 178.

[5] The history of the joint-stock company has been the subject of a significant upswing in scholarly attention over the past fifteen years. Historians have examined companies as forms of business organization, as political entities, as subjects of literature, and as vehicles for investment. These works have enhanced our appreciation of the economic and cultural significance of the company in the nineteenth century, but most of them touch only tangentially on the subject of fraud. Leaving articles and chapters aside, the major books include: Timothy L. Alborn, *Conceiving Companies: Joint-Stock Politics in Victorian England* (London, 1998); Ron Harris, *Industrializing English Law: Entrepreneurship and Business Organization, 1720–1844* (Cambridge, 2000); James Taylor, *Creating Capitalism: Joint-Stock Enterprise in British Politics and Culture, 1800–1870* (Woodbridge, 2006); Rob McQueen, *A Social History of Company Law: Great Britain and the Australian Colonies, 1854–1920* (Farnham, 2009); Ranald C. Michie, *Guilty Money: The City of London in Victorian and Edwardian Culture, 1815–1914* (London, 2009); Paul Johnson, *Making the Market: Victorian Origins of Corporate Capitalism* (Cambridge, 2010); Mark Freeman, Robin Pearson, and James Taylor, *Shareholder Democracies? Corporate Governance in Britain and Ireland before 1850* (Chicago, IL, 2012).

[6] G. R. Searle, *Morality and the Market in Victorian Britain* (Oxford, 1998), 78–81.

tion was one thing, legal assimilation another. These practices might be frowned upon, but were they actually illegal? If they were, would there be anyone willing and able to set the law in motion against the perpetrators when unlimited shareholder liability meant that victims of company frauds could lose everything they possessed?

These were not trivial questions, for company fraud was anything but a peripheral feature of Victorian life. Countless thousands were touched personally, as shareholders, as depositors in banks and building societies, as policyholders in insurance companies, as employees, and as contributors to relief funds for the victims of fraud. A handful of the most notorious wrongdoers, such as George Hudson, John Sadleir, and Jabez Balfour, together with their fictional analogues such as Mr Merdle and Augustus Melmotte, are still well known and continue to attract the attention of biographers and television dramatists.[7] But whereas the history of corruption has been explored in great detail, with the battle against 'Old Corruption' now established as a central feature of nineteenth-century political narratives, the study of fraud in this period has lagged behind.[8]

CAPITALISM AND THE LAW

Indeed, when it comes to exploring the relationship between the development of capitalism and the law, eighteenth-century historians have been more active than their nineteenth-century counterparts.[9] At the heart of their accounts is the rise of the so-called 'bloody code'—the mass of laws passed by the legislature swelling the number of penal crimes on the statute books. Historians such as E. P. Thompson and Douglas Hay, influenced by Marxist conceptions of the law as an instrument of class oppression, believed that these statutes, many of which defended new forms of property, were designed to foster capitalist development and maintain the subjugation of the labouring poor.[10] Yet others have criticized this functionalist view of the law, rejecting the idea 'that the criminal law was the instrument of any single interest or class'.[11] The vast majority of property crimes did not come before the courts but were resolved by extra-legal and 'informal sanctioning systems' applied by kin, community, religious, or other social networks. When the criminal

[7] A. J. Arnold and S. McCartney, *George Hudson: The Rise and Fall of the Railway King: A Study in Victorian Entrepreneurship* (London, 2004); James O'Shea, *Prince of Swindlers: John Sadleir M.P. 1813–1856* (Dublin, 1999); David McKie, *Jabez: The Rise and Fall of a Victorian Rogue* (rev. repr., London, 2005). *Little Dorrit* (BBC1, 2008) [drama] and *The Way We Live Now* (BBC1, 2001) [drama], featuring Merdle and Melmotte respectively, continue to receive the BBC treatment.

[8] The key text in this revival of interest in 'Old Corruption' is Philip Harling, *The Waning of Old Corruption: The Politics of Economical Reform in Britain, 1779–1846* (Oxford, 1996).

[9] Peter King, *Crime, Justice, and Discretion in England, 1740–1820* (Oxford, 2000), 3.

[10] E. P. Thompson, *Whigs and Hunters: The Origin of the Black Act* (London, 1975); Douglas Hay, et al., *Albion's Fatal Tree: Crime and Society in Eighteenth-Century England* (London, 1976).

[11] Joanna Innes and John Styles, 'The Crime Wave: Recent Writing on Crime and Criminal Justice in Eighteenth-Century England', in Adrian Wilson (ed.), *Rethinking Social History: English Society 1570–1920 and its Interpretation* (Manchester, 1993), 249.

law was invoked—which was a decision not for government officials but the victims themselves—it was less a tool of oppression than a process of accommodation between the different social groups involved.[12]

This point applies all the more when we switch from inter-class to intra-class disputes—particularly within the middle class—which are far less-studied.[13] Nearly thirty years ago, David Sugarman and G. R. Rubin warned against the assumption that legal structures fostered economic development in industrializing Britain, and underlined the lack of 'substantial *empirical* analysis' into the relationship between law and business.[14] Accounts which present the law as handmaiden to business interests are inadequate, not least because the nineteenth-century legal profession 'cannot be seen as some homogenous entity pursuing a consistent policy of support for one set of ideals rather than another . . . it could not be identified with any particular school of thought'.[15] The relationship between commerce and the law also resists easy generalization because, as Weber pointed out, 'modern capitalism prospers equally . . . under legal systems containing rules and institutions which considerably differ from each other'.[16] There is 'no single "capitalist" form of law'; a point not lost on scholars who have explored the law of private nuisances.[17] These disputes, often centring on industrial pollution, or in the famous case of *The Mayor, Aldermen and Burgesses of the Borough of Bradford v. Pickles* (1895), the right of an individual to divert water flowing through his land to force a neighbour to buy at an inflated price, involved collisions between monied groups, such as water companies, industrialists, landowners, and municipal corporations.[18] Using simplistic concepts of 'capitalist' forms of law to analyse such cases is entirely inadequate. The same can be said of the joint-stock economy. What would a 'pro-capitalist' form of law look like here: one that turned a blind eye to directorial misbehaviour? Or one that punished it in defence of capitalist investors?

Something of the complexity of legal disputes between stakeholders in the joint-stock economy is conveyed in excellent work on civil litigation arising from the emergence of the company in the nineteenth century.[19] The role played by the

[12] King, *Crime, Justice, and Discretion*, 10, 371.

[13] David Sugarman and G. R. Rubin, 'Towards a New History of Law and Material Society in England, 1750–1914', in G. R. Rubin and David Sugarman (eds), *Law, Economy and Society, 1750–1914: Essays in the History of English Law* (Abingdon, 1984), 64–5.

[14] Ibid. 4.

[15] R. Cocks, 'Victorian Barristers, Judges and Taxation: A Study in the Expansion of Legal Work', in Rubin and Sugarman (eds), *Law, Economy and Society*, 467.

[16] Quoted in Sugarman and Rubin, 'Towards a New History', 115.

[17] Ibid. See also Innes and Styles, 'Crime Wave', 219.

[18] A. W. B. Simpson, *Victorian Law and the Industrial Spirit* (London, 1995); Michael Taggart, *Private Property and Abuse of Rights in Victorian England: The Story of Edward Pickles and the Bradford Water Supply* (Oxford, 2002); Joshua Getzler, *A History of Water Rights at Common Law* (Oxford, 2004).

[19] Paddy Ireland, 'Capitalism without the Capitalist: The Joint Stock Company Share and the Emergence of the Modern Doctrine of Separate Corporate Personality', *Legal History*, 17 (1996), 40–72; R. W. Kostal, *Law and English Railway Capitalism, 1825–1875* (rev. repr., Oxford, 1997); Michael Lobban, 'Nineteenth Century Frauds in Company Formation: *Derry v. Peek* in Context', *Law Quarterly Review*, 112 (1996), 287–334; Lobban, 'Commercial Morality'.

criminal courts in such disputes, however, is hazier.[20] In the only book until now on nineteenth-century company fraud, George Robb argued that lawyers and legislators failed to rise to the challenges posed by the spread of fraudulent financial dealings, with company directors and managers accused of bad behaviour rarely punished. He attributes this inertness to the impact of laissez-faire ideas, and in particular to the class bias which pervaded law and politics: whereas light-fingered labourers and pilfering clerks felt the full force of the criminal law, company directors were not jailed because they were too powerful, or because disgrace was considered ample punishment. Serious attempts to tackle corporate wrongdoing, he argues, did not come until deep into the twentieth century, following Labour's election victory in 1945.[21]

These conclusions complement dominant interpretations of the course of company law in the nineteenth century which see the adoption of an extremely permissive system with few investor protections as the result of a dogmatic commitment to liberal political economy, and the business interests of parliamentarians.[22] And they have been supported and amplified in several shorter studies. Peter Johnstone echoes Robb in arguing that the law struggled to deal with fraud throughout the Victorian period and only provided civil remedies; criminal sanctions were a feature of the twentieth century, he argues.[23] V. A. C. Gatrell notes that while there were criminal prosecutions for embezzlement, 'it was clerks... and not managers or directors who were caught... [f]ew big fish were attended to by policemen' until after 1945.[24] Paul Johnson identifies a transition from harsh treatment of those tainted with fraud in the early nineteenth century—citing the infamous Lord Cochrane scandal of 1814—to a more tolerant attitude by the end of the century, which he ascribes to parliament's embrace of 'the morality of Mammon', and acceptance of fraud as the inevitable price of a dynamic, risk-taking economy.[25] Michael Lobban emphasizes 'the weakness of the criminal sanctions' against fraud, and asserts that criminal prosecutions of company promoters 'were rare indeed; even where they were instituted, the success rate was

[20] Historians of nineteenth-century crime tend to note the problem of company fraud, but only in passing: Emsley, *Crime and Society*, 6–7; Martin J. Wiener, *Reconstructing the Criminal: Culture, Law, and Policy in England, 1830–1914* (Cambridge, 1990), 244–5, 260–1, 310.

[21] George Robb, *White-Collar Crime in Modern England: Financial Fraud and Business Morality, 1845–1929* (Cambridge, 1992), ch. 7. This interpretation owes much to the first wave of sociologists and criminologists to study company fraud in the 1940s. In their view, the history of the fight against commercial fraud 'has been a race between the crook and the lawmaker, in which the latter has mostly played the part of "also ran"': Hermann Mannheim, *Criminal Justice and Social Reconstruction* (1946; repr. London, 2001), 121–2.

[22] For examples of this thesis, see P. L. Cottrell, *Industrial Finance, 1830–1914* (London, 1980); McQueen, *Company Law*; Johnson, *Making the Market*.

[23] Peter Johnstone, 'Serious White Collar Fraud: Historical and Contemporary Perspectives', *Crime, Law & Social Change*, 30 (1999), 107–30.

[24] V. A. C. Gatrell, 'Crime, Authority and the Policeman-State', in F. M. L. Thompson (ed.), *The Cambridge Social History of Britain, 1750–1950*, 3 vols (Cambridge, 1990), iii. 270–1.

[25] Paul Johnson, 'Civilizing Mammon: Laws, Morals and the City in Nineteenth-Century England', in Peter Burke, Brian Harrison, and Paul Slack (eds), *Civil Histories: Essays Presented to Sir Keith Thomas* (Oxford, 2000). These conclusions are further developed in his more recent study: Johnson, *Making the Market*, chs 4, 7.

low'.[26] On the other hand, Sarah Wilson has placed more emphasis on the 'discovery' of commercial crime in mid-century and the moral panic it engendered. She argues that 'the public space provided by the criminal court' began to be used in the mid-Victorian period 'for deliberating degrees of unacceptability and unlawfulness in company promotion and management'.[27]

Taking Wilson's insight as a starting point, this book argues that historians have not taken Victorian fraud trials seriously enough, and consequently we are missing a vital piece of the jigsaw when it comes to the relationship between commercial society and the law in the nineteenth century. In providing for the legitimate and regulated expression of collective disgust, the criminal law can be seen as part of the cement holding society together, as Durkheim observed. Setting the boundaries between criminal and non-criminal behaviour is one of the ways in which a society defines itself both ideologically and morally.[28] Exploring how the criminal law was extended to companies reveals much about how the Victorians dealt with the knotty moral problems engendered by rapid economic development. Criminal law is never a neutral or straightforward response to wrongdoing; rather, it is socially constructed, embodying particular values and interests in specific contexts. To understand it, as Lucia Zedner argues, we need to ask 'why certain activities are deemed criminal and not others and why at some times and not others; who creates the rules and in whose interests; and who enforces them and with what consequences'.[29]

This book asks these questions of companies and the criminal law in the nineteenth century, and the picture that emerges is rather different to the dominant view. By means of an analysis of an unprecedented range of nineteenth-century criminal cases, the book reverses the established trajectory and contends that the state demonstrated a *growing* interest in policing behaviour in the corporate economy in the nineteenth century. At its heart is a hitherto untold account of the process by which fraud was defined and criminalized through the century. Over this period there was profound disagreement as to whether commercial frauds were private affairs between management, shareholders, and creditors, or public matters, which warranted discussion and resolution in the public spaces of press, parliament, and the courts. However, frequent commercial scandals meant that business behaviour was subjected to an increasing level of public scrutiny, with

[26] Michael Lobban, 'Commercial Morality and the Common Law: or, Paying the Price of Fraud in the Later Nineteenth Century', in Margot Finn, Michael Lobban, and Jenny Bourne Taylor (eds), *Legitimacy and Illegitimacy in Nineteenth-Century Law, Literature, and History* (Basingstoke, 2010), 126–7.

[27] Sarah Wilson, 'Law, Morality and Regulation: Victorian Experiences of Financial Crime', *British Journal of Criminology*, 46 (2006), 1079. See also Sarah Wilson, 'In Defence of Respectability: Financial Crime, the "High Art" Criminal and the Language of the Courtroom, 1850–1880', in Ian Inkster (ed.), *The Golden Age: Essays in British Social and Economic History, 1850–1870* (Aldershot, 2000), 199–215.

[28] Lucia Zedner, *Criminal Justice* (Oxford, 2004), 7, 76–7; James A. Colaiaco, *James Fitzjames Stephen and the Crisis of Victorian Thought* (London, 1983), ch. 5; Thomas Max Safley, 'Business Failure and Civil Scandal in Early Modern Europe', *Business History Review*, 83 (2009), 43.

[29] Zedner, *Criminal Justice*, 39–40.

wide-ranging debates on how to define fraud, how to punish it, and, increasingly, whether the state should take on responsibility for criminal prosecutions.

Historians have tended to present debates on the regulation of fraud as a two-sided contest, between 'state' and 'business', with 'business' holding sway in the laissez-faire Victorian era, and the 'state' gradually gaining ground in the collectivist twentieth century. This is a simplification and in this book, battles over regulation are shown to be multi-cornered contests involving government, parliament, lawyers, judges, directors, shareholders, customers, creditors, stock exchanges, chambers of commerce, and the press. Recognizing the diversity of these interest groups helps us to understand the complex ethical and political issues underpinning debates on fraud: negligent and greedy shareholders could be seen as sharing the moral guilt with scheming businessmen; state-sponsored prosecutions would embroil the state in partisan feuds at a time when it was seeking to achieve legitimacy by standing above sectional interests.[30] The tangled web of interests involved, and the resulting moral ambiguity, provides a better explanation than laissez faire or class bias for the diffidence with which the state sometimes dealt with fraud in contrast to other types of crime, such as forgery.[31] To illustrate this, it is worth considering legal responses to commercial transgressions in the early years of capitalist development following the Glorious Revolution.

FRAUD IN THE LONG EIGHTEENTH CENTURY

The prominent place accorded to forgery in the 'bloody code' is well known. No less than 278 separate acts dealing with forgery were passed during George III's reign alone, many inflicting the ultimate punishment.[32] While scholars have recently argued that the idea of a 'bloody code' was the invention of early nineteenth-century reformers and that eighteenth-century law was not as sanguinary as it appeared, the severity with which forgery was treated is nonetheless very striking.[33] Until the late seventeenth century, forgery was a misdemeanour punished by pillory and fine, or a spell of confinement, under an Elizabethan act of 1563. But in 1697, Bank of England paper was protected by a capital statute, a protection subsequently extended piecemeal to other chartered corporations. A general measure followed in 1729 after the vulnerability of private paper credit was exposed by a major scandal the previous year involving an affluent and respectable banker and a clergyman. This was a flexible and open-ended statute which tried to encompass

[30] Harling, *Old Corruption*; Martin Daunton, *Trusting Leviathan: The Politics of Taxation in Britain, 1799–1914* (Cambridge, 2001).

[31] For more on conflict between shareholders and creditors in the wake of fraud, and the role of the state in mediating between them, see James Taylor, 'Company Fraud in Victorian Britain: The Royal British Bank Scandal of 1856', *English Historical Review*, 122 (2007), 700–24.

[32] Randall McGowen, 'Making the "Bloody Code"? Forgery Legislation in Eighteenth-Century England', in Norma Landau (ed.), *Law, Crime and English Society, 1660–1830* (Cambridge, 2004), 122.

[33] Phil Handler, 'Forgery and the End of the "Bloody Code" in Early Nineteenth-Century England', *Historical Journal*, 48 (2005), 683–702.

the full range of paper instruments then in use, and despite the fact that judges were usually intolerant of vagueness in criminal statutes, the measure formed the basis of many successful prosecutions. The protection of private credit was now thought to be in the public interest. As one judge put it, 'Forgery is what concerns every Englishman: as paper-credit is come to that height it is now, the utmost care ought to be taken to preserve that credit'.[34] Therefore, convicted forgers were as unlikely as murderers to receive a pardon, and were more likely to go to the gallows than highway robbers.[35] Though not all forgers were affluent—among the large numbers prosecuted by the Bank of England following the introduction of one and two pound notes in 1797 were several from poor backgrounds—the bulk were from the middle or higher ranks.[36] The importance of protecting credit in the fast developing financial system trumped the influence of class.[37]

Contrast this with legal responses to offences involving the joint-stock company, an important component of this new financial system. There was a series of company booms beginning in the 1690s. The number of companies in existence leapt from eleven to ninety-three from 1689 to 1695; capital investment doubled from £4 million in 1695 to £8 million in 1703, and rose to over £20 million by 1717.[38] But this was not a steady expansion; rather, rapid growth was periodically undercut by dramatic crises often tainted with accusations of foul play. The most famous, of course, was the 'bubble' year of 1720 when shares in the South Sea Company briefly rose to massive premiums on the back of a scheme to consolidate the national debt, stimulating increases in the stock of the other chartered corporations, and prompting the opportunistic formation of nearly 200 smaller companies to cash in on the public's appetite for investment. When confidence sagged, the shares collapsed amidst allegations of market rigs and bribery. But there were other corporate scandals too. The Charitable Corporation was a philanthropic enterprise designed to help the industrious poor by means of cheap loans. Chartered in 1707 with a capital of £30,000, it inflated its capital to £600,000 by repeated share issues, from which the directors benefited personally. Mismanagement, embezzlement, and insider lending undermined the firm until in 1731, John Thomson and George Robinson, the cashier and banker, absconded to France, taking with them large sums of the corporation's money. This triggered the unravelling of further scandals involving the York Buildings Company, the Derwentwater Trust, and, again, the South Sea Company.[39]

[34] Randall McGowen, 'From Pillory to Gallows: The Punishment of Forgery in the Age of the Financial Revolution', *Past & Present*, 165 (1999), 107–40.

[35] Randall McGowen, 'Managing the Gallows: The Bank of England and the Death Penalty, 1797–1821', *Law and History Review*, 25 (2007), 243; Frank McLynn, *Crime and Punishment in Eighteenth-Century England* (1989; repr. London, 2002), 134.

[36] McGowen, 'Managing the Gallows'; Peter King, *Crime, Justice, and Discretion in England, 1740–1820* (Oxford, 2000), 307.

[37] Emsley, *Crime and Society*, 255.

[38] Julian Hoppit, *A Land of Liberty? England, 1689–1727* (Oxford, 2000), 336–7.

[39] Thomas Keymer, 'Parliamentary Printing, Paper Credit, and Corporate Fraud: A New Episode in Richardson's Early Career', *Eighteenth-Century Fiction*, 17 (2005), 183–206; Beverly Lemire, *The Business of Everyday Life: Gender, Practice and Social Politics in England, c. 1600–1900* (Manchester, 2005), ch. 3.

The companies involved in these scandals were incorporated by the state—granted a separate legal personality and other privileges including limited liability by crown charter or parliament, or both and their boards often contained members of parliament. This meant that when abuses in them were discovered, outraged public opinion looked to parliament to act. Parliament was deluged with petitions demanding retribution following the collapse in the value of South Sea stock in 1720; a series of articles in the *London Journal* summed up the public mood: 'Let us pursue to disgrace, destruction, and even death, those who have brought this ruin upon us, let them be ever so great, or ever so many.'[40] And when a scandal was considered sufficiently heinous, parliament responded to public pressure, co-ordinating investigation, interrogation, and punishment. While Walpole was dubbed 'Skreen-Master General' by critics in the aftermath of the South Sea scandal for his efforts to protect some court favourites, many suffered in the witch-hunt which parliament conducted. The papers of the company were seized, the directors required to make a full statement of accounts, and both Houses established enquiries. Parliament ordered the confiscation of a large proportion of each director's estates to help compensate the victims, and they were barred from sitting on the boards of other companies. Directors who were also parliamentarians faced further punishment: four were expelled, and the Chancellor John Aislabie, who was heavily implicated, was also expelled and briefly sent to the Tower of London. Directors who held Crown offices were dismissed.[41] The punishments following the Charitable Corporation scandal were less severe, but still significant. The Commons appointed a committee of investigation, and expelled Robinson, the absconding banker, together with Sir Archibald Grant and Sir Robert Sutton from their ranks; two directors of the Derwentwater Trust suffered the same fate. Expulsions were recognized as rare and damning punishments, and were not repeated until the expulsion of John Wilkes in 1764.[42] Meanwhile diplomats were tasked with trying to discover the whereabouts of Thomson, who was eventually compelled to return, relinquishing most of his spoils.[43] Finally, parliament passed a bill establishing a lottery which raised £80,000 to relieve the corporation's smaller shareholders.[44]

These early corporate scandals precipitated ad hoc solutions from parliament designed to inflict retribution and to appease public opinion. But they did not tend to generate legislation criminalizing the dubious practices which the scandals exposed. The most famous exception—and it was not really an exception at all—was the measure later dubbed the 'Bubble Act' of 1720. Passed not after, as sometimes believed, but at the height of the speculative boom, the act was the result of lobbying by the South Sea Company which sought to channel investment into its own scheme at the expense of the smaller companies. The act sought to put down

[40] Hoppit, *Land of Liberty*, 405–6.
[41] Virginia Cowles, *The Great Swindle: The Story of the South Sea Bubble* (London, 1960), ch. 6.
[42] Keymer, 'Parliamentary Printing', 199.
[43] Lemire, *Business of Everyday Life*, 71.
[44] Keymer, 'Parliamentary Printing', 202.

'dangerous and mischievous undertakings' which tended to 'the common grievance, prejudice and inconvenience of great numbers' of people. The 'dangerous and mischievous undertakings' were any enterprises which 'presumed to act as if they were corporate bodies... without any legal authority, either by Act of Parliament, or by any Charter from the Crown'. The definition of acting as a corporate body was 'raising or pretending to raise transferable stock': doing so without authority was deemed 'a publick nuisance', and would be treated as a *praemunire*, a non-capital criminal offence punishable by imprisonment and the forfeiture of property to the crown, while brokers trading in these shares would be fined £500.[45] These provisions were not designed to tackle fraudulent companies as such, but to ban all unincorporated companies, and though this may have been the aim of the South Sea Company in 1720, it was not necessarily the considered policy of parliament. And so the act proved 'practically a dead letter'. Sometimes represented as stifling corporate development for a century, more recently historians have shown that it was widely ignored by businessmen and very rarely invoked, generating only one criminal prosecution in the eighteenth century, when Francis Caywood was sentenced to imprisonment during the King's pleasure for selling shares in an unchartered company promoting trade to the North Seas in 1722.[46]

Beyond the largely empty threat of the Bubble Act, then, the criminal law did not intrude in the eighteenth-century joint-stock economy. In an age when, as we have seen, parliament was not normally shy of contributing statutes creating new forms of criminal activity, this reticence requires explaining. It may have been partly due to the limited impact of corporate crises in the eighteenth century. Despite all the hyperbole following the collapse of the South Sea Scheme in 1720, it actually triggered far fewer bankruptcies than either of the general trade depressions which struck a decade before and a decade afterwards.[47] Contemporary descriptions of speculative manias stressed their all inclusive nature ('Professions & shops are forgot... Nobility, Ladys, Brokers, & footmen all upon a level') but this was an exaggeration, with the bulk of such activity found in London, and largely restricted to the rich.[48] There were bigger threats to the nation's economic health than an occasional corporate failure.

Another factor was the difficulty encountered when trying to define crimes in the joint-stock economy. At the end of 1720, nearly everyone agreed that the South Sea Company directors had done wrong, but *what* exactly had they done wrong? Could offences as novel and as elusive as manipulating the market price of shares really form the basis of criminal sanctions?[49] Ignorance, prejudice, and self-interest

[45] 6 Geo. I c. 18, ss. 18–21; Stuart Banner, *Anglo-American Securities Regulation: Cultural and Political Roots, 1690–1860* (Cambridge, 2002), 76.

[46] Ron Harris, 'The Bubble Act: Its Passage and Its Effects on Business Organization', *Journal of Economic History*, 54 (1994), 623–4; Banner, *Securities Regulation*, 78; *Rex v. Caywood* (1722) 1 Stranger, 472.

[47] Julian Hoppit, 'Financial Crises in Eighteenth-Century England', *Economic History Review*, 39 (1986), 39–58.

[48] Hoppit, *Land of Liberty*, 335.

[49] The difficulty posed to legislators by the novelty of the legal problems spawned by companies is stressed in William Holdsworth, *A History of English Law*, 17 vols (London, 1922–66), viii. 213–18.

characterized at least some of the responses to market crashes and this did not provide a sound basis on which to base legislative innovations.[50] More important still was the moral ambiguity associated with behaviour in the joint-stock economy. Though pamphlets, the press, the pulpit, and parliament resounded through the century with condemnations of 'stockjobbers' and their manipulations of the market, it was hard to paint them as villains on the same scale as forgers, whose intention to defraud was much harder to dispute.[51] Thus, their defenders could legitimately point to the public benefits they generated: thanks to them, assets were readily convertible to cash, for their existence meant that 'every man was always sure of finding a purchaser for his stock whenever he had a mind to sell'.[52] Further contributing to the moral ambiguity was the feeling that, unlike the victim of a forgery, those who had speculated and lost had brought their fate upon themselves: such was the dominant flavour of many representations of stock market speculation, such as Hogarth's *Emblematical Print on the South Sea Scheme* (1721), which presented investors as wild gamblers overtaken by a mania for quick gains. The obvious way for such investors to protect themselves was to stop spinning the wheel of fortune and return to more wholesome pursuits. So, although these years saw repeated legislation by parliament to regulate and limit 'stockjobbing' following downturns, notably in 1697, 1708, and, most famously, 'Barnard's Act' of 1733, these imposed fines rather than invoking the criminal law, and were poorly enforced. Later attempts to stiffen the law between 1746 and 1773 did not receive royal assent, so that the stock market remained 'to all intents and purposes... unpoliced and unregulated'.[53]

This situation was challenged in the nineteenth century by the significant growth of the joint-stock economy. Beginning in 1806–08, promotional booms became a regular feature of the economic cycle, raising fears about the soundness of an economy increasingly dependent on joint-stock finance. In this first boom, the moribund Bubble Act was revived by an enemy of a leading company promoter, Ralph Dodd, who had bought shares in two of Dodd's schemes expressly in order to prosecute him. The London Distillery Company and the London Paper Manufacturing Company were not incorporated, but their prospectuses advertised transferable £50 shares and held out the prospect of limited liability to the public. In November 1807, the case was taken up by Sir Vicary Gibbs, the Attorney General, and it was decided by Chief Justice Lord Ellenborough the following May. Ellenborough ruled that Dodd's limited liability promise was 'a mischievous delusion,

[50] Helen Julia Paul, 'Politicians and Public Reaction to the South Sea Bubble: Preaching to the Converted?' *Discussion Papers in Economics and Econometrics, no. 923*, School of Social Sciences, University of Southampton, 2009.

[51] H. V. Bowen, '"The Pests of Human Society": Stockbrokers, Jobbers and Speculators in Mid-Eighteenth-Century Britain', *History*, 78 (1993), 38–53.

[52] The words of an opponent of Sir John Barnard's 1733 bill against time bargains in the Lords, quoted in Banner, *Securities Regulation*, 104.

[53] Bowen, 'Pests of Human Society', 51–2; Banner, *Securities Regulation*, 89. By contrast, offences in the joint-stock economy which were more easily defined and more clearly immoral, such as forging documents conferring the power to transfer shares, were tackled, this particular transgression being made punishable by death by an act of 1722: Banner, *Securities Regulation*, 82.

calculated to ensnare the unwary public', but he allowed the promoter to go free, partly because the act had not been enforced for so long, partly because the prosecution was initiated by someone who had not been deluded by the projects, and who should have taken other steps against Dodd before trying to apply criminal sanctions.[54]

Though the case sparked a number of further actions over the next few years, these were mostly civil actions framed under the section of the Bubble Act permitting those injured by a scheme to sue for treble damages.[55] They met with mixed results, and the prohibition placed on companies by the Bubble Act did not ultimately play a major role in shaping nineteenth-century legal approaches to the joint-stock economy. Indeed, the act was repealed at the height of a second boom in 1825, and subsequent attempts at criminalizing fraud focused on specific acts by promoters and managements rather than condemning companies per se as illegal. These attempts began in earnest following this second boom, and they form the subject of this book.

CRIMINALIZING FRAUD

It is worth clarifying what is outside the scope of the chapters which follow. John P. Locker and Barry Godfrey have shown that it was in the nineteenth century that the workplace was first identified as a 'locus for criminality'. But workplace appropriation by company employees, though occasionally discussed, is not the main focus of this book.[56] Nor is it concerned with frauds perpetuated on companies by customers, whether forgeries of Bank of England notes or bogus claims by policyholders in insurance companies.[57] What the book concentrates on is fraudulent conduct by company management to the detriment of shareholders, customers, or the wider public. In other words, this is a book about the role played by the criminal law in intra-class disputes rather than in the inter-class conflicts which have tended to preoccupy historians of crime. This intentionally comprises a wide range of activities, from at one end of the scale the promotion of 'bubble' companies with no legitimate existence designed to secure subscriptions from overeager investors, to the concealment of losses in balance sheets issued by bona fide but strug-

[54] *Rex v. Dodd*, 103 ER 670, discussed in Harris, *Industrializing English Law*, 236–7, and Taylor, *Creating Capitalism*, 94, 101–2.

[55] There was one further criminal prosecution, in 1811, of the directors of the Birmingham Flour and Bread Company, for raising subscriptions in an 'unlawful undertaking, tending to the common grievance'. The King's Bench jury, supported by Ellenborough, found in favour of the defendants. The company did not come under the Bubble Act as it was formed with 'laudable motives'—chiefly, to reduce the price of bread to consumers—and transfers of its shares were restricted: *Rex. v. Webb*, 104 ER 658. For more on the civil actions, see Harris, *Industrializing English Law*, 238–41, and Taylor, *Creating Capitalism*, 102–4.

[56] John P. Locker and Barry Godfrey, 'Ontological Boundaries and Temporal Watersheds in the Development of White-Collar Crime', *British Journal of Criminology*, 46 (2006), 979.

[57] For the insurance industry, see Timothy Alborn, *Regulated Lives: Life Insurance and British Society, 1800–1914* (Toronto, 2009).

gling businesses at the other end. Anything which was termed 'fraudulent' by contemporaries and was discussed as possible grounds for criminal prosecution is relevant to the discussion. The range of offences included allows an analysis of where the boundary lines were drawn between the acceptable, the immoral, and the criminal, and underlines the fact that fraud and criminality were unstable categories, socially constructed, and evolving over time.[58]

The argument is developed by means of contextualized case studies of frauds and reactions to them.[59] The case study approach is essential: as not all frauds are the same it is impossible to understand fraud at the macroeconomic level alone.[60] The main aims are to explore what provoked victims of company failures to instigate criminal proceedings, how these actions fared in the courts, and the reasons for, and consequences of, political interventions in this process. With London the financial centre of the country, metropolitan cases inevitably preponderate, but important scandals from other towns and cities are also covered. This is particularly important in order to highlight tensions between standards of commercial morality in different parts of the country, as well as to demonstrate the genuinely national reach of statutory prohibitions later in the century.[61] England and Scotland had different legal systems, and this book, while focusing on the former, also discusses business and law north of the border; moreover, Scottish judges and magistrates exerted a strong influence on English developments, which is highlighted in later chapters. Events in Ireland also feature at several key junctures. Despite the focus on the criminal law, the book places criminal sanctions in the context of other forms of punishment, in particular the financial penalties that could be levied in the civil courts, and extra-legal punishments incurred as a result of public exposure of wrongdoing. There is a tendency to belittle the idea that public humiliation and loss of reputation could be serious forms of punishment, yet this overlooks the enormous shaming power publicity was thought to possess.[62] This was all the more so when the concept of 'public opinion', associated with the growing strength of the middle classes and the development of the newspaper press, was rapidly developing.[63]

Indeed, one of the chief sources used in this study is the press. Newspapers were central agents in the creation of scandals, but they are not useful solely for their editorial judgements. They are an unrivalled repository of information on the

[58] Jennifer S. Davis, 'Prosecutions and their Context: The Use of the Criminal Law in Later Nineteenth-Century London', in Hay and Snyder, *Policing and Prosecution*, 425.

[59] Justification for this approach, which could be termed 'legal archaeology', is given in A. W. Brian Simpson, *Leading Cases in the Common Law* (Oxford, 1995), 1–12.

[60] Per H. Hansen, 'Introduction: Special Issue on Scandals and Panics', *Business History Review*, 83 (2009), 3.

[61] The former point is explored in David Moss, 'Business and Banking: Ethics and White-Collar Crime in Norwich, 1825–1831', *Albion*, 29 (1997), 373–98.

[62] This is examined in James Taylor, 'Commercial Fraud and Public Men in Victorian Britain', *Historical Research*, 78 (2005), 230–52.

[63] Hannah Barker, *Newspapers, Politics, and Public Opinion in Late Eighteenth-Century England* (Oxford, 1998).

development of the joint-stock economy, carrying reports of annual general meetings, financial news in regular 'City columns', and, most important of all, extensive reports of both civil and criminal court cases. This kind of legal coverage was 'a new and striking feature' of the nineteenth-century press, and was not continued in the twentieth century, when such reports became much briefer.[64] Although the state improved its collection and dissemination of criminal statistics through the century, these data do not differentiate company frauds from the (far more numerous) offences by individuals, and so are of limited use when trying to locate relevant cases. Recent newspaper digitization projects, on the other hand, have made identifying important but hitherto ignored trials possible.

Once cases have been located, press reports also represent the best way of investigating them. In the nineteenth century, magistrates' courts kept registers of cases heard but these did not include records of what was said. As a result, magistrates themselves relied upon the press for a record of the details of cases before them: in 1855, the London alderman Sir Peter Laurie noted in his diary of a particularly lengthy case heard over seventeen sittings that 'all the newspaper reports were cut and kept as a memorandum to be used if necessary'.[65] The press is also invaluable when investigating cases once they were committed for trial. Civil cases receive more coverage than criminal ones in the runs of published law reports, and the main series devoted to the latter is very patchy.[66] For cases tried at London's Central Criminal Court, there is the published quasi-official *Proceedings of the Old Bailey*, recently digitized. These are a valuable record of evidence presented, but they do not generally contain the speeches made by lawyers and judges, nor details of the jury's decision-making process, which limits their usefulness. Going beyond published sources, the National Archives contain records of criminal trials throughout England and Wales, but these do not usually include transcripts of what was said in court. By contrast, the press contains lengthy reports of a host of cases which provide a more complete view of the activities of the criminal courts than can be gleaned from any other source. They were usually the work of trained lawyers.[67] *The Times*'s chief legal correspondent at this time, the barrister William Finlason (or 'Old Fin' as he was affectionately known), was 'the prince of reporters, and a lawyer of great learning', in the judgement of one eminent contemporary.[68] And so when in a 1904 Commons debate a hard-pressed Attorney General wanted to cite

[64] Chantal Stebbings, 'Benefits and Barriers: The Making of Victorian Legal History', in Anthony Musson and Chantal Stebbings (eds), *Making Legal History: Approaches and Methodology* (Cambridge, 2012), 77.

[65] Entry for 27 April 1855, *Journal of Sir Peter Laurie*, ed. Elizabeth Shepherd (Tunbridge Wells, 1985), 133.

[66] *Cox's Criminal Cases*, published between 1843 and 1941. One legal historian has stressed the importance of reading both newspaper and law reports owing to the different emphases of each, but the spotty coverage of cases in the latter means this is not always possible: Graham Ferris, 'Larceny: Debating the "Boundless Region of Dishonesty"', in Judith Rowbotham and Kim Stevenson (eds), *Criminal Conversations: Victorian Crimes, Social Panic, and Moral Outrage* (Columbus, OH, 2005), 70–86.

[67] Ferris, 'Larceny', 71.

[68] Edward Clarke, *The Story of My Life* (New York, 1919), 86–7.

a judge's words from a fraud trial of yesteryear to justify his decision not to prosecute in a similar case, he read from *The Times*'s report of the trial.[69]

As well as newspapers, both digitized and undigitized, a host of other sources have been used to provide the context essential for understanding the cases. Debates on companies and criminality have been traced through the extensive periodical and pamphlet literature. Political opinion is explored through parliamentary debates and parliamentary papers, supplemented with published and occasionally unpublished private correspondence and diaries. Popular engagement with fraud is examined by means of cultural sources: chiefly novels, but also poems and cartoons. Perhaps surprisingly, financial fraud did have considerable popular resonance. Anna Clark has suggested that what made sex scandals in the Georgian era so potent was that 'unlike complicated and hard-to-follow financial scandals, they can be told through familiar stories of broken hearts, broken families, broken marriages'.[70] In fact, when describing frauds, lawyers, politicians, and journalists alike frequently borrowed novelistic conventions and melodramatic tropes to ensure that cases struck emotional chords with the public.[71] There is little evidence of lack of popular interest in nineteenth-century financial scandals.

Because the aim of the book is to explain how, when, and why company frauds were criminalized in the nineteenth century, the chapters are arranged chronologically. Earlier thematic approaches to the topic have obscured crucial shifts and discontinuities and have given rise to a generalized view of an inadequate legal response over the entire century. The chapters are therefore divided into three parts, 'Toleration', 'Criminalization', and 'Enforcement', each representing a distinct phase. Responses to fraud in the 1820s and 1830s, covered in 'Toleration', had much in common with attitudes prevalent in the eighteenth century. Governments did not see the prevention or punishment of fraud as their responsibility, while magistrates and judges were more inclined to condemn greedy investors than swindling company promoters and directors. 'Criminalization' explores the 1840s to the 1860s, which saw the first attempts to define and outlaw offences associated with the promotion and management of companies. But prosecutions remained the responsibility of the victims, and when they were attempted, judges interpreted the legislation narrowly. 'Enforcement' encompasses the period from the 1870s down to the end of the century, years when the state gradually took the leading role in enforcing the law, and the judiciary came to adopt a stricter approach to wrongdoing in the boardroom. The approach to fraud developed in the Victorian era was, with refinements and modifications, to remain in place for much of the twentieth century, discussed in the Epilogue.

The aim of the book is not to present a mirror image of the existing consensus, or to claim that the Victorian state saw off the threat posed by fraud: clearly, it did not. The book does, however, argue that on the rap sheet against lawyers and legislators, the charges of negligence and moral bankruptcy should be discounted, and suggests that their intentions can be presented in a rather more positive light.

[69] Hansard, 4s, 129: 163 (2 February 1904). For more on this case, see the Epilogue.

[70] Anna Clark, *Scandal: The Sexual Politics of the British Constitution* (Princeton, NJ, 2004), 3.

[71] Taylor, 'Commercial Fraud'.

PART ONE

TOLERATION

2

The Morals of Mania: The 1820s

Early in 1826, the nineteen-year-old aspiring poet Elizabeth Barrett Browning wrote a letter to her uncle, Samuel Moulton-Barrett, chiding him for not visiting her for so long. She was glad to hear that he intended to leave London soon, and assured him that his promised visit 'must pay a hundred pr. cent on my angel-like patience; which payment...will be a FUND of joy to us all'.[1] Elizabeth's letter teasingly alluded to the source of Moulton-Barrett's distraction: the stock market boom of the mid 1820s. The owner of indebted Jamaican estates, he had lent his name to a variety of joint-stock schemes in an attempt to recover his fortunes.[2] The boom, which had begun in 1822 with heavily oversubscribed loans to Central and South America and continental Europe, spread to joint-stock companies from 1824.[3] Some, such as the Real del Monte Mining Company, exploited the public's enthusiasm for all things Latin American, others were formed for a range of domestic purposes.[4] One stockbroker counted a total of 624 companies promoted in 1824 and 1825, with a paper capital of no less than £372 million.[5]

As Member of Parliament for Richmond, Yorkshire, Moulton-Barrett's name was valuable to company promoters who needed to manufacture boards of directors which both inspired confidence among investors, and had the political influence to secure acts of incorporation or other privileges from parliament. He was not the only parliamentarian to capitalize. Robert Wilmot-Horton, Under-Secretary of State for War and the Colonies, boasted to his fellow country gentleman and MP Edward Littleton of having made £12,000 from the sale of shares, and that he could make £50,000 if he liked. Beguiled, Littleton 'beseeched' him for a directorship in one of his companies, and on returning to London in 1825, he 'found all the world mad about Schemes...No man thinks of the result, as no man buys shares to keep them.'[6] What was increasingly referred to as a 'mania' di-

[1] Elizabeth Barrett Browning to Samuel Moulton-Barrett, *c.* January 1826, *The Brownings' Correspondence*, ed. Philip Kelley and Ronald Hudson, 18 vols (Winfield, KS, 1984–), i. 234–5.

[2] D. R. Fisher (ed.), *History of Parliament: The House of Commons, 1820–1832*, 7 vols (Cambridge, 2009), iv. 448–50.

[3] Frank Griffith Dawson, *The First Latin American Debt Crisis: The City of London and the 1822–25 Loan Bubble* (Yale, 1990).

[4] Mining schemes were heavily promoted in puffing pamphlets. See, for example, William Rawson, *The Present Operations and Future Prospects of the Mexican Mine Associations* (London, 1825).

[5] Henry English, *A General Guide to the Companies Formed for Working Foreign Mines* (London, 1825), 30–1.

[6] Hatherton Diary, September 1824–March 1825, in C. R. Fay, *Huskisson and his Age* (London, 1951), 142–4.

vided social elites: though men like Moulton-Barrett and Wilmot-Horton embraced it, others worried about the effects on the economy and on national morality. The Duke of Wellington privately dismissed the companies as 'bubbles invented for stockjobbing purposes', and predicted 'a general crash', while Lord Colchester, former Speaker of the House, condemned 'the monstrous speculations and bubbles'.[7] The sight of noblemen, gentlemen, and merchants all playing the market led *The Times* to fear for 'the moral character of the people of England'.[8]

The mania also raised legal issues which had lain dormant since the last period of sustained company formation nearly twenty years earlier.[9] Whilst the promoters of some schemes approached parliament in 1824 for incorporating acts, the majority took the cheaper route of trading as unincorporated companies, even though this risked running foul of the Bubble Act of 1720.[10] Indeed, the illegality of unincorporated companies seemed to be confirmed by the courts in 1825. Three decisions in quick succession by Chief Justice Charles Abbott and Lord Chancellor Eldon in February and March refused to enforce contracts involving unincorporated companies and their shares, thus effectively depriving such companies of access to the law.[11] The rulings were intended to place a brake on company promotions, but their actual impact was unexpected. The legality of their companies called into question, promoters and directors bombarded parliament with petitions for corporate privileges—no fewer than 297 during the 1825 session.[12] Under this deluge, the government adopted the quickest fix, the repeal of the Bubble Act, achieved by July.[13] The victory of the directors was short-lived, however. Share prices had peaked in early 1825, and market confidence subsequently drooped, before a full-blown commercial crisis in December which swept most of the companies out of existence.[14]

This chapter focuses on the legal aftermath of the crash. Many shareholders had lost heavily and general meetings became tumultuous and sometimes violent affairs as they tried to find out what had happened to their investments. They had a number of possible recourses: bringing their cases to the criminal courts, to the civil courts, or to parliament. Though convinced of the justness of their cause, shareholders found their own behaviour placed under the microscope, which threatened to undermine their attempts at redress.

[7] *The Journal of Mrs Arbuthnot, 1820–1832*, ed. Francis Bamford and the Duke of Wellington, 2 vols (London, 1950), i. 382; Lord Colchester to Lord Amherst, 23 June 1826, *The Diary and Correspondence of Charles Abbot, Lord Colchester*, ed. Charles, Lord Colchester, 3 vols (London, 1861), iii. 441.

[8] *The Times*, 5 November 1825.

[9] See Introduction.

[10] Geo. I c. 18, s. 18.

[11] The cases concerned the Equitable Loan Bank Company (*Josephs v. Pebrer*), the British Annuity Company (*Van Sandau v. Moore*), and the Real del Monte Mining Company (*Kinder v. Taylor*): James Taylor, *Creating Capitalism: Joint-Stock Enterprise in British Politics and Culture, 1800–1870* (Woodbridge, 2006), 108–9; *Morning Chronicle*, 10 March 1825.

[12] Bishop Carleton Hunt, *The Development of the Business Corporation in England, 1800–1867* (Cambridge, MA, 1936), 52.

[13] 6 Geo. IV c. 91.

[14] English, *General Guide*, 106.

A HORRIBLE SPECIES OF GAMBLING

As the number of companies multiplied in 1825, some began to question the sanity of the speculating public. The 'morbid appetite for schemes' had become an 'epidemic', wrote one merchant.[15] The *Examiner* likened the public's appetite for shares to 'a fever in the body'; the *Leeds Mercury* thought it more like 'a species of frenzy'.[16] One of the most consistent critics of the mania was John Garratt, the Lord Mayor of the City of London. From his platform in the justice room of the Mansion House, Garratt rarely missed an opportunity to criticize the contagion. In a case in July involving a mining clerk who refused to leave his company's employment, he 'supposed the man's brain was turned by the Stock Exchange mania, which still rages'. Later that month, Garratt thought that a case in which a boy had taken a letter of allotment for shares in another mining company and sold it to a broker without the knowledge of the owner, 'shows one of the bad effects of the horrible species of gambling on the Stock Exchange'. In August Garratt noted that 'he could not take up a newspaper without bursting into laughter, at the extraordinary multitude of new speculations', but hoped that the mania was now coming to an end.[17] His wish was soon fulfilled. The boom years had rested on easy credit from both the Bank of England and the country banks; when confidence began to waver, the Bank of England protected itself by sharply restricting credit. With money suddenly scarce, many of the joint-stock promotions looked vulnerable, and new share issues had few takers.[18] By the end of October the 'bubbles' were rapidly bursting.[19]

One of the immediate repercussions was an increase in Garratt's workload, as disappointed speculators came to Mansion House crying foul. England had no public prosecutor—an official who to mainstream political opinion smacked of continental oppression and centralization—and so the large majority of prosecutions had to be organized and financed by private parties.[20] The question these speculators posed the Lord Mayor was whether the sometimes dubious strategies adopted by company promoters and directors to sell their shares, and their mishandling of shareholders' money, left them liable to prosecution under the criminal law. Whereas civil cases were decided by the most senior judges on the bench, rulings on the issue of City criminality were usually made, at least in the first instance, by one man. As chief magistrate for the City, the Lord Mayor heard cases brought to him by aggrieved parties daily, deciding which ones to send to the Old Bailey for trial.[21] Prominence in the business community rather than familiarity

[15] *Remarks on Joint Stock Companies by an Old Merchant* (London, 1825), 28.

[16] *Examiner*, 13 February 1825; *Leeds Mercury*, 15 January 1825.

[17] *The Times*, 9, 16 July, 27 August 1825.

[18] Dawson, *Debt Crisis*, 110.

[19] *Newcastle Courant*, 29 October 1825.

[20] For an excellent explanation of how the system of private prosecution worked, see Douglas Hay and Francis Snyder, 'Using the Criminal Law, 1750–1850: Policing, Private Prosecution, and the State', in Douglas Hay and Francis Snyder (eds), *Policing and Prosecution in Britain, 1750–1850* (Oxford, 1989).

[21] The process of examination before lay magistrates is detailed in David Bentley, *English Criminal Justice in the Nineteenth Century* (London, 1998), 29–32. See also Hay and Snyder, 'Criminal Law', 16–19.

with the law was the chief qualification for the role and, serving just a one-year term, there was little opportunity to acquire legal expertise. As a result he was dependent on the advice of his fellow aldermen and, in particular, his chief clerk.[22] In the final months of his term of office, Garratt, a goldsmith by trade, found himself required to arbitrate on a series of complicated disputes. His decisions were entirely in keeping with the rulings earlier that year by the Chief Justice and the Lord Chancellor. All three saw the public's thirst for quick gains as a bigger threat to economic stability—and to commercial morality—than the sharp practices resorted to by company management. As a result, their actions sought to dampen down enthusiasm for speculation rather than provide redress for those who considered themselves defrauded.

There were two main legal bases which could theoretically sustain a criminal prosecution for company fraud. The first was an act of 1757 which made obtaining money by false pretences with intent to defraud a crime liable to a maximum punishment of transportation for seven years.[23] The second was the common law of conspiracy. Most notoriously used against combinations of workmen in the nineteenth century, conspiracy was an elastic concept which provided the means by which acts not criminal by statute could be criminally prosecuted, provided they were committed by two or more people. Conspiracy to defraud had been accepted as a common law misdemeanour since at least the fourteenth century.[24] Investors tried to invoke these laws, but Garratt and his fellow aldermen denied that they were applicable to joint-stock disputes. A gentleman who had invested heavily in an unnamed company on the strength of its prospectus, which had 'promised wonderful things', lost his money when the shares collapsed. In October, he came to Mansion House alleging that his money had been 'obtained under no other than false pretences' and asked the magistrates to summon the company's bankers to explain why they would not return his money. Alderman John Thorp, sitting in for Garratt, 'did not think the case was one in which the Chief Magistrate could interfere', and advised the complainant to recover his money in the law courts. The complainant 'pressed very hard for a summons', but Thorp held firm. Garratt gave similar advice to investors who had lost money in companies for running steamships and selling fish.[25]

While these attempts were all easily seen off, a more organized effort was made by the shareholders of the failing Gwennappe Tin and Copper Mining Company, 'eight or ten' of whom descended on Mansion House requesting summonses for the company's directors, bankers, and secretary. The scene, reported *The Times*, was 'a very extraordinary one', as the applicants described many of 'the tricks of the

[22] The Lord Mayor, 'usually some trader or merchant, but little acquainted with the laws he has to administer... must, in most instances, depend entirely upon the advice of his chief clerk': *Gentleman's Magazine* (May 1844), 542. As is shown below, this did not always happen.

[23] 30 Geo. II c. 24, s. 1.

[24] Mark C. Curthoys, *Governments, Labour, and the Law in Mid-Victorian Britain: The Trade Union Legislation of the 1870s* (Oxford, 2004), 85; Michael Levi, *The Phantom Capitalists: The Organization and Control of Long-Firm Fraud* (London, 1981), 150–4.

[25] *The Times*, 25 October, 9 November 1825.

stock-market' which they had learned through bitter experience. The company was started just three months earlier, and after the issue of a glowing prospectus with several respectable names listed as directors, the shares had reached a small premium, then quickly fell. The 'rig' in the market having failed, the directors lost interest in the company, and when approached by the shareholders, refused to refund their money. Francis Hobler, the Lord Mayor's chief clerk, suggested that the law of conspiracy was flexible enough to enable them to indict the directors for a conspiracy to defraud, which would 'soon induce the great multitudes of men who had lent their names to deceptions of the kind, to refund to the public'.[26] Hobler, who had been in the Lord Mayor's office since 1803, was a popular and respected legal expert, but Garratt had no hesitation in overruling him.[27] Garratt took a dim view of the shareholders' behaviour. They accused the directors of not seriously pursuing a scheme of mining, but he accused the shareholders of the same thing: it was obvious that they had bought the shares speculating for a rise, at which point 'they would have sold them, and put the ready money in their pockets, leaving the company and its concerns to take care of themselves'. He firmly told the men that he could do nothing for them.[28]

Garratt reached the end of his mayoralty in November in self-congratulatory spirits, expressing satisfaction that by having exposed the machinations behind the flotation of fraudulent companies, he had 'contributed to abate the furious rage for speculation'.[29] But in refusing to apply the criminal law to any of these companies, he was criticized by the *Morning Chronicle*, the most outspoken of the opposition papers.[30] Though it did not defend speculators, it was uneasy that the promoters of the abortive schemes—some of them members of business and political elites—were seemingly immune from legal repercussions. It thought the 'city feeling' displayed in Mansion House was dangerous, and would encourage a decline in standards of commercial morality, with disastrous results to the nation.[31]

A more immediate disaster was about to strike, however. The credit squeeze led to panic, and runs brought down dozens of the country banks, which in turn triggered commercial bankruptcies on a large scale—224 in December 1825 alone. As the crisis spread, the Bank of England reversed its policy and began lending extensively in an attempt to save the banking system, coming perilously close to having to suspend payments itself. The episode left many bewildered: one experienced bill broker wrote that he had not witnessed such a calamity in his 36 years in Lombard Street, and reflected that 'if the Bank Directors had not seen the thing in its true light & given the prompt and immediate assistance they did, the game would have been up'.[32] The crisis killed off any remaining appetite for companies. Shares plummeted

[26] Ibid. 31 October 1825; *Morning Chronicle*, 31 October 1825.
[27] *Morning Chronicle*, 2 November 1803; *Gentleman's Magazine* (May 1844), 542.
[28] *The Times*, 1 November 1825.
[29] Ibid. 5 November 1825.
[30] Robert Harrison, rev. M. Clare Loughlin-Chow, 'John Black', *ODNB*.
[31] *Morning Chronicle*, 31 October 1825.
[32] Quoted in David Kynaston, *The City of London: Volume 1, A World of Its Own, 1815–1890* (London, 1994), 71.

in value. Investors who had counted themselves rich now found themselves poor and, in many cases, facing further calls on their shares.[33] Stunned by the sudden turn of events, shareholders began summoning general meetings and holding inquiries into their companies' affairs, post-mortems which generated mass press coverage. As a result, the question of criminality—considered and rejected by Garratt and his fellow magistrates in the autumn of 1825—returned with a vengeance in 1826.

THE ROCKET-MAN

The first company to attract attention was the Arigna Iron and Coal Mining Company, established to work mines in County Roscommon, Ireland. This was one of several schemes for Irish improvement formed in a blaze of philanthropy during the boom.[34] In common with other mining schemes, its shares were quoted at hefty premiums through late 1824 and early 1825, but by November had fallen from their peak of £25 to a miserable £4.[35] Consequently, the shareholders called a special general meeting to investigate the company's affairs in early December, just as the commercial panic was reaching its height. They had a raft of grievances centring on three key issues: first, the boards' alleged mismanagement; second, the profits made by the directors by speculating in the company's shares; third, the money paid by the directors for the mines—and the profit they made on this deal.[36]

The meeting created a sensation partly because of the involvement of several public men. The chairman Sir William Congreve was the developer of the Congreve rocket, deployed during the Napoleonic Wars by the British military. Referred to mockingly as 'the rocket-man' by the Whig lawyer Henry Brougham, his inventions brought him widespread fame, and he had organized the grand firework displays celebrating the peace of 1814 and the coronation of George IV in 1821. The king's influence helped him gain a seat in parliament, where he naturally supported the Tory interest.[37] Two other Tory MPs also featured on the board. James Brogden, a wealthy merchant, patronized by the Duke of Northumberland, had sat in parliament since 1796, and had been chairman of the Committee of Ways and Means since 1813.[38] John Bent, another government adherent who had made money in the City, had been in parliament since 1818.[39] Two of the company's three trustees were also MPs: Samuel Moulton-Barrett, Elizabeth's busy uncle, and

[33] Companies typically issued shares with a high face value but initially only required a small amount to be paid per share, allowing further 'calls' to be made in the future.

[34] *Morning Chronicle*, 19 November 1824.

[35] Ibid. 13 January 1825; *Morning Post*, 12 November 1825.

[36] *The Times*, 7 December 1825.

[37] He was MP for Gatton 1812–16, then for Plymouth from 1818 to his death: Roger T. Stearn, 'Sir William Congreve', *ODNB*.

[38] Roland G. Thorne (ed.), *History of Parliament: The House of Commons 1790–1820*, 5 vols (1986), iii. 259–61.

[39] Ibid. 183–4; Fisher, *House of Commons*, iv. 253.

his fellow Whig Peter Moore.[40] Feted as a master of getting bills through the Commons, Moore's support helped to secure the Arigna's act of parliament in 1825.[41]

The most incendiary accusation made at the meeting was that the directors had falsely stated the purchase price of the company's mines. Though telling shareholders that they had paid £25,000, they had in fact only paid £10,000, and the difference of £15,000 was secretly distributed among the board, with Congreve receiving £2,500 and the other eleven a little over £1,000 each. The directors did not deny the facts, but defended their actions. Bent and Brogden pleaded ignorance, believing that the money had come from the sale of shares to which they were entitled. Congreve was bolder, admitting that 'he knew there was to be a premium, or he would not have joined the company', but claiming it was 'done in many instances', including in the South American mining companies, and that it was an 'honourable' transaction. Unimpressed, the shareholders moved to appoint a committee to take over the company's affairs and launch legal proceedings against the directors, but the board had taken the precaution of packing the meeting with their supporters, and the motion was rejected.[42]

Victory was short-lived, however. Whilst the board had tried to contain the scandal by barring reporters from the meeting, a detailed report of proceedings appeared in the next day's *Times*, based on copious notes made by several of the shareholders.[43] Papers across the political spectrum heaped contempt on the directors. The *Morning Chronicle* did not conceal its disgust at what was 'esteemed correct and honourable' in the City.[44] In a long poem satirizing 'The Bursting of the Bubbles', the Tory *Age* mocked the men:

> For Congreve, McLean, Mr Bent, and the rest,
> Were *bent* on enriching their pockets,
> And therefore the bubble *went off*, like the best
> Of Sir William's combustible rockets.[45]

Another Tory paper, *John Bull*, thought that Bent and Brogden's protestations of innocence stretched credulity, and insisted that out of 'regard for the reputation of the individuals principally concerned... *the matter cannot rest where it is*'.[46]

There was little chance of this. The shareholders, outmanoeuvred at the general meeting, now sought legal advice. Their solicitor reported in January 1826 that he had consulted Anthony Hart, a distinguished practitioner of the Chancery Bar for

[40] For more on the role of trustees in companies, see Mark Freeman, Robin Pearson, and James Taylor, *Shareholder Democracies? Corporate Governance in Britain and Ireland before 1850* (Chicago, IL, 2012), 55–7.

[41] *Hull Packet*, 20 May 1828. He was also involved in the successful repeal of the Bubble Act: see Ron Harris, 'Political Economy, Interest Groups, Legal Institutions, and the Repeal of the Bubble Act in 1825', *Economic History Review*, 50 (1997), 675–96.

[42] *The Times*, 7 December 1825; *Morning Chronicle*, 9, 27 December 1825; *Report from the Select Committee on the Arigna Mining Company*, PP 1826–27 III. 10.

[43] *The Times*, 7 December 1825.

[44] *Morning Chronicle*, 9 December 1825.

[45] *Age*, 18 December 1825. General McLean was another of the directors.

[46] *John Bull*, 12 December 1825.

many years, and soon to become Lord Chancellor of Ireland.[47] Hart believed that the transaction was 'grossly fraudulent', and advised that the shareholders would be able to recover the £15,000 in a court of equity. The solicitor also took counsel's opinion on whether the abstraction of the money was punishable as a criminal offence: he was told that as the intention of the directors was clearly to defraud the company, they could be indicted for a conspiracy. The shareholders, keen to see their money returned, preferred the first option, and authorized their solicitor to proceed with an action in Chancery.[48]

John Bull had predicted that unpleasant as these exposures were, more were lurking around the corner.[49] Sure enough, attention began to switch to other companies established by the Arigna men. One article published in *The Times* found that Brogden sat on the boards of eleven companies, Bent seven, and Congreve six.[50] That these men had traded on their position so extensively was transforming a financial scandal into a political one.[51] The call was taken up by radicals. Both Congreve and Brogden had appeared in John Wade's *Black Book* of 1820, and the revelations slotted into traditional radical concerns about corruption in public life.[52] Alderman Robert Waithman, a leading reformer who had previously served as MP for the City of London and Lord Mayor, attempted to persuade the Court of Common Council—the main decision-making body of the City of London—to petition the House of Commons for an inquiry into joint-stock companies. The projectors of many companies established them purely in order to inflate the share price and make a quick profit, which he called 'downright barefaced fraud', and several MPs were implicated. However, he was outvoted by his fellow councilmen, who seemed to feel less strongly than he did.[53]

Nevertheless, the fight was taken up by the radical MP for Westminster, John Cam Hobhouse, who raised the subject in the Commons. Soon after the parliamentary session began in February 1826 he presented a petition from a London merchant who had lost money in a failed mining venture, for a select committee to inquire into the companies of the boom.[54] Hobhouse depicted the mania as a national disaster, attributing much of the current commercial distress to joint-stock companies: 'every one of the shares in those bubbles which was thrown on the market was a bad piece of currency'. Worse, the crash had caused a crisis of trust in the market, because so many previously respected figures had been implicated, undermining 'the hitherto untarnished character of the English

[47] *Gentleman's Magazine* (December 1831), 566; Daire Hogan, 'Sir Anthony Hart', *ODNB*.

[48] *The Times*, 7 January 1826.

[49] *John Bull*, 12 December 1825.

[50] *The Times*, 25 January 1826. See also letter from 'Argus', ibid. 26 February 1827.

[51] The precedent of the parliamentary enquiry into the Charitable Corporation in 1731 was cited: ibid. 25 January 1826. See also ibid. 10 January, 13 February 1826; *Glasgow Herald*, 16 January 1826.

[52] John Wade, *The Black Book: Or, Corruption Unmasked!* (London, 1820), 21, 29. The book, a powerful salvo in the battle against 'Old Corruption', sold over 50,000 copies in its various editions: Philip Harling, 'John Wade', *ODNB*.

[53] *The Times*, 1 March 1826.

[54] *Journals of the House of Commons*, 81: 87 (21 February 1826).

merchant'.[55] He also pressed Sir John Copley, the Tory Attorney General, on the state of the law. The repeal of the Bubble Act left the public vulnerable, and the government needed to introduce a new measure to protect the public from future frauds.[56] But Copley signalled the government's uninterest in either investigating or reforming the joint-stock economy, arguing that the law as it stood was 'sufficient to reach any fraudulent attempts, by any number of persons forming themselves into illegal companies'.[57]

A FLAWED CRUSADER

The man who, above all others, would decide whether the law could indeed reach joint-stock fraud was the Lord Mayor. William Venables, a successful wholesale stationer with moderate Whig leanings and no legal background, succeeded Garratt in November 1825.[58] Shortly after taking office, he had echoed Garratt's line on companies and the law. While condemning gambling in shares, he was adamant that 'the Chief Magistrate had nothing to do with the punishment of persons who acted improperly with respect to them'.[59] But this statement of intent did not stop disappointed investors approaching him with their grievances through 1826, and in fact his policy was not quite as inflexible as his words suggested. The principles on which Venables operated are revealed by his contrasting handling of two cases which came before him in the spring of 1826.

In March John and Nicholas Bell, two tea dealers from Huddersfield, approached Venables with a complaint. They had met a Quaker, William Goundry, who was employed by a major tea merchant known by the Bells.[60] Goundry introduced himself as managing director of the Equitable Tea Agency Company ('capital £500,000'), and invited the Bells to invest. They bought £20 of the company's shares, and placed an order for tea. But when the promised dividends on the shares did not materialize, the Bells came to Mansion House. The case was suspicious enough for Venables to issue a summons, but Goundry did not appear. An officer was sent to his counting house, but returned to say that the house—in a parlous state, and showing little sign of recent business activity—was deserted but for a down-at-heel porter. Venables sent him back to fetch the porter, who revealed that Goundry *was* the company: he never saw any meetings of directors, and no subscribers ever visited. Venables concluded that the company was 'got up for the purposes of fraud', to take in 'a few inexperienced individuals'. If Goundry ignored

[55] Hansard, 2s, 14: 644–7 (21 February 1826). Hobhouse had been an outspoken opponent of the companies of the boom during the previous session: see, for example, ibid. 12: 1048–56 (16 March 1825).

[56] Ibid. 14: 416 (15 February 1826), 644–7 (21 February 1826).

[57] Ibid. 416 (15 February 1826).

[58] Fisher, *House of Commons*, vii. 547–50.

[59] *The Times*, 14 November 1825.

[60] Though it later transpired that Goundry had been expelled in 1814 after declaring bankruptcy amidst accusations of fraud.

a second summons, he would issue a warrant for his arrest. This did the trick, and the next day, Goundry materialized to answer questions. Having no solicitor, he failed to prove that the company had any real existence, and Venables ruled that there was a case of obtaining money under false pretences to answer and that it needed to go before a jury. Unable to afford bail, Goundry was imprisoned until the trial.[61]

The following month saw Venables act quite differently in a second case. During the boom, the Alliance Granite and China Clay Company had raised £3,000 from eager investors without even issuing a prospectus; their money was used to buy a quarry from a member of the board. One of the investors, a surgeon named Brooks, came to Mansion House to complain that this was another Arigna—the director had obtained the quarry for just £550 but sold it to the company for £2,100, and the board had divided the proceeds between them. Furthermore, the directors were accused of using £700 to buy the company's shares, thus artificially inflating their price. The directors had done nothing to work the mine, and it was, Brooks claimed, 'as gross a case as any which had been brought before his Lordship'. After consulting with Hobler, Venables ordered the directors to answer the charge of 'obtaining money under the false pretence of carrying on a company'. The following day, three of the directors obliged, presenting a robust defence. The company was formed 'in the firmest hope of success', and was calculated to yield at least 50 per cent profit when in operation. Though it was currently at a standstill, this was because of the impossibility of making calls owing to the recent credit squeeze: all bona fide companies were in a similar bind. Venables believed the directors, and thought that the case 'differed essentially from that of Goundry', but he agreed to hold a further meeting. Two days later, Mansion House heaved with 'persons interested in joint stock companies'. Brooks and a fellow shareholder, William Clark, made a series of allegations, but without evidence of conspiracy, causing Hobler to explain to them that it was lawful for a man to buy land cheaply and 'sell it at 50 times the sum' if he could. It was different for 'two men to make a bargain with the view of getting hold of the property of others', but the collusion had to be demonstrated before the law could interpose. Venables agreed that there was no evidence of sinister intent, and thought that 'the complainants were themselves much to blame for the mode in which they parted with their money'. Rather than sitting through any more 'interminable' detail, he dismissed the case, instructing the parties to resolve their differences at a general meeting.[62]

To some, it seemed that the City was looking after its own. In a scathing commentary, the *Morning Chronicle* claimed that Goundry's error was to operate on too small a scale. He would have been safer had he chosen to associate himself 'with two or three Lords, or, at least, a dozen or two of Members of Parliament'. His scheme had not raised enough money to pay for lawyers: it was well established that 'if there be but enough of money to spend, the law is quite adequate to the protection of the most desperate plunderers'. Standing alone, and without the resources a Congreve or

[61] *The Times*, 30, 31 March, 1 April 1826.
[62] Ibid. 22, 24, 26 April 1826.

a Moore could command, he would be found guilty, and would 'give the venerable Judges of the land an opportunity of boasting its efficacy to reach offenders'.[63] But there was more to Venables' decisions than this. His interpretation of the law was based on a distinction between real and fictitious companies, reflecting the certainty with which Christian economists distinguished between 'solid commerce' and 'excrescent trade'.[64] Goundry claimed to have established a real company with a capital of half a million pounds, but it had no offices, no directors, held no meetings, its only existence being in his mind. The false pretences were in such a case demonstrable. But when there was a real company, with all the paraphernalia that implied, established with some hope of success, then it fell outside the Lord Mayor's jurisdiction, and disputes between its members were a private matter.

The difficulty of applying the criminal law even to cases of fictitious companies became clear at Goundry's trial at the Old Bailey in May. Even though Goundry was hardly a City player, the financial community recognized that the trial might establish boundaries between criminal and non-criminal behaviour in the promotion of companies. As a result, the courtroom was 'excessively crowded with gentlemen from Capel Court'; reporters could not remember seeing 'so many "Bulls" and "Bears" in the Old Bailey before'.[65] In the event, however, the trial was an anticlimax. Goundry faced five counts of obtaining money by false pretences, but his defence objected to the form of the indictment. All the counts accused Goundry of defrauding John *and* Nicholas Bell, but he had never dealt with Nicholas, only John. The prosecution requested that such an important case not be thrown out on a technicality, but the Common Serjeant, Thomas Denman, determined that the flaw in the phraseology of the counts was fatal and Goundry walked free.[66]

The decision did not discourage one man from continuing to press for criminal prosecutions. William Clark, a stockbroker and shareholder who had made allegations against the board of the Alliance Granite Company alongside Brooks, had invested in a range of joint-stock companies during the boom and held the directors responsible for his losses. At the start of the year, he had taken the unusual step of bypassing Mansion House and going to the Court of Oyer and Terminer for bills of indictment against the directors of the Imperial Plate Glass Company, Richard Ireland and Richard Mott, together with a clerk, for conspiracy to defraud. Clark alleged that the men had sold him fabricated shares in the company, and as a result, he had lost £2,000. Clark's strategy worked, and a grand jury found true bills against the three, who were bailed before facing trial.[67] He then tried to rally shareholders in other companies behind a policy of criminal prosecution. The

[63] *Morning Chronicle*, 4 April 1826.

[64] The words are Thomas Chalmers's, cited in Boyd Hilton, *The Age of Atonement: The Influence of Evangelicalism on Social and Economic Thought, 1785–1865* (Oxford, 1988; repr. 2001), 121–2.

[65] *Morning Chronicle*, 16 May 1826. 'Bulls' and 'bears' were popular terms for speculators on the stock market.

[66] *Rex v. Goundry* (1826), *Morning Chronicle*, 16 May 1826, *The Times*, 16 May 1826. The Common Serjeant was deputy to the Recorder of London, the most senior permanent judge at the Old Bailey.

[67] *The Times*, 19 January, 5 April 1826.

board of the Equitable Loan Bank Company, which featured Brogden, Bent, Congreve, and Moulton-Barrett, had spent all but £69 of the company's money, but it had not actually started business. The directors' main priority seemed to have been speculating in the company's shares, and they had made big profits selling out when they were at a large premium.[68] At a general meeting in April, Clark told his fellow shareholders that while he would prefer 'mild measures' to induce the directors to do the right thing, he feared that 'the only plan to be adopted with effect against fraudulent directors, was to bring them before the Lord Mayor'.[69]

Fast becoming a 'corporate gadfly', Clark was also involved in other scandals which erupted over the summer, featuring a familiar cast of characters.[70] John Wilks, the solicitor son of the Arigna's auditor, was active in promoting domestic mining companies, and had assembled an impressive board for the Cornwall and Devon Mining Company. Moore was the chairman; Moulton-Barrett was one of the deputy chairmen, and three other MPs were also found, including no less than Henry John Temple, Viscount Palmerston, Secretary at War since 1809.[71] Palmerston had been under no illusions as to Wilks's nature, writing to his brother-in-law when the company was being formed that 'I am sure [Wilks] is a bit of a rogue if nature writes a legible hand; at the same time he is a clever fellow and as long as his interest goes hand in hand with ours will probably do well by us'.[72] Getting involved with Wilks was a decision he came to rue. As the company's solicitor, Wilks had cut a lucrative deal for himself, leasing the mines from their owners for £79,500, but charging the company £121,000 for them. Worse still, though £54,000 was subscribed, Wilks fell behind with the payments to the mine owners, and under the terms of the leases, the mines therefore reverted to them. At a general meeting, Clark accused the absent Wilks of defrauding the company, and Moore, Moulton-Barrett, and four other directors of accepting secret payments from Wilks. He asked his fellow victims to decide 'whether they were to submit to the robbery, or whether they should proceed to recover what they had lost by legal means, and endeavour to have the satisfaction of seeing the guilty parties brought to the Old Bailey': rabble-rousing which received much applause.[73] Clark went on to make similar accusations against the management of the Welsh Iron and Coal Mining Company, another Wilks promotion, whose board also featured Moore, Moulton-Barrett, and Palmerston.[74]

The revelations attracted blanket press coverage through the summer and autumn of 1826. Amusement was the dominant response in some quarters,

[68] Ibid. 7 April 1826.

[69] Ibid. 21 April 1826.

[70] 'Corporate gadflies', a type of shareholder activist, were a familiar sight in 1930s America: see Janette Rutterford, 'The Shareholder Voice: British and American Accents, 1890–1965', *Enterprise and Society*, 13 (2012), 120–53.

[71] *The Times*, 15 April 1825.

[72] *The Letters of the Third Viscount Palmerston to Laurence and Elizabeth Sulivan, 1804–1863*, ed. Kenneth Bourne (London, 1979), 175. Wilks was not shy of approaching Cabinet ministers with his proposals, writing to Sir Robert Peel requesting that he become president of his Provincial Bank for England and Wales: letter of 24 February 1826, ff. 273–4, British Library, Peel Papers, Add.40385.

[73] *The Times*, 28 July, 16 August 1826; *Morning Post*, 16 August 1826.

[74] *The Times*, 28 August 1826.

prompting comic verse satirizing the excesses of the bubble-blowers.[75] Others were more indignant, the *New Monthly Magazine* noting the 'very disgraceful disclosures' in the City: general meetings had exposed 'such a system of fraud and knavery, as cannot, even in the present inexplicable, contradictory, and absurd state of our laws, escape well-merited punishment'.[76] Indeed, autumn saw a renewed flurry of complaints presented to the Lord Mayor at Mansion House, but in every case Venables, his patience growing ever thinner, declined to act. After dismissing a complaint against the Rio de la Plata Mining Association on the grounds of lack of evidence of guilty intent, he had to sit through a prolonged dispute between Wilks and his former partner, Frederick Verbeke.[77] Wilks's refusal to surrender the Welsh Iron Company's share transfer book had escalated into a violent feud between the two men, and after a succession of lengthy hearings, in which Verbeke was backed by William Clark, Venables dismissed the case, and was heard to groan 'Messrs. Wilks and Verbeke, Messrs. Wilks and Verbeke, the Lord deliver me from Messrs. Wilks and Verbeke'.[78]

When complainants were clearly speculators who had been caught out, Venables had little time for their grievances, particularly when he suspected they were simply threatening criminal actions to collect debts. The day after dismissing Wilks's application a solicitor came to Mansion House to apply for summonses against the promoters of yet another mining scheme, the Waldeck Company, for conspiracy to defraud and obtaining money under false pretences. Before he could go any further, Venables asked him whether he had strong legal grounds for his case, 'because the applications have been so numerous relative to these joint stock companies, without their coming to any thing; and I should not be inclined to listen to another application, unless the parties can say positively that they are certain their claims are far stronger'. He eventually allowed the solicitor to continue, but when witnesses were produced who had invested in the company, Venables tore them down from the moral high ground. One, who was a clerk, had bought fifty shares, but admitted under questioning that he did not have the money to make such a purchase; a second Venables dismissed as a 'stock-jobber' who had bought the shares for speculation. On further questioning, the solicitor admitted that the Lord Mayor's help was sought 'as the cheapest and most summary for the parties': he had hoped that taking the case to Mansion House would force the promoters to come to terms with the investors. Venables said that he would not allow disappointed speculators to use the law 'to force an accommodation', and accordingly dismissed the complaint.[79]

By the time the Cornwall and Devon Company's affairs were presented to Venables, he was thoroughly sick of joint-stock disputes. A respectable-looking

[75] *Glasgow Herald*, 11 September 1826; *Examiner*, 24 September 1826.

[76] *New Monthly Magazine and Literary Journal*, 18 (September 1826), 353.

[77] *The Times*, 21 September 1826. Wilks with his partner Verbeke were solicitors to at least seven companies; his father to a further nine: Ron Harris, *Industrializing English Law: Entrepreneurship and Business Organization* (Cambridge, 2000), 263 n. 37.

[78] *The Times*, 7 September, 4 October 1826.

[79] Ibid. 5 October 1826.

mechanic called Menet came to plead his case. With tears in his eyes, he explained that during the boom, he had seen the company's prospectus, and was drawn in by the names of Palmerston and Moore. An interview with Moore at the company's offices persuaded him of the safety of investing his life's savings of £300. But rather than yielding dividends, the investment became a liability, with the board making large calls on the shares which Menet could ill afford. Venables 'expressed his sorrow at the condition of the poor man, but could give him no relief'. He had brought his troubles on himself, as many others had done during the boom, by committing himself 'before he had made adequate inquiries respecting the nature of the plan'. Venables told the man to go to the company's solicitors and explain to them his position: they might be sympathetic.[80]

This hardening attitude in Mansion House discouraged shareholders from following Clark into further battles. In September, he urged the Alliance Granite shareholders to back a prosecution of the directors, but having received little help from the Lord Mayor earlier in the year, they were sceptical. One responded that he would 'much rather have the money he had paid as deposits, than go to the Old Bailey for satisfaction', which the reporter noted was 'the general feeling of the room'.[81] Clark had vowed 'to destroy every spurious company he could reach', but his authority was weakening.[82] At a meeting of the Cornwall and Devon Company, details of his past were revealed. Wilks told the shareholders that Clark had been 'compelled to visit the Lunatic Asylum a couple of years ago', and accused him of being 'hired to attack companies'. Clark admitted that he had 'been affected in the intellect' as a result of a falling out with his former employer, Joseph Timperon, which had caused him serious financial loss, but that he had fully recovered, and he denied that he had ever received a farthing for his exertions at general meetings.[83] Clark was subsequently sued successfully by Timperon for having published a series of malicious libels against him, and while no punishment was recorded, the affair served to further weaken his credibility.[84]

But Clark still had one card left to play. His prosecution of the Imperial Plate Glass directors, delayed by its transferral to the Court of King's Bench so that it could be tried before a special jury, took place in January 1827. The switch in location, requested by the defendants, was their attempt to secure as sympathetic a body of jurymen as possible, an act of 1825 stipulating that special juries would consist only of bankers, merchants, and men of the rank of esquire or above.[85] And although the defendants were hardly members of the capital's financial elite—Richard Ireland was a glass manufacturer and upholsterer, Richard Mott a

[80] Ibid. 17 October 1826.
[81] Ibid. 14 September 1826.
[82] Ibid. 18 November 1826.
[83] Ibid. 16 August 1826.
[84] Ibid. 27 October 1826. Clark later said that he had never been brought up for judgement: ibid. 15 January 1827.
[85] 6 Geo. IV c. 50, s. 31. Though in the absence of strict definitions of these occupational categories, it seems that men of lower status continued to serve in some instances: James Oldham, 'Special Juries in England: Nineteenth-Century Usage and Reform', *Journal of Legal History*, 8 (1987), 155–6.

fishmonger, Peter Stainsby a bank clerk—the trial was a high-profile affair occupying the finest lawyers of the day. The presiding judge was Chief Justice Abbott. The prosecution was conducted by Thomas Denman, the judge in Goundry's case, and a leading Whig lawyer who was Queen Caroline's Solicitor General in 1820 and had been Common Serjeant of the City of London since 1822.[86] Ireland's defence was in the hands of another Whig lawyer, James Scarlett, 'the most successful advocate of his day'. No one was immune to his persuasiveness—a common joke was that he had 'developed a machine which made judges nod their assent at his arguments'—and, unfortunately for Clark, his influence over Abbott was 'so marked as to become a subject of complaint at the bar'.[87] Stainsby's defence was led by John Gurney, who knew his way around the law of conspiracy, having conducted the successful prosecution of Lord Cochrane for the supposed stock exchange hoax of 1814 and the Cato Street Conspirators in 1820.[88] Clark charged the three men with conspiracy to defraud him of £2,000 by selling him 238 shares which were over and above the 2,000 shares which the company's prospectus stated it would issue. But it seemed that his main grievance was that the defendants had sold out their shares when they were at 8 per cent premium, breaking an understanding previously reached that they would wait till they reached 25 per cent. This prompted 'such an inundation of the market' that Clark, who had bought at a premium, was left facing large losses. Denman portrayed Clark's loss as 'not merely a question between him and the defendants', but as 'a gross fraud' on the public.[89]

The defence lawyers attempted to get the case thrown out on the grounds of the illegality of the company and its shares. Scarlett said that the indictments mentioned a company legally constituted with shares, but the company never had an act of incorporation, and though a deed of settlement was prepared, it was never signed. As a result, it was only a projected company with intended shares—scrip.[90] Abbott, who had accepted this line of argument when ruling in favour of the defendant in the Equitable Loan Bank civil lawsuit in 1825, said that 'as a lawyer, he might be disposed to say these papers were not shares', but decided to allow the trial to continue. More fatal to the prosecution's case was the fact that the defence lawyers were able to cast considerable doubt on Clark's motives and character. He was a stockbroker who, by his own admission, 'trafficked a good deal in the shares of joint stock companies'. He had bought the shares speculating for a rise, but had lost. Alluding not so subtly to Clark's well-publicized mental health problems, Scarlett was able to play on familiar critiques likening speculation to madness to devastating effect: 'there were men in whom selfishness prevailed to such an insane

[86] Gareth H. Jones and Vivienne Jones, 'Thomas Denman', *ODNB*.

[87] G. F. R. Barker, rev. Elisabeth A. Cawthon, 'James Scarlett', *ODNB*.

[88] J. A. Hamilton, rev. Catherine Pease-Watkin, 'Sir John Gurney', *ODNB*.

[89] *Rex v. Mott* (1827) 172 ER 236, *Morning Chronicle*, 15 January 1827, *The Times*, 15 January 1827.

[90] Successful subscribers to a scheme were sent letters of allotment; on paying a deposit, these were exchanged for scrip, which were in turn swapped for shares when subscribers signed the deed of settlement and began paying calls. Speculation in scrip could be frantic: W. A. Thomas, *The Provincial Stock Exchanges* (London, 1973), 30–40.

degree, that they thought when they lost money that they had a right to recover it by any means. This was really pursuing selfishness to the verge of insanity'.[91]

Things got worse still for Clark. The chief weakness with his case was that whilst it appeared that the company had indeed issued more than the advertised 2,000 shares, there was no evidence that the shares sold to Clark were fabricated, quite the reverse. The evidence strongly suggested they were part of the original 2,000 shares, as at that stage only 1,265 shares were shown to have been on the market. Consequently, Abbott instructed Denman to drop all twenty-three counts charging a sale of fabricated shares to Clark, leaving just the final count, a general charge that the defendants conspired to fabricate shares for the purpose of defrauding the public, to go to the jury. In his summing up, Abbott told the jury that they could still convict if they believed that the defendants had conspired to issue more shares than advertised in the company's prospectus, as this was a crime 'cognizable by that Court, notwithstanding the inherent defects of all associations of that nature'. However, as the charge was conspiracy, the jury had to find at least two of the men guilty. Ireland had delegated to Mott the power to authorize further share issues, and while Abbott thought that in doing this, Ireland had acted 'very improperly', there was no evidence that he knew of the over-issue of shares. There was even less evidence against Stainsby, whose bank had issued just 1,886 shares—it was the company's other bankers who had issued shares over and above the 2,000 permitted. Abbott told the jury that unless they thought either Ireland or Stainsby guilty, they must also acquit Mott. The jury deliberated for just five minutes before acquitting all three defendants.[92]

IN THE POCKET

Clark was defeated, and this was the final attempt to criminally prosecute directors of the 1825 boom. With a stern gatekeeper in the form of the Lord Mayor imposing a narrow definition of fraud, few cases made it to trial. When they did, they either fell on legal technicalities, or were fatally hamstrung by a lack of evidence proving guilty intent. Nor did shareholders find it easy to hit directors in their pockets by means of civil litigation. Early in the crisis, *The Times* told shareholders that if they found evidence of fraud, 'the persons resorting to such means ought and might be prosecuted, and compelled to return what they had so fraudulently obtained'.[93] But this was an idealized view of the law. The first problem facing shareholders was the uncertain legal standing of joint-stock companies so soon after the repeal of the Bubble Act, which made civil actions complicated, time-consuming, and expensive. This was the experience of the Arigna shareholders who

[91] *Morning Chronicle*, 15 January 1827; *The Times*, 15 January 1827. Public concern over the problem of malicious prosecutions was at its height in the early nineteenth century: Douglas Hay, 'Prosecution and Power: Malicious Prosecution in the English Courts, 1750–1850', in Hay and Snyder (eds), *Policing and Prosecution*, 377–89.

[92] *Morning Chronicle*, 15 January 1827; *The Times*, 15 January 1827.

[93] *The Times*, 13 February 1826.

launched a Chancery suit against their directors in early 1826 for making secret profits from the mine purchase.[94] The defendants managed to delay proceedings by raising a series of legal objections, and the case was not finally decided until May 1831. It continued over several days and was vigorously argued by both sides, with a total of thirteen counsel engaged by the two factions. One by one, however, Vice Chancellor Sir Lancelot Shadwell dismissed the objections raised by the defendants. Ignorance of the source of the money was no defence, while objections that the mines were worth the £25,000 paid was not material, for there was still a misrepresentation. Shadwell found for the plaintiffs with costs, but the shareholders had had to wait five and a half years for their reward.[95]

Others received swifter justice. At the end of 1826, a shareholder in the Imperial Distillery Company managed to recover his £100 investment from the directors. Vice-Chancellor Sir John Leach ruled that the company was not established with genuine intentions but was 'a snare to make persons subscribe to that which was intended for the private emolument of the directors, who were to make a profit by the sale of the shares'.[96] Yet such victories were not the norm.[97] One reason was that many of the companies of the boom had run up large debts, which left shareholders vulnerable to legal actions from directors seeking to enforce calls on shares, and from creditors demanding repayment. The shareholders of the Cornwall and Devon Mining Company threatened both civil and criminal proceedings against their directors, but the latter were able to turn the tables by making a call on the shares, and promising that legal action would be taken against anyone resisting payment.[98] This proved an effective strategy: attendance at the shareholders' meetings plummeted, which Clark attributed to the directors' threats: many shareholders feared that 'if they made themselves conspicuous in any proceeding against the directors, the latter would select them for litigation'.[99] Subsequently, neither side could use the law to land a blow against the other. First, the directors tried and failed to enforce their calls in the courts since the meeting which authorized the calls was not legally constituted.[100] But the shareholders proved similarly unable to harness the law against their directors. In 1828, an attempt by a shareholder to

[94] Ibid. 27 February 1826.

[95] *Hichens v. Congreve* (1831) 58 ER 157, *Standard*, 31 May 1831, *The Times*, 31 May 1831.

[96] *Green v. Barrett* (1826) 57 ER 495, *The Times*, 8 November 1826. Leach cited the case of *Colt v. Woollaston* (1723) in which the plaintiffs successfully recovered their investment in one of the bubbles of 1720, a project for extracting oil from English radishes.

[97] Earlier that year, a shareholder had recovered his investment in the Bristol and Northern Railway, a projected company which did no business, though the defendant was not a director but a fellow shareholder who had sold him the shares: *Kempson v. Saunders* (1826) 172 ER 165. Lobban cites this case, and two others, as evidence that the courts were very willing 'to protect the naïve investor' and displayed little in the way of '[d]our evangelicalism'. But there were clear limits to the protections afforded by the courts, as some of the following cases suggest. Michael Lobban, 'The Politics of English Law in the Nineteenth Century', in Paul Brand and Joshua Getzler (eds), *Judges and Judging in the History of the Common Law and Civil Law: From Antiquity to Modern Times* (Cambridge, 2012), 124–5.

[98] *The Times*, 21 October 1826.

[99] Ibid. 18 November 1826, 27 January 1827.

[100] *Moore v. Hammond* (1827) 108 ER 519, *Morning Chronicle*, 1 May 1827, *Morning Post*, 7 May 1827.

recoup his £525 investment from two of the directors on the grounds of fraud failed. Chief Justice Abbott, denying the collective responsibility of the board of directors, ruled that there was no evidence of fraud against either of the defendants, so the shareholder's case fell.[101]

The law offered more facilities to creditors of companies than to shareholders, and actions brought by creditors were usually successful when a legitimate debt could be proven.[102] Sometimes creditors targeted directors, but they were not usually too concerned from whom they recovered—directors and shareholders were all partners in the eyes of the law, and all equally liable. So when shareholders in the Imperial Distillery Company were sued at the Court of Common Pleas in 1829 by an engineer for over £2,300 for work done on behalf of the company in 1825, the jury found the shareholders liable for the full amount. The shareholders' lawyers secured a retrial on the grounds that their clients had parted with their shares before the work was done, had not signed the deed of settlement, and had not held themselves out to the world as partners, but the original verdict was confirmed.[103] Talk of legal action therefore soon dissipated after the initial exposures in many of the scandal-struck companies, as suing directors seemed less of a priority than fending off litigious creditors.[104]

Nevertheless, a final possibility for redress remained. The fact that so many of the directors implicated in the frauds and failures were MPs raised the possibility that parliament would act against the worst offenders. Following Hobhouse's questions in February 1826, the subject was not debated further that session, which was cut short in May due to elections. The directors at the heart of the scandals fared relatively well as the pre-reform political system insulated politicians from public opinion. Brogden was MP for the pocket borough of Launceston, in the gift of the Duke of Northumberland. Brogden retained his patron's support, and was returned unopposed.[105] Richmond was in the pocket of Thomas, first Baron Dundas, a Whig landowner, who saw no reason to remove his friend and neighbour Moulton-Barrett.[106] Congreve had become Member for Plymouth as nominee of the Prince of Wales, high steward of the town, who since 1806 had chosen one of the constituency's two MPs. In 1826, local interests were disinclined to upset this arrangement, and Congreve was returned unopposed.[107] Other directors did less well. At Totnes, Bent was obliged to step aside to accommodate the son of the Earl of Darlington, but the decision had nothing to do with the joint-stock scandal.[108] Moore, by contrast, was a direct casualty of the scandal. Coventry, where he had been member since 1803, had a relatively democratic franchise which

[101] *De Lisle v. Kay* (1828), *The Times*, 3 December 1828.

[102] *Clay v. Langslow* (1827) 173 ER 1076, *Bristol Mercury*, 19 March 1827; *Lawler v. Kershaw* (1827) 173 ER 1093, *The Times*, 17 October 1827.

[103] *Fox v. Clifton* (1830) 130 ER 1479, *The Times*, 24 October, 11, 30 November 1829, 1 July 1830, 8 July 1831.

[104] At the Equitable Loan Bank, for example, shareholders were preoccupied liquidating the claims of creditors, not fully accomplished until August 1829: *The Times*, 4 May, 18 December 1826, 19 May 1827, 28 November 1842.

[105] Fisher, *House of Commons*, ii. 159–60.

[106] Ibid. iii. 281. [107] Ibid. ii. 283–5. [108] Ibid. 300–1.

included many artisans, and Moore came bottom in a four-cornered contest.[109] However, in a spectacular twist, Wilks, who had not previously sat in parliament, stood for the corrupt borough of Sudbury as an independent 'constitutional Briton' and, thanks to his munificence to the voters, was successfully returned.[110]

The presence of several of the tarnished directors in the new parliament of 1826 made the bubbles a warm political topic. Even though the *Morning Chronicle* reflected that the shareholders were gamblers, and gamblers sometimes lost, it thought 'there are rules which ought to be observed in every game; and it appears that many of the winners have but too often been foul players'.[111] This sense of foul play meant that pressure for investigation built through the autumn, and the press confidently predicted that parliament would institute 'a severe and active enquiry'.[112] The radical alderman Robert Waithman, returned to parliament in the elections, spearheaded the move for enquiry, and when the new parliamentary session commenced in November he wasted little time raising the issue. He complained that, unlike in 1720, parliament had taken no steps to punish the projectors of the fraudulent schemes. He singled out Brogden, as chairman of the Committee of Ways and Means, insisting that he explain his conduct before being allowed to continue in the role.[113] Brogden resigned three days later, but Waithman kept up the pressure, presenting a petition from the Arigna shareholders calling for an enquiry.[114] Waithman claimed that the Arigna Company was just one of several which needed to be investigated, and moved for a general committee to enquire into the mania as a whole. He highlighted the 'immense sums' lost through fraudulent companies, and whilst investors may have been foolish, it was 'the duty of the legislature to protect the foolish and the simple, the silly and the ignorant, against the arts and insidious devices of the crafty and the knavish'.[115]

The government rejected a general investigation as unnecessary, and potentially damaging to the economy. Leader of the Commons George Canning thought that it would be taken as an indictment of joint-stock companies as a whole, whereas many had proven to be 'useful speculations' in which 'persons of the most unimpeachable characters' were involved. Canning consented to a select committee, but, crucially, it would be tasked with investigating the Arigna only. If the allegations were proven, then other companies could be investigated in due course.[116] In pursuing this line, the government, rather than shielding particular individuals as in 1720, was shielding

[109] Ibid. iii. 130.
[110] Ibid. vii. 778.
[111] *Morning Chronicle*, 7 September 1826.
[112] *Age*, 10, 24 September 1826; *Morning Herald*, repr. in *Royal Cornwall Gazette*, 4 November 1826; *Morning Chronicle*, 14 November 1826.
[113] Hansard, 2s, 16: 72–3 (21 November 1826).
[114] Ibid. 137–42 (24 November 1826); *Journals of the House of Commons*, 82: 91 (5 December 1826).
[115] Hansard, 2s, 16: 243–55 (5 December 1826). During these debates, Congreve wrote an unrepentant letter to Peel. His main defence—that he was justified in taking a cut, and that he insisted that the profits be shared by the whole board—did not really help his cause: letter of 24 November 1826, ff. 88–92, British Library, Peel Papers, Add.40390.
[116] Hansard, 2s, 16: 255–7 (5 December 1826).

the joint-stock system as a whole which, bemired in scandal, was vulnerable to attack. Now, all awaited the results of the committee's investigations.[117]

These were certainly thorough, with thirty-two witnesses interviewed, including Brogden, Bent, and Congreve. The committee probed the allegedly fraudulent share traffic which took place in the three months following the company's formation. Such was the public enthusiasm for the shares that two of the directors, Henry and Joseph Clarke, were rumoured to have realized as much as £25,000. However, the committee was unable to find records verifying these claims, and whilst it thought the claims very probable, the 'intricacy' of the deals and the lack of evidence meant it did not detail them at length. Unsurprisingly, the committee focused instead on the issue which had attracted the most press comment—the division of the £15,000 profit secured on the sale of the Arigna property. Though the committee members were not asked to comment on its legality, 'they cannot in a moral view designate it otherwise than as a deliberate fraud'. It was so objectionable because it was secret, having been carefully concealed from the shareholders. The committee thought that the deal originated with the former owner of the mines and the Clarkes, admitting that it could not find any direct evidence that Congreve was aware of the details of the fraud. Nevertheless, it thought that he was too implicated in the company's affairs to be able to plead ignorance, and that it 'must impute to him, either a too ready dismissal of scruples... or a want of sufficient sensibility to obligations'.[118] Stopping short of accusing Brogden and Bent of lying, the committee nevertheless noted that their testimony exhibited 'so many marks of hasty and imperfect recollection, as to inspire little confidence in the precise exactness of its details'. But in the absence of clear evidence to the contrary, it accepted their defence that they were ignorant of the true source of the £15,000 and assumed the money to have derived from the sale of shares. Nevertheless, this was not a moral exculpation: such a reservation of shares for the board's benefit, though practised in other joint-stock companies, was 'altogether improper and unjustifiable'.[119]

Despite this censure, the report did not say what action, if any, parliament should take. Rumours in London suggested that Waithman intended to move for the expulsion of both Congreve and Brogden, 'and for the prosecution of the original concocters of this bubble by the Attorney-General'.[120] But the report, critical though it was, did not accuse the MPs of conceiving the fraud, and it was too measured in its conclusions to sustain a crusade. In fact, for all its criticisms, the report punctured the campaign against the men. Revealingly, *The Times*, which had been so outspoken in its attacks on the MPs, quietly dropped the subject after the report was published. Waithman's critics, such as the Tory *John Bull*, heaped scorn on him for pursuing an unjust vendetta against his enemies.[121]

[117] *Age*, 10 December 1826.

[118] *Select Committee on the Arigna Mining Company*, 11–13, 13–14, 16–17, 23–4.

[119] Ibid. 24–32.

[120] N. S., 'Letter upon Affairs in General, from a Gentleman in the "Country" to a Gentleman in "London"', *Monthly Magazine, or, British Register*, 3 (May 1827), 526.

[121] *John Bull*, 9 April 1827.

Undaunted, days after the report's publication Waithman renewed his attack on fraudulent companies in the Commons, presenting a petition from subscribers to the Cornwall and Devon Mining Company, accusing the directors of making secret profits from the sale of the mining property and fraudulently manipulating the share price.[122] Waithman singled out Wilks, elected to the Commons last summer, but he also pointed out that a total of ten of the company's directors were 'noblemen, baronets, and members of that House'. He called upon members to vindicate the honour of parliament by inflicting 'condign punishment' on anyone taking part in the fraud. But enthusiasm for further investigation was waning, with even Waithman's fellow radical Daniel Whittle Harvey doubting that parliament was the best forum to investigate the matter. Palmerston, embroiled in the affair as one of the directors, questioned the petitioners' motives. They were not the helpless victims of fraud, but failed speculators. 'It was not honest for individuals to subscribe nominally to an undertaking', he observed, 'then, when they found that they could not make a miserable profit by trafficking in the shares, to attempt to withdraw themselves from all responsibility'.[123]

The crusade was doomed. When Waithman subsequently moved for a select committee, he faced a wall of opposition. Henry Brougham thought that the House should not 'erect itself into a court of criminal jurisdiction to try those offences' when they were being dealt with by other, more suitable, courts. Ultimately, they were private, not public, affairs, and it was not parliament's business to collect 'all the gossip of the town'.[124] The banker Hudson Gurney, an independent MP and an authority on economic matters, argued along similar lines. He did not defend Wilks, even noting in his diary that evening that he was a 'great rogue'.[125] But he thought it beyond the jurisdiction of the House to inquire into what were private affairs: 'it was evidently impossible that the House of Commons could make themselves the auditors of private accounts'. Even Robert Grant, the Tory chairman of the Arigna committee, opposed appointing another one. Waithman withdrew his motion, and did not subsequently revisit the subject in the Commons.[126] After the Arigna witch-hunt, MPs shelved the idea of using parliament as a surrogate court.

REGULATION BY REPUTATION

Given the sensation of the collapse of 1825, the results, measured in terms of criminal prosecutions, civil actions, or parliamentary enquiries, might seem slight. Yet this was not a society tolerant of morally dubious behaviour by its public men. Reputation was the currency of business, and several reputations were destroyed by involvement in fraudulent companies. This, ultimately, was

[122] *Journals of the House of Commons*, 82: 399 (9 April 1827).
[123] Hansard, 2s, 17: 299–343 (9 April 1827).
[124] Ibid. 848–50 (15 May 1827).
[125] Peter Osborne, 'Hudson Gurney', *ODNB*; Fisher, *House of Commons*, vii. 778.
[126] Hansard, 2s, 17: 845–53 (15 May 1827).

how the joint-stock economy was to be regulated. In April 1827, at a meeting of the Imperial Distillery Company, in which Wilks, Moore, and Moulton-Barrett were involved, William Clark boasted that he had 'succeeded in covering these directors with shame, and driving them out of society'.[127] Clark was perhaps guilty of a degree of self-aggrandizement here. MPs whose involvement with the fraudulent companies was marginal did not suffer long-term effects to their reputations. Moulton-Barrett retired from parliament in 1827, but this was to take control of his substantial West Indian estates. He died in Jamaica ten years later, leaving his niece a substantial legacy.[128] Palmerston had not been a 'bubble-monger': confident the Cornwall and Devon Company would be profitable, he purchased shares in it for his son; when it proved a failure, he paid his liabilities.[129] Thus, his involvement did not impair his political prospects. Bent was more directly involved than either Moulton-Barrett or Palmerston, but having stood down from parliament in 1826, was able to fade into the background, re-inventing himself as a Sussex squire.[130]

Nevertheless, there was some truth to Clark's claim, as those whose names were more closely associated with the frauds faced the loss of their reputations as well as their fortunes. Moore, a leading figure in Whig society, was reduced to a figure of contempt.[131] Association with the bubbles plagued him during his ill-fated election campaign, during which the new cry of 'No Stock Jobbing!' supplemented the more familiar 'No Popery!'[132] The Tory press eagerly reminded voters of Moore's embarrassing business interests, the *Age* lambasting him for having 'assumed the directorship of an almost countless number of… bubbles'.[133] It regarded his defeat as 'a proper retribution on the most consummate impudence and ignorance that ever one man was clothed with'.[134] His ousting left him vulnerable to creditors' suits, and in March 1827 he was arrested at the behest of bankers for non-payment of a £5,000 bond which he had signed as a director of the Cornwall and Devon Company.[135] He complained to the press that 'without any previous notice, I was awoke out of my sleep, and at the age of seventy-four, was arrested by Sheriffs' officers'.[136] On his release in June, he moved to France in order to avoid further actions, and he died there a year later, leaving just £300.[137] The *Age*'s verdict? '[R]ats die in holes and corners'.[138]

[127] *The Times*, 23 April 1827.

[128] Marjorie Stone, 'Elizabeth Barrett Browning', *ODNB*; Fisher, *House of Commons*, vi. 448–50.

[129] Henry Lytton Bulwer, *The Life of Henry John Temple, Viscount Palmerston, with Selections from his Diaries and Correspondence*, 3 vols (London, 1871–4), i. 150.

[130] Fisher, *House of Commons*, iv. 253.

[131] E. A. Smith, 'Peter Moore', *ODNB*.

[132] Fisher, *House of Commons*, iii. 133.

[133] *Age*, 4 June 1826; *Hull Packet*, 20 June 1826.

[134] *Age*, 18 June 1826. See also *John Bull*, 19 June, 4 September 1826; *Morning Post*, 29 June 1826.

[135] *Age*, 11 March 1827; *Bell's Life in London and Sporting Chronicle*, 11 March 1827; *The Times*, 12 March 1827.

[136] *Bell's Life in London and Sporting Chronicle*, 18 March 1827.

[137] *Jackson's Oxford Journal*, 5 May, 12 June 1827; Fisher, *House of Commons*, vi. 433.

[138] *Newcastle Courant*, 17 May 1828; *Age*, 18 May 1828.

Congreve's fall was equally dramatic. A baronet, equerry to the king, comptroller of the royal laboratory, major-general, honoured by Tsar Alexander of Russia and Charles XIV of Sweden, he found himself squeezed from the companies whose boards he had graced. The *Age*, which had pilloried Moore, a Whig, was just as contemptuous of the Tory Congreve who had allowed his urge to speculate to 'degrade the dignity of his rank, and the talents by which he has signalized his name, and placed himself so high in office, into a mere stock-jobbery reputation—an avocation which, however lucrative to himself, has visited hundreds of other people with positive ruin'.[139] Though the patronage of the king secured his re-election, the unfavourable Arigna report raised expectations that he would vacate his seat, and indeed he announced his intention to retire two months after its publication.[140] With the Chancery action hanging over him, he left for the Continent, his departure mocked in the press.[141] Less than a year later he was dead, aged just 55.[142] He did not manage to salvage much from his career of speculation, leaving just £100 to his wife and children.[143] Obituaries acknowledged his scientific achievements, but classed him 'with those individuals of previous respectability, the influence of whose example decoyed so many weaker minds to ruin'.[144]

Wilks, the enterprising solicitor, had used his ill-gotten wealth to buy his way into high society. He maintained an extravagant lifestyle, hosting entertainments at his mansions in Middlesex and Ramsgate, and spent £3,000 securing his election to parliament before the extent of his frauds had been exposed.[145] But soon after his moment of triumph his world began to unravel. He fought hard to retrieve his reputation through the second half of 1826, firing off letters to the press to defend his character and threatening his critics with legal action, but the negative commentary mounted.[146] In November he had to fend off accusations of forgery which saw him hauled before the Lord Mayor.[147] His reputation was such that he 'seldom showed his face in the House of Commons', and it was well known that only his status as a Member prevented his imprisonment for debt.[148] He had been dropped by his companies and without employment, and facing further legal actions, a relation promised him a modest annuity on condition that he quit the country. He resigned his seat and moved to Paris in March 1828, where he continued his career of speculation, promoting a string of unsuccessful companies, and nearly being expelled from the country after spreading false

139 *Age*, 4 June 1826.

140 *John Bull*, 18 June 1827. He did not retire, however, and a replacement was only elected after his death: Fisher, *House of Commons*, ii, 285.

141 *Bell's Life in London and Sporting Chronicle*, 1 July 1827; *Plymouth Herald*, repr. in *Jackson's Oxford Journal*, 30 June 1827.

142 *Caledonian Mercury*, 29 May 1828; *John Bull*, 2 June 1828.

143 Fisher, *House of Commons*, iv. 717–18.

144 *Gentleman's Magazine* (August 1828), 178–9.

145 Fisher, *House of Commons*, vii. 778.

146 *Examiner*, 3, 10 September 1826; *The Times*, 20, 26 September 1826.

147 *The Times*, 27 September, 24 October, 4, 7 November 1826.

148 Ibid. 13 December 1826; *Ipswich Journal*, 21 February 1846.

rumours on the Bourse.[149] His obituaries noted that his debt to nature was 'the only liability he ever settled'.[150]

It might seem that Brogden emerged more or less unscathed: unlike Moore, Congreve, and Wilks, he was not forced into exile, and, retaining the patronage of the Duke of Northumberland, he was able to remain in parliament until retiring in 1832. But involvement in the scandal 'effectively destroyed Brogden . . . as a public figure'.[151] He failed to retain the support of the Tory leadership: early in 1826, soon after the scandal broke, he wrote to Canning requesting an interview, which Canning, returning his letter, angrily declined. He was forced to relinquish the chairmanship of Ways and Means by Sir Robert Peel—a major blow as it paid £1,200 a year—and did not subsequently hold office. After the Arigna committee published its report, he complained in parliament of his 'persecution' at the hands of Waithman and the unfairness of being tried by a committee of 'country gentlemen and . . . young officers' rather than commercial men. The ordeal, which he likened to 'the Star-chamber inquisitions', had reduced him to 'a state of despair'.[152] The experience soured him, and clearly played on his mind for the rest of his life: he complained shortly before his death in 1842 that he had been done 'a very great injustice' by the select committee, and that he had been made the scapegoat to save the skin of Palmerston and other speculating ministers.[153]

CONCLUSION

Despite the terrible impact of the 1825 crash, contemporaries were quick to detect the hand of God at work. Anyone who turned to evangelical preachers to understand what had happened would find them almost glorying in the destruction wrought. Speculation and covetousness had corroded commercial morality; the crash was divine retribution for the nation's sins. While such extreme views were not uniformly held, they were detectable in the growing association between business failure and personal guilt—bankruptcies were not random events 'but the logical outcome of sin'.[154] This helps to explain the very limited extent to which the courts and parliament were prepared to intervene on behalf of the victims of the crash. The interposition of the law would actually undermine the workings of divine providence, for if left alone, the market would expunge itself of its unsound and fraudulent elements. Speculators would learn the error of their ways and return to wholesome enterprise, whilst those who tempted them would be driven from society and prevented from forming more companies. Reinforcing this tendency was a belief, prevalent on the bench, in the hortatory function of the law. As P. S. Atiyah has pointed out, judges in the nineteenth century were more concerned

[149] Richard Davenport-Hines, 'John Wilks', *ODNB*; *Gentleman's Magazine* (June 1846), 649–50.
[150] *Ipswich Journal*, 21 February 1846.
[151] Fisher, *House of Commons*, iv. 346.
[152] Hansard, 2s, 17: 850–2 (15 May 1827).
[153] Fisher, *House of Commons*, iv. 344–7.
[154] Hilton, *Age of Atonement*, 132–3.

with the influence of their decisions on long-term behaviour than with doing justice in individual cases: harsh decisions could play a crucial role 'in educating people how to behave'.[155] Nowhere was this more apparent than in decisions on joint-stock cases at all levels in the law courts.

The lack of formal sanctions against fraud should not, therefore, be taken as proof of 'class law'. It is certainly true that the criminal law could deal with petty thefts, most often committed by members of the lower orders, in brutal fashion. At the same Old Bailey sessions which saw Goundry acquitted, prisoners found guilty of burglary, horse theft, and sheep stealing were all sentenced to death.[156] Yet respectable criminals were dealt with in the same way, for the state still executed many well-to-do men (and occasionally women) for forgery in the early nineteenth century.[157] Bookending the commercial crisis were the high-profile executions of Henry Fauntleroy, a private banker, in 1824, and of Joseph Hunton, a wealthy merchant, in 1828.[158] The key issue was not the social status of the offender but the nature of the offence. Forgery, unlike the kinds of acts committed by joint-stock directors, was regarded as unambiguously criminal. For one, forgery was easier to prove—Fauntleroy had not even bothered pleading not guilty as the evidence, 'in his own handwriting, was indeed unanswerable'—and the intent of the forger was rarely in doubt.[159] Moreover, the victims of forgery, unlike those who bought shares in companies, were seen as entirely innocent, as they were not motivated by greed, nor could they be accused of gullibility. This explains the discrepancy in the criminal law's treatment of company fraudsters and forgers. Whereas voices in parliament and in the commercial community began to doubt the justice of allowing forgery to remain a capital offence in the 1820s, all were agreed that it was a serious crime against the public which warranted severe punishment. Conversely, there was widespread doubt that the criminal law could be applied to the joint-stock sector, with the Lord Mayor effectively acting as a gatekeeper, preventing the law from being used (or abused) by disaffected shareholders. Only two cases progressed to the criminal courts, and their outcomes suggested that it was too much of a stretch to make the law reach this kind of offence.

Although the statutory prohibition on joint-stock companies had been removed in 1825 with the repeal of the Bubble Act, this did not mean that the state was willing to promote investment in this kind of enterprise, which still carried the stigma of gambling and speculation. Those who took the plunge and did invest did so at their own risk, and disputes between members were considered private, not public, matters. This was not an inevitable conclusion: other industrializing nations took a different approach, highlighted by events in the US which had also seen a period of speculative 'mania' in 1824–5, followed by a crash in July 1826.

155 P. S. Atiyah, *The Rise and Fall of Freedom of Contract* (Oxford, 1979), 394–7.
156 *The Times*, 16 May 1826.
157 Phil Handler, 'Forgery and the End of the "Bloody Code" in Early Nineteenth-Century England', *Historical Journal*, 48 (2005), 690.
158 Ibid. 691–2; Richard Davenport-Hines, 'Henry Fauntleroy', *ODNB*.
159 Davenport-Hines, 'Fauntleroy'.

Several interconnected New York financial institutions failed owing hundreds of thousands of dollars, and the press called for criminal actions against 'these harpies, who practice upon the credulity of the ignorant and fatten upon the spoils of the widow and orphan'. The District Attorney of New York City responded by prosecuting several of the directors, including leading Republicans, for conspiracy.[160] Four were found guilty, and in his sentencing speech, the judge articulated a different view of the role of the criminal law in the joint-stock economy from that prevalent in Britain. New York was 'the emporium of the nation', and in its 'moneyed institutions' was centred much of the wealth of the nation. But these institutions could only thrive under the guardianship of 'incorruptible agents', and given the temptations they offered for fraud, and the destructive effects of such frauds, 'considerations of public policy call loudly, whenever such cases occur, for infliction of exemplary punishment upon the offenders'. The *Morning Chronicle* thought that the outcome set an example to the English courts, showing that, in America at least, judges 'dare to do their duty when flagrant transgressors come before them'.[161]

Though the one- and two-year sentences were subsequently overturned—indicating that difficulty making the criminal law penetrate the boardroom was not a uniquely English one—the judge's words suggest a different approach to the joint-stock economy. In New York, judges seemed willing to advance an economic case for prosecution, accepting the need for the criminal law to police moneyed institutions in the interests of the public. In England, shareholders were still seen as partners in private concerns who had no particular right to invoke the 'public' interest. There was great reluctance to adapt the law, either criminal or civil, to suit the interests of 'speculators' and 'stockjobbers'. Finally, in New York there was an official—the District Attorney—tasked with conducting prosecutions in the public interest, whereas in England prosecutions were left to the victims, who, though willing to threaten criminal actions to try to force directors to come to terms, were rarely minded to follow through with their threats. It was a pattern which was to be repeated after the next company mania a decade later.

[160] Eric Hilt, 'Wall Street's First Corporate Governance Crisis: The Panic of 1826', Working Paper 14892, National Bureau of Economic Research (2009).

[161] *Morning Chronicle*, 5 February 1827.

3

Mismanagement or Fraud? The 1830s

One of the more momentous consequences of the economic crisis of the mid 1820s was a major revision of England's banking code. Though joint-stock banks were prohibited in England from 1707 and in Ireland since 1783, no such restriction existed in Scotland following the lapse of the Bank of Scotland's monopoly in 1716.[1] As a result, larger banks began to flourish in Scotland towards the end of the century, and eighteen banks with over a dozen partners were operating by 1825.[2] Despite reverses such as the Ayr Bank failure in 1772, the Scottish banking system earned a reputation for stability, and the contrasting fortunes of banks north and south of the border when the 1825 crisis hit were striking: whereas around seventy banks in England and Wales fell, very few in Scotland followed.[3] Lord Liverpool's ministry, which had already liberalized banking law in Ireland before the crisis, was convinced that England had fared badly because its small country banks were ill-equipped to withstand financial pressure.[4] The Prime Minister questioned the wisdom of a system in which any 'small tradesman, a cheesemonger, a butcher, or a shoemaker, might open a country bank; but a set of persons with a fortune sufficient to carry on the concern with security were not permitted to do so'.[5] The result was an act, closely modelled on the legislation for Ireland, reforming the Bank of England's charter, permitting the establishment of joint-stock banks sixty-five miles outside of London.[6]

The government's hopes that the reform would stabilize the banking sector initially seemed justified: not one of the twenty-eight new banks formed up to 1832 failed. Improving economic conditions from 1833, together with a further relaxation of the law that year which permitted joint-stock banks inside London, quickened the pace of formations.[7] Eighty-nine new banks were established between 1833 and 1836, fifty-nine of these in the boom year of 1836.[8] These years also saw

[1] P. L. Cottrell and Lucy Newton, 'Banking Liberalization in England and Wales, 1826–1844', in Richard Sylla, Richard Tilly, and Gabriel Casares (eds), *The State, the Financial System, and Economic Modernization* (Cambridge, 1999), 78; Howard Bodenhorn, 'Free Banking in Ireland', in Kevin Dowd (ed.), *The Experience of Free Banking* (London, 1992), 138–9; Lawrence H. White, 'Free Banking in Scotland before 1844', in Dowd, *Free Banking*, 158.

[2] White, 'Free Banking in Scotland', 169. Some doubt the extent to which many of these banks can legitimately be described as 'joint-stock': Cottrell and Newton, 'Banking Liberalization', 82.

[3] Philip Ollerenshaw, *Banking in Nineteenth-Century Ireland: The Belfast Banks, 1825–1914* (Manchester, 1987), 22.

[4] Bodenhorn, 'Free Banking in Ireland', 144–5; Ollerenshaw, *Banking*, 9–10; Cottrell and Newton, 'Banking Liberalization', 79–80.

[5] Hansard, 2s, 14: 19 (2 February 1826).

[6] 7 Geo. IV c. 46.

[7] 3 & 4 Will. IV c. 98.

[8] Cottrell and Newton, 'Banking Liberalization', 84.

continued development in Scottish and Irish banking, with eighteen new companies established in Scotland between 1826 and 1844, and eight in Ireland.[9] The huge extension of currency and credit caused by the bank boom stimulated further economic activity: a contemporary collector of prospectuses counted a total of 300 joint-stock ventures promoted in the period 1834–37 with a nominal capital of £135 million.[10] Railways were a particular favourite among investors: this was 'the City's first railway boom', with the number of companies listed on the stock exchange nearly trebling between the summers of 1835 and 1836.[11] But with rapid growth came instability: 1834 saw the first joint-stock bank failure in England, followed by several more when confidence collapsed at the end of 1836.

Banking historians have tended to dwell upon the long-term success of joint-stock banking rather than the short-term problems.[12] But this obscures the tremendous psychological impact the banking boom and bust of the 1830s had on contemporaries. The boom revived memories of the 'bubbles' of 1824–25 and commentators were quick to assimilate the new promotions to familiar narratives of speculative mania and unchecked greed. And when joint-stock banks failed, the effects could be devastating. There may have been fewer joint-stock bank failures than country bank failures, but those that did fall sometimes had enormous debts—£3.3 million in the case of the Northern and Central Bank of England, £2.1 million for the Commercial Bank of England—which sent shockwaves through commercial districts.[13] Although the joint-stock company had largely slid from the political agenda after 1827, this chapter will show that the events of the mid 1830s brought it back with a bang. An extended post-mortem into the banking bust took place, with a succession of parliamentary investigations, more wide-ranging than that of 1826, attempting to diagnose what had gone wrong. The committees were assiduous in sifting the details, bringing to light evidence of scandalous behaviour in several joint-stock banks. Major reform to curb abuses in the banking sector seemed a certainty, but appearances were deceptive.

AN EXPERIMENTAL LAW

The fashion for companies in the mid 1830s brought back memories of 1825, and by the middle of 1836, the anxiety in parliament was palpable. At the end of his budget speech in May, Whig Chancellor Thomas Spring Rice urged the public to treat the new joint-stock banks with 'vigilance, caution, and prudence'. His concerns were echoed by his colleague, the President of the Board of Trade and MP for

[9] S. G. Checkland, *Scottish Banking: A History, 1695–1973* (Glasgow, 1975), 372–3; Ollerenshaw, *Banking*, 32.

[10] *First Report of the Select Committee on Joint Stock Companies*, PP 1844 VII. appendix 4.

[11] David Kynaston, *The City of London: Volume 1, A World of Its Own, 1815–1890* (London, 1994), 102.

[12] Edward Victor Morgan, *The Theory and Practice of Central Banking, 1797–1913* (Cambridge, 1943), 19–20; Cottrell and Newton, 'Banking Liberalization', 83–5.

[13] S. Evelyn Thomas, *The Rise and Growth of Joint Stock Banking* (London, 1934), 668–9.

Manchester Charles Poulett Thomson, who thought that banks were multiplying so quickly that they would inevitably cause mischief. The Whigs were not alone in their fears. The leader of the opposition, Sir Robert Peel, warned that history showed that the country was 'subject to vicissitudes arising from excessive speculation', and that the good times might not last. He likened the schemes currently being promoted to the 'mad projects' of 1825, and thought that the rapid spread of banks required a legislative response.[14] The following week, the backbench Liberal MP William Clay, a loyal government supporter, moved for a select committee to investigate the banking sector. Coming from a mercantile background, Clay was no enemy to joint-stock banks, but believed that among the legitimate projects lurked many 'bubble companies'.[15] The act of 1826 had not set up any regulatory code beyond requiring banks to register with the Stamp Office in London the names and addresses of their shareholders, the names of their public officers, the location of their branches, and where their bills and notes were issued.[16] Spring Rice assented. The act of 1826 had been 'an experimental law', so it was appropriate, ten years on, that parliament should investigate the results of that experiment, though he insisted on a committee of secrecy, as the inquiry would be dealing with commercially sensitive information. He stressed that the government's actions should not be construed as an attack on the joint-stock principle, which was 'one of the great discoveries of modern times'. But it was parliament's responsibility to ensure that the country was not 'imposed upon' by bubbles.[17]

Chaired by Spring Rice, the committee of secrecy interviewed sixteen witnesses connected with joint-stock banks through June and July, and circulated questionnaires to every bank in England and Wales. While it found some evidence of banks formed as vehicles for speculation, it concluded that a bigger problem than the bubbles were banks established for legitimate purposes, but which were badly managed.[18] There was a chasm between good governance in theory and the reality at some banks. The advocates of joint-stock banks boasted about their transparency: unlike private banks, they were 'more open to public inspection and information—there is no mystery about them'.[19] The company constitution—the deed of settlement—set out the rights and responsibilities of management and owners. Directors delegated the day-to-day running of the company to paid managers, but monitored them and made sure they acted in the company's interests. Rigorous accounts would be kept, with bad debts written off and honest appraisals of profit and loss ascertained. Dividends would be paid out of profits actually made. Important decisions concerning the life of the company would be made by the shareholders at general meetings.

[14] Hansard, 3s, 33: 672, 690, 686–7 (6 May 1836).

[15] Francis Watt, rev. H. C. G. Matthew, 'Sir William Clay', *ODNB*; Hansard, 3s, 33: 843 (12 May 1836).

[16] 7 Geo. IV c. 46, ss. 4–8.

[17] Hansard, 3s, 33: 859–66 (12 May 1836). Clay's speech was subsequently published as a pamphlet: William Clay, *Speech of William Clay, Esq., MP, on Moving for the Appointment of a Committee to Inquire into the Operation of the Act Permitting the Establishment of Joint-Stock Banks* (London, 1837).

[18] *Report from the Secret Committee on Joint Stock Banks*, PP 1836 IX. p. v.

[19] *Mercantile Journal*, repr. in *Bristol Mercury*, 13 August 1836.

This was the theory, but the committee uncovered an alternative reality at the Norwich and Norfolk Bank, established in 1827 and recently sold on to the East of England Bank in controversial circumstances. First, its promoters were inexperienced and negligent. The bank's founder was Samuel Bignold, a notable player in Norwich civil society, manager of the Norwich Union Fire and Life Insurance companies and formerly the town's Tory mayor.[20] His reassuring presence won lots of custom for the bank, but despite holding the title of resident director, he was little involved in the bank's affairs.[21] The managing director, Edward Booth, was left to determine lending policy, and contracted heavy debts much exceeding the paid-up capital of £23,000. The second problem was the method of accounting used by the bank. Balance sheets prepared for the board showed the profits made, but did not have the losses deducted.[22] Shareholders were not allowed to see even these flawed balance sheets: though Bignold claimed that they would have been given financial information had they requested it, this was contradicted by Robert Gilbert, one of his fellow directors who had recently quit the board. At one meeting, the shareholders meekly 'put forward . . . that they should like to have a balance-sheet if they could', but dropped the matter when Booth curtly informed them that this was not how banks operated and would be 'injurious to the concern'.[23] With the losses concealed, the bank was free to declare robust dividends of between 4 and 7 per cent, entirely unjustified by the bank's miserable performance. These dividends enabled it to issue many of its reserved shares to the public at a 10 per cent premium even after the losses had started to accrue.

The final failing identified was the manner in which the bank's business had been transferred earlier in 1836 to the East of England Bank, without notifying the public or consulting the shareholders. How little the management cared about good governance was suggested by a flippant comment by the bank's chief clerk, Thomas Nimmo. When asked whether the company's deed of settlement contained any provisions for how the company was to be wound-up, he replied: 'I can only answer that question by saying, I shall have great pleasure in referring to it, but I do not think I have read it through in my life.'[24] Despite Bignold's claim that the bank had always sought to do the best by its shareholders, the fact that he was a trustee of the East of England, and Nimmo a sub-manager, left the impression that the deal was chiefly intended to benefit the bank's board and officers.[25]

Bignold and Nimmo defended themselves spiritedly. The committee pressed the pair hard on the bank's accounting methods, arguing that keeping bad debts off the balance sheet was deceptive. Nimmo explained that this was done because it was 'impossible to know the precise amount' of the bad debts, so part of the profits were carried annually to an 'undivided profits' account to meet bad debts

[20] Robert Blake, 'Sir Samuel Bignold', *ODNB*.
[21] *Secret Committee on Joint Stock Banks* (1836), 166.
[22] Ibid. 12–14. [23] Ibid. 19.
[24] Ibid. 25. [25] Ibid. 171–4.

as accounts were closed. The committee challenged Nimmo to explain how the amount of undivided profits could be ascertained without first deducting the losses sustained. Nimmo, a Scotsman, felt himself under attack from a roomful of City figures, and accused his questioners of double standards, citing a famous London forgery from the 1820s:

> I was asked whether, from my experience in banking, I conceived that any such statement would not be a delusion. Perhaps gentlemen living in London may be more able to give explanation on that point; but in the case of Fauntleroy there was a bad debt of 360,000*l*. Perhaps some gentleman can tell whether the Bank of England deducted that from their profits for the year.[26]

When the committee took issue with the bank's dividends, Bignold was defiant. He believed the directors were fully justified in declaring dividends on the strength of the bank's longer-term prospects: 'we always had our hopes of better times', he explained.[27] Not declaring a dividend would have damaged the bank's credit-worthiness and brought about a collapse, as even Gilbert recognized.[28] Bignold was untroubled by accusations of concealment, arguing that the shareholders knew about the bank's predicament because it was impossible to keep losses in a provincial bank quiet: 'I know that it was as much known to every proprietor as if they had turned over the leaves of the ledgers.'[29] Finally, on the deal with the East of England Bank, Bignold maintained that publicizing the negotiations risked triggering a run. Instead, most of the shareholders had 'individually applied for information', and were happy with a 'smooth and quiet' transfer.[30]

With the case for the defence argued so vigorously, the committee's interim report in August stopped short of designating any of these practices—reckless lending by an unsupervised manager, creative accounting, paying dividends out of capital, secret takeovers—'fraudulent'. It did, however, talk of 'evils', 'mismanagement', and 'irregularity' which required legislative intervention, the details of which it would consider next session, if renewed.[31] The edited evidence was reprinted extensively in the London and regional press in September, and the Norfolk and Norwich case attracted censure from Liberal and Conservative papers alike, though they followed the committee's lead and did not use the term 'fraud'. The *Morning Chronicle* took it as 'a specimen of the wild manner in which some of these joint stock banks transacted business'; the *Morning Post* thought that banks which lost their capital and yet paid dividends to prolong their existence operated on principles 'surely not to be patronised and upheld by the financial

[26] Ibid. 25–7. [27] Ibid. 171–2. [28] Ibid. 18. [29] Ibid. 169.

[30] Ibid. 172. There was also a political subtext, with Bignold, a Tory, probably feeling ambushed by a committee dominated by Whigs. For more on Bignold's business affairs, see Roger Ryan, 'Banking and Insurance', in Carole Rawcliffe and Richard Wilson (eds), *Norwich since 1550* (London, 2004), 368.

[31] *Secret Committee on Joint Stock Banks* (1836), v.

guardians of the nation'.[32] But others accused the committee of bias. An anonymous writer to *The Times* wondered why James Pattison, a governor of the Bank of England and member of the committee, 'considers the shareholders in joint-stock banks entitled to more information than is ever afforded by the directors of the Bank of England to their proprietors, from whom any kind of balance-sheet or account has always most studiously been withheld'.[33] Indeed, what stopped the Norwich and Norfolk case generating more heat was the fact that, to many, the Bank of England seemed the bigger villain. By the time the committee reported, the Bank had been placing the brakes on the economy for several weeks, ramping up the discount rate and refusing to discount American bills following a sharp downturn in the US economy.[34] This meant that the currency dimension of the banking debate began to dominate. There was much anger at the Bank's 'constant tampering with the currency': the scarcity of money was clearly a man-made problem.[35] With the good times of the past few years drawing to a close, businessmen prepared for a rough ride.[36]

CRISIS

Just as in 1825, the Bank's credit squeeze had a dramatic impact on the banking system, but whereas in 1825 the main victims were the country banks, in 1836 the new joint-stock banks were in the firing line. The first to feel the pinch was one of the new Irish institutions, the Agricultural and Commercial Bank of Ireland. Formed in 1834 by Thomas Mooney, a Dublin baker, the Agricultural and Commercial aspired to be 'the poor man's bank'.[37] Although it had an immense advertised capital of £5m (£1m more than the largest four Irish banks combined), unlike its rivals it had a low share denomination—£5, with just £1 paid up per share—enabling it to accumulate what was by the standards of the day a huge proprietary of over 2,000.[38] The bank branched rapidly but this rapid expansion was predicated on the continuance of good times and the restriction of credit in autumn 1836 hit it hard.[39] Confidence in the bank began to sag, and the announcement of a call at the October general meeting sparked a run. With the Banks of Ireland and England refusing its requests for aid, it was obliged to suspend payment on 16 November.[40]

[32] *Morning Chronicle*, 17 September 1836; *Morning Post*, 19 September 1836.
[33] 'Monumethensis', letter to *The Times*, 4 November 1836.
[34] Ollerenshaw, *Banking*, 41; Kynaston, *City of London*, 107.
[35] *Morning Herald*, repr. in *Jackson's Oxford Journal*, 10 September 1836; *London Dispatch and People's Political and Social Reformer*, 17 September 1836. Others presented the Bank's actions as a prudent response to changing economic conditions: *Morning Post*, 19 September 1836.
[36] *Manchester Times*, 3 September 1836.
[37] G. L. Barrow, 'Justice for Thomas Mooney', *Dublin Historical Record*, 24 (1970), 177.
[38] Ollerenshaw, *Banking*, 39; *A Return of Joint Stock Banks in Ireland*, PP 1836 XXXVII. Even by 1875, English provincial banks had an average of just 322 shareholders: Charles R. Hickson and John D. Turner, 'The Genesis of Corporate Governance: Nineteenth-Century Irish Joint-Stock Banks', *Business History*, 47 (2005), 187 n. 16.
[39] *Report from the Secret Committee on Joint Stock Banks*, PP 1837 XIV. 155.
[40] Hickson and Turner, 'Genesis of Corporate Governance', 182–3.

That this was not just an Irish problem was graphically demonstrated at the start of December when the Northern and Central Bank of England was forced to approach the Bank of England for a massive cash injection. The Bank agreed, provided the applicant withdrew its notes from circulation and closed most of its branches. *The Times* called it 'one of the most remarkable incidents that perhaps, taken in itself and its probable consequences, has ever occurred in the money-market'.[41] Formed, like the Agricultural and Commercial, in 1834, the bank, with its head office in Manchester, had, by means of a low share denomination of £10, acquired over 1,000 shareholders, the second-largest proprietary in the UK banking sector.[42] It too had adopted an aggressive expansionist strategy and, like its Irish cousin, did not have the resources to withstand the contraction of credit. The deal with the Bank caused relief on the money market.[43] But much remained mysterious. Were these two banks innocent victims of monetary pressure, had they been mismanaged, or were they in fact fraudulent from the start? Commentators, such as *The Times*, who had fought shy of describing the Norwich and Norfolk as fraudulent now wondered whether the recent failures were in fact frauds on the public, and predicted that the crisis would lead to 'some legislative interference of a very decided character'.[44] Others went further. In *Blackwood's Edinburgh Magazine*, the Tory commentator Alfred Mallalieu called for a searching inquiry into all UK banks. Seeing the bank boom as a symptom of phoney 'Whig-Radical prosperity', he pulled no punches in his critique of the sector, which he saw as riddled with fraud. He claimed to have enough information on other cases to fill the entire issue with stories of 'fraud and trickery more flagrant than the annals of swindling—even those of 1825–26—could parallel; but of which, to this day, the ensnared stockholders remain in a state of ignorance'. He drew parallels with the investigation following the South Sea Bubble, which saw 'national honour vindicated, and society restored to more healthy action by the unflinching excision of its diseased members', and wanted nothing less now.[45]

Given the public disquiet, it was unsurprising that the government signalled its intention to renew the banking committee in the King's Speech at the start of the 1837 session.[46] When the issue came before the Commons in early February, however, the debate was more vexed than it had been the previous May. Radicals thought that the joint-stock banks were being scapegoated for problems caused by the Bank of England, and wanted the investigation opened up to include currency management; others opposed

[41] *The Times*, 2 December 1836.
[42] *An Account of all Places where United or Joint Stock Banks have been Established under the Act 7 Geo. IV. c. 46*, PP 1836 XXXVII; *A Return of Joint Stock Banks in Ireland*, PP 1836 XXXVII.
[43] *The Times*, 24 December 1836.
[44] Ibid. 17 November 1836, 5 January 1837. See also 'Joint-Stock Banks', *Monthly Repository* (January 1837), 109–12.
[45] [Alfred Mallalieu], 'Whig-Radical Prosperity', *Blackwood's Edinburgh Magazine*, 41 (February 1837), 147.
[46] Hansard, 3s, 36: 3 (31 January 1837).

investigating joint-stock banks at all, arguing that it was best to let them learn by experience. But with Peel's support, Spring Rice secured renewal on his own terms: the committee would not investigate the Bank of England, but its remit would be widened to include Irish joint-stock banks. The investigation, the Chancellor promised, would be the prelude to legislation 'for the protection of the banks themselves, of the people, and for the general protection of the credit and currency of the country'.[47]

The reappointed committee took evidence from a further fourteen banking and legal witnesses between February and July 1837. This time, much of the evidence gathered related to the two recent suspensions, both of which made the Norwich and Norfolk Bank look like a model of good governance. The Agricultural and Commercial Bank was established by men with practically no banking experience.[48] The company advertised a nominal capital of £5 million, but when it started trading, its paid-up capital was miniscule, no more than £3,000.[49] The bank allowed credit accounts to its customers on insufficient security—nearly £100,000 was loaned in this way.[50] The bank also had a policy of discounting small high-risk bills of as little as £5 for its shareholders, and this was one of the chief attractions which enabled the bank to build such a large shareholding base.[51] Dubious transactions were hidden in the mess which was the bank's accounts. The chairman James Dwyer would admit no more than that the bank's books may not have been kept 'in that regular state which bankers or merchants would wish', but this was a huge understatement.[52] When the bank hired a new accountant, Thomas Brierly, he could make no sense of the bank's books.[53] Whilst balance sheets were issued to shareholders, these listed £114,000 in overdue bills as available assets, even though some of the bills were more than a year overdue. Furthermore, £83,000 in overdrawn cash accounts without collateral security was also listed as immediately available.[54] This made a mockery of the bank's 5 per cent dividends.

It was a similar story at the Northern and Central Bank, except here some of the revelations were even more startling. Henry Moult, the chairman, admitted that none of the directors had any banking experience. The easy-money climate of the mid 1830s encouraged the bank to adopt a simple business model: obtaining money on discount in London and lending it at higher rates in the country, as was the case with many other banks.[55] The bank soon got into difficulties because it loaned too much money, especially to its own shareholders and directors.[56] The Bank of England's investigation showed that the directors owed the bank over a quarter of a million pounds. Even the bank's clerks had been allowed to run up debts of £13,975.[57] When pressed, Moult conceded that directors were allowed to

[47] Ibid. 155–203 (6 February 1837).
[48] *Secret Committee on Joint Stock Banks* (1837), 205.
[49] Ibid. 140, 243–4. [50] Ibid. 155. [51] Ibid. 217.
[52] Ibid. 140. [53] Ibid. 201, 213. [54] Ibid. 214–15.
[55] Ibid. 43–8. [56] Ibid. 67, 5. [57] Ibid. 98, 102.

overdraw massively, to a 'shameful' extent in one case, and applications were only rarely turned down. Worse, directors used their shares in the bank as security for the loans, all the more dubious because they had not paid for them, but had debited their accounts for them.[58] This not only undermined the security of the loans, it also diminished the bank's paid-up capital.[59] The directors also secretly allocated additional shares to themselves, and six of them used these shares for speculation, selling at a premium in 1836.[60]

The bank's bookkeeping lacked transparency, a deliberate strategy. James Lyle, the bank's accountant, kept a private ledger in his possession at all times, in which some of the heavier loans to directors, and their sales of shares, were recorded.[61] The dividends declared by the bank, ranging from 5 to 8 per cent, concealed the true state of its finances. Lyle admitted that the amount of bad debt was systematically underestimated for the purposes of dividend calculation. The accounts were never audited, and balance sheets were not presented to shareholders. The lack of transparency was also evident during the bank's negotiations with the Bank of England at the end of 1836, when the board exaggerated its assets and underestimated its liabilities, deceiving the Bank as to the extent of aid required. Having agreed to help on the understanding that £400,000 was the maximum amount needed, the Bank eventually advanced £1.3 million.[62]

However, as in the case of the Norwich and Norfolk Bank, a different construction could be placed on some of these transactions. Lyle highlighted the importance of understanding the commercial culture which gave rise to the Northern and Central's policy. Formerly an accountant at the National Bank of Scotland, he had seen how discounting worked in Edinburgh. Customers would leave bills, they would be inspected by the directors and either passed or declined, and customers would return to hear the verdict. But 'if such a system were tried in Manchester it would fail completely; no one would come near you': here, bills presented were instantly cashed.[63] Even the London and Westminster manager J. W. Gilbart, who distanced himself from many of the Northern and Central Bank's practices, confirmed that this was simply the Manchester way rather than rogue practice. Similar observations were made about the Agricultural and Commercial Bank's credit policy which was dictated by the commercial culture of Ireland.[64] When the bank's general inspector was asked whether discounting small bills was legitimate business, he drew a distinction based on commercial cultures: 'Not in England, I should say; but in Ireland it appeared to be the practice'.[65] There were also justifications for the lack of transparency. Lyle defended the private ledger, the main purpose of which, he said, was to keep sensitive accounts from the clerks. He

[58] Ibid. 15–16. [59] Ibid. 45. [60] Ibid. 12–23. [61] Ibid. 52–3.
[62] Ibid. 78–101. [63] Ibid. 92. [64] Ibid. 155.
[65] Ibid. 229. For more on the clash between commercial cultures in different parts of the country, see David J. Moss, 'Business and Banking: Ethics and White-Collar Crime in Norwich, 1825–1831', *Albion*, 29 (1997), 373–98.

understood that this was done in other banks.[66] The directors of the Agricultural and Commercial were unrepentant about the lack of information given shareholders. At the October general meeting, the directors knew that they had exhausted the amount of credit available from the London banks, but feared that admitting the truth would spark the run which they were trying to avoid.[67]

Both banks were able to point to factors beyond their control to explain their suspensions, chiefly the economic downturn and lack of shareholder support. Before the crisis, the Northern and Central directors had agreed on a new strategy of closing branches and reducing accounts, and Moult believed that this would have saved the bank 'if it had not been for the great pressure of the times'.[68] When the Bank of England raised interest rates, the bank found itself with its resources tied up in loans and unable to get access to ready money. The directors tried every option to stave off disaster: they made 'continual applications' to those who had overdrawn their accounts to repay what they owed, but few heeded the appeal. Overtures to some of the bank's wealthier shareholders yielded no result, for few of them had any ready money, while making further calls on shares was not an option because they were fully paid up.[69] Selling some of the bank's 20,000 unissued shares was not practical: as one of the directors pointed out, the company's shares were already unpopular, and glutting the market would have simply undermined confidence.[70] Lack of shareholder support was even more pronounced at the Agricultural and Commercial. Its shares did have an uncalled margin, and the bank had hoped to raise £157,000 from the call made at the October 1836 general meeting, but only £23,000 was received.[71] If the call had been paid, suspension would have been averted.[72]

Pierce Mahony, legal representative of a group of Agricultural and Commercial shareholders, had little hesitation in accusing some of the directors of 'fraud and gross misconduct', but other witnesses stopped short of such claims.[73] William Goodier, an auditor appointed after the Agricultural and Commercial's suspension to investigate its accounts, claimed that the bank could not have been conducted any more disastrously, but used the term 'gross mismanagement' rather than 'fraud' to describe the board's actions.[74] Gilbart too was critical of the balance sheet presented by the bank shortly before its suspension, but when pressed by the committee, refused to label it fraudulent.[75] In drawing the line between mismanagement and fraud where they did, the commercial community undercut the case for serious reform and helped to limit the repercussions of the crisis.

[66] *Secret Committee on Joint Stock Banks* (1837), 52. [67] Ibid. 165.
[68] Ibid. 41. [69] Ibid. 6–7. [70] Ibid. 82. [71] Ibid. 181–2.
[72] Ibid. 163. [73] Ibid. 240–1. [74] Ibid. 218–20. [75] Ibid. 120.

BACKLASH

Indeed, as the committee approached the conclusion of its hearings in June 1837, there were signs that government enthusiasm for thoroughgoing banking reform was waning. When Spring Rice presented his budget at the end of the month, he struck an optimistic note, observing that the commercial crisis was 'now rapidly passing away', and made no reference to the issue of joint-stock banking.[76] The City column of *The Times* found this odd given the extensive sittings of the committee over the past four months, and surmised that the Chancellor was refraining from criticizing the banks because the 'directors and proprietors of these banks have acquired great weight and influence in particular districts', and he did not want to risk offending them on the eve of elections precipitated by the recent death of William IV.[77] Although some on the committee, Clay among them, wanted to issue a report recommending a course of reform before parliament prorogued, Spring Rice persuaded them to wait until the following session, when the committee would complete its investigations.[78] The mass of evidence collected to date was therefore printed without a report.

Spring Rice's decision was probably influenced by the fact that the evidence gathered by the committee over two sessions did not point to any obvious legislative solution to the banking sector's governance problems. Clay's favoured remedies—limited liability, publicity, and audit—were supported by some witnesses but criticized by several others, particularly limited liability, widely seen as an inducement to reckless gambling.[79] Moreover, the sense of scandal was dissipating, not least because the directors of the two banks still seemed to enjoy the confidence of the majority of their shareholders. The mood at the general meetings of the Northern and Central immediately following the suspensions had not been particularly venomous: though the board came in for serious criticism, it seems that contesting liabilities in the courts, let alone punishing the directors, was not seriously considered.[80] In August 1837, the directors called for 'the cordial good-will and co-operation of the shareholders at large', and it seemed that there was a mood to pull together. One shareholder's motion of censure against the directors failed to receive a seconder, with one fellow investor arguing that 'it was unwise to dwell longer on that which was not profitable'.[81] The bank discharged its debt to the Bank of England in January 1838, the same month that the Agricultural and Commercial Bank reopened after its losses proved to be less substantial than originally expected.[82]

So when the committee's evidence was published in October 1837, the press was temperate in its judgements. It printed extracts, sometimes noting the light

[76] Hansard, 3s, 38: 1714–28 (30 June 1837).

[77] *The Times*, 3 July 1837.

[78] Hansard, 3s, 38: 1733–4 (30 June 1837).

[79] John D. Turner, '"The Last Acre and Sixpence": Views on Bank Liability Regimes in Nineteenth-Century Britain', *Financial History Review*, 16 (2009), 119–21.

[80] *Manchester Guardian*, 25 January, 25 February 1837.

[81] Ibid. 2 September 1837.

[82] *The Times*, 10 January 1838. The bank was to fail a second time, and permanently, in 1840: Ollerenshaw, *Banking*, 43.

they shed on 'the gross abuses and nefarious practices' in the sector.[83] But there were signs of a backlash. The *Manchester Times* thought it had been a mistake for the committee to focus on the two problem banks: to call it 'an inquiry into the working of the Joint Stock Banking system, is about as ridiculous as to call an examination of a lunatic hospital an inquiry into the human understanding'.[84] By December, a year after the suspensions, *The Times* referred to the 'almost forgotten subject of the Northern and Central Bank'.[85]

But if the scandal had largely passed, the banks' liabilities remained, and these sparked government action of an unexpected nature. Whereas reforms to protect shareholders and customers against rogue banks had seemed a certainty in early 1837, what actually emerged was legislation to protect banks against their shareholders and customers. Events convinced the government that enforcing payments was more pressing than banking regulation. The Northern and Central Bank was owed money by rafts of customers, and though the bank sometimes had to resort to the courts to recover, these actions were initially unproblematic, and in some cases were not even defended.[86] However, in November 1837, an action against a customer, Abraham Franklin, for a dishonoured bill of exchange, hit troubled waters in the Court of Exchequer. Franklin's counsel, the Liberal MP William Maule, made an unusual plea. He claimed that his client's contract with the bank was unenforceable because two of the bank's shareholders were clergymen, and an act of 1817 forbade all 'spiritual persons' from carrying on 'any trade or dealing for gain or profit'.[87] The bank's counsel, the Tory barrister and former Solicitor General Sir William Follett, argued that this measure largely re-enacted an old piece of legislation from Tudor times which only applied to trading at fairs and markets; the idea that it applied to joint-stock companies was ludicrous. Maule, who was also counsel to the Bank of England, and who therefore might have been keen to limit the operation of joint-stock banks, indulged in some anti-banking rhetoric, claiming that the trading done by joint-stock banks was 'of all others the most pernicious; he who engages therein is nothing but a "money-changer", that class which was driven out of the temple ignominiously'. As such, he concluded, there was no doubt that the act did apply.[88] It seemed a desperate strategy, and the *Manchester Guardian*'s reporter thought it 'tolerably clear... that the decision will be in favour of the bank'.[89] But in January 1838, the judges, led by James Scarlett, now Lord Abinger, gave their opinion that the act of 1817 did more than simply consolidate old legislation—it amended it—and that the inclusive form of words used—'any trade or dealing for gain or profit'—meant that the act did include banking. The judges realized the inconvenience their decision would cause, but were unable to 'put a forced construction on the act of parliament'.[90]

[83] *The Times*, 1 November 1837.
[84] *Manchester Times*, 11 November 1837.
[85] *The Times*, 18 December 1837.
[86] See, for example, *Hall v. Taylor* (1837), *Manchester Guardian*, 19 August 1837.
[87] 57 Geo. III c. 99, s. 3.
[88] J. D. FitzGerald, rev. Hugh Mooney, 'Sir William Henry Maule', *ODNB*.
[89] *Manchester Guardian*, 22 November 1837.
[90] *Hall v. Franklin* (1838) 150 ER 1141, *Manchester Guardian*, 3, 7 February 1838.

The Northern and Central Bank immediately sent a deputation to meet with Manchester's two MPs, one of whom was President of the Board of Trade Poulett Thomson, to lobby for a change in the law. The MPs were sympathetic and persuaded the government to act.[91] Just one week after Abinger's decision, Spring Rice told parliament it was essential that the law be altered, not only for the sake of the Northern and Central Bank, but for all joint-stock companies. Under the current law, 'parties might be ruined to an extent scarcely calculable...a door would be opened to fraud, and considerable difficulty and derangement would be created in the commercial world'.[92] The spectre of hosts of unscrupulous debtors exploiting the law to resist paying their lawful debts was sufficiently terrifying to spur the bill through both Houses in a fortnight, and the measure received royal assent in February.[93]

But by now the directors of the Northern and Central were facing another problem, this time caused by their shareholders. Though the bank had paid off its debt to the Bank of England, the shareholders' prospects were bleak, as the board's asset valuations had proved far too optimistic. In February 1838 one shareholder wrote to his 'fellow-sufferers' via the press, urging them to demand 'a correct and tangible statement' before the forthcoming half-yearly general meeting, rather than the 'very illusory statement' they had previously been given. At the meeting, the shareholders learned that value of the assets estimated at the last meeting had fallen by a further £45,000. Now, the mood turned decisively against the management, a motion that the profits made by several of the directors from trafficking in the bank's shares be returned, together with the silver plate voted to the board (obtained 'under false pretences'!) was passed unanimously 'amidst loud applause'.[94]

The mutinous mood of shareholders was brought to the government's attention by the secret committee, which interviewed its final set of witnesses between May and July 1838. In the course of the examinations, the committee collected further evidence on the two problem banks, and the issue that made them sit up and pay attention was the huge difficulty faced by the Northern and Central Bank in collecting debts from its shareholders.[95] One hundred of the shareholders (including two of the former directors, one of them Moult) owed £443,000, and refused to pay it. The bank had brought an action against one of the biggest debtors, but was advised by legal authorities including the Attorney General Sir John Campbell to abandon it. The common law remedy for the recovery of a debt did not apply when the debt was contracted between a partnership and one of the partners, a situation not altered by the 1826 act.[96] Taking the case to Chancery was not a feasible option as all partners had to be listed as a party to the suit, which was not practicable. One of the bank's inspectors told the secret committee that the process

91 *Manchester Guardian*, 24 February 1838.
92 Hansard, 3s, 40: 818 (6 February 1838).
93 Ibid. 918–22 (8 February 1838), 1130–1 (15 February 1838); 1 & 2 Vict. c. 10.
94 *Manchester Guardian*, 27, 31 January, 21, 24 February 1838.
95 *Report from the Secret Committee on Joint Stock Banks*, PP 1837–38 VII. 111.
96 Ibid. 1–3.

of winding-up had consequently been halted: 'we dare not proceed in law or equity...We are stuck fast now, and cannot move till we have relief from the Chancellor'.[97]

When the committee issued its final report in July 1838, it made a vague recommendation that parliament consider the whole evidence gathered by the committee over the past three sessions with a view to comprehensive reform. But it identified the inability of the Northern and Central to collect debts from its shareholders as the more pressing issue, urging immediate legislation. If parliament did not act, 'a most serious blow might be struck at commercial credit, likely to produce the most calamitous consequences'.[98] So, for the second time that session, the government hurried to the aid of the joint-stock banks, introducing a bill to amend the acts of 1825 and 1826 for Ireland and England. The measure, to continue in force until the end of the 1839 session, and which would subsequently be renewed, allowed the public officers of banks to sue shareholders for debts on the same terms as non-shareholders. Attracting little debate in either House, it received royal assent in August.[99]

Nevertheless, the question of liability remained live, as shareholders in both the Northern and Central and the Agricultural and Commercial continued to resist, crying fraud. Therefore it was left to the courts to decide whether fraud could be proved, and if so, whether it absolved shareholders from their liabilities. The answer was equivocal. In one action, an investor named Stainbank tried to recoup his £384 investment claiming that he had been induced to purchase at a heavy premium on the strength of representations made by the manager, Thomas Evans, and because of the dividend of 7 per cent. He sued one of the directors, John Fernley, as he had since discovered that the shares he bought had belonged to him, a fact which had been concealed from him at the time. In February 1839, Vice-Chancellor Sir Lancelot Shadwell ruled that the directors had made false representations to induce people to buy their shares at an unjustified price, the sale was voided, and Fernley was ordered to repay the money.[100] The victory encouraged other shareholders to try their luck in the courts, but with less success. A second investor, Seddon, had bought £7,000 in shares on the strength of fraudulent representations in the directors' reports, and now sought to recover from the public officer of the bank, together with Moult and Evans. The matter came before Shadwell in June 1840, and seemed very similar to the Stainbank case. Yet there was a crucial difference. Seddon was suing the men as representatives 'of the entire company as it exists in the year 1840, not as it existed in 1836', and not for frauds they committed personally. Shadwell therefore ruled that he had no remedy against them personally for a fraud committed by others.[101] Attempts by shareholders in the Agricultural and Commercial Bank to retrieve their losses were met with similarly mixed results.[102]

[97] Ibid. 108–9.
[98] Ibid. iii–iv.
[99] *The Times*, 31 July 1838; 1 & 2 Vict. c. 96, s. 1.
[100] *Stainbank v. Fernley* (1839) 59 ER 473, *The Times*, 14 February 1839.
[101] *Seddon v. Connell* (1840) 59 ER 534, *The Times*, 12 June 1840.
[102] *Thorpe v. Hughes* (1838) 40 ER 1112, *Morning Post*, 29 March 1838; *Hughes v. Thorpe* (1839) 151 ER 278.

The exhibition of shareholders trying to wriggle free from their liabilities only reinforced public antipathy towards them which, though not as pronounced as after the mania of 1825, was nevertheless apparent.[103] Legislation to protect them came to be seen as less desirable than private solutions to problems of corporate governance. The *Manchester Times* recast the banking problem as a private issue, driving a wedge between shareholders' interests and the wider public interest. It reminded its readers that '*The public has not lost one shilling by the failure of these banks*'. The shareholders had brought their losses upon themselves by electing men unworthy of trust and allowing them free rein. 'No act of parliament can provide against such a contingency; the remedy is with the shareholders themselves.' The main function of the voluminous evidence gathered by the secret committees and the extensive press coverage was not to act as a roadmap for legislation but as a warning to shareholders of the necessity of taking care of their interests more carefully.[104]

The government agreed. If its commitment to thoroughgoing banking reform was cooling in 1837, it had altogether died by 1838. In the debate following Spring Rice's budget speech in May, the Chancellor told the House that no legislative measure could liberate trade from the vicissitudes attendant on excesses of speculation and depression; nothing he could do could protect people from the effects of what he called 'commercial vibrations'.[105] In July, he noted the lack of further failures among the joint-stock banks, which, considering the tough economic climate, convinced him 'that the principle of joint-stock banks was good, and would prove beneficial to the country'.[106] Not even a further currency crisis in 1839, followed by a spate of further joint-stock bank failures (nine stopped payment in 1839–41), encouraged a rethink.[107] The lack of reform became a handy stick with which the Conservatives could beat the Whigs, but for many, especially radicals, the events of 1839 confirmed that the currency question, rather than the governance question, was the main issue, and that the Bank of England, rather than the joint-stock banks, was the institution requiring the most urgent reform.[108]

However, following the pair of acts on joint-stock banks, there was one final intervention in 1840 which again highlighted the government's priorities. One of the banks which fell in early 1840, the Walsall and South Staffordshire Banking Company, had generated a considerable fuss in the West Midlands due to irregularities in the accounts of T. F. Wood, the bank's manager. The directors accused Wood of embezzling two parcels of notes totalling over £7,000, and

[103] There was particular condemnation of small shareholders who, it was believed, were short-termist, speculative, and incapable of holding boards to account: Timothy L. Alborn, *Conceiving Companies: Joint-Stock Politics in Victorian England* (London, 1998), 105–15.
[104] *Manchester Times*, 11 November 1837. See also *The Times*, 10 August 1838.
[105] Hansard, 3s, 42: 1417–18 (18 May 1838).
[106] Ibid. 44: 718–20 (27 July 1838).
[107] Thomas, *Joint Stock Banking*, 315–17, 668–9.
[108] See the comments of Lord Stanley and Sir James Graham: Hansard, 3s, 51: 910–11 (30 January 1840), 52: 709 (27 February 1840).

local magistrates committed him for trial.[109] But when the case came before Walsall Quarter Sessions in July, the prosecution collapsed because Wood was also a shareholder, and in law, could not steal from himself. The decision sent panic through the sector: as it was the policy of most banks to appoint shareholders as managers, 'every joint-stock bank might be robbed by a manager, without the latter running any risk of criminal prosecution'.[110] The response of the banks was speedy, with a deputation sent to new Chancellor Francis Baring to argue the case for intervention.[111] The bankers' case was simple: Irish banks already possessed the legal right to criminally prosecute their shareholders under the Irish Bankers Act of 1825, and all that was required was the extension of this law to England and Wales.[112] Attorney General Campbell did not object to the proposed extension, and an opportunity to change the law arose because a bill renewing the 1838 act enabling banks to sue their shareholders was currently in parliament. Baring inserted the relevant lines from the Irish act into the bill in committee stage, and it received royal assent at the end of the session.[113]

This was the third time in three years that the government had responded rapidly to problems faced by the joint-stock banks and once again the intervention was designed to help directors. Previous interventions had supported their attempts to recover from customers and shareholders; this one helped them discipline their employees. By contrast, the wider issue of how the banks were governed by their directors was kicked into touch. And while the law was tightened up to ensure that the criminal law could reach company servants, it was striking that, for all its scandalous elements, the crisis did not generate a public debate on whether acts by *directors* should be punished criminally.

[109] The legal distinction between embezzlement and larceny is explained in C. H. S. Fifoot, *Judge and Jurist in the Reign of Victoria* (London, 1959), 93. The first general act against embezzlement, to clear up the legal ambiguity over whether a servant appropriating money or goods received from a third party was committing an offence, was passed in 1799: 39 Geo. III c. 85. The maximum punishment was transportation for fourteen years. For the background to this act, see Graham Ferris, 'Larceny: Debating the "Boundless Region of Dishonesty"', in Judith Rowbotham and Kim Stevenson (eds), *Criminal Conversations: Victorian Crimes, Social Panic, and Moral Outrage* (Columbus, OH, 2005), 77; Barry S. Godfrey and John P. Locker, 'The Nineteenth-Century Decline of Custom, and its Impact on Theories of "Workplace Theft" and "White Collar" Crime', *Northern History*, 38 (2001), 268–70.

[110] *Wolverhampton Chronicle*, repr. in *Sheffield and Rotherham Independent*, 28 March 1840; *The Times*, 18 July 1840.

[111] *A Record of the Proceedings of the Committee of Deputies from the Joint Stock Banks of England, Wales, and Ireland* (London, 1845), 36–7; *Newcastle Courant*, 24 July 1840.

[112] The act made it possible for the public officer of a bank to prosecute any shareholder who 'shall steal or embezzle' any bank property, 'or shall commit any fraud, forgery, crime, or offence, against or with intent to injure or defraud' the bank: 6 Geo. IV c. 42, s. 20.

[113] 3 & 4 Vict. c. 111. The act did facilitate the successful prosecution of some managers: in July 1842, for example, the Carlisle and Cumberland Banking Company prosecuted a branch manager, Joseph Atkinson, for embezzling £653. Despite also being a shareholder, he was sentenced to transportation for ten years: *Reg. v. Atkinson* (1842) 174 ER 619, *Morning Chronicle*, 28 July 1842, *The Times*, 28 July 1842, *Lancaster Gazette*, 15 April 1843. The case was subsequently reported as establishing that shareholder-employees could be prosecuted, but in fact such prosecutions remained difficult into the 1850s. William Oldnall Russell and Charles Sprengel Greaves, *A Treatise on Crimes and Misdemeanors*, 2 vols (8th American edn, Philadelphia, PA, 1857), ii. 105.

A REGULAR GAMBLING SYSTEM

Criminal actions against directors were also conspicuous by their absence in the wider joint-stock economy in the 1830s. Whereas in the mid 1820s London magistrates had had to deal with gaggles of disappointed investors, very few cases were presented in the aftermath of the 1830s mania. Though the railway boom established the long-standing link in the public mind between this new sector and fraudulent practices, no railway directors were brought before magistrates on criminal charges.[114] Those rendered desperate by their unsuccessful railway speculations were more likely to take other steps. A young man named Edwin Bates had inherited over £2,000 from his father, and had travelled to London to become an artist. But instead of painting, he had become embroiled in the mania, speculating unsuccessfully in a variety of schemes, and investing more in an attempt to retrieve his losses. Deciding that railways were the answer to his problems, he took fifty shares in the Northern and Eastern Railway Company for £365. However, the shares plummeted, and when they reached £150, he determined to sell out and use what remained of his fortune to settle down to art. Unfortunately, the secretary Charles Rowcroft persuaded him not to sell, because the shares were bound to rise again. Nevertheless, the shares continued their descent, bottoming out at just £19. An outraged Bates wrote threatening letters to the directors demanding restitution; in one such, he 'wish[ed] to God that you were comprised in one man, that I might have one chance to punish by my single arm the villany of the whole body'. Fearful for their safety, the directors sought a warrant for Bates's arrest, and he appeared before Lord Mayor Thomas Kelly at Mansion House in June 1837. Kelly was not sympathetic, telling him that he was wrong to believe that the directors knew he would lose by the speculation.

> They are not at all responsible. You entered into a regular gambling system without knowing any thing about it. If you had gained, other persons must have been losers; and if every man who had purchased shares were to raise up his arm because he sustained severe losses, the city of London would be a scene of confusion and bloodshed.[115]

The directors pressed their case against Bates, and Alderman William Venables, the former Lord Mayor, supported them. Bates, Venables argued, was not justified in taking the law into his own hands: 'If the directors of any company were to behave dishonestly, they would soon be corrected by the public reprobation, and in one way or other by the law.'[116] Bates pleaded guilty and was imprisoned for one year.[117]

[114] R. W. Kostal, *Law and English Railway Capitalism, 1825–1875* (rev. repr., Oxford, 1997), 18–23. Though others argue that the link is overdone: Sybil Jack and Adrian Jack, 'Nineteenth-Century Lawyers and Railway Capitalism: Historians and the Use of Legal Cases', *Legal History*, 24 (2003), 65–6.

[115] *The Times*, 9 August 1837.

[116] Ibid. 18 September 1837.

[117] *Reg. v. Bates* (1837), *The Times*, 23 September 1837, 9 January 1844.

Venables' optimism as to the power of the law to bring dishonest directors to book was possibly misplaced. The laws against obtaining money by false pretences and conspiracy to defraud protected creditors and shareholders on paper, but not in practice, even in the most egregious cases.[118] For example, in 1837, John Jones, an agent of the East London Gas and Coke Company, ordered three dozen chairs from William Leadbitter, a London furniture maker. As a reference, he gave the name of Mr T. Camp, the managing director of the gas company. Leadbitter called on the company's offices on Abchurch Lane, and saw 'several persons, who had the appearance of clerks, sitting at desks with large account-books before them'. He asked to see Camp, who turned out to be 'a well-dressed man', who vouched for Jones. Leadbitter provided the chairs on credit, but subsequently discovered that Jones had sold the chairs within three hours of receiving them and had no intention of paying for them. On making further inquiries, he was told that the men he had met on Abchurch Lane were a gang of swindlers and Jones's accomplices. Leadbitter obtained a warrant for Jones's arrest, but when he was taken into custody, Jones declared that he had 'committed no offence that the law could take cognizance of, and that he was simply indebted to the complainant for the goods he had bought'.[119]

His confidence was justified. When the case came to Union Hall police court at Southwark, the magistrate James Traill observed that despite the fact that Jones had obtained the chairs by false pretences, and that there was a conspiracy between him and the gang at Abchurch Lane, a jury would not convict since Leadbitter had made insufficient inquiry before entrusting his property. In the absence of criminal precedents, Traill was relying upon principles derived from the treatment of fraud at common law. The key question in contractual disputes was whether the plaintiff was justified in relying upon the defendant's representations, or whether he should have made his own inquiries. Whereas in the eighteenth century the courts had tended to treat reliance on a promise as reasonable, in the nineteenth century judges backtracked from this principle. Though fraud could nullify a contract, P. S. Atiyah has shown that 'the concept of fraud was whittled down a good deal' during the nineteenth century, with judges becoming reluctant to protect those whom they saw as guilty of gross negligence.[120] So, Leadbitter's retort that he had been fooled by the appearance of the offices, populated by clerks at desks, which had made him believe 'that everything was right', cut no ice with Traill. Despite the fact that another tradesman gave evidence that he had been swindled in the same way, Jones was discharged.[121]

It was not that Leadbitter lacked the social standing to bring the 'company' to account; even the Duke of Wellington was powerless to make the criminal law reach such fraudsters. In March 1838, the Duke received a letter inviting him to

[118] The statutory crime of obtaining money by false pretences was restated in the consolidating Larceny Act of 1827: 7 & 8 Geo. IV c. 29, s. 53.

[119] *The Times*, 7 August 1837.

[120] P. S. Atiyah, *The Rise and Fall of Freedom of Contract* (Oxford, 1979), 188–9, 468–9.

[121] *The Times*, 7 August 1837.

become a patron of the London Equitable Loan Company and General Deposit Bank. He wrote back promptly to decline, and he was therefore surprised when, six weeks later, he received a letter from a man named Cheshire who wanted to check that Wellington really was its patron, as claimed in the company's prospectus, before buying shares. An angry Duke went to Sir Frederick Roe, chief magistrate at Bow Street, to see whether the company could be made criminally liable for using his name against his wishes. Roe made some enquiries, and established that the prospectus contained other falsehoods: the company claimed its bankers were the Bank of England, but the Bank's secretary told Roe that this was untrue. Wellington assured Roe that he was willing to prosecute the men, and the magistrate considered whether 'some legal means might not be devised to bring the parties to justice by whom those false representations had been practised'. But he concluded that they were not criminally liable because there was no evidence that Cheshire had parted with money on the strength of the prospectus. Wellington would have to be satisfied with a public disavowal of any connection with the company.[122]

Traill and Roe were cautious about applying the criminal law even to the shady margins of the joint-stock economy. However, outside the capital, there was a case where magistrates proved bolder. In the mid 1830s, John Allen, an affluent resident of Oxford, had become acquainted with a local man, Vincent Vaughan, and had loaned him £2,500 on the security of the latter's furniture and effects. Over a sumptuous dinner at the Star Hotel at Oxford, Vaughan had introduced Allen to his friend, Baron Charles De Behr. De Behr purported to be son of a Swiss Marquis, and president of the Cachoeira Gold, Silver, and Copper Mining Company in Brazil. Vaughan wanted to repay his debt to Allen by giving him the opportunity to invest in this promising concern. Though its shares were highly sought after, De Behr had a block of £3,000 he was willing to sell Allen, who subsequently agreed to take them, waiving the £2,500 debt to Vaughan and paying a further £500 in cash. One of Allen's friends subsequently alerted him that the company might not have been such a sound investment, and on making further enquiries, Allen discovered that he had been swindled. The firm De Behr claimed did his banking business had never heard of the Cachoeira Company, while the Alien Office confirmed that De Behr was no baron. Allen swore an information against Vaughan and De Behr—the first step towards a prosecution—on the strength of which they were arrested and brought before magistrates at a crowded Henley-on-Thames town hall. A German Jew, De Behr had been trading in the early 1830s as a wine merchant in the City, but had spent two years in debtors' prison. On his release in 1836 he had reinvented himself as Baron De Behr, and was believed to have duped many in London before relocating to Oxford. The magistrates committed both men for trial on counts of conspiracy to defraud and obtaining money by false pretences. Unable to meet bail, they were moved to Oxford Castle to await trial, and at the Quarter Sessions in October, true bills were found against the pair.[123] The trial was scheduled for the Oxfordshire Spring Assizes, but there is no record that the trial took place, either in

[122] Ibid. 7 June 1838; *Morning Post*, 7 June 1838.
[123] *Standard*, 24 August, 20 October 1837; *Morning Post*, 25, 28 August 1837.

the press or in the assizes records, suggesting that Allen may have had a change of heart and dropped his prosecution.[124] It is possible that De Behr, seeing Allen was in earnest, mustered the resources to compensate him for his losses: such was the vulnerability of the private prosecution to compromise.

CONCLUSION

The joint-stock bust of the 1830s led to a negligible amount of activity in the criminal courts of Britain. Nor was there much demand for legal reforms to extend the reach of the criminal law into the boardroom. In contrast to the previous crisis in 1825–26, the shareholders of the failed banks proved unwilling to pursue their directors into the criminal courts. This may partly have been because magistrates had closed the door so decisively against such prosecutions in the 1820s. Another factor may have been the firmer social ties between shareholders and directors in some provincial banks compared with the metropolitan companies with more geographically diffuse shareholder bases which were the focus following the crisis of 1825. This time there was no 'corporate gadfly' in the mould of William Clark to flit from company to company agitating for action. The absence of shareholder pressure for punishment made it easy for politicians to ignore this aspect of the crisis; what made it easier still was the fact that the bank failures, though dramatic, were ultimately seen as private matters between shareholders and directors. What was of more pressing interest to the public than the governance crisis was the currency crisis, and this helped the banks. Whereas radicals had led the charge against the bubbles of 1825, radicals in the 1830s were much more sympathetic to the joint-stock banks, which they were inclined to see as valiant Davids taking on the monopolistic Goliath of the Bank of England. They were therefore unlikely to probe the dubious behaviour exposed by the failures too deeply. Finally, the investigations into the failures demonstrated that many of the practices thought of as fraud in some quarters were actually more ambiguous than they at first seemed. Some, such as easy overdrafts and indiscriminate discounting, could be ascribed to dissimilar business cultures in different parts of the country; others, such as lack of transparency in accounting and poor management of reserves, could be laid at the door of the Bank of England itself.[125]

Although the Whig government declined to submit the banking sector to serious reform in the 1830s, it would be wrong to characterize the administration as entirely dormant when it came to problems in the wider joint-stock economy. Its policy was to extend access to corporate privileges, but responsibly, guarding

[124] The pair are listed in the Oxfordshire Quarter Sessions Calendar of Prisoners for Michaelmas 1837, but they do not appear in the Crown Minute Books, Indictment Files, or Criminal Depositions for the Oxford Circuit in Lent 1838. Calendar of Prisoners for Michaelmas Sessions 1837 and Lent Assizes 1838, Oxfordshire History Centre, QS1837/4/A7/1; Oxford Circuit: Crown Minute Books, 1833 Lent–1842 Summer, TNA ASSI 2/32; Oxford Circuit: Indictment Files, Oxon, 1838 Lent, ASSI 5/158/11; Oxford Circuit: Criminal Depositions and Case Papers, 1836–40, ASSI 6/4.

[125] Thomas, *Joint Stock Banking*, 317.

against the abuse of these privileges by vetting the firms which applied for them, and by withholding access to the hazardous principle of limited liability. So, acts promoted by Poulett Thomson in 1834 and 1837 enabled the Board of Trade to grant letters patent part-incorporating companies, but the Board adopted a conservative policy when determining which companies should be so favoured, the idea being that the public would be protected by the wisdom of government ministers.[126] The proposition that all companies be allowed these privileges by right—recommended by a report on the law of partnership commissioned by Poulett Thomson in 1837—was considered far too dangerous.[127] Paradoxically, it was to take a fresh wave of frauds in the early 1840s to trigger this step.

[126] 4 & 5 Will. IV c. 94; 1 Vict. c. 73. See James Taylor, *Creating Capitalism: Joint-Stock Enterprise in British Politics and Culture, 1800–1870* (Woodbridge, 2006), 125–34.

[127] *Report on the Law of Partnership*, PP 1837 XLIV.

PART TWO

CRIMINALIZATION

4

Baffling Fraud: The 1840s

In September 1843, the resident director of the City of London Convalescent Fund Pension Society and Savings Bank, a Welshman named John Stanley Humphery, appeared at Mansion House to answer charges of obtaining goods under false pretences. Humphery's firm boasted an illustrious set of subscribers and patrons, including Queen Victoria, the Duke of Wellington, and the King of Belgium; moreover, he claimed to be the nephew of the Lord Mayor, John Humphery, who was also president of the society. Impressed with his credentials, a succession of tailors had furnished him with suits on credit: one testified that he reasoned that 'as there was so many great names upon the prospectus, I might look upon that as a guarantee'. When Humphery refused to pay any of the tailors, one of them issued a warrant for his arrest. With Lord Mayor Humphery hearing the case against his alleged nephew—whom he denied ever laying eyes on before—proceedings soon took a farcical turn. When Humphery produced what he claimed was a letter from his 'uncle', the paper turned out to be an unpaid bill for a suit, to the delight of the audience.

Despite the comedy, there were serious issues at stake, not least for the capital's tradesmen, who crowded into Mansion House for the examinations. The defendant claimed that he was the victim of an attempt to 'violate the law, by turning what would have been at most a debt into a penal offence', a defence previously deployed with success by others accused of fraud. But the Lord Mayor thought there was 'something beyond a mere debt in all this business', and probed the affair thoroughly. Though mounting a spirited defence, Humphery—real name Humphries—was unable to prove that his society had any existence beyond the prospectus which he carried around in his pocket (the printing bill for which he had never paid). He had fitted out businesses premises in July (neglecting to pay the carpenter), but his landlord testified that no business was done there. Having failed to secure subscribers to his society, Humphries changed tack, using the firm's name to obtain personal credit. At the fourth examination, Alderman John Johnson, standing in for the Lord Mayor, concluded that Humphries had clearly 'represented a society which had no existence', and as a result, he would have to 'take a turn in Bridewell for three months'. He was led down 'evidently shocked at the sentence'.[1]

[1] *The Times*, 28 September, 3, 10, 17 October 1843. Summary justice dispensed by magistrates was increasingly common in the nineteenth century: David Bentley, *English Criminal Justice in the Nineteenth Century* (London, 1998), 19–20.

Given the difficulties previously experienced in applying the law of false pretences to some pretty barefaced swindles, this outcome represented something of achievement, even if there was the suspicion that the summary justice dispensed may have been as much for Humphries' impudence in claiming kin with the Lord Mayor as for getting up a sham company.[2] Indeed, faced with a series of frauds in the 1840s, magistrates were to show themselves a little more willing than before to intervene in cases of pretended or real companies. Few cases reached the Old Bailey, however, as the onus was still on victims to finance prosecutions, which they were generally unwilling to do when the criminality of such frauds was far from established in law. A more significant change was seen in the attitude of government to company fraud. If the 1830s had been characterized by complacency about joint-stock morality, best demonstrated by the lack of any serious reform of the banking sector following the scandalous failures of the mid 1830s, in the 1840s fraud came to be seen by government as a problem which could and should be solved by legislative intervention. The exposure of a massive insurance company fraud in 1841 sparked select committees under the Whig and Conservative governments. Whereas previous crises in the 1820s and 1830s had led to investigation without legislation, this time, it was a different story, with three acts designed to bring companies fully within the law—both civil and criminal—for the first time.

INVESTMENT GURUS AND AGONY AUNTS

In early 1839 a radical Glasgow newspaper, the *Scotch Reformers' Gazette*, ran a series of articles exposing the Independent West Middlesex Assurance Company as a fraud. The company, though recently formed, was doing large amounts of business throughout the country thanks to its cut-price rates, an extended network of agents, and blanket advertising in the newspaper press.[3] But its low rates began to attract suspicion. Peter Mackenzie, the editor of the *Gazette*, had investigated the company and found it was run by a 'band of swindlers': the names of the managers listed in its advertisements were fake, its claims to have a capital of a million pounds were false—it had no shareholders—and anyone who entrusted it with their money was sure to lose it.[4] Although the company survived these attacks, the possibility of government intervention was raised in June when Sir James Gibson Craig, the prominent Edinburgh Whig and legal advisor to the Scottish Widows' Fund and Life Assurance Society, got involved. Having read Mackenzie's articles, he suggested that the editor write to Fox Maule, Under-Secretary of State at the Home Office and another Scot, to see if something could be done. Mackenzie did so, but to his 'deep mortification' received a dismissive reply. Maule had referred the issue

[2] See the cases of William Goundry in Chapter 2, and John Jones in Chapter 3.

[3] James Taylor, 'Numbers, Character and Trust in Early Victorian Britain: The Independent West Middlesex Fire and Life Assurance Company Fraud', in Tom Crook and Glen O'Hara (eds), *Statistics and the Public Sphere: Numbers and the People in Modern Britain, c. 1800–2000* (New York, 2011), 185–202.

[4] *Scotch Reformers' Gazette*, 9, 30 March, 6, 13, 27 April, 11, 25 May 1839.

to Poulett Thomson, President of the Board of Trade, but Thomson was 'of opinion that the Government cannot interfere in the matter'.[5] This response confirmed what had been evident following its handling of the banking scandals of the mid 1830s: the Whig government did not think offences in the joint-stock sector required the intervention of the executive or the legislature.

However, this stance was challenged at the beginning of 1841 when the Independent West Middlesex Company collapsed, its managers fleeing to the Continent.[6] The following weeks saw tragic scenes as desperate annuitants, many of them old women, who had trusted everything they had to the company, flocked to the offices to try to find out what had happened; '[o]ne appeared to be quite exhausted with fatigue, another quite convulsed with crying'.[7] Press reports confirmed what Mackenzie had alleged: the founders of the company really were swindlers. The two main movers were William Hole and Thomas Knowles; Hole had been an unsuccessful tavern-keeper, tallow-chandler, and estate agent, while Knowles had been a footman and small shopkeeper; both had spent stretches in debtor's prison.[8] But the West Middlesex Company had been their ticket to fortune, with estimates of the total invested by the public in four years ranging from £150,000 to more than £250,000. Even though much of this was eaten up by advertising costs, agents' commissions, and payments to annuitants and policyholders to keep the scheme going, the gang netted themselves a tidy profit.[9]

Now Mackenzie renewed his efforts to mobilize the forces of law. On 16 January he wrote to his fellow Scot, Sir Peter Laurie, a City magistrate and former Lord Mayor of London, calling his attention to the fraud. Laurie was a good choice: always interested in reform and originally destined for the Church of Scotland, he was a paternalist Tory dedicated to good causes, having campaigned for better treatment of prisoners and improvements to asylums.[10] Laurie believed it was 'one of the most extensive swindling concerns' ever known, and five days later, he read out Mackenzie's letter in the justice room of Mansion House to warn the public against such schemes.[11] Though he 'deeply regretted that he had not the power of dealing with' those responsible, he invited anyone with information on the company to write to him: 'if he could not get hold of the individuals who had been perpetrating all this mischief', he would 'set before the eyes of the world the extent of the villainies they had committed'. Politicizing the issue, he argued that it showed the need for legislation introducing compulsory registration for all insurance offices, and ensuring the solvency and responsibility of their managers. More

[5] Letter from Fox Maule to Peter Mackenzie, 1 July 1839, East Dunbartonshire Archives, GD185/3/3; Peter Mackenzie, *Reminiscences of Glasgow and the West of Scotland*, 3 vols (Glasgow, 1866), ii. 622–3.

[6] The firm's advertisements used the term 'managers' rather than 'directors'.

[7] *The Times*, 28 January 1841; *Scotch Reformers' Gazette*, 6 February 1841.

[8] *Glasgow Argus*, repr. in *Caledonian Mercury*, 18 January 1841.

[9] *Bristol Mercury*, 23 January 1841; *Freeman's Journal*, 27 January 1841; *Derby Mercury*, 7 April 1841.

[10] Anita McConnell, 'Sir Peter Laurie', *ODNB*.

[11] Entry for 11 February 1841, *Journal of Sir Peter Laurie*, ed. Elizabeth Shepherd (Tunbridge Wells, 1985), 98.

immediately, he urged the company's victims to lobby their MPs for a parliamentary investigation.[12]

Meanwhile, Mackenzie renewed his own efforts, writing again to Maule, and this time receiving a fuller reply. But the government remained uninterested in pursuing a criminal prosecution. Maule agreed that the swindlers' conduct was 'atrocious and fraudulent', and Henry Labouchere, Thomson's successor at the Board of Trade, had 'well considered the case', but he had concluded that 'there do not appear sufficient grounds to institute or sustain a criminal charge'. For Maule, the solution to fraud was individual vigilance rather than state intervention, believing that 'it will not be easy to restrain such companies, if the public will not look into the nature of their establishment before entrusting their money to them'. But Maule did hint that the government would do something, albeit reluctantly:

> Seeing the mischief which this company has been able to commit—and that the public when tempted by large profits have not the sense or the prudence to consider the risques which they run—it may be that the Government, difficult as the question is, will endeavour to find some protection for those whom such schemes are likely to entrap.[13]

Sure enough, a fortnight later Labouchere announced the appointment of a select committee to investigate the law on joint-stock companies with the aim of preventing fraud.[14] The committee began interviewing witnesses in May, and the Independent West Middlesex was the hottest topic. Despite Maule's diffidence on the subject, the committee showed an interest in whether company frauds came under criminal law, pressing Laurie, the first witness, on the question. The magistrate conceded that what the managers had done could be construed as obtaining money under false pretences and that they could also be tried for conspiracy.[15] Doubts remained over his jurisdiction over offences perpetrated outside the City, yet Laurie subsequently announced that if the managers came into the City, he would try his best to have them apprehended, charged, and sent to the Central Criminal Court.[16]

In the space of a few months, a single company scandal had seemingly transformed the terms of the public debate on companies and the law. The government had appointed a committee specifically tasked with investigating means of preventing frauds, while Mansion House, hitherto an obstacle to the criminal prosecution of company directors, was home to a magistrate who signalled his intention 'to go to the verge of the limits of his authority... to bring such wholesale plunderers to justice'.[17] But the returns were disappointing. The summer parliamentary

[12] *The Times*, 21 January, 8, 19 February, 18 March 1841. A group of Scottish MPs, including Joseph Hume, were prominent in pressuring the Whig government to act: Mackenzie, *Reminiscences*, ii. 629. But Laurie, typically, attributed the appointment of the committee to his own exertions, and those of his nephew: entry for 13 May 1841, *Journal of Sir Peter Laurie*, 99.

[13] Letter from Fox Maule to Peter Mackenzie, 18 March 1841, East Dunbartonshire Archives, GD185/3/8.

[14] Hansard, 3s, 57: 842 (2 April 1841).

[15] *First Report of the Select Committee on Joint Stock Companies*, PP 1844 VII. 8–10.

[16] *The Times*, 27, 31 May 1841.

[17] Ibid. 27 May 1841.

elections cut short the select committee, which interviewed just seven witnesses over three sittings, and did not issue a report. It was not renewed when parliament reconvened after the victory of Peel's Conservative Party, and the question of reform was shelved. The West Middlesex managers stayed out of Laurie's clutches, and the question of criminal proceedings faded, though the victims obtained verdicts in civil lawsuits against two of the managers unwise enough to return to the country.[18]

The West Middlesex case seems to have altered how the speculating public viewed the magistracy. Some even came to see Laurie as an investment guru: in April he was obliged to point out that 'it was quite impossible that he could answer the many letters he received requesting him to state what companies were good and what bad'.[19] Others who felt themselves the victims of fraud were encouraged by the publicity given to the West Middlesex case to bring their grievances to the magistrates' courts in numbers not seen since the mid 1820s. Some magistrates, like Sir James Duke, who also sat in the Commons as a Liberal, were reluctant to get involved. Duke's line was that if people would 'improvidently embark in speculations which they afterwards saw reason to regret, they must get out of them as well as they could' without bothering the magistrates.[20] Others, however, proved more willing to listen to cases, acting as 'agony aunts', and dispensing help and advice to investors in a bind.

Laurie was the most progressive of them all, underlined by his handling of the Westminster Loan and Investment Joint-Stock Company. This looked like a re-run of the West Middlesex case: the company advertised heavily throughout the capital, drummed up business through well-paid agents, offered rates inconsistent with safety, its advertised capital was non-existent, and its prospectuses listed names of made-up directors, or real men whose names were used without permission. Under a barrage of criticism in *The Times*, it folded in July 1842, and soon after, the depositors and shareholders came to Laurie to present their case. But so did the manager, and main power behind the company, Charles Kerry Nicholls. Armed with a barrister, Nicholls claimed his company was nothing like the notorious West Middlesex. Rather than pillaging his company, he had lost money by its failure; far from fleeing the country, he stayed in order to defend himself. His barrister complained that the investigation was taking place in a criminal instead of a civil court, where 'it obviously belonged', and thought that 'Sir Peter was a little warped by his heroic desire to serve all the world'. Laurie, though, was undeterred, and after listening to the evidence, concluded that Nicholls and his accomplices had exposed themselves to a criminal action. He therefore advised the victims to take legal advice to 'see how their evidence could be shaped', and to prosecute the men at the next session of the Old Bailey, 'to see what 23 of their countrymen sitting as

[18] *Grover v. Williams* (1841), *The Times*, 7 April 1841; *Napper v. Hole* (1842), *The Times*, 2 April 1842; *Larkin v. Hole* (1844), *The Times*, 16 March 1844; *Snow v. Hole* (1845), *The Times*, 10 March 1845; *Select Committee on Joint Stock Companies*, 95.

[19] *Morning Post*, 15 April 1841.

[20] *The Times*, 30 August 1841.

a grand jury would say to their tale'.[21] Nevertheless, the victims did not follow this advice and instead turned on each other, the depositors and other creditors successfully suing the shareholders for recovery of their money.[22]

Some magistrates were therefore beginning to see a role for the criminal law in prosecuting company frauds, but if they thought a company was a genuine business, they refused point-blank to allow the complainants access to criminal remedies.[23] Only when a magistrate was persuaded that a company was a bubble scheme without any real existence would he invoke the criminal law, as Johnson did with Humphries. And for such prosecutions to happen, the victims needed to co-operate, something they were rarely willing to do. As a result, dramatic scandals following in the wake of the West Middlesex affair tended to be exposed in forums other than the magistrates' courts. These included the case of Thomas Saunders Cave, a failed mining speculator who succeeded in attracting £368,000 in subscriptions from fifty-four well-to-do investors.[24] Though the mines did exist, they were catastrophically unproductive, costing far more to run than they yielded, and Cave, who lived the high life whilst the money lasted, eventually bankrupted himself. The case attracted publicity because of comments made by one of the Bankruptcy Commissioners, who called it 'one of the most extraordinary cases' that had ever come before the court, yet Cave's victims eschewed a criminal prosecution.[25] A second mining venture brought about smaller losses, but a larger scandal, due to the involvement of a City of London alderman. The Talacre Coal and Iron Company was formed in 1839 to operate mines in the north-west, but went bust in under three years. Nevertheless, the company's permanent chairman and solicitor, Alderman Thomas Wood, had profited handsomely: having paid £75,000 for the mines, he sold them to the company for £110,000; investors were lured by the exhibition of Talacre coal which was in fact taken from another, superior mine.[26] Because of Wood's mayoral ambitions, the accusations were investigated by a committee of his fellow aldermen, which reached the damning conclusion that the company 'appeared to have been got up as a speculation presenting no probabilities of profit, and calculated to benefit no person except those by whom it had been concocted'.[27] The scandal was enough to prevent him becoming Lord Mayor despite five attempts, but he never faced criminal charges.[28]

[21] Ibid. 13, 15, 21, 28 July 1842; *Morning Post*, 28 July 1842.

[22] *Smith v. Vanderlin* (1842), *The Times*, 9 November 1842; *Smith v. Steele* (1842), *The Times*, 16 November 1842; *Griffiths v. Taylor* (1843), *The Times*, 28 January 1843.

[23] See, for example, the outcomes of cases involving the North Staffordshire Colliery Company, the Wheal Trevenon mine, the British Central American Land Company, and the Union Flint Glass Company: *Morning Post*, 15 April 1841; *The Times*, 23 April 1841; *Morning Chronicle*, 1 May 1841; *The Times*, 21, 26 August 1841.

[24] Justin Brooke, 'Thomas Saunders Cave, Speculator Extraordinary', *British Mining*, 43 (1991), 11.

[25] Charles Williams, *Re Saunders* (1841), *The Times*, 15 December 1841.

[26] *Morning Post*, 14 October 1841; *The Times*, 23 September 1842, 26 June 1843.

[27] *The Times*, 26 June 1843.

[28] Alfred P. Beaven, 'Notes on the Aldermen, 1701–1838', in *The Aldermen of the City of London: Temp. Henry III–1912* (London, 1908), 195–211 <http://www.british-history.ac.uk/report.aspx?compid=67,248>.

PREVENTION OR PUNISHMENT?

The badly tarnished reputation of joint-stock companies in the early 1840s is traceable in the culture of the period.[29] Until now, novels and plays had only rarely satirized companies, but the subject became a fictional staple from the early 1840s.[30] The influence of the West Middlesex is obvious in William Makepeace Thackeray's *The History of Samuel Titmarsh and the Great Hoggarty Diamond*, which features the Independent West Diddlesex Fire and Life Insurance Company, whose collapse causes its promoter, John Brough, to flee to Calais.[31] The 'Diddlesex' also appeared on the stage. In 1841, the disreputable impresario Renton Nicholson launched his famous Judge and Jury Society at the Garrick's Head and Town Hotel, which put on performances satirizing 'the follies of the day', presided over by Nicholson in his incarnation as 'Lord Chief Baron Nicholson'.[32] One of its first performances was a farce telling the story of the 'West Diddlesex'. The show proved a hit with London audiences, being performed for upwards of 130 nights; thereafter, 'Diddlesex' became common shorthand for a fraudulent project.[33] Charles Dickens too probably had the West Middlesex in mind when he wrote *Martin Chuzzlewit*, featuring the fraudulent Anglo-Bengalee Disinterested Loan and Life Assurance Company, whose capital would be '[a] figure of two, and as many oughts after it as the printer can get into the same line'.[34] Others novels contained more general commentaries on the growing public taste for speculation: Samuel Warren's *Ten Thousand a-Year* described the 'monstrous passion for JOINT-STOCK COMPANIES' which fuelled absurd schemes like the Artificial Rain Company and the Gunpowder and Fresh Water Company.[35] In the preface to *George St. George Julian, The Prince*, Henry Cockton warned his readers that many of the banks, societies, and companies being formed were 'utterly rotten'.[36]

Fraud was thus seen as a pressing problem in the early 1840s, and a variety of remedies were proposed. Some identified private solutions, focusing on the moral lessons to be drawn from the catastrophes. The evangelical understanding of the trade cycle, so influential in these years, was relevant here. According to this line of thought, economic crises were to be welcomed as they stripped the improvident and unsound elements out of the economy, leaving only 'wholesome' enterprise.[37] So, commenting on Cave's Cornish mines and the West Middlesex Company, *The*

[29] Ranald C. Michie, *Guilty Money: The City of London in Victorian and Edwardian Culture, 1815–1914* (London, 2009), ch. 1.

[30] John R. Reed, 'A Friend to Mammon: Speculation in Victorian Literature', *Victorian Studies*, 27 (1984), 183–4.

[31] The novel first appeared in instalments in *Fraser's Magazine* from September 1841.

[32] G. C. Boase and K. D. Reynolds, 'Renton Nicholson', *ODNB*.

[33] Mackenzie, *Reminiscences*, ii. 629–30.

[34] Charles Dickens, *Martin Chuzzlewit* (1844; repr. Ware, 1994), 396. The novel was serialized from January 1843.

[35] [Samuel Warren], 'Ten Thousand a-Year', *Blackwood's Edinburgh Magazine*, 49 (March 1841), 401–2.

[36] Henry Cockton, *George St. George Julian, the Prince* (London, 1841), v–vi.

[37] Boyd Hilton, *The Age of Atonement: The Influence of Evangelicalism on Social and Economic Thought, 1785–1865* (Oxford, 1988; repr. 2001), 134–5.

Times was incredulous that anyone could be found to support such mad schemes. These 'incautious investors' were 'themselves the chief cause of the evil they deplore', and the morality of commerce would improve only once they learned wisdom through experience.[38] Some industry insiders also favoured private solutions. Andrew Meek, accountant to the North of England Joint Stock Banking Company, firmly believed that if shareholders could be persuaded to become more active in monitoring their companies' affairs, banks could be raised out of 'the state of degradation' where they currently languished, and legislative interference averted.[39]

However, an alternative viewpoint was developing which posited legislation as essential for a better-functioning system. Prominent figures from within the joint-stock economy were among the keenest advocates of intervention. Swinton Boult, secretary to the Liverpool Fire and Life Insurance Company, opposed unnecessary interference but thought that a system of compulsory registration for all companies would help root out unsound schemes.[40] John Augustus Beaumont, managing director of the County Fire Office, went further, hoping for legislation 'to enforce a fair and honest disclosure of the proceedings of public companies'.[41] Even the Committee of Deputies from the Joint-Stock Banks was 'deeply impressed with the importance of an early revision' of the banking code.[42]

Peel's Conservative ministry proved responsive, signalling its intention to deal both with banks and the wider joint-stock economy. As banks had been thoroughly investigated following the crisis of the mid 1830s, Peel announced in 1842 that they would be dealt with by the executive government.[43] By contrast, the joint-stock sector more generally had been less exhaustively dissected, with a report on the law of partnership in 1837 and the curtailed 1841 select committee on companies being the only significant investigations to date. As a result, in 1843 the government decided to revive the lapsed committee. Under the chairmanship of the new President of the Board of Trade, William Gladstone, the committee recalled the seven witnesses from 1841 to give further evidence, and summoned sixteen more—an assortment of barristers, solicitors, bankers, and merchants—to give their views. This time, as well as commenting on the West Middlesex case, witnesses discussed other recent failures, and were invited to recommend anti-fraud measures.

Several witnesses believed that the criminal law had a part to play, and suggested three main reforms. The first was the establishment of a public prosecutor for England, along the lines of Scottish law, which had a prosecutor in the form of the Lord Advocate. Conspiracy prosecutions were complex, cumbrous, and hugely

[38] *The Times*, 16 December 1841.

[39] Andrew Meek, *Observations on the Government of Joint Stock Banks in England* (London, 1841).

[40] Swinton Boult, *The Law and Practice relating to the Constitution and Management of Assurance, Banking, and other Joint Stock Companies* (London, 1841), 27–34.

[41] John Augustus Beaumont, *Thoughts and Details on Life Insurance Offices, in a Letter to the Shareholders and Insured in the Provident Life Office* (London, 1842), 24–5.

[42] *A Record of the Proceedings of the Committee of Deputies from the Joint Stock Banks of England, Wales, and Ireland* (London, 1845), 51.

[43] Hansard, 3s, 61: 842 (7 March 1842).

expensive, all of which deterred the victims. Responsibility for them should therefore be taken out of their hands and vested in a government official.[44] A second suggestion was to reform the law so that directors could be prosecuted for misappropriating company money. Henry Bellenden Ker, a barrister who had authored the 1837 report on partnerships, highlighted a discrepancy in the law which meant that whereas robbery 'of a mere trifle' by a clerk was punishable by transportation, a company director could steal £10,000 and only be liable for the debt because he was legally in possession of the property as a trustee. These 'aggravated breaches of trust' should be criminalized, Ker believed.[45] The third suggestion was to criminalize the unauthorized use of names on company prospectuses, a device used with success by the Independent West Middlesex, the Westminster Loan, and others.[46]

But most of the witnesses focused on preventative measures, and even the supporters of criminal penalties believed that the legislature ought to prioritize prevention over punishment, which was 'very little remedy to the sufferers'.[47] The committee agreed, and though its report stated that it was 'expedient to make provision for prosecuting the directors or officers' of companies that were conducted fraudulently, it did not elaborate, and its main concern was clearly prevention.[48] The first step to preventing fraudulent practices was to define them, and the report furnished a catalogue of fourteen types of deception, ranging from falsehoods in prospectuses to fabricating accounts and declaring unjustified dividends.[49] The language was harder than that used in the committee's predecessor on banks: whereas this had discussed 'evils', 'mismanagement', and 'irregularity', the new report did not shy away from using the term 'fraud'.[50] Nor did it recoil from presenting a bold plan to prevent fraud. The solution was publicity. Here, the committee was influenced by wider currents in early nineteenth-century liberal thought. Secrecy was coming to be seen as an instrument of vested interests against the public good; publicity was a means of subjecting corrupt forms of governance to public scrutiny and evaluation. Jeremy Bentham had led the way in theorizing publicity in this way: 'In the darkness of secrecy, sinister interest and evil in every shape, have full swing...Where there is no publicity there is no justice'. Publicity was 'the surest of all guards against improbity'.[51] These ideas influenced a range of government policies after 1832, such as the creation of the Statistical Department of the Board of Trade in 1832, the reduction of the newspaper stamp in 1836, putting Hansard on public sale in 1838, and the introduction of the Penny Post in 1840.[52] The principle linking them was a desire to harness the regulatory power of public opinion.

[44] *Select Committee on Joint Stock Companies*, 10, 36, 85.
[45] Ibid. 195.
[46] Ibid. 231, 16–17.
[47] Joseph Parkes, ibid. 231.
[48] Ibid. xiv.
[49] Ibid. ix–x.
[50] *Report from the Secret Committee on Joint Stock Banks*, PP 1836 IX. p. v.
[51] Jeremy Bentham, 'Constitutional Code', in *The Works of Jeremy Bentham*, ed. John Bowring, 11 vols (Edinburgh, 1843), ix. 493; Jeremy Bentham, 'Draught of a New Plan for the Organization of the Judicial Establishment in France', *Works of Jeremy Bentham*, iv. 316.
[52] David Vincent, *The Culture of Secrecy: Britain, 1832–1998* (Oxford, 1998), 3–4.

These ideas were also influencing the economic sphere. Fraud was only possible, so witnesses before the committee argued, because disreputable directors could take advantage of the anonymity afforded by the joint-stock company form to keep their true identities concealed. If the public knew with whom they were dealing, they would only do business with honest men who deserved their trust. The committee seized upon the idea, and made it the centrepiece of their report. The compulsory publication of the names and addresses of the directors and shareholders, and the capital and constitution of the company, 'would baffle every case of fraud which has come under the notice of your committee'.[53]

Sadly, however, faith in the power of publicity derived from a widely held but false assumption: that those who perpetrated company frauds were not respectable merchants, but low-class imposters. The belief derived from the West Middlesex gang who were small tradesmen, and became entrenched by subsequent fictional representations. In *Martin Chuzzlewit*, the seemingly respectable director of the Anglo-Bengalee, Tigg Montague, is actually the petty thief Montague Tigg, who finances his company from the proceeds of a stolen watch. Brough, the director in *Samuel Titmarsh*, was initially a poor clerk, who rose on the back of his company promotions. In *George St. George Julian*, the projector of some of the wildest schemes of the age, Horatio Oswald Tynte, 'walked upon his toes and twisted his hips at every step, and spoke with a pseudo-aristocratic drawl', which made it clear that he was 'not a gentleman'.[54]

Nevertheless, in June 1844 the government introduced a bill regulating joint-stock companies based on the committee's recommendations, together with two further bills, one concerned with the winding-up of companies, the other with the regulation of joint-stock banks. Despite the great changes they embodied, the measures met with little opposition, passing with few amendments. Taken together, they represent the birth of modern company law.[55]

The acts embodied four innovations designed to ensure honest management. The first, of course, was publicity. This was to be achieved by compulsory registration of all companies with a new Board of Trade Registrar.[56] Before companies could advertise, they had to pay £5 for provisional registration, giving details of the name and business of the company, and the names, addresses and occupations of the promoters, and later, of the directors, officers, and subscribers.[57] They would only obtain the full set of rights granted by the act when they completely registered,

[53] *Select Committee on Joint Stock Companies*, v.

[54] Cockton, *George St. George Julian*, 37.

[55] Hansard, 3s, 76: 273–82 (3 July 1844), 1178–85 (22 July 1844). Though this was a revolution which did not reach Scotland, as the acts did not apply to companies north of the border.

[56] The principle of registration dated back to the 1786 Registration Act for recording information about the owners of ships, but really took off after 1815, being extended to savings banks (1817), joint-stock banks (1826), friendly societies (1829), and building societies (1836), and was included in the letters patent acts of 1834 and 1837 which extended the availability of corporate privileges: Ron Harris, *Industrializing English Law: Entrepreneurship and Business Organization, 1720–1844* (Cambridge, 2000), 274–6.

[57] 7 & 8 Vict. c. 110, s. 4. Prospectuses had to be registered, but this requirement was scrapped by an act of 1847 following lobbying from company promoters: 10 & 11 Vict. c. 78, s. 4.

by submitting a deed of settlement signed by the shareholders.[58] Completely registered companies had to make twice-yearly returns of all changes to the shareholder list.[59] They also had to register audited balance sheets within a fortnight of each general meeting.[60] The Registrar's offices were open to the public, who could inspect any of the returns for a shilling.[61] Financial penalties for non-compliance were stipulated throughout the act; using names without permission was penalized financially, by a £10 fine, rather than criminally.[62] In return, companies were granted a secure legal existence, enjoying all the privileges of incorporation—including a separate legal personality—except limited liability, which was still regarded as a dangerous principle only to be granted on a case-by-case basis. These were major concessions, but the lack of a secure legal status for companies had come to be seen as an incentive to commercial immorality.[63] The reforms would take companies out of the legal limbo in which they had hitherto operated, and ensure that their affairs were conducted fairly and in the open.

The second innovation was enforcement of minimum standards of corporate governance. The Companies and Banks Acts contained similar provisions here. Both stipulated that general meetings be held at least once a year; that shareholders be able to call extraordinary general meetings; and that the members of the board be rotated regularly so that they could not hold office indefinitely.[64] Shareholders were to elect auditors, who would examine the accounts and report on them to the general meeting.[65] Shareholders in companies and banks would receive the balance sheet at their annual meeting, but shareholders in companies had the further right to inspect the books of the company.[66] Banks were more heavily regulated in other respects, however, with their capital not to be less than £100,000, with shares of not less than £100. Banks could not start business until all the shares were subscribed for, half the capital paid up, and the deed of settlement executed by all the shareholders.[67]

The third innovation was regulation of company liquidation. Hitherto, there was no special procedure for this and disputes over company assets were taken to the equity courts, with all the expense, uncertainty, and delay this could involve. With unincorporated companies treated in law as large partnerships, actions were frequently

58 7 & 8 Vict. c. 110, ss. 7, 21.

59 Ibid. s. 11.

60 Ibid. s. 43.

61 Ibid. ss. 18–20.

62 Ibid. s. 65. Publicity requirements for joint-stock banks were less demanding, with the Stamp Office continuing to receive the annual returns of members, directors and branches, making them available to the public on payment of a shilling. However, in addition to registering these returns, banks also had to print and display the names and addresses of all their members 'in a conspicuous place' at head office: 7 & 8 Vict. c. 113, ss. 16–17.

63 When taken to court, promoters pleaded the illegality of their schemes in order to shed their liabilities to investors: *Blundell v. Winsor* (1837) 59 ER 238; *Garrard v. Hardey* (1843) 134 ER 648.

64 7 & 8 Vict. c. 110, schedule A; 7 & 8 Vict. c. 113, s. 4.

65 7 & 8 Vict. c. 110, ss. 38–43; 7 & 8 Vict. c. 113, s. 4.

66 7 & 8 Vict. c. 110, ss. 33–37, 49–50, 57.

67 7 & 8 Vict. c. 113, ss. 2, 5. The Joint-Stock Banks Act was extended to Scotland and Ireland in 1846: 9 & 10 Vict. c. 75.

complicated by the need to include the names of all shareholders.[68] The select committee had recommended that the process be reformed, but failed to suggest how this might be achieved.[69] Nevertheless, the subject was taken seriously enough by the government to warrant a separate act, designed to extend bankruptcy law to companies by locating the winding-up of companies in the Court of Bankruptcy.[70] There were two objectives. The first was to help creditors by making the process of winding-up easier and quicker, extending their remedies against company property. This was possible now that companies had been given a separate legal personality: a company could be declared bankrupt without the bankruptcy extending to its individual members.[71] Any creditor could petition for the bankruptcy of a company, either provisionally or completely registered. Judgements obtained by creditors were to be executed first against the property of the company and only against individual shareholders if the company's property was inadequate to meet the claims.[72] The second objective was to serve the wider public interest by applying to companies what was already the procedure in cases of bankrupt individuals: shining a light into the affairs of insolvent concerns, establishing the causes of failure, and exposing any abuses.[73] To achieve this, the act charged the Court of Bankruptcy with investigating company failures, empowering it to summon anyone involved for examination, and to order them to produce any documents it wanted to see.[74]

The fourth, and potentially most radical, innovation was the extension of the criminal law to company directors, only hitherto reachable by the law of conspiracy and false pretences. For the first time, there was a statutory, and seemingly far-reaching, crime of fraud. The Joint-Stock Companies Act stipulated that

> if any such Director or other Officer of any Joint Stock Company registered under this Act wrongfully do or omit any Act, with Intent to defraud the Company or any Shareholder therein, or falsify or fraudulently mutilate or fraudulently make any Erasure in the Books of Account or Books of Register, or any Document belonging to the Company, then such Director or Officer shall be deemed to be guilty of a Misdemeanor.[75]

The Winding-up Act contained a similar section referring more specifically to the circumstances prior to and after a declaration of bankruptcy. Again borrowing from the laws on private bankruptcy, it stipulated that any member of a company declared bankrupt who, after or 'in contemplation of' the bankruptcy, tampered

[68] Victor M. Batzel, '"The General Scope of the Act": A Study of Law, Moralism, and Administration in England, 1844–1910', *Canadian Journal of History*, 22 (1987), 350–1; V. Markham Lester, *Victorian Insolvency: Bankruptcy, Imprisonment for Debt, and Company Winding-up in Nineteenth-Century England* (Oxford, 1995), 222. Even banks, which had a more secure legal status than some other types of company, sometimes failed to secure dissolution because of the need to make all the shareholders party to the suit: see *Deeks v. Stanhope* (1844) 60 ER 278.

[69] *Select Committee on Joint Stock Companies*, xiv.

[70] Hansard, 3s, 76: 559 (10 July 1844).

[71] Ibid. s. 2.

[72] 7 & 8 Vict. c. 110, s. 66; 7 & 8 Vict. c. 113, s. 10.

[73] 7 & 8 Vict. c. 111, s. 1.

[74] 7 & 8 Vict. c. 111, ss. 15, 19. A similar act was passed for Ireland the following year: 8 & 9 Vict. c. 98.

[75] 7 & 8 Vict. c. 110, s. 31.

with any of the company's books, or made false entries in them 'with Intent to defraud the Creditors', was guilty of a misdemeanour. While the Companies Act did not set a punishment, the Winding-up Act fixed a maximum penalty of a three-year jail sentence with or without hard labour.[76]

As well as establishing these offences, the legislation also provided for the active involvement of the state in prosecuting them. But this stopped well short of the public prosecutor called for by some. The Winding-up Act stipulated that once the Court of Bankruptcy had investigated, it would report to the Board of Trade on the causes of failure, noting 'any special circumstances relating to the formation or management of the affairs of such company'.[77] If it saw fit, the Board would forward the report and relevant papers to the Attorney General, who could order a Treasury prosecution of any of the directors or officers of the company.[78] Different provisions were made in the Joint-Stock Companies Act, which stipulated that prosecutions could only be commenced 'in the name and with the consent of' the Attorney General.[79] Neither act set out any criteria by which the Attorney General would assess whether or not to authorize proceedings, but these provisions seemed to anticipate a role for the government in prosecuting fraud, something which the Whigs had been singularly unwilling to accept in 1841 following the Independent West Middlesex failure.

The legislation was generally well received by the press. The *Manchester Guardian* got over its philosophic antipathy to government interference, arguing that the 'small amount of control possessed by the proprietors in these companies over the directors, coupled with the fact that many of the former are persons not at all conversant with business' made it necessary. It thought the legislation was likely to protect the public, and singled out the parts of the act extending the criminal law to companies for particular notice.[80] *The Times* thought the legislation 'really necessary', designed as it was for 'the suppression of the trade in bubble-companies'. It had confidence that the central principle of the legislation was sound. 'Publicity is all that is necessary. Show up the roguery, and it is harmless'.[81] Company directors and lawyers also praised the legislation, while J. W. Gilbart, manager of the London and Westminster Bank thought that, by defending existing firms from 'reckless competitors', the Bank Act would advance the joint-stock banking interest.[82] Yet the legislation was to achieve far less than its supporters hoped.

[76] 7 & 8 Vict. c. 111, s. 30.

[77] Ibid. s. 25.

[78] Ibid. s. 27.

[79] 7 & 8 Vict. c. 110, s. 77.

[80] *Manchester Guardian*, 24 July 1844. Others were less willing to see the principle of laissez faire sacrificed. The *Westminster Review* thought the acts went too far down the path of centralization, arguing that *caveat emptor* 'provides a far better preventive of possible fraud than a cartload of statutes': Anon., 'The Legislation of 1844', *Westminster Review*, 42 (December 1844), 324.

[81] *The Times*, 4 July 1844. See also *Morning Post*, 4 June 1844.

[82] James Burchell, *The Joint Stock Companies Registration Act* (London, 1844); George Henry Lewis, *The Liabilities Incurred by the Projectors, Managers and Shareholders of Railway and other Joint-Stock Companies Considered: and also the Rights and liabilities arising from Transfers of Shares* (London, 1845); James William Gilbart, *The Letters of Nehemiah: Relating to the Laws Affecting Joint Stock Banks, and the Effects Likely to be Produced, by the Measures of Sir Robert Peel, upon the System of Banking in London, and Throughout the Country* (London, 1845), 16.

THE RAILWAY MANIA

After 1844, magistrates continued to tolerate the use of the police courts to air joint-stock grievances, but they preferred giving advice to exercising their magisterial powers, so that the criminalization of fraud was not made a reality. This was true even of Laurie who, despite being more concerned than most with frauds, held traditional views on speculation. When his personal wealth reached £100,000, he congratulated himself in his diary for his slow and steady approach: he had 'never run risks by being eager for great interest, for when there are great gains there are always great risks'.[83] When he suspected others of running such risks, his sympathy had definite limits.[84] And it soon became clear that far from making directors amenable to the criminal law, the legislation of 1844 actually provided a pretext for magistrates to pass the buck to other authorities. In December 1845, a country gentleman named Gregory approached Alderman John Musgrove at Guildhall with an alleged case of obtaining money by false pretences. On the strength of a prospectus, Gregory had applied for shares in the Direct Birmingham, Oxford and Brighton Railway, paying £52 10s deposit. Though he received a letter of allotment, he never received his scrip because the project was subsequently abandoned. But Musgrove failed to see any false pretence: Gregory had applied to the company, not the other way around. In Musgrove's view, it was 'not a proper case for the interference of a magistrate', and castigated him for trying to shrink from his pecuniary responsibilities. Moreover, if fraud was alleged, 'the justice-room would not be a proper place for the inquiry' because the Winding-up Act gave 'the power of inquiry to the Bankruptcy Court', which would report any criminal matters to the Board of Trade.[85]

Gregory's case was one of many arising from the collapse of the railway share market at the end of 1845. Speculation in railways had grown through the previous year, becoming a 'mania' in the eyes of many commentators by the autumn.[86] Confidence soared in 1845 but broke at the end of the year; share prices tumbled, and many projected schemes were abandoned. By January 1846, no less than 549 provisionally registered lines had been scrapped, 'leaving nothing behind them but a mass of liability'.[87] In this climate, countless disputes arose between shareholders (or in many cases scripholders), promoters, directors, and creditors, and some of these were taken to the police courts. Despite the widespread belief that the market for railway shares was riddled with deception and deceit, the criminal law was

[83] Entry for 18 April 1843, *Journal of Sir Peter Laurie*, 104–5.

[84] See his decisions in the cases of the General Benefit Assurance Office and the Heir-at-Law Society: *The Times*, 17, 21 October 1844, 12 March 1845. He seems to have adjudicated in joint-stock disputes less frequently after 1845, partly because of recurring anal abscesses, the leeching and lancing of which left him housebound for months at a time. It is possible his ailments made him less patient with the grievances of speculators: *Journal of Sir Peter Laurie*, 114–15.

[85] *The Times*, 8 December 1845.

[86] *Era*, 15 September 1844; *Freeman's Journal*, 21 October 1844; *Liverpool Mercury*, 22 November 1844.

[87] *The Times*, 9 January 1846.

barely applied to those behind the schemes, only proving adequate to catch charlatans operating on the fringes of the market.[88]

One such operator was Benjamin Brown, a self-proclaimed 'railway projector', a 'shrewd-looking man' of 44. In fact, he was a carpenter and builder by trade, but had been employed by a railway engineer as an 'enquirer', to probe the respectability and solvency of share applicants. He had seen an opportunity to benefit from his inside knowledge when spotting an advertisement in *The Times*. Charles Jacobs, a draper, was offering £50 to anyone who could find him a permanent situation at a railway. Brown contacted Jacobs, representing himself as projector of several railways, including the Prince of Wales London and Oxford Railway, and the London and Windsor Railway. He told Jacobs he could get him a job as a secretary on one of his lines in return for £50 upfront and a bill of exchange for a further £50. Jacobs paid the money, but received no job, and swore an information against Brown. Confident that he was out of the reach of the law, Brown told the police constable who arrested him that 'I can't think how Mr Jacobs could be so cruel, when I have been so kind to him; but never mind, let him do his best, he can only make a debt of it'. Initially, it seemed Brown was right. Thomas Henry, the presiding magistrate at Lambeth police court, showed little sympathy for the draper, remarking that 'it was really astonishing that any person should have been so soft as to part with his money under such circumstances'. But the prosecution was able to build a convincing case of obtaining money by false pretences against Brown. He purported to be the projector of two registered companies, but George Taylor, the Assistant Companies Registrar, testified that the Prince of Wales line was not registered, and although the London and Windsor was, Brown's name did not feature anywhere as promoter or provisional director. Moreover, other victims wrote to say that Jacobs had attempted to defraud them in a similar way. On this evidence, Henry committed Brown for trial. When it reached the Old Bailey in January 1846, the trial proved relatively straightforward. In his summing up, the judge, Commissioner Edward Bullock, dismissed much of the defence case, and the jury took only a short time to find Brown guilty. He was sentenced to hard labour for twelve months.[89]

The episode probably did some good: the police reported that Brown's arrest had led to 'several persons absconding from their late haunts, and "making themselves scarce" in the metropolis'.[90] But it was an isolated case, which underlined that the criminal law was only able to deal with confidence tricksters who concocted imaginary companies. When cases involving real promoters and directors came to magistrates, accusations of obtaining money by false pretences, whether made by shareholders or creditors, were brushed aside and the complainants told to turn to

[88] When forgery was added to the charges against a defendant, cases did end up in criminal courts: see, for example, the trials of stockbrokers John Faulkner (acquitted) and Horatio West (convicted) for forgery of railway scrip: *The Times*, 24 September 1846; *Daily News*, 21 June 1847.

[89] *Reg. v. Brown* (1846), *The Times*, 29, 30 December 1845, 2, 10 January 1846; *OBP Online*, January 1846, trial of Benjamin Brown (t18460105-439) <www.oldbaileyonline.org> version 6.0.

[90] *The Times*, 2 January 1846.

the civil law for redress.[91] When complainants followed this advice, they found that the judges in their cases usually exercised similar moral judgements against them. After initial uncertainty and confusion caused by the volume of cases and the novel principles involved, the clearest thread that emerged in the decisions of judges in civil cases was condemnation of speculators and a desire to prevent them from recouping their losses, even in cases of misrepresentation.[92]

Moral considerations also shaped responses to the most scandalous episode associated with this period of speculation. One of the most powerful railway operators was George Hudson, the 'Railway King'. As chairman of four of the biggest companies of the railway boom—the York and North Midland, the York, Newcastle and Berwick, the Eastern Counties, and the Midland Counties—he was the personification of the new joint-stock economy in the 1840s.[93] Of relatively humble origins, his rapid rise unsettled many of his contemporaries. For Absalom Watkin, a Manchester merchant, Hudson was 'a greasy-butcher-looking fellow, with a tremendous bump of self-esteem'; for the Whig MP and man of letters Thomas Babington Macaulay, he was 'a bloated, vulgar, insolent, purseproud, greedy, drunken blackguard'.[94] Yet he was courted by investors because of his seemingly miraculous ability to generate vast profits from his railway schemes. He managed to buy his way into the social and political elite, purchasing estates in Yorkshire and a mansion in Knightsbridge, and winning election to parliament as Conservative representative for Sunderland in 1846.[95] But he found it increasingly difficult to sustain his railway empire after the initial crisis at the end of 1845. With rumours of dubious practices freely circulating, shareholder confidence slowly evaporated. In early 1849 they appointed committees of investigation which by the end of the year had produced a dozen reports, most of them unfavourable. The share prices of his four companies plummeted between 40 and 70 per cent, and before the last of the reports, 'Hudson's reputation was broken'.[96]

Despite the fact that the Midland Counties Committee effectively exonerated Hudson, committees at the other three companies accumulated a stack of damning evidence against the Railway King. The findings fell into two categories: first were cases of misappropriating company funds and related breaches of trust. The committees identified five instances where Hudson had taken sums totalling

[91] See allegations made against the Great Manchester, Rugby, and Southampton Railway, the London and Norwich Direct Railway, and the Derby and Liverpool Railway: ibid. 2, 6, 25 December 1845, 24 January 1846.

[92] R. W. Kostal, *Law and English Railway Capitalism, 1825–1875* (rev. repr., Oxford, 1997), ch. 2. Though note that Lobban presents a more optimistic view: Michael Lobban, 'The Politics of English Law in the Nineteenth Century', in Paul Brand and Joshua Getzler (eds), *Judges and Judging in the History of the Common Law and Civil Law: From Antiquity to Modern Times* (Cambridge, 2012), 126–7.

[93] James Taylor, 'Business in Pictures: Representations of Railway Enterprise in the Satirical Press in Britain, 1845–1870', *Past & Present*, 189 (2005), 120–2.

[94] *Absalom Watkin: Extracts from his Journal, 1814–1856*, ed. A. E. Watkin (London, 1920), 247; *The Journals of Thomas Babington Macaulay*, ed. William Thomas, 5 vols (London, 2008), ii. 67.

[95] Michael Reed, 'George Hudson', *ODNB*.

[96] A. J. Arnold and S. McCartney, *George Hudson: The Rise and Fall of the Railway King: A Study in Victorian Entrepreneurship* (London, 2004), 180–1.

£159,000. In addition, they uncovered other misdeeds: Hudson had secretly allocated shares to himself, sold shares to his companies for more than their market value, and broken by-laws by contracting personally with companies which he directed.[97] The second set of findings concerned the falsification of balance sheets used to justify unwarranted dividends. At the York and North Midland between 1846 and 1848 profits had been deliberately overstated by about £68,000, an eighth of total profits reported. A similar story was told at the York, Newcastle and Berwick where a fifth of the stated profits were false. In both cases, the statements did not turn losses into profits, but were designed to conceal the decline in profitability from the earlier 1840s, sustaining Hudson's reputation for financial wizardry. However, at the Eastern Counties, the committee unearthed false accounting on a far grander scale. No less than half the published profits—over £350,000—were false. The company had not recovered from massive losses made during the construction phase—before Hudson arrived—but Hudson fiddled the figures to create the impression that he had worked a miracle.[98] In the hierarchy of Hudson's crimes, the false balance sheets and dividends were considered 'scarcely less culpable than his more direct tampering with the property and interests of the shareholders'.[99]

As the charge sheet against Hudson swelled with each additional report, the press became increasingly outspoken in its censure, describing Hudson's acts as 'enormous frauds'.[100] 'Corruption upon such a large scale as he has been charged with is unknown in this country since the South Sea Bubble,' thought the *Observer*.[101] Tellingly, cartoons depicted him as a common thief, fleeing from duped investors with his bag of swag (see Figure 4.1). The revelations were so appalling that they had repercussions beyond Hudson's empire, undermining confidence in the sector as a whole, and sparking calls for government audit of railway accounts. In September 1849, George Cornewall Lewis, parliamentary under-secretary at the Home Office, wrote to a friend that railway speculations were 'unfairly depressed by the exposure of Hudson's proceedings, which has made people think that *no* railway management is to be trusted'.[102]

But could Hudson be made criminally liable for his frauds? There was some legal backing for this view. In an appeal case in the House of Lords earlier that year, Lord John Campbell, previously Attorney General under the Whigs, had condemned in the strongest possible terms the declaration of dividends out of capital rather than profits. Directors who did this were guilty of 'a gross fraud', and were 'not only civilly liable to those whom they have deceived and injured', but in Campbell's

[97] Ibid. 185–92.

[98] The Midland Committee found no evidence of false or fraudulent accounting: there had been no need, as this was a line that remained profitable throughout the period. Ibid. 193–8.

[99] *The Times*, 10 July 1849.

[100] Ibid. 26 December 1849. For other uses of the 'f' word, see *Observer*, 29 April 1849; *Manchester Guardian*, 15 September 1849.

[101] *Observer*, 20 May 1849.

[102] George Cornewall Lewis to Sir Edmund Head, 4 September 1849, in *Letters of the Right Hon. Sir George Cornewall Lewis, Bart. to various Friends*, ed. Gilbert Frankland Lewis (London, 1870), 211.

Figure 4.1 'The Last Royal Flight; Or, Good-Bye to the Railway King', *Puppet-Show*, 3 (1849), 93

opinion, were 'guilty of a conspiracy for which they are liable to be prosecuted and punished'. Lord Brougham backed his judgement, saying that where such payments were made with fraudulent intent, there was 'good ground for having recourse to a much severer proceeding than a mere civil action'.[103] These words were noted by some of Hudson's shareholders. A Liverpool shareholder of the York, Newcastle and Berwick Railway named Wylie reminded his fellows of the Law Lords' statement, and announced he would prepare a motion 'that legal proceedings should be instituted against every one of the directors', which was greeted with 'loud applause'.[104]

Wylie's stance may have been popular with his fellow victims, but outside the meeting, there were few calls for Hudson to face prosecution. Although some saw the way in which Hudson calculated his dividends as unambiguously corrupt, with accountancy in its infancy, there were serious disagreements among practitioners on how to apportion charges between capital and revenue.[105] Moreover, there was no legislative definition of 'profits', so paying dividends out of profits was not easy to classify in law.[106] All railway companies faced similar dilemmas, and Hudson's solutions were far from unique, as he was quick to point out. When he took over at the Eastern Counties, the line was in a mess, there were frequent accidents, and significant expenditure was needed to improve the line. He did not think it 'improper to charge a considerable amount of that to capital rather than to revenue'. There were no laws against this; indeed a clause permitting the payment of interest to shareholders out of capital, at least during construction, was a standard feature of acts incorporating railway companies. Consequently, Hudson did not see 'why one law should apply to the Eastern Counties, and another to other companies'.[107]

Even Hudson's appropriation of his companies' money was not as black and white as it first seemed. As A. J. Arnold and S. McCartney argue, this needs to be seen in the context of the very different remuneration climate of the nineteenth century. While private entrepreneurs could make fantastic wealth, company directors were more akin to municipal officeholders who gave gratuitous service out of a sense of duty to their local community. Payment for directors was typically minimal in joint-stock companies, and could be restricted to fees for attendance at boards. Hudson was expected to work tirelessly to earn bumper profits for his shareholders without receiving any significant reward in return.[108] The point was

[103] These points were made during the unsuccessful attempt by a shareholder in the Forth Marine Insurance Company to escape liability for calls on his shares citing fraudulent misrepresentation by the directors. *Burnes v. Pennell* (1849) 9 ER 1181, *The Times*, 17 July 1849.

[104] *Leeds Mercury*, 27 October 1849.

[105] For a discussion of this, see *Morning Chronicle*, 22 June 1849.

[106] And nor was there such a definition until 1980: Dean Ardern and Maxwell Aiken, 'An Accounting History of Capital Maintenance: Legal Precedents for Managerial Autonomy in the United Kingdom', *Accounting Historians Journal*, 32 (2005), 24–5.

[107] Hansard, 3s, 105: 586–7 (17 May 1849). For more on these acts of incorporation, see Mark Freeman, Robin Pearson, and James Taylor, *Shareholder Democracies? Corporate Governance in Britain and Ireland before 1850* (Chicago, IL, 2012), 121.

[108] Arnold and McCartney, *Hudson*, 199. See also Robin Pearson, 'Shareholder Democracies? English Stock Companies and the Politics of Corporate Governance during the Industrial Revolution', *English Historical Review*, 117 (2002), 840–66.

acknowledged by contemporaries: the *Era* thought that Hudson did the best he could for the interests of his constituents, 'and if he served his own at the same time, we ask, which of those constituents would not have done the same thing?'[109] Few went as far as this in exculpating Hudson, but *The Times* noted that his shareholders had seemingly 'forgotten that he had his own fortunes to make as well as theirs'.[110]

The main argument against punishing Hudson was the perceived complicity of his shareholders in the creation of the bubble. Hudson had 'cheated and demoralized a nation', wrote *The Times*, but 'the full measure of contempt will be reserved, not for the idol, but the worshippers'. If they had been satisfied with 3 per cent instead of 9, 'they need never have called in Mr Hudson'.[111] Even though it was the shareholders' committees of investigation which had exposed Hudson's misdeeds, their belated activism was seen in the context of years of fawning dedication to the Railway King so long as dividends were high.[112] John Roebuck, an outspoken radical MP, was contemptuous of those who now hounded Hudson. He had seen men 'fawning' and 'cringing and almost lying on their bellies', but now when fortune changed, 'they turn basely with the tide, and swell the cry against the fallen king'.[113] At the other end of the political spectrum, the conservative essayist Thomas Carlyle reached a similar verdict, excoriating those who had bought Hudson's shares: 'set up your Brazen Calf, ye misguided citizens…worship your bellyful, you absurd idolators'.[114]

With commentators uniting in condemning the greed of middle-class investors, there was little public sympathy for a campaign of criminal prosecution, and Wylie and his fellow shareholders chose not to pursue this course.[115] Nor did their attempt to get Hudson expelled from parliament win much support.[116] Such punishments were widely regarded as unnecessary for, like the directors of the failed joint-stock schemes of 1825, Hudson faced retribution in the form of loss of reputation. While he continued to be tolerated in the north-east, he was driven out of York in disgrace, and was spurned by London society: as early as February 1849, it was made clear to him that he was no longer welcome at the house of Lord Stanley, the leader of the protectionist Conservatives, with whom he had previously been on good terms. Though retaining his seat in the Commons, he was rebuffed by his fellow MPs. One parliamentary sketch-writer described how Hudson had 'stolen, unnoticed' into the Commons where he 'seems to cower as if to escape notice'. He was

109 *Era*, 22 April 1849.

110 *The Times*, 10 May 1849.

111 Ibid. 10 May, 21 July 1849. For similar views, see *Illustrated London News*, 14 April 1849; *Lloyd's Weekly Newspaper*, 29 July 1849.

112 *Daily News*, 5 May 1849; *Manchester Guardian*, 15 September 1849.

113 Hansard, 3s, 105: 248 (10 May 1849).

114 Thomas Carlyle, 'Hudson's Statue', in *Latter-Day Pamphlets* (London, 1850), 248.

115 *Observer*, 22 July 1849; *Economist*, 27 October 1849.

116 In May 1849, the shareholders of the Eastern Counties Railway petitioned the House of Commons requesting a full enquiry into Hudson's behaviour, and his expulsion from the House. This prompted a defence from Hudson, but the subject was not subsequently debated: Hansard, 3s, 105: 581–9 (17 May 1849).

'shunned as the pestilence, or, if touched, is touched as if he were some slimy nauseous reptile'.[117] In May, Hudson's brother-in-law committed suicide, depressed by his implication in one of Hudson's share transactions. Hudson later stated that it was only his wife's loyalty that enabled him to carry on through this time.[118] Returning the bulk of the money he was accused of appropriating before the shareholder investigations began divested him of most of his assets; the remainder went defending Chancery suits filed by the York and North Midland Company which dragged on for the rest of his life. After losing immunity against imprisonment for debt when his parliamentary career ended in 1859, he spent much of the remainder of his life in cheap boarding houses in Calais, separated from his family, living off handouts from friends. When he did venture back, he was obliged to spend two spells in debtors' prison, for three months in 1865 and for a further week in 1866.[119] After his death in 1871, an obituarist noted that the world which once worshipped him 'avenged itself by excessive and savage reprobation'.[120]

THE SHOCKING PLUNDER OF THE POOR

Hudson escaped criminal prosecution because of the moral and legal ambiguity of his actions. But where morality and law were clearer cut, as in the savings bank sector, criminal sanctions were applied, sometimes with great force. Savings banks dated back to the early nineteenth century, and were first regulated by acts for England and Ireland in 1817, and Scotland in 1819.[121] They differed from many other forms of self-help in that they were established by the middle class to encourage saving by the working class. The poor depositors were entirely at the mercy of the middle-class administrators, for they had no right to participate in the management, and there were no general meetings.[122] Control was exercised by trustees and managers, who employed an actuary or secretary to take care of the day-to-day running.[123] Deposits, paid by the trustees into the Bank of England to the credit of the Commissioners for the Reduction of the National Debt, were guaranteed by the government, creating the impression that this was a risk-free form of saving, and helping savings banks to spread rapidly: by 1846, over a million depositors had invested a total of more than £30m.[124] However, the guarantee only applied to funds actually received by the Bank of England: if the bank's actuary failed to pay in the money, it was not guaranteed. By the late 1840s, a series of scandals revealed that this had happened in a number of banks. Disaster struck first in Ireland, with

[117] *Dumfries Courier*, repr. in *The Times*, 2 March 1850.
[118] Arnold and McCartney, *Hudson*, 206–7.
[119] Ibid. 218, 231–4.
[120] *The Times*, 16 December 1871.
[121] 57 Geo. III c. 105; 57 Geo. III c. 130; 59 Geo. III c. 62.
[122] Eric Hopkins, *Working-Class Self-Help in Nineteenth-Century England* (London, 1995), 48–9.
[123] Arthur Scratchley, *A Practical Treatise on Savings Banks, Containing a Review of their Past History and Present Condition, and of Legislation on the Subject* (London, 1860), 30.
[124] *Accounts of the Number of Depositors in Savings Banks, Money Received, Interest Credited, &c*, PP 1847 XXXIV. 2.

three savings banks folding in quick succession in 1848: the Tralee, the Killarney, and Dublin's Cuffe Street Bank.[125] Between them, they had liabilities of £138,000 against assets of just £18,000. The trustees had not exercised sufficient control over their actuaries, who were free to extract large sums from the coffers, disguised by simple falsification of the books. The press was astonished at 'the shocking plunder of the poor and industrious classes', the 'atrocious system of fraud and robbery' that had been exposed.[126] The revelations prompted runs across Ireland and a longer-term loss of confidence in savings banks as a whole.[127] The repercussions were felt in Westminster, with Irish members securing a select committee to investigate the failures, and parliament eventually agreeing to provide £30,000 to reimburse the poorest Cuffe Street Bank depositors.[128]

The problem was widely seen as an Irish one, but these illusions were soon shattered. George Haworth, actuary of the Rochdale Savings Bank for over twenty years, was a cotton master and Quaker known for his 'uprightness and strict integrity', and his generosity, particularly towards his employees, made him well liked. But when he died in November 1849, the trustees discovered deficiencies of over £70,000—nearly three-quarters of the bank's total deposits. Haworth had kept a private ledger and cash book containing over a thousand accounts, the money in which Haworth used for his own purposes rather than depositing it with the bank. Haworth had been so respected, and the scale of his embezzlement so large, that the revelations became a major national news item. They also prompted 'a degree of scrutiny and vigilance hitherto unknown' in the savings banks sector.[129] Many cans of worms were opened: trustees uncovered defalcations at twenty-two banks over the next eight years.[130] The hall of shame included John Johnson, a wealthy colliery owner, who had abstracted over £10,000 from the St Helen's Savings Bank, Thomas Smurwaite, a well-respected wine and spirit merchant, who had taken over £3,000 from the Scarborough Savings Bank, and David Jardine, proprietor of the town's biggest drapery business, who misappropriated £2,000 from the Dartford Savings Bank.[131] In most cases, the actuaries had used parallel books in the same manner as Haworth at the Rochdale Bank: a simple strategy with devastating results.

Some actuaries, like Jardine, faced only civil suits from trustees; others fled the country when their defalcations were exposed.[132] But with the embezzlements so

[125] Cormac Ó Gráda, 'Savings Banks, Famine and Financial Contagion: Ireland in the 1840s and 1850s', *Irish Economic and Social History*, 36 (2009), 28–9; Cormac Ó Gráda, 'The Early History of Irish Savings Banks', Working Paper WP08/04, University College Dublin Centre for Economic Research (2008).

[126] *Morning Chronicle*, 27 April 1848; *Cork Examiner*, repr. in *Liverpool Mercury*, 2 May 1848.

[127] Ó Gráda, 'Savings Banks', 30.

[128] Ó Gráda, 'Early History'.

[129] H. Oliver Horne, *A History of Savings Banks* (London, 1947), 126–8; *Wigan Times*, repr. in *The Times*, 14 January 1850.

[130] Horne, *Savings Banks*, 128.

[131] *Standard*, 14 January, 11 February 1850; *Morning Post*, 15 January 1850; *The Times*, 29 January 1850.

[132] The manager of the Killarney bank, David Murphy, only escaped prosecution by fleeing to America when his defalcations were exposed: *Freeman's Journal*, 24 April 1848; *Morning Chronicle*, 27 April 1848.

obviously facilitated by their negligence, trustees were under some pressure to redeem themselves by prosecuting the culprits, and they initiated several successful prosecutions.[133] Although sentences varied enormously, it was clear that these crimes were taken seriously. John Johnson was prosecuted along with his brother and sub-actuary William for embezzlement and conspiracy to defraud the St Helen's depositors. At the trial before Baron Edward Alderson at a densely crowded Liverpool Assizes, the pair pleaded guilty to conspiracy and the prosecution, believing that neither man had taken the money with a felonious intention, decided not to press the embezzlement charges. The men therefore got off relatively lightly with a six-month sentence.[134] Others fared less well. At his trial at York Crown Court before Baron Robert Rolfe in March, Smurwaite pleaded guilty to embezzlement. Rolfe told the actuary that, employed 'to protect the property of the poor', he had betrayed his trust, and deserved to be transported, but on account of his age and infirmities, he would sentence him to two years' imprisonment.[135] Harsher still was the sentence given to the actuary of the Ulverston Savings Bank, Samuel Donaldson.[136] At the trial in February 1851 at Lancaster Assizes before Justice Cresswell Cresswell, the jury found Donaldson guilty of embezzlement, and he was sentenced to transportation for seven years.[137] An even stiffer penalty was handed down in Ireland, where prosecutions were co-ordinated by the Irish Attorney General.[138] At Tralee Assizes the solicitor John Lynch, actuary of the Tralee Savings Bank, admitted embezzling upwards of £20,000 from the bank over the course of nearly two decades, and was sentenced by Judge Nicholas Ball to transportation for fourteen years.[139]

So, while the exposure of frauds in the railway sector in the late 1840s led to no attempts at criminal prosecution, the savings bank scandal produced a spate of prosecutions, most of which were successful. Why was there such a difference in the legal responses? First, the legal standing of actuaries in savings banks was different to that

[133] Encouraging this trend was the touchy subject of trustee liability for fraud. Until 1844, trustees were liable to depositors in case of wilful neglect or default, but the Savings Bank Act of that year freed trustees from liability except where it was voluntarily assumed. One commentator noted that 'all the great frauds with this class of bank have occurred since that date': William Lewins, *Her Majesty's Mails: An Historical and Descriptive Account of the British Post-Office* (London, 1864), 268–9.

[134] *Reg. v. Johnson* (1850), *The Times*, 1 April 1850, *Morning Post*, 1 April 1850, *Daily News*, 1 April 1850, *Morning Chronicle*, 2 April 1850.

[135] *Reg. v. Smurwaite* (1850), *Morning Post*, 18 March 1850, *Sheffield and Rotherham Independent*, 23 March 1850.

[136] *Huddersfield Chronicle*, 14 December 1850.

[137] *Reg. v. Donaldson* (1851), *Lancaster Gazette*, 22 February 1851.

[138] From the 1840s, private prosecutions in Ireland were very rare. John McEldowney, 'Crown Prosecutions in Nineteenth-Century Ireland', in Douglas Hay and Francis Snyder (eds), *Policing and Prosecution in Britain, 1750–1850* (Oxford, 1989), 436.

[139] Lynch confessed when his frauds were discovered by the bank's treasurer, who seized his papers, and swore a criminal information against him, after which the prosecution was taken up by the Irish government: *Select Committee on Savings Banks (Ireland)*, PP 1849 XIV. 46–57; *Reg. v. Lynch* (1848), *Freeman's Journal*, 26 July 1848. The select committee appointed to investigate the Cuffe Street Bank recommended the prosecution of the cashier for embezzlement by the Attorney General for Ireland. But at the trial in December 1850 the defendant was able to present evidence that his disbursements were authorized by the bank's trustees and was consequently acquitted: *Reg. v. Hughes* (1850), *Freeman's Journal*, 4 December 1850.

of railway directors like Hudson: whereas considerable doubt existed as to whether company directors, as trustees of shareholders' money, could be made criminally liable for misappropriating funds of which they were legally in possession, such doubts did not apply to the employees of savings banks, who could be prosecuted for embezzlement. So, even when these employees were affluent and respected figures in local communities, there was little difficulty holding them to account in the criminal courts. Second, savings banks were established in order to inculcate thrift amongst the working classes. They were predicated on trust by working-class savers in middle-class administrators. When this trust was abused, public disgust was accompanied by anxiety lest such abuses would discourage workers from saving, retarding the project of 'improving' the masses. A decade after Haworth's frauds were discovered, young men and women in Rochdale were still saying 'We will spend our money rather than George Haworth shall have it.'[140] Press commentary reveals a genuine sympathy with the victims and a visceral condemnation of the perpetrators, in stark contrast to the limited sympathy extended to middle-class victims of railway frauds. The *Cork Examiner*, for example, reviled Lynch, who had been 'living *en prince* on the fortunes of children, the provision of old age, the substance of widows, the support of orphans'.[141] After the Rochdale Bank disclosures, *The Times* was moved to note that

> To the owner of thousands the loss of a few hundred pounds is rather a metaphysical than a real inconvenience—it deprives him of no enjoyment, it debars him from no luxury. Take away from the labourer the small but hard-earned savings of his long life of sleepless toil, and he is left exposed to the direst stings of penury, and to the worst suggestions of despair.

There was a practical dimension too: the paper thought it was impossible to exaggerate the contribution made by savings banks to 'social order'. A deposit in a savings bank gave 'a stake in the country', but this was threatened when frauds were exposed, the news of which 'passes like an electric shock through every cottage and hired lodging in the empire'.[142] Moreover, frauds were dangerous because they gave validity to radical critiques of capitalism: the Chartist *Northern Star* commented that the Irish banks frauds, 'were supposed to be exceptional cases'; the Rochdale scandal was written off in the same way; but the sequence of frauds subsequently revealed proved that 'the system was rotten throughout'.[143]

Class was a factor in criminal responses to fraud in financial institutions, but not in the way that is often claimed. Historians have suggested that joint-stock company directors escaped prosecution because of a biased legal system which provided one law for the rich and another, harsher, one for the poor.[144] In fact, the class of

[140] Horne, *Savings Banks*, 127.

[141] *Cork Examiner*, repr. in *Liverpool Mercury*, 2 May 1848.

[142] *The Times*, 4 December 1849.

[143] *Northern Star*, 26 January 1850.

[144] George Robb, *White-Collar Crime in Modern England: Financial Fraud and Business Morality, 1845–1929* (Cambridge, 1992), 147, 163–4; Paul Johnson, 'Civilizing Mammon: Laws, Morals, and the City in Nineteenth-Century England' in Peter Burke, Brian Harrison, and Paul Slack (eds), *Civil Histories: Essays Presented to Sir Keith Thomas* (Oxford, 2000), 319; Rob Sindall, 'Middle-Class Crime in Nineteenth-Century England', *Criminal Justice History*, 4 (1983), 32.

the victims mattered more than the class of the offenders. Where victims were blameless working-class investors, prosecutions were initiated and judges and juries had little hesitation in finding middle-class embezzlers guilty and, in some cases, passing stiff sentences. Undoubtedly there were limits to the efficacy of the law. Prosecutions in England were left to private parties and in some cases they declined to act and, as with joint-stock frauds, the government did not step in to fill the gap.[145] Some judges saw this as proof of the need for a public prosecutor.[146] Nevertheless, the stack of prosecutions of savings bank officers between 1848 and 1851 underlines that the criminal law was more likely to respond to frauds on working-class investors than their middle-class counterparts.[147]

CONCLUSION

On the face of it, the 1840s was a decade of change inspired by a series of major frauds. Magistrates began to take a more active role in the wake of joint-stock scandals, beginning with the Independent West Middlesex Company. The legislature conducted a wide-ranging investigation of the joint-stock economy as a whole for the first time. And in 1844 it passed a set of thoroughgoing reforms designed to regulate companies from the cradle to the grave, which included criminal punishments for directors and managers. But, as with so much in the joint-stock economy, appearances were deceptive. Magistrates continued to display their traditional conservatism when dealing with joint-stock cases. They extended their role to dispensing advice and occasionally twisting arms to produce settlements of disputes, but despite Sir Peter Laurie's bluster, they clearly preferred civil solutions, and the legislation conveniently allowed them to pass responsibility onto other courts. Although the government had high hopes for the legislation, it failed to prevent fraud. 'The tacit influence of a better system', wrote Peel of the Joint-Stock Banks Act, 'would compel the adoption by the old companies of similar principles—and thus purify the whole system, old and new'.[148] But the act contained such restrictive provisions that it brought new promotions to a virtual standstill, while existing banks continued to

[145] A disincentive to prosecution was the expense: the prosecution of Donaldson, for example, cost the Ulverston Savings Bank over £400: *Lancaster Gazette*, 6 March 1852.

[146] See Commissioner Edward Holroyd's words in *Re Jardine* (1850), *Morning Post*, 24 December 1850.

[147] There were earlier precedents which further emphasize this point. In 1842, Captain Henry Belstead, secretary of the Richmond Savings Bank, and a well-connected member of the Surrey Militia, was sentenced to two years' imprisonment for embezzling £1,500, in a prosecution by the bank's trustees: *Reg. v. Belstead* (1842), *The Times*, 23 November, 14, 20 December 1842. In 1847, Basil Henry Stronsberg, manager of three building societies, was charged at Guildhall with embezzling small sums. Alderman William Hughes ordered Stronsberg to pay twice what he owed the bank. The prisoner had no money, so the alternative punishment was levied: three months' hard labour. Hughes explained that he wanted to make Stronsberg 'an example to the officers of other building societies, and tend to the due protection of the savings of the industrious classes in future': *The Times*, 19, 30 July 1847.

[148] Letter from Peel to Gladstone, 23 April 1844, quoted in Bishop Carleton Hunt, *The Development of the Business Corporation in England, 1800–1867* (Cambridge, MA, 1936), 96 n. 21.

operate under the old law. Just ten banks were formed under the act between 1844 and 1857; one of them was the Royal British Bank, whose subsequent career, discussed in the next chapter, highlighted the inability of the new law to prevent fraud.[149]

Nor did the Winding-up Act facilitate the exposure and punishment of fraud. Though it allowed creditors to take proceedings against companies in Bankruptcy, it respected their right to proceed against individual shareholders in Chancery. With all partners equally liable for the entire debts of the company, it made more sense for creditors to fasten on rich individual shareholders rather than rely on the company's assets, and this is what they usually did.[150] As Michael Lobban comments, despite the fact that the law gave the company a separate corporate personality at its formation, 'its members were treated as partners when the firm failed'.[151] With this option kept open for creditors, the legislation was rarely employed and its impact was slight: in the three years following the act, it seems that just four companies were wound up under its provisions.[152] Directors of two of these companies were publicly examined, and accusations of 'irregularity', 'abuses', and 'reckless and improvident trading' made, but the Bankruptcy Commissioners refrained from imputing dishonesty to the directors and so the issue of criminal prosecution did not arise.[153]

The Joint-Stock Companies Act clearly had the greatest impact of the three measures, but it was not the silver bullet against fraud its advocates had imagined. Although it brought all companies within the law, the experience of the railway mania showed that provisional registration did not prevent investors losing their money in opportunistic schemes. The criminalization of certain fraudulent practices, embodied in both the Companies Act and the Winding-up Act, remained theoretical; the very few attempted prosecutions of promoters and directors were under the existing law of conspiracy and false pretences. But if Hudson's exposure failed to change anything, scandals in another sector in the 1850s were to have a bigger impact.

[149] Timothy L. Alborn, *Conceiving Companies: Joint-Stock Politics in Victorian England* (London, 1998), 114.

[150] See evidence of John Malcolm Ludlow, *Report from the Select Committee on Investments for the Savings of the Middle and Working Classes*, PP 1850 XIX. 5.

[151] Michael Lobban, 'Joint Stock Companies', in *The Oxford History of the Laws of England*, 13 vols (Oxford, 2003–), xii. 625.

[152] From evidence presented in reports by the Registrar of Joint Stock Companies between 1846 and 1848. In two further cases, both railways, the petition for winding-up was rejected by the Court: *Abstract of Report by the Registrar of Joint Stock Companies to the Committee of Privy Council for Trade, for the year 1847*, PP 1847–48 LI. 12.

[153] These were the Forth Marine Insurance Company—which subsequently became the subject of *Burnes v. Pennell*—and the Tring, Reading, and Basingstoke Railway Company: *The Times*, 9 February 1846, 24 May 1847.

5

Criminalizing Fraud: The 1850s

The legislation of the 1840s was confidently predicted to thwart fraud and protect investors. But, as we have seen, the exposure of large-scale fraud in the railway sector at the end of the decade shook this faith. Further revelations in the 1850s demolished it altogether. It became evident that government-imposed publicity and disclosure was not enough to combat those determined to deceive, while the theory began to develop that unlimited liability, long enforced as the default in the belief that it discouraged fraud, was actually making the problem worse. These new beliefs inspired a series of reforms between 1855 and 1858 which conceded general limited liability, and represented a retreat from the project of prevention. But a simultaneous sequence of banking scandals put pressure on government to take punishment more seriously. Hitherto, only the most egregious types of 'fictitious' company, existing solely on paper, and promoted by confidence tricksters, had been successfully prosecuted. Other practices by the managements of genuine companies, such as issuing false balance sheets and paying dividends out of capital, though attracting censure, had not yet yielded prison terms. But the hammer blows dealt to the law by the banking failures prompted the government to take significant steps towards the criminalization of fraud. Whether the courts would play along, however, was another matter.

FRAUD IN THE SPOTLIGHT

In 1844, Peel's government had accepted the need to make better legal provision for the winding-up of joint-stock companies, but the act of that year did not provide a satisfactory solution. As a result, a new measure was passed four years later.[1] As one of the bill's architects, the barrister John Malcolm Ludlow, noted, the 1844 act tackled winding-up solely from the point of view of creditors—only they could activate it, and it said nothing about the apportioning of contributions among shareholders.[2] The new law sought to rectify this. So, whereas the 1844 act had given *creditors* the power to initiate winding-up in *Bankruptcy*, the 1848 act enabled *shareholders* to petition for winding-up in *Chancery*. The hope was that shareholders 'would act quickly when a company began to get into financial trouble and

[1] 11 & 12 Vict. c. 45.

[2] John Malcolm Ludlow, *The Joint-Stock Companies Winding-up Act, 1848* (London, 1850), xxxi.

cut their losses' by approaching the court before the situation became disastrous.[3] The act, further revised in 1849, protected the rights of creditors, and did not prevent them from suing individual shareholders; a proposal to restrict this right was heavily defeated in the Commons.[4] Unlike its predecessor, the act was extensively used. By the end of 1849, a total of eighty-seven companies, the majority of them railway schemes, were in the process of being liquidated in Chancery.[5] The amount of winding-up business continued to swell; by late 1851, it had 'blocked up' the Chancery Masters' offices, delaying the rest of their work.[6]

The 1848 act empowered Masters to summon and examine anyone with information on a company being wound up, which meant that hearings were not always dry, technical affairs, but sometimes became the means by which scandalous episodes were disclosed.[7] This was not lost on the press, and columns reporting winding-up proceedings became a staple of the London dailies. The exhibition of failures and frauds in Chancery exposed just how little the Joint-Stock Companies Act had done to improve commercial morality. Registration and publicity had been embraced in 1844 as a panacea to 'baffle' fraud; now it seemed that they were limp instruments with which to combat the ingenuity of the unscrupulous. The problem was that while the act imposed all kinds of safety measures, from the registration of shareholders' names to the publication of balance sheets, it created no machinery to ensure that this information was accurate, rendering it 'almost worthless' to the public.[8] The Companies Registrar himself, Francis Whitmarsh, was deeply frustrated by the way the act worked, and in February 1850 sent a 38-page memo to the Board of Trade recommending reforms to give the regulations teeth, ranging from making provisional registration more difficult to obtain, to tougher penalties for incorrect or incomplete returns.[9]

Critics argued that by increasing the circulation of dubious or false information, the legislature had actually facilitated fraud. Unsound insurance companies, the trigger which in the early 1840s had prompted the legislation, were an even bigger problem a decade later. In the first ten years of the act, 335 life insurance offices were provisionally registered, only 149 of which were actually founded; of these, 90 had subsequently folded, leaving just 59 still in business.[10] Walter Pateman, publisher of the *Post* magazine for the insurance industry, claimed that the legislation

[3] V. Markham Lester, *Victorian Insolvency: Bankruptcy, Imprisonment for Debt, and Company Winding-up in Nineteenth-Century England* (Oxford, 1995), 223.

[4] Hansard, 3s, 98: 1415–16 (25 May 1848); 12 & 13 Vict. c. 108.

[5] *Manchester Times*, 21 November 1849.

[6] *Daily News*, 31 October 1851. There are no official returns of the numbers of companies wound up in these years: returns made retrospectively in 1861 are incomplete, leading Lester to wrongly claim that 'it does not appear that large numbers of companies were formally dissolved by courts in the first few years of the new system's operation'. Lester, *Victorian Insolvency*, 225; *Returns from the Official Managers and Liquidators of every Joint Stock Company Wound-up or Winding-up under the Joint Stock Companies Winding-Up Acts*, PP 1861 XXXIV.

[7] 11 & 12 Vict. c. 45, ss. 37, 63.

[8] *The Times*, 26 October 1849.

[9] Memorandum from Francis Whitmarsh to Board of Trade (7 February 1850), TNA, BT 1/477/431/50.

[10] Hansard, 3s, 124: 1327–8 (8 March 1853).

was 'the cause of all the bad offices being projected', for it enabled them to advertise that they were 'Empowered by Act of Parliament', when in fact they were merely registered under the 1844 act, which was no security at all.[11] One promoter who knew how to exploit this to the full was Augustus Collingridge, who promoted a series of schemes which all ended in Chancery. One of them, the Merchant Traders' Ship Loan Insurance Company, failed in 1848 owing £60,000. Winding-up revealed that most of the names on the deed of settlement were obtained by touring 'the lowest purlieus and pothouses' and paying a shilling per signature. Only two of the subscribers were solvent, which left them liable for the company's entire debts. Sir William Horne, the Chancery Master, blamed the Joint-Stock Companies Act for the fraud, while the barrister Francis Roxburgh thought that the case showed why the act should be 'struck out from the statutes at large'.[12]

The act's other key ingredient was enforcement of unlimited liability, long viewed as a bulwark against fraud. But Chancery exposures undermined faith in the principle. Ludlow argued that the working of the acts provided evidence 'of the reckless speculation and barefaced fraud which have prevailed to an enormous extent in this country under unlimited liability'.[13] Unlimited liability encouraged what Edwin Field, a solicitor also involved in the drafting of the 1848 act, called 'mischievous credit', given in the full knowledge that it was being improperly used, while the shareholders, 'whose whole fortunes were involved had very little chance of knowing'. The unethical creditor stood to gain immense sums, intervening to close the company 'just at the moment when he can stop it to his own advantage; he goes as far as he dare go, and then stops it'. Field cited the example of the North of England Joint Stock Banking Company, which came to Chancery in 1848. Although it had a capital of just £150,000, it was able to secure credit on a vast scale, incurring liabilities of £1.9 million. When it was wound up, its shareholders were plunged into a 'vortex of ruin'.[14]

Field's experiences had taught him that 'there are such things as dishonest creditors as well as dishonest debtors'.[15] Indeed, there were signs of a wider recalibration of moral attitudes to creditors and shareholders. Some judges felt that the law they were required to implement was unjust. Perhaps swayed by his experiences as a railway director, the Bankruptcy Commissioner Robert Fane advocated limited liability as a fairer principle, asking 'why...should the law be so harsh against contributors [the shareholders], and so tender to creditors?...Why is one to be enriched and the other ruined?'[16] Such views influenced the wider public, the *Daily News* noting the plight of shareholders under the winding-up acts: 'lawyers and assignees wage a sort of war against [them] as if they were a race of wild animals to be rooted out and pursued without remorse to death'.[17]

[11] *Report from the Select Committee on Assurance Associations*, PP 1852–53 XXI. 262–3.
[12] *Daily News*, 12 February 1852.
[13] *Report from the Select Committee on the Law of Partnership*, PP 1851 XVIII. 170.
[14] *Select Committee on the Law of Partnership*, 145–50; Alexander Gordon, rev. Catherine Pease-Watkin, 'Edwin Watkins Field', *ODNB*.
[15] *Select Committee on the Law of Partnership*, 145.
[16] Ibid. 76; G. C. Boase, rev. H. J. Spencer, 'Robert George Cecil Fane', *ODNB*.
[17] *Daily News*, 31 October 1851.

The act of 1844 had failed to prevent fraud. It had also failed to punish it. Dishonest promoters and directors could still defraud without fear of the criminal law. The section of the Companies Act making fraud by directors and officers a misdemeanour seemed to have been forgotten by the early 1850s. And while the 1848 Winding-up Act reiterated the section in its predecessor making the falsification, mutilation, or destruction of any book a misdemeanour (though reducing the penalty from three to two years), there was a significant difference. The procedures in the earlier act for reporting bad cases to the Board of Trade and authorizing prosecution by the Attorney General were omitted; instead it was the official manager appointed to administer the winding-up who was tasked with carrying out any criminal prosecutions he deemed necessary.[18] As these would be funded out of the company's assets, the option was less attractive to the victims than prosecution by the Attorney General. Thus, although the flood of cases reaching Chancery was receiving much publicity in the press, Chancery Masters had no authority to refer fraud cases to a higher level. All they could do was make an occasional wry comment on their lack of powers, as in the case of the General Commission, Ship, Loan, and Insurance Company—another of Collingridge's schemes—when Horne observed that 'the more he saw of these concerns the more they reminded him of the necessity of placing the offices of Masters in Chancery in juxtaposition or communication with either the police or the Central Criminal Court'.[19]

The only joint-stock fraud prosecution in the first half of the 1850s was based on the law of false pretences, rather than the laws of 1844 and 1848, and did not emerge from the equity courts, but via the government's emigration agent, Captain James Lean, responsible for supervising and assisting emigration to the colonies.[20] Demand for emigration to Australia grew substantially in the early 1850s following the discovery of gold in New South Wales and Victoria in 1851, with several companies formed to capitalize on the gold rush.[21] One was the Australian Gold and General Mining and Emigration Company, based in the City of London. The company's prospectus, listing several respectable names as directors, had appeared in several London dailies, and a number of working men had paid deposits for transit.[22] But the owners of the vessels they were due to sail on denied all knowledge of the company and its directors, prompting the men to complain to Lean. Lean tried to get them their money back, but had been rebuffed, and he therefore brought the case to Mansion House, flanked by several of the victims. The presiding magistrate, Sir Robert Carden, a Conservative with strong paternalist leanings, who was active in children's charities, made his views clear from the start.[23] 'Many

[18] 11 & 12 Vict. c. 45, ss. 114, 51.

[19] *Daily News*, 25 March 1851.

[20] David Feldman and M. Page Baldwin, 'Emigration and the British State, ca. 1815–1925', in Nancy L. Green and Francois Weil (eds), *Citizenship and Those Who Leave: The Politics of Emigration and Expatriation* (Urbana, IL, 2007), 140–1.

[21] Peter Stearns, 'Prosperity and Industrial Emigration from Britain during the Early 1850s', *Journal of Social History*, 22 (1988), 340.

[22] See, for example, *The Times*, 10 June 1852; *Morning Post*, 11 June 1852; *Daily News*, 17 June 1852.

[23] Peter M. Claus, 'Sir Robert Walter Carden', *ODNB*.

a poor family' had been lured into 'a snare in which all they have been able to scrape together is swallowed'. He issued summonses for all the men listed in the prospectus, and over the course of a fortnight, five directors—including a lord and a major—together with the company's mineralogist, Henry Montague, and its superintendant of shipping, Cornelius Tripe, appeared, all armed with lawyers. Carden instructed Charles Pearson, the City Solicitor, to take over the prosecution at the expense of the Corporation of London because the victims were not equipped 'to take the necessary measures in a case which might be made complex and perplexing by professional ingenuity'.[24] Pearson's investigations established that Montague and Tripe were the main movers behind the company. Some of the men listed as directors and officers had discussed forming a company with the pair, but there was no evidence to implicate them in the frauds committed in their name: Montague and Tripe had received money from would-be emigrants without their knowledge or consent. On this evidence, Carden committed the duo for trial for obtaining money by false pretences at the Old Bailey.[25]

The trial, which took place over two days in September, saw the clash of several of the most eminent barristers of the day, including William Bodkin for the prosecution and William Ballantine for the defence. The case revolved around the intentions of the defendants. Bodkin contended that 'the transaction was in reality a fraud from the beginning to the end'. The company was unregistered, and had no real existence, yet the defendants advertised it and received money on its behalf. Although the pair had made inquiries about chartering a vessel, this was probably done 'with a view to get up some kind of answer to a charge such as that which was now preferred against them'. Ballantine countered that these inquiries were genuine, and the deal would have been completed but for the signatures of four of the directors, which the defendants were unable to obtain at that juncture. The company was a '*bonâ fide*' speculation, but an unsuccessful one, with Tripe and Montague scapegoats for the directors, who had left them 'to suffer all the disgrace'. The jury believed the prosecution's version of events, however, and found both men guilty.[26] In sentencing the pair, the Recorder James Stuart-Wortley, a Peelite MP, took the fraud very seriously partly on moral grounds—it was a 'heartless and cruel' case—but also because of its 'great public importance'. It was imperative to deter others tempted to exploit the emigration mania, but even more important to make an example of those who would defraud the public 'under the pretence of getting up a company', a practice which was 'not new in this country'. He therefore sentenced the pair to seven years' transportation.[27] It was the first Old Bailey conviction for false claims made in a company prospectus.[28]

[24] The City Solicitor was the Corporation's criminal prosecutor.

[25] *The Times*, 22, 26 July, 2, 5, 7 August 1852. The directors acted on Pearson's suggestion that they contribute to a fund to help the victims' passage to Australia.

[26] *Reg. v. Montague* (1852), *The Times*, 21, 22 September 1852.

[27] *The Times*, 25 September 1852.

[28] Such prosecutions had already taken place in France. In 1838, a banker and an ironmaster were sentenced to three years' imprisonment for false claims made in the prospectus of the Compagnie des Mines de Saint-Bérain et de Saint-Léger, a coal mining company, though this too was an isolated prosecution, a product of the 'supercharged atmosphere' which followed the exposure of widespread

Heavy though the sentence was, it was an isolated example of a prosecution of a joint-stock swindle, deriving from the willingness of the government's emigration agent to adopt the case, and a magistrate's decision to use the Corporation of London's funds to bankroll the prosecution. Carden's paternalist instincts mirrored Sir Peter Laurie's in the 1840s, and his readiness to use the criminal law to protect vulnerable working-class emigrants did not have implications for the wider joint-stock economy, where the majority of victims were middle-class and presumed capable of looking after themselves.[29] This seemed to have been generally understood, for Carden's actions did not prompt a renewed flood of joint-stock victims into London's police courts. While shareholders at general meetings sometimes threatened their directors with criminal proceedings, they did not follow through in the early 1850s.[30] Thus, *The Times* was moved to comment in 1852 that the joint-stock company was 'a form of proceeding peculiarly calculated... for the evasion of all civil and criminal responsibility for the most questionable acts'.[31]

THE CHANGE IN THE LAW

Dissatisfaction with the legislative settlement of 1844 had grown so pronounced that parliament was ready to subject the law on companies to further investigation in the early 1850s. Robert Slaney, a backbench Liberal MP interested in improving the condition of the poor, secured the appointment of select committees in 1850 and 1851 on outlets for the savings of the middle and working classes, and the law of partnership.[32] Both were essentially opportunities for Slaney to agitate for what Ludlow dismissively called his 'special hobby'—the legalization of *en commandite* companies, popular in France, in which the liability of directors and managing partners only was unlimited, the rest of the investors enjoying limited liability.[33] 1853 saw the appointment of two further investigations: a select committee on the life insurance industry, and a royal commission on the law of partnership, the former reporting that year, the latter in 1854.[34] The specific objects of enquiry—whether limited liability should be made generally available, and in what ways the

abuses among French companies: Charles E. Freedeman, *Joint-Stock Enterprise in France, 1807–1867: From Privileged Company to Modern Corporation* (Chapel Hill, NC, 1979), 63–5.

[29] Lobban detects a 'paternalistic approach to the naïve investor' among Tory judges in civil cases around this time, and this was even clearer in the police courts, with complainants generally standing a better chance if the magistrate was a Conservative, as Laurie had been. Michael Lobban, 'The Politics of English Law in the Nineteenth Century', in Paul Brand and Joshua Getzler (eds), *Judges and Judging in the History of the Common Law and Civil Law: From Antiquity to Modern Times* (Cambridge, 2012), 127.

[30] See, for example, the general meeting of the British Australian Gold Mining Company: *Daily News*, 31 December 1853.

[31] *The Times*, 28 July 1852.

[32] Ernest Clarke, rev. H. C. G. Matthew, 'Robert Aglionby Slaney', *ODNB*.

[33] John Malcolm Ludlow, *The Autobiography of a Christian Socialist* (London, 1981), 195.

[34] *Select Committee on Assurance Associations*; *First Report of the Commissioners appointed to Inquire and Ascertain how far the Mercantile Laws in the Different Parts of the United Kingdom of Great Britain and Ireland may be Advantageously Assimilated*, PP 1854 XXVII.

registration and publicity requirements of 1844 could best be reformed—had the problem of fraud at their heart. The same questions kept recurring: would limited liability improve or degrade standards of commercial morality? Could government regulations prevent fraud? Or did all such regulations in fact make shareholders more vulnerable by lulling them to sleep?

These questions split witnesses before the various investigations but the recent scandals had weakened the credibility of arguments that unlimited liability prevented fraud. Consequently, Palmerston's Whig Ministry took decisive action in the middle of the decade, promoting measures in 1855 and 1856 making limited liability generally available, and recasting the 1844 act along permissive lines.[35] The 1855 bill, introduced by Edward Bouverie, Vice-President of the Board of Trade, was a relatively brief amending measure, allowing companies registering under the 1844 act to limit their liability, though imposing a number of restrictions and safeguards, and excluding insurance companies and firms with shares of under £10.[36] But when Bouverie was replaced at the Board by the Liberal lawyer and journalist Robert Lowe, there was a more ambitious recasting of the law. Lowe introduced a bill designed to replace the previous acts with a single measure. But this was much more than a mere consolidating statute: it represented an overhaul not only of the minutiae of company law, but of the philosophy underpinning it as well. When he introduced the measure in February 1856, Lowe did not conceal his contempt for previous legislation, bemoaning the fact that companies always seemed to be legislated for 'in a state of excitement': this had been the case with the Bubble Act in 1720, and no less true in 1844, when the select committee appeared to have acted 'in a state of mental perturbation scarcely less violent than that which prevailed in the days of George I'. Knee-jerk regulation only exacerbated the problem of fraud, and Lowe signalled a complete change of direction, 'entirely repudiat[ing] as the basis of legislation the principle upon which the present Joint-Stock Companies Act is founded—that it is in the power of the Government to prevent the institution of fraudulent companies'. Frauds would continue to occur, but this was 'a necessary incident of a large commercial society', and was 'an evil which cannot be met or cured by way of anticipation by any legal enactment whatever'.[37] So, Lowe's bill, which passed with minimal opposition, dispensed with the compulsory provisions for publication of balance sheets and audit of accounts, and scrapped the two-stage system of provisional and full registration which had been abused by companies only provisionally registering.

While some commentators took Lowe's rhetoric at face value, finding it 'monstrous' that '[e]very protection' against fraud should be stripped away, the act was not the straightforward exercise in deregulation it appeared.[38] It set out a detailed model constitution running to eight pages, providing for the presentation and

[35] James Taylor, *Creating Capitalism: Joint-Stock Enterprise in British Politics and Culture, 1800–1870* (Woodbridge, 2006), 148–75.
[36] 18 & 19 Vict. c. 133, s. 1.
[37] Hansard, 3s, 140: 116–17, 124 (1 February 1856).
[38] *Law Times*, 26 July 1856.

audit of accounts, and even offered a template for balance sheets.[39] These regulations were regarded as the default, and would be taken to apply to a company unless its constitution explicitly made alternative provisions.[40] Moreover, the main body of the act contained a number of safeguards against fraud. Directors were made personally liable for dividends paid when a company was insolvent. Shareholders representing one-fifth in number and value of the shares were able to appoint a Board of Trade inspector to examine a company's affairs and report back to the Board, an idea borrowed from the New York code.[41] Alternatively, a simple majority of shareholders could appoint their own inspectors at a general meeting.[42]

In addition, the process for winding up companies was radically overhauled, with the rights of shareholders and creditors reconfigured once more in an attempt to make the process cheaper, fairer, and more effective. Creditors of limited companies were barred from pursuing actions against individual shareholders and could henceforth only look to company assets in satisfaction of their debts.[43] To compensate, creditors were given more summary redress against companies, and were allowed to petition for winding-up when a company could not pay a debt of over £50.[44] Shareholders could petition for winding-up if a company had not commenced business within a year of incorporation, when the number of shareholders fell below seven, or when three-quarters of the capital had been lost. In addition, shareholders were now allowed to dissolve their companies outside the courts in what was termed 'voluntary' winding-up, though this did not prevent creditors from instituting proceedings in either Bankruptcy or Chancery.[45] While insurance companies were excluded from the act (in deference to the opinion of the 1853 committee which believed that they needed to be legislated for separately), as were banks, the safeguards and regulations were extended to Scotland for the first time—the nation having been exempt from both the act of 1844, and the series of winding-up acts.

Nevertheless, these protections against fraud did not include further innovations in criminal law. The 1856 act retained the provision introduced in 1848 rendering the falsification or mutilation of the books of a company being wound up punishable by up to two years' imprisonment, and empowered liquidators to bring criminal prosecutions with the sanction of the court. But it scrapped the moribund clause in the 1844 Companies Act making acts of fraud a misdemeanour and did not replace it with any other provision for criminal punishment.[46] However, this period of reform took place against a background of business scandal which soon prompted a rethink.

[39] 19 & 20 Vict. c. 47, table B.
[40] 19 & 20 Vict. c. 47, s. 9.
[41] Ibid. ss. 14, 48; Hansard, 3s, 140: 134 (1 February 1856).
[42] 19 & 20 Vict. c. 47, s. 51.
[43] Ibid. s. 61.
[44] Ibid. ss. 67–9. Lowe presented this as a quid pro quo: Hansard, 3s, 140: 135–6 (1 February 1856).
[45] 19 & 20 Vict. c. 47, ss. 102–5.
[46] Ibid. ss. 79, 90.

ONE CONTINUOUS LIE

At the end of June 1855, when Bouverie's limited liability bill was receiving its second reading, the biggest commercial story in the papers was the sensational failure of the long-established private bank Strahan, Paul, and Bates. The two senior partners, Sir John Dean Paul and William Strahan, were members of old and wealthy families well known in the capital; the former was prominent in the evangelical wing of the Church of England. A West End rather than a City bank, its customers were mostly noblemen and wealthy commoners who kept large balances. But as far back as 1816 the partners' antecedents had begun secretly borrowing their customers' money, and from the late 1840s, the bank got into further difficulties when it started financing Welsh coalmines. By 1849 the bank was insolvent, but rather than closing its doors, the partners tried to retrieve the situation by speculative Italian railway loans, and financing a plan to drain Lake Capestang in the south of France. These loans were funded by fraudulently converting over £100,000 in securities deposited by the bank's unsuspecting customers. Word began to leak, and a run on the bank prompted its closure on Saturday 9 June. Its total debts were £750,000.[47]

One of the bank's customers, the Reverend Dr John Griffith, prebendary of Rochester Cathedral, had lost £22,000 but was not ruined, and he considered it 'his duty to do that which many of his fellow sufferers are unable to do—namely, to bring these culprits to the bar of a court of justice'. Consequently, the three partners appeared at Bow Street police court, the press noting that no proceeding had produced so much excitement for many years. 'Every available corner from which a view of the prisoners could be obtained was eagerly taken'. At a subsequent hearing, the public were so desperate to catch a glimpse of the defendants that 'the scuffle for admission was literally violent'.[48] Griffith's prosecution was framed under the 1827 Larceny Act which made it a misdemeanour for a banker entrusted with money or securities to convert them to his own use 'in violation of good faith'.[49] The evidence against the men was plain, and in October 1855 the Old Bailey jury took just twenty minutes to convict all three. Whilst it pained the judge, Baron Edward Alderson, to have to sentence men who had held such an elevated social position, he could not conceive of a worse case of embezzlement, so he had no choice but to impose the sentence reserved for the worst cases—transportation for fourteen years. It was a highly charged moment: Alderson made his speech 'with deep emotion'; the prisoners 'seemed astounded by their sentence', while Griffith was observed shedding tears at the outcome.[50] But outside the court, the result was acclaimed both as warning to others tempted to commit similar crimes, and as proof that the law was class-blind.[51]

[47] D. Morier Evans, *Facts, Failures and Frauds: Revelations Financial Mercantile Criminal* (1859; repr. New York, 1968), 106–14; Richard Davenport-Hines, 'Sir John Dean Paul', *ODNB*; *Morning Chronicle*, 12 June 1855.

[48] *Daily News*, 23, 28 June 1855.

[49] 7 & 8 Geo. IV c. 29, s. 49.

[50] *Reg. v. Strahan* (1855) 7 Cox 85, *The Times*, 29 October 1855.

[51] See, for example, *Morning Post*, 29 October 1855; *Belfast News-Letter*, 30 October 1855; *Leeds Mercury*, 30 October 1855.

Though it concerned a private rather than a joint-stock bank, the case gifted the advocates of limited liability a devastating example of the inability of unlimited responsibility to secure honesty in commerce. While the opponents of the government's bill alleged that it would encourage fraud, Bouverie retorted that it would be 'quite as fair to argue from the unfortunate case which had lately occurred in the City and other similar cases, that the Legislature ought to put a stop to those transactions conducted on the unlimited liability principle'.[52] The protections afforded by unlimited liability were illusory; the principle was 'a broken reed'.[53]

Just as the Strahan case provided the backdrop to the passage of Bouverie's bill, a second scandal unfolded as Lowe's bill made its way through parliament. On Sunday 17 February, shortly after the bill's second reading, the body of John Sadleir MP was found on Hampstead Heath. Reports the next day confirmed that he had committed suicide by taking prussic acid.[54] He had been a major business and political figure, involved in banking in Ireland and England, financing foreign railway and mining schemes, serving in the Commons as an independent Liberal MP, and had been Junior Lord of the Treasury in Lord Aberdeen's coalition ministry.[55] Consequently, that Monday clubland was ablaze with excitement, and many Members travelled to Hampstead 'to glean further particulars of the distressing affair', and to view the body.[56] Initially, it was presumed that Sadleir's suicide was triggered by sudden and catastrophic business reverses encountered in the previous few weeks, and early reports were sympathetic.[57] But soon the precise reasons emerged. He had been speculating unsuccessfully on the stock exchange for some time—it was believed he lost £120,000 on a single sugar speculation in the autumn of 1855—and had pillaged the companies with which he was involved to fund his gambling.[58] The biggest victim was the Tipperary Joint-Stock Bank, managed by his brother James, also an MP, its closure hastened by Sadleir's massive overdraft of £288,000.[59] With the exception of the London and County Joint-Stock Bank, which he had until recently chaired, 'most of the institutions connected with him were seriously damaged or destroyed'.[60] Within a week of his death, the press suspected that his frauds and forgeries could total £1 million: the most extensive ever committed by a single individual.[61]

As we saw in the previous chapter, one of the reasons few demanded to see George Hudson punished for his railway frauds was because his greedy shareholders were thought to share the moral blame. The Tipperary Joint-Stock Bank shareholders were viewed differently, however. This was not a time of collective

[52] Hansard, 3s, 139: 326 (29 June 1855).
[53] *Liverpool Mercury*, 3 July 1855. See also *Standard*, 23 June 1855; *Railway Record*, repr. in *Morning Post*, 25 June 1855.
[54] *The Times*, 18 February 1856.
[55] *Daily News*, 18 February 1856; James O'Shea, 'John Sadleir', *ODNB*.
[56] *Observer*, 24 February 1856.
[57] See, for example, *Daily News*, 18, 20 February 1856; *Glasgow Herald*, 22 February 1856.
[58] James O'Shea, *Prince of Swindlers: John Sadleir M.P. 1813–1856* (Dublin, 1999), 401.
[59] Though involved in the bank's formation in 1838 and initially acting as its solicitor, John was not a board member: O'Shea, *Prince of Swindlers*, 22–3, 422–3.
[60] O'Shea, *Prince of Swindlers*, 409.
[61] *Morning Advertiser*, 22 February 1856.

mania for high profits; they had not been 'looking for 60 per cent. and unquestionable security'.[62] Moreover, correspondence uncovered in court during an attempt by the bank's English shareholders to contest their liabilities revealed that they had been victims of premeditated and cynical deception. A letter written by John in December 1855 instructed James how to manufacture a balance sheet to maintain the trust of the bank's shareholders. John advised him to list the paid-up capital, which in reality was £40,000, as £100,000: 'therefore the requisite number of shares to make this account square should be entered'. An increase of £30,000 in customers' balances 'should be made to appear'. The accounts needed to be 'adjusted' so as 'to work out enough of profit' to enable the bank to pay the required 6 per cent dividend and 3 per cent bonus, and to leave 'a good sum' for the reserve fund. On the basis of this statement, John predicted that the English shareholders would double their present holdings, thus stabilizing the bank.

More sensationally still, Sadleir justified these deceptions with reference to the practice of his contemporaries:

> Now, I know many of the English joint-stock banks, in order to give a good appearance to their balance, have constantly trebled the amount of their balances, &c., by making a series of entries, whereby they appeared to have assets and liabilities to four times the amount they really possessed or had. This has been always kept very quiet, and what at first was a kind of fiction became gradually to be *bonâ fide*... There is nothing to prevent the Tipperary Bank from doing what has been done in the _____ Bank and the _____ Bank, and the _____ Bank, and that is all I advise.[63]

This wilful flouting of safeguards intended to protect investors scandalized public opinion. The letter showed that 'in certain hands... the whole account may be made one continuous lie from the beginning to the end', wrote *The Times*. The figures would be 'beautifully congruous', but it was 'not the figures but the facts which must be tested, and how are the customers and shareholders to get at the facts?'[64] It was a question that the paper did not answer.

The shock was sufficient to place punishment firmly on the agenda. Although John had put himself beyond the reach of the law, the question of what would happen to the management—above all James—remained. Some urged the shareholders to prosecute James for complicity in his brother's frauds—they 'owe it to themselves and to the cause of public justice'.[65] But given the lack of precedents for such prosecutions, many assumed that the criminal law was unable to reach him.[66] This view was spectacularly challenged in June when the Irish Master of the Rolls, Thomas Cusack Smith, who had a reputation for recklessness, stated that the actions of the Tipperary management were 'tainted with the most extraordinary fraud', and accused the Irish government of dereliction of duty in not prosecuting any of them.[67]

[62] *The Times*, 10 March 1856.
[63] *The Times*, 21 June 1856. The names of the other banks were redacted in press reports.
[64] Ibid. 23 June 1856.
[65] *Leinster Express*, repr. in *The Times*, 10 March 1856.
[66] *Daily News*, 10 March 1856; *Morning Chronicle*, 11 March 1856.
[67] Daire Hogan, 'Thomas Berry Cusack Smith', *ODNB*.

If ministers continued to do nothing, the public would charge them with 'connivance at conspiracy'. He claimed that the law was clear, citing Campbell's 1849 ruling in *Burnes v. Pennell* that paying dividends out of capital was not only a civil but a criminal offence.[68]

The accusations, coming from a senior Irish judge, caused a stir, but his interpretation of the law was open to question. While *Burnes v. Pennell* was sometimes cited, it had never been successfully acted upon, and it seemed that party politics—Smith was a Conservative and no friend of the Palmerston administration—was clouding the legal debate. What had begun as a financial scandal was becoming a political one, with the Conservative press seizing on Smith's claims, highlighting the close links between the Sadleirs and the Aberdeen and Palmerston ministries, and suggesting that political loyalties were behind the government's inaction.[69] When it transpired that a nervy James Sadleir had fled to France, the government faced a chorus of condemnation in parliament orchestrated by Irish Conservatives.[70]

However, John Fitzgerald, the Attorney General for Ireland, successfully defended himself by giving his critics a lesson in the law. Commercial frauds were private affairs and responsibility for prosecuting them rested with the victims rather than the state. To date, the victims had made no moves to pursue a criminal action, instead focusing on what they could recover from the directors during winding-up proceedings. James had been examined privately by Chancery Master Jeremiah Murphy with the aim of discovering property available to the estate. Afterwards, Murphy had expressed the opinion that there was insufficient evidence to support a criminal prosecution.[71] Fitzgerald agreed, explaining that the reach of the law was far more circumscribed than his Conservative critics believed. Allowing John such a large overdraft may have been a gross breach of trust by James, but it was not criminal. 'The director of a public company may publish false accounts, may misrepresent its balances, and there is no law, unfortunately, to make him amenable.'[72] Nevertheless, even though such frauds could not be punished directly, an alternative course became available when John's letter was found. On the basis of the letter, Fitzgerald concluded that James could be indicted for a conspiracy to pass off Tipperary Bank shares to English shareholders by means of false representations. And so, despite the fact that a panel of Irish legal authorities, including the Solicitor General for Ireland and a former Conservative Attorney General for Ireland, advised against prosecution, Fitzgerald, after consulting with Sir Alexander Cockburn, his English counterpart, overruled them. He did so because of the magnitude of the case, and the shock it had given to public credit. A warrant was issued for Sadleir's arrest, but he had left the country: not because of government delay, Fitzgerald maintained, but because Smith's public statements had spooked him.[73]

[68] *Standard*, 6 June 1856; *Daily News*, 5 June 1856.
[69] *Standard*, 6 June 1856.
[70] Hansard, 3s, 143: 381–3 (4 July 1856), 399–401 (7 July 1856), 652–74 (11 July 1856).
[71] Ibid. 880–1 (15 July 1856).
[72] Ibid. 667 (11 July 1856).
[73] Ibid. 877–94 (15 July 1856).

Fitzgerald's opponents backed down, admitting that he had successfully rebutted all charges; the Liberal press now rounded on Smith for making false allegations against the government and for sparking Sadleir's flight.[74] But despite the warrant, the government could not get hold of James because his crimes did not come within the extradition treaty between Britain and France, which covered only murder, attempted murder, forgery, and fraudulent bankruptcy.[75] He was punished by other means, though, being expelled from parliament in 1857 and, as Fitzgerald noted, condemning himself to 'exile for life'.[76]

The government's decision to initiate proceedings against Sadleir, though certainly influenced by political pressure, and not resulting in prosecution, was nevertheless significant.[77] It needs to be understood in the context of a shift in legislative priorities from prevention of fraud to punishment of fraud detectable in the limited liability debates. When piloting his bill through the Commons, Bouverie stated that 'it was the duty of the legislature to prevent fraud, not by prohibiting a class of transactions, many of which were honest and advantageous to the public and the parties concerned, but by taking care that fraud, wherever it existed, should be detected and punished'.[78] When the bill reached the upper house, Lord Denman, son of the late chief justice, tried to reassure its opponents that it was not an incitement to fraud: 'persons who were inclined to commit frauds . . . might be certain that some criminal law would be passed to meet their cases if necessary'.[79] The uncertainty over Sadleir's criminality, coming so soon after the Strahan case which had seen justice swiftly and devastatingly dispensed, highlighted for many the necessity of such a law, especially when the immorality of the Sadleirs seemed plainer than of the private bankers.[80] At the heart of the inconsistency was the law of trust. The misappropriation of company funds by directors of joint-stock companies, who stood as trustees of this money, was viewed by the law not as a theft, but as a debt, and therefore not criminally punishable. Even before the Sadleir case broke, the government was aware of the problem, and when introducing his bill, Lowe had stated that a reform to the law of trustees to tackle the problem of misappropriation, while outside his province, 'would be one of the greatest boons that could be conferred on society'.[81] Whilst the Sadleir case did not derail Lowe's bill, there was some disquiet that the government had decided to set 'commerce entirely free' at the precise moment when such gross frauds were being uncovered.[82] As the scandal unfolded, therefore, pressure for a change in the criminal law mounted.[83]

[74] Ibid. 889 (15 July 1856); *The Times*, 14 July 1856; *Observer*, 14 July 1856; *Manchester Guardian*, 17 July 1856.

[75] Hansard, 3s, 144: 709 (16 February 1857).

[76] Ibid. 710 (16 February 1857). He lived the rest of his life in Zurich, surviving on a small annuity provided by his wife's family, though his wife chose not to join him: O'Shea, *Prince of Swindlers*, 456–7.

[77] One historian calls Fitzgerald's actions 'unprecedented': O'Shea, *Prince of Swindlers*, 429.

[78] Hansard, 3s, 139: 326 (29 June 1855).

[79] Ibid. 1923 (7 August 1855).

[80] *Morning Chronicle*, 11 March 1856.

[81] Hansard, 3s, 140: 493 (8 February 1856).

[82] *Daily News*, 10 March 1856.

[83] *Freeman's Journal*, 5 March 1856; *Daily News*, 10 March 1856; *The Times*, 29 April 1856.

Later that session Attorney General Cockburn introduced a measure to bring misappropriation of trust property within the criminal law.[84] Some believed that the bill was 'evidently prompted' by recent banking frauds, and that it would apply to the directors of joint-stock companies.[85] Nevertheless, it was far from apparent that the measure was designed to tackle company frauds. When introducing the bill, Cockburn did not allude to bank frauds; the bill itself ran to just five clauses, and did not mention banks or joint-stock companies, let alone misrepresentation in balance sheets.[86] Though the bill was withdrawn before it reached the Lords, further scandals meant that the matter would not rest there.

THE EMBEZZLEMENT MANIA

These halting steps towards reform were made against a skittish commercial backdrop. Were the Sadleirs rotten apples or were they indicative of a broader commercial malaise? Soon after John's suicide there was a severe run on the London and County Bank, which Sadleir had chaired, but it survived as it was sound and had wisely secured its loan to its chairman.[87] At the end of April, false rumours spread by a group of disgruntled clerks led to a near-fatal run on the St Martin's Provident Institution, during which £90,000 was withdrawn.[88] The publication of John's letter in June stoked the rumour mill. If he was to be believed, then creative accounting was rife among English banks. While *The Times* reminded its readers that Sadleir was hardly the most reliable authority, it suggested that joint-stock bank shareholders 'would do well to satisfy themselves that their trust is rightly placed'.[89]

One bank in particular looked shaky. Towards the end of April 1856, the newly established *Joint Stock Companies' Journal* began publishing a series of articles on the affairs of an unnamed London bank which it claimed was insolvent, but was concealing its true state from the public.[90] The identity of the bank was suggested by a number of increasingly heavy hints: the Royal British Bank, chartered in 1849. While the journal had a small circulation, the rumours reached the shareholders, who grilled the board at the company's general meeting in early August. Though the directors managed to orchestrate a vote of confidence, the whispers continued, and there was 'a sort of indefinable impression that something was not quite right'.[91] The value of the company's shares nosedived at the end of the month, and a run on the bank's deposits followed.

[84] Hansard, 3s, 141: 432 (3 April 1856).

[85] *Morning Chronicle*, 13 March 1856; Joseph Napier, Hansard, 3s, 143: 1392 (24 July 1856).

[86] *A Bill to Amend the Law Relating to the Criminal Appropriation of Property held by Persons as Trustees or Bailees*, PP 1856 II; Hansard, 3s, 143: 1113–14 (21 July 1856).

[87] O'Shea, *Prince of Swindlers*, 419.

[88] *Observer*, 27 April 1856.

[89] *The Times*, 23 June 1856.

[90] *Joint Stock Companies Journal*, 26 April, 3, 10, 17, 24 May 1856.

[91] *Observer*, 7 September 1856.

The bank succumbed and closed its doors in September. The rumours proved correct. The bank had been speculating unsuccessfully in Welsh iron mines; the manager, Hugh Innes Cameron, and several of the directors had been secretly draining the bank of its funds in the form of large loans; it had been paying dividends out of capital for years.[92]

This was the third big bank failure in little over a year, and the cumulative impact was tremendous. From the start, the British Bank was viewed as part of a trend, following the 'gigantic...swindle' of Strahan, Paul, and Bates, and the 'thunderclap' of the Tipperary Bank.[93] The press concluded that this was not a series of unlinked cases but a failing system which needed to be fixed. This explains the outspoken tone of even the earliest reports. The *Observer* found it 'impossible to find words to describe the intense indignation of the public'.[94] 'Better for the small tradesman to tie up his earnings in a stocking and hide it in his bed', wrote *The Times*, than 'to become a depositor in banks conducted on such lax principles, on such a negation of principle'.[95]

While some attention was devoted to the question of how to improve bank governance, with proposals for public audit particularly prominent, the seeming rigour of the 1844 Joint-Stock Bank Act under which the British Bank operated meant that there was scepticism about the efficacy of legislative solutions.[96] Consequently, the focus from the start was on punishment, and pundits had little hesitation labelling what the management had done as criminal.[97] There was a new urgency in debates, a growing sense of moral panic. Accepted categories of reliability and respectability had become destabilized; the press was beginning to talk of the 'embezzlement mania', and urged decisive action to enforce honesty in management and to restore confidence in the nation's financial institutions.[98] Some kind of deterrent was desperately needed: the board 'should be made examples of, for the benefit of their brother joint-stock directors'.[99] Outrage was particularly strong because of the outward respectability of the board, which at various points had boasted four Liberal MPs and an alderman: John Macgregor, formerly of the Board of Trade, respected financial author and MP for Glasgow; Humphrey Brown,

[92] James Taylor, 'Company Fraud in Victorian Britain: The Royal British Bank Scandal of 1856', *English Historical Review*, 122 (2007), 704.

[93] *The Times*, 9 September 1856.

[94] *Observer*, 7 September 1856.

[95] *The Times*, 9 September 1856. For the crisis in confidence brought about by the British Bank failure, see Timothy L. Alborn, 'The Moral of the Failed Bank: Professional Plots in the Victorian Money Market', *Victorian Studies*, 38 (1995), 210–11.

[96] The *Observer* was particularly enthusiastic about schemes for public or professional audit: 7, 21 September 1856; *The Times* was sceptical: 12 September 1856.

[97] *Observer*, 7 September 1856; *The Times*, 9 September 1856.

[98] Jane Garnett, 'Commercial Ethics: A Victorian Perspective on the Practice of Theory', in Christopher Cowton and Roger Crisp (eds), *Business Ethics: Perspectives on the Practice of Theory* (Oxford, 1998), 124; *Joint Stock Companies Journal*, repr. in *Morning Chronicle*, 24 November 1856; *Blackburn Standard*, 17 December 1856.

[99] *Daily Telegraph*, 6 September 1856. Reading the 1850s press it is hard to agree that middle-class crime 'went unnoticed by the Victorians': Rob Sindall, 'Middle-Class Crime in Nineteenth-Century England', *Criminal Justice History*, 4 (1983), 26.

merchant and MP for Tewkesbury; the barrister John Stapleton, MP for Berwick; Southwark MP and glass manufacturer Apsley Pellatt; and Richard Kennedy, formerly physician-general in the Indian army and a City alderman. Brown had borrowed over £70,000 from the bank, Macgregor nearly £14,000, while Cameron, the manager, owed over £30,000. The apparent inability of the criminal law to reach this kind of offence was lamented in editorials: '[w]e hear it asked on every side are there no means of consigning the offending directors of the Royal British Bank to the hands of justice?'[100]

But who would set the law in motion? Not the victims. The possibility of criminal prosecution was raised at a depositors meeting in early October when one aggrieved depositor said that the directors 'would never have their deserts until they were brought to the bar of a criminal court'. Another told the meeting that he had offered £200 to an eminent firm of solicitors to bring the directors to the Old Bailey.[101] While such comments were well received by fellow victims, they did not spark a general movement to prosecute, for the depositors and shareholders were locked in a bewildering and expensive legal struggle.[102] Shareholders petitioned for the bank to be wound up in Chancery under the acts of 1848–49 (Lowe's recently passed act did not apply to banks), but depositors petitioned for the bank to be wound up in Bankruptcy under the original 1844 act.[103] Both courts were permitted to operate concurrently, which most commentators thought would achieve little beyond enriching the lawyers.[104] In the months that followed, the victims turned on each other. Shareholders formed an association for mutual defence and contested their liability for the bank's debts on the grounds of fraud; depositors lost their patience and began exercising their right under the 1844 Winding-up Act to milk individual shareholders for what they were owed. Shareholders responded by fleeing the country.[105] The last thing on either side's mind was spending more money on criminal litigation.

However, the government was listening to the public outcry. Sir Richard Bethell, who replaced Cockburn as Attorney General when the latter was made Chief Justice in November 1856, told the Commons in early March 1857 that he had been preparing a bill to punish fraudulent trustees which he had hoped to introduce, but which had had to be delayed because of the forthcoming general election. He assured that House that if he were re-elected, he would introduce it when parliament reassembled.[106] Unlike Cockburn, Bethell made it clear that his bill applied to company directors as well as trustees, and encompassed all companies and not solely joint-stock banks: the recent frauds had highlighted a problem which transcended the banking sector.[107]

[100] *The Times*, 24 September 1856. See also *Law Times*, 27 September 1856.
[101] *The Times*, 7 October 1856.
[102] The legal dispute is summarized in Taylor, 'Company Fraud', 705–10.
[103] *The Times*, 26 September, 10 October 1856.
[104] *Law Times*, 25 October 1856.
[105] Ibid. 27 December 1856.
[106] Hansard, 3s, 144: 2111–12 (9 March 1857).
[107] Ibid. 2405 (17 March 1857).

Shortly after the election, which saw Palmerston's Whig government returned, Bethell introduced his bill. He had framed it to take into account the various forms of breach of trust, and several sections explicitly addressed joint-stock company frauds, which Bethell noted had been 'so frequent and so gigantic'.[108] The bill went much further than the inoperative clause in the 1844 Joint-Stock Companies Act, and criminalized three types of behaviour by management. The first consisted of crimes of larceny and embezzlement. It was a misdemeanour for any 'Director, Public Officer, or Manager' of a company to 'fraudulently take or apply, for his own use, any of the money or other property' of the company (larceny) or to receive 'any of the money or other property' of the company for anything other than payment of a just debt, and 'with intent to defraud' omit to record this in the company's books (embezzlement).[109] The second concerned the falsification of company books: management could not 'with intent to defraud, destroy, alter, mutilate, or falsify any of the books, papers, writings, or securities' of the company, or 'make or concur in the making of any false entry, or any material omission in any book of account or other document'.[110] The third addressed the dissemination of false statements: no director or officer could 'make, circulate, or publish, or concur in making, circulating, or publishing, any written statement or account which he shall know to be false in any material particular, with intent to deceive or defraud any member, shareholder, or creditor', or with intent to induce anyone to become a shareholder or creditor.[111]

Unlike the 1844 act, Bethell's bill specified punishments, making use of the new category of penal servitude, introduced in 1853 as a replacement for sentences of transportation and intended to be particularly harsh.[112] The bill had originally stipulated a maximum penalty of seven years' penal servitude for these offences, but this was reduced in committee, following fears that it was too severe, to a maximum of three years' penal servitude, or imprisonment for a maximum of two years with or without hard labour.[113] This did not necessarily represent an excessively tender approach to fraud: in agreeing to the amendment, Bethell explained that this would make the law consistent with other countries such as France, where the punishment of fraudulent trustees was limited to 'two or three years'.[114] Moreover, the willingness to impose penal servitude at all showed that these offences were being taken seriously: white-collar criminals were to be incorporated in '[t]he desire to punish', which became 'so dominant a characteristic of Victorian Britain after 1850'.[115]

Other than this, most of the debate concerned the sections dealing with private trustees; the sections of the bill addressing joint-stock companies elicited practically no discussion, such was the consensus that had been generated by the banking

[108] Ibid. 145: 679–82 (21 May 1857). [109] 20 & 21 Vict. c. 54, ss. 5–6.
[110] Ibid. s. 7. [111] Ibid. s. 8.
[112] Ibid. s. 10; Clive Emsley, *Crime and Society in England, 1750–1900* (2nd edn, Harlow, 1996), 277–8.
[113] Hansard, 3s, 146: 1190–1 (9 July 1857).
[114] Ibid. 1191 (9 July 1857).
[115] W. R. Cornish and G. de N. Clark, *Law and Society in England, 1750–1950* (London, 1989), 584.

scandals, though Scottish members negotiated an opt-out.[116] The act was hailed as a major achievement. One accountant declared that the public owed 'a large debt of gratitude' to the government, and believed it would drive up standards of governance and transparency across the joint-stock economy.[117] England had lagged behind 'all other civilised nations', wrote *The Times*, but now the 'vulgar sophism' that the law should not interfere with commerce had been demolished.[118]

The act could not be applied retrospectively to the British Bank directors, but another means was found to bring them to a criminal court. Because the bank was being wound up under the act of 1844 as well as those of 1848–49, the bank's management would be investigated by the Court of Bankruptcy, and commentators anticipated that this would lead to greater exposure of the 'shameless villainy' perpetrated by the bank than regular winding-up proceedings in Chancery.[119] Such hopes proved well founded. The extensive interrogations of the directors and officers before Commissioner Edward Holroyd stretched through March and April 1857, and despite the rival appeal of a general election, were exhaustively reported in the press. They reinvigorated flagging interest in the case and rekindled indignation that the culprits seemed unlikely to face criminal prosecution.[120]

On their own, the interrogations would have been sufficient to rouse public opinion. What gave them added edge was the failure of yet another joint-stock bank just as proceedings were getting under way. The London and Eastern Banking Corporation, a new bank established in 1854, announced in the middle of March that it would go into liquidation.[121] It transpired that the bank had loaned practically its entire paid-up capital of £250,000 to Colonel William Waugh, one of its directors, most of which he had sunk into unprofitable potteries. A further £50,000 had been loaned to three other directors and the manager, and total liabilities approached £400,000.[122] The case seemed to confirm what the previous failures had suggested about the commercial morality of the country. 'The management of our joint-stock establishments is becoming a disgrace to the country and a scandal to the world,' wrote *The Times*.[123]

As the examinations of the British Bank directors progressed, the press began baying for retribution, demanding that the letter of the law be 'strained to the utmost' to enable a prosecution.[124] In early May, the creditors' solicitor John Linklater, who had conducted the interrogations, upped the pressure on the government. He argued that there was 'already quite sufficient upon the records of this Court to insure a

[116] Chantal Stebbings, *The Private Trustee in Victorian England* (Cambridge, 2002), 182–3; 20 & 21 Vict. c. 54, s. 18.

[117] Henry Lloyd Morgan, *Personal Liabilities of Directors of Joint Stock Companies under the Fraudulent Trustees' Act* (3rd edn, London, 1858), 20.

[118] *The Times*, 23 May 1857. See also *Illustrated London News*, 30 May 1857; *Weekly Dispatch*, 31 May 1857; *News of the World*, 7 June 1857; *Manchester Guardian*, 25 August 1857; *Observer*, 31 August 1857.

[119] *Observer*, 28 December 1856.

[120] Ibid. 15 March 1857.

[121] *The Times*, 18 March 1857.

[122] Ibid. 26 March 1857; Evans, *Facts, Failures and Frauds*, ch. 11.

[123] *The Times*, 1 April 1857.

[124] *Observer*, 3 May 1857; *Lloyd's Weekly Newspaper*, 3 May 1857.

certain conviction if a prosecution be instituted'.[125] Suddenly, the press was hopeful: 'Who is to be transported?' asked *Lloyd's Weekly Newspaper*.[126] But the last word would be Commissioner Holroyd's. His track record suggested that he would take the case seriously: after all, he had helped draw up the 1844 act under which these examinations were taking place, and in 1850 he had gone on record as supporting a public prosecutor.[127] So it proved. The examinations had been adjourned till late June because one of the directors was unavailable, but as delay would 'defeat the ends of justice' he took the unusual step of bringing forward his final judgement by six weeks. For Holroyd, the causes of failure were clear: he did not believe 'that a scene of greater recklessness, fraud, and criminality of conduct in the management of a banking establishment was ever exhibited in a court of justice'. He directed transcripts of the examinations to be sent straight to the Attorney General so that the government could institute criminal proceedings.[128]

This placed the ball firmly in Bethell's court, and the next day a fellow Liberal MP asked him whether the government would prosecute the directors. Bethell was cautious: he needed to see the papers and take legal advice before making a decision. The press, heedless of legal niceties, mocked his caution and urged him to act immediately.[129] The criticism stung. Six days later, when introducing his bill to punish fraudulent trustees, he tartly observed that he would not 'be dictated to by a newspaper'. Nevertheless, he had decided that 'he would try, without a moment's delay', to pursue the bank gang under the law of conspiracy.[130] So, on 5 June, warrants were issued for the arrest of the entire board and Cameron, the manager. It was known that some of them had followed Sadleir's example and fled the country, but the authorities were determined to bring them back: they could not risk losing the subjects of the public's ire a second time. The resulting manhunt was widely reported. Brown evaded capture for some time 'by wearing green spectacles and a wig, which most effectually altered his personal appearance', but eventually surrendered himself. Alderman Kennedy was tracked down in the south of Germany just as he was about to leave for Italy. Cameron was the last to be found, eventually being captured in Switzerland. Like Brown, he had taken steps to disguise his appearance, having grown a moustache and long white beard since the bank's failure 'which would prevent his most intimate friends from recognizing him except upon a close scrutiny'. The arrests were well received, widely portrayed as a blow struck by the law against over-mighty bankers in the name of defenceless investors.[131]

[125] *Re The Royal British Bank* (1857), *The Times*, 5 May 1857.

[126] *Lloyd's Weekly Newspaper*, 10 May 1857.

[127] Ludlow referred to 'Mr Holroyd's Winding-up Act' of 1844: Ludlow, *Winding-up Act*, xxxix. For Holroyd's comments on a public prosecutor, see *Re Jardine* (1850), *Morning Post*, 24 December 1850.

[128] *Re The Royal British Bank* (1857), *The Times*, 15 May 1857.

[129] Hansard, 3s, 145: 310–11 (15 May 1857); *The Times*, 16 May 1857; *Daily News*, 16 May 1857; *Liverpool Mercury*, 18 May 1857.

[130] Hansard, 3s, 145: 680 (21 May 1857).

[131] *Observer*, 28 June 1857; *The Times*, 29 June 1857. Macgregor was not among them, having died in April 1857.

The trial of the six directors and the manager took place before a special jury of commercial men at the Court of Queen's Bench in February 1858.[132] The 'elaborate' indictment against them, framed by Bethell himself, contained six counts of conspiracy to publish a false balance sheet with intent to deceive and defraud the shareholders, inducing them to keep their shares and to become or continue customers of the bank.[133] By law, conspiracy could be proven without any overt acts committed, but the prosecution set out a series of acts, including paying a dividend of 6 per cent when no profits were made, buying shares with the bank's money to maintain their price, and issuing new shares knowing the bank to be failing, to allow the jury to 'draw an inference as to the object of the conspiracy'. Owing to the number of defendants and the complex body of evidence, the trial lasted thirteen days. But the crux of the prosecution's case, led by Sir Frederick Thesiger, twice Attorney General in Conservative administrations, and William Atherton, a Liberal and standing counsel to the Admiralty, was simple, and revolved around proving three key points. First, that the bank was insolvent, second, that the defendants knew this, and third, that they lied about it to the shareholders.[134]

It was unfortunate for the defendants that the judge was John Campbell, now Lord Chief Justice, who had famously made clear his views on paying dividends out of capital in *Burnes v. Pennell* in 1849. His Scottish Presbyterian background—his father was a minister in the Church of Scotland for fifty-one years, and he had originally intended to follow in his father's footsteps—may have influenced his view of the role of the law in the joint-stock economy. Although historians have identified a link between Calvinist theology and the development of capitalism and economic individualism in Scotland, there were other factors shaping religious attitudes to business.[135] Discipline was a key feature of Presbyterianism, and in the Scottish Reformation the church was structured to enforce it. For John Knox, the key was 'ecclesiastical discipline uprightly administered, as God's Word prescribes, whereby vice is repressed, and virtue nourished'.[136] Cases of misconduct were investigated and publicly punished at Kirk Sessions, with witness statements and decisions carefully recorded in minutes which mimicked legal language. The rich and powerful did not escape these exercises in public discipline, and Campbell did not belittle the vices of the rich defendants before him.[137] While his summing up eschewed overt reference to religious precepts, he strove to reduce the case to 'a few

[132] The men had been arrested following an *ex officio* information filed by the Attorney General, which meant that they could be tried at the Court of Queen's Bench without having to be committed by magistrates: David Bentley, *English Criminal Justice in the Nineteenth Century* (London, 1998), 84.

[133] Thomas Arthur Nash, *The Life of Richard Lord Westbury*, 2 vols (London, 1888), i. 207–8.

[134] *Reg. v. Esdaile* (1858) 175 ER 696, *The Times*, 15 February, 1 March 1858. Evans, *Facts, Failures and Frauds*, 280–390. The trial began under a Whig ministry and concluded under a Conservative one after Palmerston's government was defeated in the Commons over its Conspiracy to Murder Bill.

[135] The literature is summarized in Callum Brown, *The Social History of Religion in Scotland since 1730* (London, 1987), 137–8.

[136] Alistair Mutch, 'Theology, Accountability and Management: Exploring the Contributions of Scottish Presbyterianism', *Organization*, 19 (2012), 369.

[137] Ibid; Diarmaid MacCulloch, *Reformation: Europe's House Divided, 1490–1700* (London, 2003), ch. 14.

plain points', which made his views tolerably clear. He told the jury that the balance sheet excluded debts known to be bad to the extent of at least £100,000, which could only conceivably be justified if there was a reserve fund to cover them. In this case, the reserve fund was but £339; it was therefore 'a false account'. This established, the main job of the jury was to decide who knew the figures were false. Knowledge signified guilt; ignorance innocence. His final instructions to the jury left little scope for acquittal: 'though it would be a great satisfaction to him if they could say they were not guilty', he 'was sure they would not shrink from their duty, but would give a verdict which would be satisfactory to their consciences and to the country'. Nevertheless, assessing the extent of each defendant's knowledge proved tricky: it took nearly four hours' deliberation and much disagreement before the jury finally returned a guilty verdict for all seven men, but recommending four of them to mercy.[138] Being tried by their commercial peers rather than by an ordinary jury had not saved them: their acts had been placed beyond the pale.

In his sentencing speech, Campbell's view of the law as a crucial disciplinary instrument in the capitalist economy became clear. Though exonerating the men of having conceived the bank with fraudulent intent, they had for years carried on 'a system of deliberate fraud', circulating false documents to deceive the public. This was more than a breach of contract with the bank's shareholders or customers: it was 'a criminal conspiracy to do what inevitably leads to great public mischief, in the ruin of families, and reducing the widow and orphan from affluence to destitution'. The defence offered by some of the men's lawyers—that what the management had done was common practice—only made punishment *more* necessary. 'Unfortunately, a laxity has been introduced into certain commercial dealings, not from any defect in the law, but from the law not being put in force'. This had degraded commercial ethics, for 'practices have been adopted, without bringing a consciousness of shame, and I fear without much loss of character among those with whom they associate'. Campbell hoped that it would now be understood that these practices were illegal and would be punished by law. However, because this was the first prosecution of its kind, he decided to pass less severe sentences than he otherwise would have done. He allowed John Stapleton, who joined the bank late in its career, to escape with a shilling fine, but the other six all got custodial sentences. Brown, Cameron, and Edward Esdaile, the bank's governor, were sentenced to one year's imprisonment in the Queen's Prison; the other three to between three and nine months.[139] Foreign commentators were impressed, the *New York Times* noting that similar crimes would not have been punished at all in New York, where the conspiracy trials of the 1820s had not been followed through with further fraud prosecutions. Despite the fact that the sentences were relatively short, the men's disgrace was assured: 'when they come out of prison it will not be to associate again with honorable men'.[140]

[138] *The Times*, 1 March 1858.
[139] Ibid.
[140] *New York Times*, 19 March 1858. For more on the damage done to the reputations of the bank's directors, see James Taylor, 'Commercial Fraud and Public Men in Victorian Britain', *Historical Research*, 78 (2005), 230–52.

FALSE PROMISE

Domestic commentators were less impressed. The newspapers had wanted retributive sentences and did not get them, and they now made their displeasure known. The radical press thought it was a 'sham verdict' and 'an impudent and palpable mockery of justice', and many voices in the mainstream press agreed.[141] Campbell vented his frustration in his diary, claiming that all at the bar recognized that he had acted throughout with 'patience, discrimination and firmness'.[142] But worse was to follow. In April, the men's lawyers moved for a retrial on the grounds of misdirection and that the verdict was against evidence.[143] The appeal won some sympathy among the Queen's Bench judges, and Campbell had 'the most unpleasant work to go through which I have ever encountered since I became a judge' trying to persuade them to refuse the rule. 'For a fortnight I was most wretched, passing sleepless nights and losing my appetite for food.' Finally, he won the last doubter round, and was able to reject the appeal in 'a very elaborate judgment' in the name of the whole court.[144]

Campbell claimed that this judgement 'brought me more credit than any former judicial performance'. Nevertheless, the appeal seems to have raised misgivings within government, for one of the defendants was subsequently granted a free pardon, and three others were released early, so that only Cameron and Esdaile served their full terms.[145] This must have made some wonder whether it had all been worth the vast cost—the final bill came to £20,000.[146] In an age of retrenchment, when governments were attempting to reduce burdens on the taxpayer and stand above sectional interests, such prosecutions seemed unjustifiably expensive, and embroiled ministers in complex disputes involving contested legal principles.

Thus it is perhaps unsurprising that Bethell's decision to prosecute was not emulated by his Conservative successors, in power from late February 1858. This was not through lack of controversial failures. Though Colonel Waugh, the architect of the spectacular collapse of the London and Eastern Bank, was declared an outlaw for not attending personal bankruptcy proceedings, he retired to the Continent and never faced criminal prosecution.[147] The 1857 commercial crisis which began in the US and struck Britain in October brought down three more banks heavily involved in the American market.[148] The Liverpool Borough Bank, the

[141] For radical opinion, see *People's Paper*, 6 March 1858; *Reynolds's Newspaper*, 7 March 1858. For mainstream criticism, see *The Times*, 1 March 1858; *Daily Telegraph*, 1 March 1858; *Illustrated London News*, 6 March 1858.

[142] Diary entry for 2 March 1858, *Life of John, Lord Campbell*, ed. Mrs Hardcastle, 2 vols (London, 1881), ii. 357.

[143] *The Times*, 21 April 1858.

[144] Diary entry for 9 May 1858, *Life of John, Lord Campbell*, ii, 358; *Reg. v. Brown* (1858), *The Times*, 6 May 1858.

[145] *Law Times*, 19 June, 10 July 1858, 5 March 1859.

[146] Hansard, 3s, 156: 384 (31 January 1860).

[147] Taylor, 'Commercial Fraud', 249–50.

[148] George Robb, *White-Collar Crime in Modern England: Financial Fraud and Business Morality, 1845–1929* (Cambridge, 1992), 63.

Northumberland and Durham District Bank, and the Western Bank of Scotland failed in October and November 1857, while the City of Glasgow and Wolverhampton Banks suspended payment but later reopened.[149] Subsequent shareholder investigations identified serious abuses, including hefty loans made on poor securities, falsified balance sheets, and dividends paid out of capital—the Western Bank had paid 9 per cent just months before its collapse. Of course, these were the same offences discovered in the Tipperary and British Bank cases, which had roused the Liberal administration to action, but the Conservatives did not follow suit.

When it became apparent that the British Bank prosecution had been a one-off, the disappointment was palpable. *Town Talk* complained that fraudulent joint-stock banks were being allowed to swindle with impunity. It looked forward to the day when the law would stand up to the 'blustering bully', but in the meantime, had to satisfy itself with a piece of wish-fulfilment in the shape of a cartoon showing a lawyer defending helpless widows against a monstrous banker (see Figure 5.1). Some detected sinister forces at work. *The Times*'s money market column claimed that the trial had been a sop to satisfy public opinion, the main aim being to shield City insiders, who were allowed to continue swindling unmolested.[150] Yet such criticisms ignored the more obvious point that the Fraudulent Trustees Act had been passed to facilitate *private* prosecutions. Whereas actions against private trustees could not be commenced without the permission of the Attorney General, the act made no such stipulation for the prosecution of company directors.[151] Thus, traditional attitudes soon slid back into place. Joint-stock frauds were held up as private rather than public offences; it was not the government's responsibility to 'hunt out crime', as the Lord Advocate John Inglis put it.[152]

If the new law was a tool for injured parties to use against errant management, the question remained whether they would choose to do so. The first attempt came quickly, in March 1858, when Arthur Oliver, a shareholder in the Carnewas Mine Company and 'gentleman of independent means', took out a summons against the manager Richard Tredinnick, charging him with issuing false accounts. On the strength of these accounts, Oliver explained to Sir Robert Carden, now Lord Mayor, he was induced to invest £187; since then, Tredinnick had been declared bankrupt. Carden took the case seriously, and as it was the first such prosecution under the act, he would remand it for a week. But when the parties reconvened, Oliver, having taken legal advice, and receiving little support from his fellow shareholders, was ready to back down. Carden was thus left to rule whether the prosecution should be proceeded with on public grounds. He decided not to for two reasons. First, as a cost-book mine, the Carnewas venture was not a public company within the meaning of the act: it was not registered in any public office

[149] *Report from the Select Committee on the Bank Acts*, PP 1857–8 V. p. xvi.
[150] *The Times*, 3 May 1858.
[151] 20 & 21 Vict. c. 54, s. 13.
[152] Hansard, 3s, 149: 1196–1210 (16 April 1858).

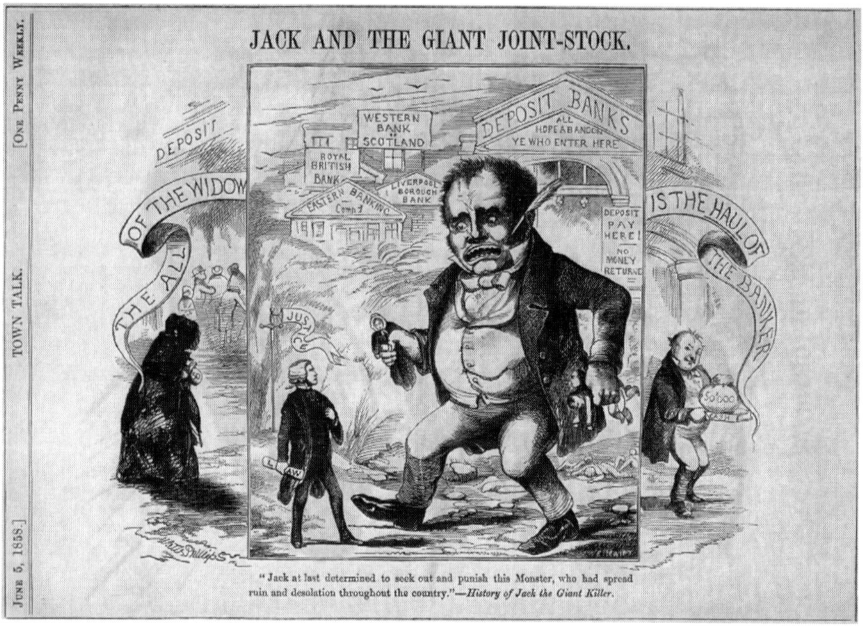

Figure 5.1 'Jack and the Giant Joint-Stock', *Town Talk*, 5 June 1858

or regulated by any public statute.[153] Second, the evidence against Tredinnick did not reveal intent to defraud: though the accounts showed debts due as paid, the defence held that this was customary practice among cost-book mines. Carden decided to dismiss the summons, nonetheless noting that it had been 'a very proper inquiry', and supporting Oliver's decision to have the matter publicly investigated.[154]

Despite Carden's sympathetic handling of the case, Oliver's example was not followed elsewhere. Angry shareholders at general meetings were often heard menacing their directors: at the Royal Surrey Gardens Company, which was unexpectedly declared bankrupt shortly after shareholders had received a 10 per cent dividend, one shareholder exclaimed 'Why the British Bank seemed to be a fool to this... The directors would be put into the witness-box and would be examined'. Yet in this, and other similar cases, shareholders did not try to deploy the new act.[155] Civil rather than criminal actions were invariably preferred. And while shareholders in civil suits had typically struggled to win over judges and juries, it seemed that the frauds of the 1850s were bringing about a change in attitudes. In

[153] For more on cost-book mines, see Ron Harris, *Industrializing English Law: Entrepreneurship and Business Organization, 1720–1844* (Cambridge, 2000), 190–2; Roger Burt and Norikazu Kudo, 'The Adaptability of the Cornish Cost Book System', *Business History*, 25 (1983), 30–41.

[154] *Morning Post*, 20, 27 March 1858.

[155] *Morning Chronicle*, 24 August 1857. See also the report of the general meeting of the Metropolitan Saloon Omnibus Company: ibid. 6 August 1857.

1858, two shareholders in the Liverpool Borough Bank sued one of its managing directors, Joshua Dixon, for issuing a report misrepresenting the bank's affairs with intent to defraud. The paper trail implicating Dixon was damning: he had submitted to the board a draft report admitting large losses, which they had rejected as 'too alarming'; the rewritten report recommended carrying money to the reserve fund and paying a dividend of 5 per cent. The difference between the two proved that Dixon's real appraisal of the bank's affairs was at odds with that actually presented to shareholders, and the special jury consequently ordered Dixon to repay the purchase money. *The Times* hailed it as 'the first instance on record in which a Director has been made liable in damages for one of those innumerable misrepresentations which have hitherto been made with such perfect impunity' and thought that enforcing this liability would encourage honesty in joint-stock companies.[156] Certainly, there is evidence that judges were starting to take shareholder protection more seriously in common law and equity suits around this time.[157]

With the principle of civil liability for misrepresentation only just beginning to gain acceptance, it was perhaps unsurprising that there were few attempts to test it in the criminal courts. Indeed, what the criminal law actually was, following the British Bank verdict, was a matter of contention. This was revealed during a Commons debate on the Western Bank of Scotland failure in April 1858. Walter Buchanan, a Glasgow MP keen to defend the bank's directors, drew a firm distinction between this bank and the British Bank. The directors of the Western Bank were not guilty of fraud because at the time of the collapse they had large deposits in the bank, they had not sought to leave the sinking ship, and had not 'helped themselves' to its funds. That they had not profited from the bank's activities was proof that they were both morally and legally innocent. But this definition of fraud was based upon a misunderstanding of the British Bank trial, as William Atherton, part of the prosecution team two months earlier, explained. People assumed that the British Bank management was charged with taking company money, but only two of the defendants had done this: they were actually tried for misrepresentation. It was immaterial that the Western Bank of Scotland directors had stuck by their sinking ship—the same was true of the British Bank directors, several of whom had even encouraged friends and relatives to invest shortly before its collapse. For a prosecution to go ahead, Atherton explained, it was merely necessary to prove that there had been misrepresentation. Then a jury would decide whether the defendants were aware of the lie. '[W]hen untruth was put forward to lure people to mischief and ruin, there was sufficient ground for investigation and careful inquiry, with the view of punishing those who had been the authors of the fraud if it could be shown they were aware of it'.[158]

[156] *Scott v. Dixon* (1858), *The Times*, 28, 30 August 1858. The jury's verdict was upheld on appeal at the Court of Queen's Bench: *Scott v. Dixon* (1859) 29 LJ Ex. 62n, *The Times*, 28 January 1859.

[157] Jean Margo Reid, 'Judicial Intervention in Accounting Behavior: A Reevaluation of the Nineteenth-Century Experience', *Journal of Accounting and Public Policy*, 6 (1987), 20–2; Michael Lobban, 'Misrepresentation', in *The Oxford History of the Laws of England*, 13 vols (Oxford, 2003–), xii. 417–25.

[158] Hansard, 3s, 149: 1211–13 (16 April 1858).

This disjunction between the crimes for which the Royal British Bank gang were condemned by public opinion and those for which they were actually tried by the law mattered enormously as it thwarted attempts to establish agreed parameters between criminal and non-criminal behaviour. Many saw misrepresentation as a lesser crime than misappropriation. The *Law Times* wondered whether there was a single bank 'in all Europe' which would issue a true balance sheet 'the certain effect of which would be to produce a panic, a run, and ruin in its most fatal form'.[159] Another problem was the centrality of intent to the act's definition of fraud. The *Bankers' Circular* argued that if Sir John Dean Paul had been tried strictly on intent to defraud, he would have been acquitted.[160] The *Scotsman* agreed, holding that recklessness, rather than intent, should be the guiding principle. Under the new law, it explained,

> It is necessary to show that A. intended specially to cheat B. before he can be touched. If a reckless fellow fire a blunderbuss into a crowded street and kill certain passengers, the administration of justice would be defeated if it were necessary to prove that when he fired he had malice against those special persons, and intended to slay them.

As a result, it was glad that the act did not apply to Scotland.[161]

Despite the 'embezzlement mania' of the mid 1850s and its dénouement in the Court of Queen's Bench, the criminal trial of company directors was not yet accepted as the natural mechanism by which justice should be delivered in the joint-stock economy. That this kind of trial had not yet found a place in the Victorian imagination is suggested by the fictional narratives of the period. The banking scandals were quickly immortalized in a range of popular novels, including Dudley Costello's *The Joint-Stock Banker*, *Little Dorrit* by Charles Dickens, and Charles Lever's *Davenport Dunn*. All three feature fraudulent joint-stock bank directors whose activities cause widespread suffering. Costello's tale centres on Meredyth Powell Jones, chairman of the Universal Guarantee and Cosmopolitan Safety Alliance Joint-Stock Bank of Central Africa. Powell Jones embodied the spirit of modern speculation, with 'a face of brass, a heart of iron, impudence that nothing can daunt, recklessness that nothing can restrain'.[162] *Little Dorrit* featured Mr Merdle, 'one of England's world-famed capitalists and merchant-princes'. His 'wonderful Bank', which he projected and managed, was hailed 'the latest of the many Merdle wonders'.[163] The 'hero' of Lever's eponymous novel is an Irish solicitor who becomes the richest man in the country through promoting a complex network of joint-stock companies at the centre of which is the Ossory Bank, with a capital of a million pounds, a royal charter, and a titled directorate.[164] All three men buy their way into social and political elites but their shaky empires collapse

[159] *Law Times*, 26 September 1857.
[160] *Bankers' Circular*, 30 May 1857.
[161] *Scotsman*, 2 December 1857.
[162] Dudley Costello, 'The Joint-Stock Banker', *Bentley's Miscellany*, 39 (April 1856), 351.
[163] Charles Dickens, *Little Dorrit*, 2 vols (1857; repr. London, 1891), i. 305, ii. 157.
[164] Charles Lever, *Davenport Dunn; or a Man of our Day* (London, 1859).

and their frauds are exposed. All are punished, though not by the law. Powell Jones fakes his own death, but later drowns at sea en route to Sweden. Merdle actually does take his life, while Dunn is murdered in a random attack on a train.[165] Of course, sensational plot twists such as these were a necessity for novelists following the well-established conventions of melodrama. Yet it says much about the still-ambiguous criminality of joint-stock frauds that while retribution was an essential element of these novels, it was never achieved by means of the law.

CONCLUSION

The 1850s are well known as a turning point in the early corporate history of Britain for the change in the law which made limited liability generally available. Less discussed is the fact that the decade also saw the first serious attempt at criminalizing company fraud, as well as the first government-directed prosecution of the board of directors of a joint-stock company. The two events were closely linked: the new harder response to fraud was prompted by the legislative shift towards deregulation, begun in 1855 and 1856, and extended by acts in 1857 and 1858 which dispensed with the conditions imposed on banks by the act of 1844 by assimilating them to the Companies Act of 1856, even allowing them to register with limited liability.[166] This legislation retreated from the idea that the state could prevent fraud by enforcing publicity and governance standards. But as prevention fell out of favour, punishment was taken more seriously, with government ministers presenting the criminalization of fraud as the natural corollary of deregulation. If it was true, as some feared, that the limited liability acts were incitements to fraud, then there had to be a countervailing disincentive.[167] The criminal prosecution of delinquent directors would offer investors 'a protection infinitely more effectual' than publicity and other such regulations.[168]

These events raise broader questions about the relationship between capitalism and the law in the nineteenth century. To resolve disputes among themselves, businessmen had long preferred self-regulatory mechanisms such as arbitration over recourse to the courts.[169] Although company constitutions often contained provision for disagreements between members to be settled by arbitrators, the rise of the joint-stock company multiplied the possible grounds for conflict, leading to an increase in civil lawsuits, most strikingly in the aftermath of the railway mania, but

[165] Before his murder, Dunn's agent boasts to a friend that the law cannot 'touch a hair of his head' and that at most he would have to spend a year or two abroad: ibid. 669.

[166] 20 & 21 Vict. c. 49 and 21 & 22 Vict. c. 91.

[167] Edward W. Cox, *The New Law and Practice of Joint Stock Companies, with and without Limited Liability* (4th edn, London, 1857), i–ii.

[168] *Morning Post*, 23 September 1856.

[169] David Sugarman and G. R. Rubin, 'Towards a New History of Law and Material Society in England, 1750–1914', in G. R. Rubin and David Sugarman (eds), *Law, Economy and Society, 1750–1914: Essays in the History of English Law* (Abingdon, 1984), 8–9; A. W. B. Simpson, *Victorian Law and the Industrial Spirit* (London, 1995), 4.

also visible in the numbers of winding-up disputes which blocked up the Court of Chancery.[170] Battles between directors and shareholders were not often taken into the criminal courts, however. This was partly because civil actions made more financial sense: defrauded investors preferred to see their money returned than justice done. But it was also because when such disputes had been taken to the criminal courts, notably in the 1820s and 1840s, magistrates and judges had been unsympathetic, arguing that they were more properly resolved in the civil courts. Sometimes presented as triggering public awareness of the problem of fraud, the exposure of widespread frauds in the railway sector at the end of the 1840s changed nothing.[171] In part this was because, for all his sins, George Hudson had not destroyed the companies he ran, nor had he ripped up the railway tracks or run his engines into the sea. They were still viable businesses which stood to generate profits for their shareholders, albeit more modest ones than they had been led to believe.[172] The bank failures of the 1850s were a different matter. Shareholders, without the shield of limited liability, were left with nothing other than liabilities to creditors which could ruin them. And they were not the only victims. It was the way in which a seemingly solid, safe bank could be turned into a black hole, swallowing wealth, disrupting credit, and destroying trust, which made bank failures seem a threat to the wider public interest. But the courts were not chiefly concerned with this public interest. Whilst drawing on an eclectic mix of sources ranging from natural law and political economy to notions of justice and convenience, judges did not always base their decisions on what was 'best for society in the abstract [or] for the economy'; indeed, one historian of the common law concludes that the courts 'backed private property, and left it to the legislature to worry about the public interest'.[173] It is unlikely that the courts alone, preoccupied with the principles of freedom of contract and *caveat emptor*, would have acted. This is what sparked the political interventions of the mid 1850s.

The Fraudulent Trustees Act and the Royal British Bank prosecution looked like evidence of a sea change in attitudes, the moment when the law finally caught up with abuses in the joint-stock sector. In reality they were the consequences of a contingent set of events—the failure of a big private bank, followed by three joint-stock banks—which created a moral panic, and an overwhelming public demand for action. The panic only temporarily overrode ingrained beliefs. These beliefs—that fraud was a private, not a public, offence which it was the responsibility of the injured parties to prosecute, and that defrauded shareholders usually brought their woes upon themselves through negligence and greed—gradually reasserted themselves towards the end of this period of instability. By the time of the Western Bank

[170] Mark Freeman, Robin Pearson, and James Taylor, *Shareholder Democracies? Corporate Governance in Britain and Ireland before 1850* (Chicago, IL, 2012), 61–3.

[171] See, for example, Sarah Wilson, 'Fraud and White-Collar Crime: 1850 to the Present', in Anne-Marie Kilday and David Nash (eds), *Histories of Crime: Britain, 1600–2000* (London, 2010), 211.

[172] *Observer*, 20 May 1849.

[173] Michael Lobban, *The Common Law and English Jurisprudence, 1760–1850* (Oxford, 1991), 90–6; Simpson, 'Victorian Law', 22. See also A. W. Brian Simpson, *Leading Cases in the Common Law* (Oxford, 1995), ch. 7.

failure, commentators were lecturing the victims that they could not expect more than 3 per cent without exertion and vigilance: they had 'the unreasonable expectation that other people will work, and hand over to them the produce'.[174] Moreover, there were doubts about the legal soundness of the British Bank convictions, and Campbell had to work hard to shore up his position in the face of an appeal. The state of the criminal law remained unclear, and investors continued to seek resolution of conflicts in the civil rather than the criminal courts. Public demand for more trials of company directors dissipated, and far from facilitating further actions, the main immediate consequence of the Fraudulent Trustees Act (albeit an unintended one), was to enable the friends of Strahan, Paul, and Bates to argue for their release after three years on the grounds that this was the maximum sentence for their crimes under the new law. Sure enough, Bates was released in October 1858 after serving three years, and Strahan and Paul after four.[175] After these inauspicious beginnings, it seemed possible that the act might simply fall into disuse.

[174] *Scotsman*, 23 October 1858.

[175] Hansard, 3s, 152: 144–7 (7 February 1859); *Leeds Mercury*, 21 October 1858; *Daily News*, 3 October 1859. Despite their sentence of transportation, the men were actually incarcerated—Strahan and Paul in Millbank, Bates in Pentonville—which was not unusual. *Globe*, repr. in *Bradford Observer*, 17 September 1857; Emsley, *Crime and Society*, 276.

6

One Law for the Rich? The 1860s

Anyone walking through the City of London on Friday 27 April 1860 would have witnessed quite a sight. The streets outside Mansion House were besieged by crowds anxious to gain admittance to the justice room. They had come to see 'a stalwart, florid-complexioned man', 48 years old, who, in spite of all the attention, seemed calm and self-possessed.[1] The man was William Pullinger, a cashier at the Union Bank of London since its formation in 1839. In 1855, he had been promoted to the post of chief cashier, and in this position of trust soon realized how easy it would be to siphon off the bank's funds for his own purposes. Responsible for his bank's account with the Bank of England, he kept two pass-books: the real one, showing the correct balance, he used with the Bank of England; the false one, showing a lower balance, was given to the ledger-keeper at the Union Bank. The difference between the two he pocketed. No one ever checked the figures until one day, distracted by a relative's funeral, Pullinger accidentally left both pass-books together in the office, and the discrepancy was spotted. On his return, he was questioned by the manager, and confessed everything. In five years he had extracted £263,000.[2]

The money had funded an extravagant lifestyle. Belying his reputation at the bank as a quiet man of steady habits, on the Stock Exchange he was known as a 'gigantic speculator', dealing in time bargains on some of the most volatile stocks; he was also a patron of the turf, owning several racehorses.[3] The case was a huge embarrassment for the directors, including the governor, the elderly Sir Peter Laurie, and they swiftly prosecuted their clerk for larceny. Pleading guilty did Pullinger little good. Baron William Channell, a judge with a reputation for severity, told him that he had been engaged in 'a long career of guilt', daily abusing the trust placed in him despite being paid a large salary of £600.[4] He therefore sentenced him to fourteen years' imprisonment for one of the offences—the maximum permitted—and to a further six years for the second, to run consecutively.[5]

This case, together with others in which company employees were given long sentences, has led some to conclude that embezzling clerks were invariably treated

[1] *The Times*, 28 April 1860.
[2] Ibid. 25 April 1860; *Nottinghamshire Guardian*, 10 May 1860.
[3] *Daily News*, 25 April 1860.
[4] J. A. Hamilton, rev. Hugh Mooney, 'Sir William Fry Channell', *ODNB*.
[5] *Reg. v. Pullinger* (1860), *The Times*, 16 May 1860. The maximum penalty for larceny and embezzlement was fourteen years' transportation under the Larceny Act, 1827 (7 & 8 Geo. IV c. 29 ss. 46–7), which also allowed imprisonment for up to three years and public or private whipping.

more harshly than other white-collar criminals, for their crimes 'bore the additional stigma of social insubordination'.[6] Yet judgements of 'class law' based on unrepresentative cases such as Pullinger are misleading. When the defalcations were for small amounts, which they usually were, sentences for clerks varied enormously according to the reasons for the crime, the perceived character of the offender, and the inclinations of the judge, but were rarely on the scale of the punishment inflicted on Pullinger. So, when a young clerk at the City Bank pleaded guilty to stealing £80 because he needed money to keep up appearances at an exclusive boating club he had recently joined, Judge Russell Gurney had little sympathy, claiming that only 'an honest mind' was needed to resist such temptation, and passed a deterrent sentence—not twenty years, though, but three years' penal servitude.[7] Other employees similarly tempted could receive slighter sentences still, as was the case with a cashier at the Havannah Cigar Company who pleaded guilty to embezzling several small sums to fund his forthcoming marriage and was jailed for six months.[8] Moreover, it was not just clerks among the ranks of white-collar criminals who could receive exemplary sentences. In 1858, the wealthy stockbroker William Oliver pleaded guilty to forging documents and misappropriating securities belonging to his clients, and was sentenced to twenty years' penal servitude, which was held up as proof of the lack of class bias in the criminal law.[9]

The key was not the class of the offender but the nature of the offence. The forgeries and falsifications of clerks often proved to be black-and-white cases when detected: Pullinger, like many other clerks who were found out, did not even attempt to mount a defence. Offences by directors were much greyer both in law and in morality, and it was this, not the social standing of the offenders, which led to the discrepancy in their treatment. Class did matter, but in a different way. Defrauded shareholders continued to prove reluctant in the early 1860s to deploy the Fraudulent Trustees Act against their directors, and the government was content to allow middle-class investors to sort out their own affairs. But when the culture of working-class thrift was jeopardized by swindling in financial institutions for the poor, government could be sparked into action. It was the standing of the victims, rather than the offenders, which determined the response.[10] However, the commercial crisis which struck in 1866 threatened to change everything. The exposure of

[6] The words are George Robb's: *White-Collar Crime in Modern England: Financial Fraud and Business Morality, 1845–1929* (Cambridge, 1992), 164. Robb also cites the cases of William Robson and Leopold Redpath, transfer clerks at the Crystal Palace Company and the Great Northern Railway respectively, who were convicted of embezzlement by means of falsified share transfers. The former was transported for twenty years, the latter for life: ibid. 53–4, 133–4.

[7] *Reg. v. Farrer* (1859), *The Times*, 26 October 1859.

[8] *Reg. v. Crouch* (1858), *The Times*, 15, 17 June 1858. Commentators often sympathized with embezzling clerks because of the temptations posed by lax supervision or poor pay: Gregory Anderson, *Victorian Clerks* (Manchester, 1976), 37–40.

[9] *Globe*, repr. in *The Times*, 27 November 1858. *Reg. v. Oliver* (1858), *The Times*, 26 November 1858.

[10] The difference between the liberal 'disclosure philosophy' in joint-stock companies and the 'paternalistic tradition' in savings banks and building societies has been noted, though not with reference to the criminal law: R. B. Ferguson and A. C. Page, 'The Development of Investor Protection in Britain', *International Journal of the Sociology of Law*, 12 (1984), 287–305.

abuses in a number of the City's biggest financial institutions prompted shareholders to bring criminal actions against their managements in unprecedented numbers. Magistrates, strict gatekeepers who usually resisted sending instances of alleged joint-stock fraud for trial, now proved more willing to treat such cases as public offences. Despite these initial victories, securing convictions was another matter.

THE MOST SACRED FUND

To understand attitudes to commercial fraud in the early 1860s it is instructive to compare the fallout from the failure of two financial institutions at the end of 1861. The outrage generated by both cases highlights the mounting intolerance of fraud, and the growing public appetite to see perpetrators punished, in contrast to the more equivocal views typical a generation earlier. Yet the different outcomes in the two cases underline the salience of class to political responses to fraud.

After a sustained run at its Pall Mall head office in October, the liquidation of the National Assurance and Investment Association was announced in November 1861.[11] Under the vigorous leadership of its managing director, Peter Morrison, the company had diversified into banking, and became known as the 'Bank of Deposit', or simply 'Morrison's bank', though it was not registered as such.[12] Morrison's guiding principles were blanket advertising (over £25,000 was spent on this), unusually high rates of interest to depositors, and aggressive branching. Trust was won by means of an aristocratic board, featuring the Marquess of Abercorn, Lord Edward Keane, and the Crimean veteran Lord George Paget. The bank attracted over 3,000 depositors, scattered not only throughout the country but also across the empire, notwithstanding warnings from some quarters that it was fraudulent.[13] The warnings proved correct: the accountants' report at the end of November showed that the company had never turned a profit, and its assets had been siphoned off into other companies managed by Morrison, until it was sucked nearly dry. Against liabilities of £365,000, the assets were expected to realize no more than £55,000.[14]

The case roused strong emotions. Some saw it as a national disaster; one clergyman urged his fellows to preach sermons and hold collections in aid of the sufferers, to 'relieve the orphan, the fatherless, and the widow'.[15] Morrison and his rented lords became public enemies: they had few defenders even among the financial community, the *Standard* reporting that City feeling was that 'immediate measures' should be taken to make the manager and directors criminally responsible.[16] Some commentators were certain that such a case of 'premeditated

[11] *Daily News*, 24 October 1861; *Standard*, 18 November 1861.

[12] *Belfast News-Letter*, 8 November 1861; *Sheffield and Rotherham Independent*, 26 November 1861.

[13] For example, see *The Times*, 18 March 1858.

[14] *Daily News*, 25 November 1861.

[15] Letter from William D. Dodge, *Royal Cornwall Gazette*, 29 November 1861.

[16] *Standard*, 27 November 1861.

villainy' could be punished by the criminal law.[17] Others, noting the lack of prosecutions after the Royal British Bank trial, were less sure that the law would reach the board.[18] They were right to be sceptical. Several factors militated against punishment, the chief one being the priorities of the victims. Previous company failures had seen the victims turn on each other rather than acting together against management, and this case was no different. The depositors, though numerous, were geographically dispersed and acted in small factions rather than uniting: there is no record of a general depositors' meeting ever being held. Each group employed its own solicitors who disagreed on how best to proceed, leading to suspicions that greedy lawyers were fomenting discord in order to milk the concern of its remaining assets.[19] One of the factions promised criminal proceedings once the question of liabilities was settled by Chancery, but nothing came of this.[20]

Of course, the British Bank case had shown that prosecutions need not originate with the victims. In that instance, the interrogations in the Court of Bankruptcy under the 1844 Winding-up Act had provided the legal catalyst. But the Bank of Deposit was wound up in Chancery, under the Winding-up Acts of 1848–49, and this made a difference.[21] The Master of the Rolls, Baron John Romilly, consented to the examination of the directors in open court, which some commentators saw as a prelude to criminal prosecution.[22] But this did not happen. First of all, the biggest catch—Morrison—had absconded, his whereabouts unknown.[23] The examinations of six of the other directors, including Keane and Paget, took place in his absence over three days in December.[24] They denied all knowledge of any wrongdoing and laid the blame on the absent Morrison, a line widely believed.[25] Moreover, it soon became clear that Romilly's responsibilities were not akin to those of a Bankruptcy Commissioner. The 1848–49 acts did not require the court to report to the government on the causes of failure, and Chancery Masters, deluged by a large volume of company business, saw it as their chief responsibility to expedite liquidations rather than ensuring that cases of alleged fraud were thoroughly sifted.[26] Romilly had taken the unusual step of allowing a public examination, but by the end of the third day, he had tired of the repetitive nature of the

[17] *Manchester Times*, 30 November 1861. For similar views, see *Daily News*, 25 November 1861; *Morning Post*, 26 November 1861; *Bury and Norwich Post*, 26 November 1861; *Hampshire Telegraph and Sussex Chronicle*, 30 November 1861.

[18] *The Times*, 25 November 1861; *Morning Chronicle*, 26 November 1861; *Saturday Review of Politics, Literature, Science and Art*, 30 November 1861.

[19] *Belfast News-Letter*, 22 November 1861.

[20] *Standard*, 25 November 1861; *The Times*, 28, 29 November 1861.

[21] It had not registered under the 1856 Joint-Stock Companies Act, and therefore was not wound up under its provisions.

[22] *Huddersfield Chronicle*, 28 December 1861; *Mercantile Test*, repr. in *Glasgow Herald*, 7 January 1862.

[23] *York Herald*, 28 December 1861.

[24] *The Times*, 18, 19, 21 December 1861.

[25] *Sheffield and Rotherham Independent*, 21 December 1861; *Standard*, 24 December 1861.

[26] The 1856 Joint-Stock Companies Act had similar provisions: 19 & 20 Vict. c. 47, ss. 77–8.

disclosures and refused to name a date for the continuation of proceedings. No specific charges against the directors emerged.[27]

Meanwhile, Morrison remained out of harm's way, prompting rumours of a cover-up: the government refused to pursue him because he knew the secrets of too many powerful people.[28] The more likely reality was that there was not a strong enough moral case to justify intervention. After the initial shock had dissipated, the public mood turned against the victims. An anonymous letter to the *Sheffield and Rotherham Independent* blamed the victims of such bank failures: 'What infatuation!...the only way to teach the multitude common sense on this subject is the suffering of loss'.[29] Leader writers queued up to lecture investors never to trust aristocratic names on prospectuses.[30] They hoped that the public would learn from the episode, but some were doubtful: once the fuss had died down, new fraudsters would find plenty 'willing to enjoy the pleasure of being cheated'.[31] The victims were a mix of tradesmen and hard-up members of the middle classes, but the one thing they had in common was that rather than contenting themselves with legitimate rates of interest, they had blindly chased higher returns heedless of risk.[32] The moral justification for intervention was therefore weak, and the case was not even raised in parliament.

There was a different result following another bank failure soon afterwards, however. The trigger was quite innocuous. In March 1861, John Tidd Pratt, the barrister employed by the government to certify the rules of savings banks, gave a lecture on self-help at Bilston, an industrial town in the Black Country. In his talk, he alluded to the local savings bank, and criticized the loose way in which it made its weekly returns to the National Debt Commissioners, stressing the importance of accurate bookkeeping and regular audits.[33] His comments sparked an administrative overhaul at the bank, new trustees and a new actuary were elected, and proper auditing procedures established. At the end of the year, the actuary found a black hole of close to £9,000 in the bank's accounts—nearly a third of its total assets—and called in the secretary, Reverend Horatio Fletcher, to explain. Fletcher admitted that he had taken the money, and Pratt advised that the bank be shut down and its remaining assets divided amongst the depositors.[34]

A well-respected local figure, Reverend Fletcher had been the incumbent of Bilston since 1825, was a magistrate, and had been closely identified with the bank since its foundation in 1838. Its business was transacted every Monday in the

[27] *Standard*, 21 December 1861; *The Times*, 21 December 1861; *Birmingham Daily Post*, 26 December 1861.

[28] *Reynolds's Newspaper*, 23, 30 March 1862.

[29] *Sheffield and Rotherham Independent*, 3 December 1861.

[30] *Standard*, 24 December 1861; *Spectator*, repr. in *Aberdeen Journal*, 25 December 1861; *Caledonian Mercury*, 27 December 1861; *Huddersfield Chronicle*, 28 December 1861; *Lloyd's Weekly Newspaper*, 29 December 1861.

[31] *Standard*, 21 February 1862.

[32] *Saturday Review of Politics, Literature, Science and Art*, 30 November 1861, *Belfast News-Letter*, 8 November 1861.

[33] *Birmingham Daily Post*, 28 March 1861.

[34] Ibid. 3, 16 January 1862.

schoolroom attached to Fletcher's church; Fletcher or his wife transported the books between the school and the parsonage.[35] How he abused this position of trust was revealed at a depositors' meeting chaired by Pratt in the middle of January 1862, attended by 400 of the bank's 1,400 depositors. Fletcher had kept depositors' books correctly, but had systematically falsified the returns to the government. For example, one week Fletcher recorded receipts of £183 and payments of £148, whereas the receipts should have been £283 and the payments £48: that week he therefore abstracted £200 for himself. Such a simple fraud was supposed to be impossible: the secretary received the money from the depositors and accounted for it to the treasurer, but both offices were held by Fletcher. The actuary never detected the frauds because, until 1861, Fletcher held this post too. Pratt's revelations provided grist to moralists across the country: Fletcher's conduct was 'shocking' and 'disgraceful'; he was 'the meanest, the most cowardly, and the most cruel of swindlers'.[36]

As in so many previous cases, the victims were keener to recoup their losses than pursue justice. The committee of management formed to wind up the bank's affairs wanted to maximize returns for the depositors by negotiating a private settlement with Fletcher, rather than launching criminal proceedings. Nevertheless, Fletcher's fate did not rest in the hands of the committee alone. After the depositors' meeting, Pratt raised the case with the law officers of the Crown, chiefly to discuss the civil liability of the bank's trustees.[37] But William Atherton, who had been involved in the British Bank prosecution and was now Attorney General under Palmerston, decided that Fletcher was criminally liable under the terms of the Fraudulent Trustees Act, and that it was 'incumbent on the Government to prosecute'. On 21 February, Atherton wrote to the Treasury authorizing proceedings, and six days later Fletcher was arrested on a warrant charging him with 'feloniously appropriating several sums of money to his own use'. At Birmingham police court, the Reverend appeared 'miserably haggard and careworn', and 'appeared deeply to feel his humiliating position'. With nothing to say in his defence, he was committed for trial.[38] 'English justice is no respecter of persons', concluded one commentator.[39]

Fletcher's trial took place over two days in March at the Staffordshire Spring Assizes before Baron Channell, the judge who had condemned Pullinger to twenty years' imprisonment. Fletcher was indicted on six specific instances of misappropriating deposits for his own use with intent to defraud. Henry Matthews, Fletcher's defence counsel, and a rising star on the Oxford circuit, marshalled a host of arguments for his client. First, he pointed out that the committee of management opposed the prosecution: a guilty verdict would be a disaster for the bank's depositors as Fletcher's living would be forfeited, depriving them of the proceeds. Second,

[35] Ibid. 28 February 1862.

[36] Ibid. 8 January 1862; *Dundee Courier and Daily Argus*, 23 January 1862; *The Times*, 17 January 1862.

[37] *Birmingham Daily Post*, 16 January 1862.

[38] *Morning Post*, 28 February 1862; *Birmingham Daily Post*, 28 February 1862.

[39] *Blackburn Standard*, 5 March 1862.

he played on Fletcher's good character and record of charitable works among his parishioners. Third, there was no evidence of intent to defraud. Though curiously silent on what Fletcher had actually done with the money, he claimed that making false accounts might be 'reprehensible' but was not proof of intent to defraud: 'supposing he had lent [the money] to a friend, expecting to receive every farthing of it again whenever the negligent trustees should call for it, he could not... be charged with intent'. But his principal line of argument was a technical one. Fletcher was not a trustee under the terms of the Fraudulent Trustees Act, and there was consequently no case to answer. As treasurer he held the money as servant of the trustees, rather than as a trustee himself. If he had misappropriated money as a treasurer, he would have to be indicted under a different statute.[40]

In his summing up, Channell praised Matthews's 'ingenious' lines of argument, but dismissed most of them. The jury had to reach a verdict based on the facts, not on suppositions of what the consequences of their verdict might be, nor on evidence of good character. On the key question of intent, he suggested to the jury that Fletcher's intentions might be ascertained from 'the number of false returns, and the time over which they extended'. However, he decided to reserve the point about Fletcher's status as a trustee so that it could be decided by a superior court if necessary. The jury found the facts of the case plain, and took just ten minutes to convict. Yet Channell agreed to Fletcher's release on bail while the technical point was decided.[41]

Disappointment greeted Fletcher's release, and it seemed that he might ultimately go free.[42] Five judges of the Exchequer Chamber discussed his case in early May but could not agree, so a decision was postponed until the following term when the case could go before all the judges.[43] In June the full court, headed by the new Chief Justice Alexander Cockburn, upheld the conviction, ruling that Fletcher was legally a trustee for the bank.[44] Fletcher returned to Staffordshire Assizes to be sentenced to two years' imprisonment without hard labour.[45] The local press argued that though the sentence seemed relatively light, Fletcher's punishment was 'really very heavy'. He was 'simply and entirely a ruined man': for a man in his position, 'no punishment can exceed the horror of detection and exposure'.[46]

This was the first successful attempt to use the Fraudulent Trustees Act in relation to a commercial institution. Why had the government chosen to act now but not in the Bank of Deposit case? After all, as *Reynolds's Newspaper* observed, the Bilston affair was just a 'flea-bite' by comparison.[47] To some extent, the Bilston scandal implicated the state more than regular joint-stock frauds. Whilst Pratt was

[40] *Reg. v. Fletcher* (1862) 9 Cox 189, *Birmingham Daily Post*, 14, 15 March 1862.
[41] *Birmingham Daily Post*, 15 March 1862; *Morning Post*, 15 March 1862.
[42] *Birmingham Daily Post*, 22 March 1862; *The Times*, 17 March 1862.
[43] *The Times*, 5 May 1862.
[44] Ibid. 9, 16 June 1862.
[45] *Birmingham Daily Post*, 23, 24 July 1862; *Sheffield and Rotherham Independent*, 23 July 1862.
[46] *Birmingham Daily Post*, 26 July 1862.
[47] *Reynolds's Newspaper*, 12 January 1862.

adamant that the negligence lay wholly with the bank's trustees, some blamed the Commissioners for not intervening and closing down the bank when the problems with its accounts were spotted.[48] There were also bureaucratic factors. Whereas the Joint-Stock Companies Registrar was a largely impotent functionary, Pratt had more powers and was a far more dynamic figure, instrumental in raising the Bilston case with the government's law officers.[49] But the main factor was the desire to nurture self-help among the working classes. This had just been underlined by Gladstone's 1861 Post Office Savings Banks (POSB) Act, designed to provide a safe outlet for small savings, and contemporary commentary gives a clue as to how seriously the investments of the poor were regarded.[50] For *The Times*, the £36 million invested in savings banks was 'the most sacred fund which exists'.[51] Frauds like the Bilston case were doubly dangerous as they weakened 'the reliance of the labouring classes upon persons above them in the social scale', and discouraged the habit of thrift.[52] Depositors in savings banks were not speculators aiming for outrageous profits, but poor people investing spare shillings. And with no say in the management, they could not be accused of negligence when they were defrauded.

The government's action in this case was unusual, but not unique. In 1863, the Treasury took on the prosecution of the secretary, treasurer, and collector of the Perseverance Life Assurance and Sick Fund Friendly Society after several of its policyholders complained of non-payment to Pratt, who was also Friendly Societies Registrar. At the start of the Old Bailey trial, the prosecution explained that given the nature of the fraud alleged, and the victims' want of means, the Treasury 'felt it their duty to take care that the matter should undergo proper investigation'. The men were indicted for a conspiracy, and the crux of the prosecution case was that the society had always been a sham, its sole purpose being 'by false pretences to induce poor persons to hand over sums of money to them which they applied to their own use'. But, as in the Bilston case, the prosecution proved far from straightforward. The defence called a series of witnesses who testified that they had been paid promptly on the death of insured parties, even after the commencement of the present legal proceedings. When the society could go on no longer, its policies were handed over to another society, demonstrating the defendants' care for their customers. The defence admitted that the society's business had been 'somewhat loosely conducted', but appealed to the jury 'as men of business and men of the world' that there was no evidence of conspiracy to defraud. Nevertheless, to the surprise of most present, including the judge, Common Serjeant Thomas Chambers, the jury found the three guilty. Chambers distanced himself from the verdict, but sentenced the men to eighteen months' hard labour.[53] As in the Bilston case, the government

48 *The Times*, 4, 6 January 1862. The scandal also led to legislation in 1863 amending the law relating to savings banks, which remained the principal act regulating the sector long into the twentieth century: H. Oliver Horne, *A History of Savings Banks* (London, 1947), 209–16.

49 Peter Gosden, 'John Tidd Pratt', *ODNB*.

50 24 & 25 Vict. c. 14. For more on the act, see Horne, *Savings Banks*, ch. 9.

51 *The Times*, 17 January 1862.

52 *Dundee Courier and Daily Argus*, 23 January 1862. See also *Aberdeen Journal*, 22 January 1862.

53 *Reg. v. Knowlden* (1863), *Standard*, 28, 29 October 1863; *Daily News*, 28, 29 October 1863.

had successfully deployed the criminal law to shore up confidence in the structures of self-help considered so important for improving the working classes.[54]

LYING IN UNITY

After the legislative flurry remodelling company law between 1855 and 1858, the pace of change slackened; nevertheless there were two consolidating acts in the early 1860s which were significant. The first came as part of a wider package of criminal law rationalization in 1861. A host of criminal statutes covering crimes against property, including the Fraudulent Trustees Act, were repealed and replaced by the Larceny Act.[55] The new measure largely restated the provisions of the 1857 act, though with one significant difference. Whereas the former had stipulated punishments of three years' penal servitude or up to two years' imprisonment, with the freedom to levy a fine as an alternative, the Larceny Act set out a harsher punishment scale of between three and seven years' penal servitude, or two years' imprisonment with or without hard labour, and removed the option of a fine. This still left acts of fraud by company management at a lower level in the hierarchy of crimes than embezzlement by company servants, the maximum penalty for which remained fourteen years, but higher than obtaining money by false pretences, now punishable by up to three years' penal servitude.[56] The penalties were further augmented by the 1864 Penal Servitude Act which raised the minimum sentence of penal servitude for all first offences to five years, seven for subsequent offences.[57]

A second consolidating measure followed in 1862, this time rationalizing the many statutes regulating joint-stock companies. Introduced by the Solicitor General, Sir Roundell Palmer, the 1862 Companies Act continued many of the permissive provisions of its predecessor of 1856, leaving most of the key constitutional decisions to companies themselves, though again setting out a model default constitution in a table at the end of the act.[58] But aside from its permissiveness—the quality most historians have stressed—it also had implications for the criminal liability of directors.[59] Pulling together provisions contained in the original act of 1856, and the amendment acts of 1857–58, it standardized the procedures for winding up, making the Court of Chancery the default authority, and providing

[54] Further evidence of this aim was the establishment in 1864 of a state annuity and life insurance scheme operated through the POSB to provide a safe alternative to fraudulent societies, though it was not a success: Dermot Morrah, *A History of Industrial Life Assurance* (Abingdon, 2006), ch. 3.

[55] The Fraudulent Trustees Act was repealed by the Criminal Statutes Repeal Act, 1861, passed at the same time as the Larceny Act. However, the act stipulated that offences committed before its passage would be tried under the former laws (24 & 25 Vict. c. 95, s. 3). This is why Fletcher was not tried under the Larceny Act.

[56] Ibid. ss. 75, 68, 88. Obtaining money by false pretences had been punishable by up to seven years under the 1827 Larceny Act: 7 & 8 Geo. IV c. 29, s. 53.

[57] 27 & 28 Vict. c. 47, s. 2.

[58] 25 & 26 Vict. c. 89, table A.

[59] For an interpretation stressing permissiveness, see P. L. Cottrell, *Industrial Finance, 1830–1914* (London, 1980), 54.

three methods for terminating companies: by the court ('compulsory liquidation'), voluntary liquidation outside the court, and voluntary liquidation under the supervision of the court. Chancery had summary powers to arrest any contributory suspected of planning to abscond, and could compel directors, managers, and officers who had misapplied or retained company money to repay it with interest. Most significantly, if it appeared that any director, manager, officer, or member was guilty of a criminal offence, the court could, either on the application of anyone interested in the winding-up or of its own volition, direct the official liquidator to prosecute, the costs to be paid out of the company's assets.[60] While many of these provisions had been first introduced in the earlier legislation, they now had a wider reach, for the new act applied not only to banks but also insurance companies, which had until now been excluded.

The new system implied that Chancery judges would be more involved in making judgements on the criminality of company officials than they had been in cases such as the Bank of Deposit. The act can therefore be seen as consistent with the Bankruptcy Act passed the previous year. Though imprisonment was losing favour as a way of dealing with insolvent debtors, attitudes to *fraudulent* debtors were stiffening. An experiment in moral regulation by means of certificates of bankruptcy introduced in 1849 was widely believed to have failed, leading to a growing conviction that fraudulent bankrupts were best dealt with by the criminal law.[61] Therefore, as well as defining the offences punishable as misdemeanours, such as concealing assets and falsifying books, in far more detail than before, the 1861 act gave the Bankruptcy Court power to punish those whose insolvency was judged to be due to 'rash and hazardous speculation, or unjustifiable extravagance in living' by imprisonment for up to a year.[62]

The Times praised the 1862 Companies Act's 'stringent provisions against delinquent directors' and anticipated that they would help to 'check practices which are the standing disgrace of our times'.[63] These hopes would be put to the test by a complex bank failure in the middle of the decade. In 1862 the management of a small London bank, the Unity Joint-Stock Mutual Banking Association, issued a balance sheet showing small profits in order to persuade its shareholders to invest in a new venture, the London and Middlesex Bank, which would take over the deposit accounts of the Unity.[64] Most of the shareholders went along with the proposal, which involved the rest of the Unity's business being wound up voluntarily by the directors, with shareholders told to expect a sizeable dividend. However,

[60] 25 & 26 Vict. c. 89, ss. 118, 165, 167–8.

[61] The act of 1849 had tried to tackle fraudulent debtors by implementing a sliding scale of certificates issued by the Bankruptcy Commissioners. These ranged from first-class for those whose failure was entirely due to 'unavoidable losses and misfortunes', to third-class for those whose failure was down to recklessness or dishonesty, the belief being that the stigma of the lower-grade certificate would be enough to police behaviour. Barbara Weiss, *The Hell of the English: Bankruptcy and the Victorian Novel* (Cranbury, NJ, 1986), 43–5; 12 & 13 Vict. c. 106, schedule Z.

[62] 24 & 25 Vict. c. 134, ss. 159, 221; James Fitzjames Stephen, *A History of the Criminal Law of England*, 3 vols (1883; repr. Abingdon, 1996), i. 231.

[63] *The Times*, 22 November 1862.

[64] *Morning Post*, 28 August 1862.

when the liquidation stalled, and when the London and Middlesex was itself absorbed a year later by the London and Westminster Bank, the shareholders revolted, appointing a shareholders' committee to sit on the directors' liquidation committee and investigate the Unity's accounts. The committee found that rather than the profit of £2,255 claimed by the balance sheet, the bank had actually lost over £133,000. The balance sheet misstated the amount of paid-up capital and the amount of deposits, and listed the preliminary expenses of the bank (over £32,000) and dishonoured bills as assets.[65]

In November 1864, the liquidation committee launched criminal proceedings against the bank's manager and secretary, Joseph Terry and Thomas Burch, for circulating a false balance sheet, their motive being to secure lucrative employment in the new bank.[66] Selecting George Lewis, a rising star in the legal firmament, to lead the prosecution proved a smart move, and after nearly two months of investigation in the justice room of the Mansion House, Lord Mayor Warren Hale committed both men for trial.[67] Initial suspicions that they were being made scapegoats for the directors were quelled when it emerged that the decision to prosecute was taken by the shareholders on the committee of liquidation, not the directors, who were present, but did not vote.[68] In fact, the directors were hugely embarrassed by the investigations at Mansion House. Several were called to give evidence, including the bank's chairman and Hale's fellow alderman, John Mechi.[69] Their testimony showed that they should never have been allowed near a bank: they had demonstrated 'negligence so gross . . . that the result could not have been more disastrous if the spirit of Innes Cameron or of Colonel Waugh had animated their deliberations'.[70] Disinclined to repeat their humiliation at the Old Bailey, the directors now threw a spanner in the works. In January 1865, they raised legal objections to the prosecution, claiming that the shareholders' committee which had voted to prosecute was a committee of *assistance* to the directors, and had no authority to authorize legal proceedings without the approval of a general meeting. By depriving the committee of the necessary funds this stalled the prosecution. Acknowledging the mistrust that now existed between directors and shareholders, they proposed resolving the affair by petitioning to have the bank wound up under the supervision of Chancery.[71]

Lewis now wrote to Home Secretary Sir George Grey requesting support. He did not anticipate that the prosecution costs would much exceed £1,000, and to justify intervention, he cited the Royal British Bank prosecution—'similar in every respect to the present'—which the Treasury had funded. But he received a terse

[65] *The Times*, 4 November 1864.

[66] Ibid.; *Standard*, 31 January 1865.

[67] *The Times*, 30 December 1864.

[68] Ibid. 16 November 1864. For articulations of the scapegoating thesis, see *Daily News*, 5 November 1864; *Sheffield and Rotherham Independent*, 7 November 1864; 'Northumbrian' in *Reynolds's Newspaper*, 13 November 1864.

[69] *The Times*, 12, 19 December 1864.

[70] *London Review*, repr. in *Trewman's Exeter Flying Post*, 21 December 1864. For Cameron and Waugh, see Chapter 5.

[71] *Morning Post*, 30 January 1865; *Standard*, 31 January 1865; *Daily News*, 25 February 1865.

reply from Thomas Baring, Grey's under secretary, that the Home Secretary was 'not aware of any peculiarity in this case to call for the special interference of the Government'. Despite two more appeals, which represented the false balance sheet as 'a crime against the whole banking and commercial community of this country', Grey remained unmoved.[72] The government, which had funded the Bilston and Perseverance prosecutions to protect working-class investors, was unwilling to contemplate subsidizing the costs faced by more affluent shareholders. It seemed that Grey's decision had killed the case: the abandonment of the prosecution was widely reported.[73] But the directors' plan of going to Chancery for a supervised liquidation gave the shareholders one last hope, thanks to the 1862 Companies Act.[74] The shareholders applied to Master of the Rolls Baron Romilly requesting that he order the prosecution be financed out of the bank's assets. He consented, and the trial began barely a fortnight later, in the middle of April.[75] The new machinery had proved sufficient to bring the case to trial, but would the law confirm the criminality of publishing false balance sheets?

The trial took place against the backdrop of a rising tide of speculation in joint-stock companies, which the prosecution counsel, Hardinge Giffard, tried to turn to his advantage, justifying the prosecution on the grounds of protecting investors. It was extremely important, 'when joint-stock associations of this description were so much on the increase', that the public should be protected from false statements. '[I]f the law did not interpose, nothing would be easier than for persons to get up public companies, and by means of false balance-sheets... the public might be defrauded to an enormous amount'.[76] Giffard's view chimed with an increasingly popular view of shareholders as powerless in the face of company management, and therefore utterly reliant on the accuracy of company statements. 'The balance-sheet is the only guide for ninety-nine shareholders out of a hundred', commented the *Daily News*.[77] But others held a more traditional view of shareholders as partners, with all the rights and responsibilities this entailed. Unfortunately for the prosecution, one of these was the judge, Justice Montague Smith, a Conservative, a commercial law specialist, and 'an accurate and painstaking' judge.[78] When it emerged during Mechi's evidence that the company's accounts were audited—as was common practice in the sector—by two shareholders appointed at the general meeting, Smith scented weakness. He argued that the defendants' willingness to submit their accounts for audit made it difficult to argue that there was any intention to deceive; Giffard retorted that the auditors were deceived along

[72] *Copy of all Correspondence between the Secretary of State for the Home Department and Messrs. Lewis and Lewis, on behalf of persons interested in the affairs of the Unity Bank, respecting the Prosecution of Messrs. Terry and Burch*, PP 1865 XXX.

[73] See, for example, *Morning Post*, 25 March 1865; *Sheffield and Rotherham Independent*, 27 March 1865.

[74] *Daily News*, 25 February 1865.

[75] *The Times*, 31 March 1865.

[76] *Reg. v. Burch* (1865) 176 ER 622, *Morning Post*, 18 April 1865.

[77] *Daily News*, 5 November 1864.

[78] David Pugsley, 'Sir Montague Edward Smith', *ODNB*.

with everyone else. Smith insisted that the one surviving auditor be called to give evidence. The auditor testified that officials never attempted to hold back any books: they were always 'readily produced' when requested. Smith thought it was 'rather remarkable under these circumstances that the alleged fraud was not discovered', and believed that 'upon this evidence the jury could hardly be expected to convict'. A majority of the jury decided to continue with the trial, but now the prosecution was hobbled, and it was no surprise when the defendants were eventually acquitted.[79]

The case had been decided on an interpretation by the judge, accepted by the jury, which conceptualized companies as large partnerships. The books were not concealed from the men chosen from among the partners to represent the whole—the auditors—and the truth of the company's finances was in these books; therefore there was no attempt to hide the truth from the partners. The verdict had worrying implications: by Smith's logic, it was difficult to see how managers could be made legally responsible to shareholders.[80] Moreover, while the falsity of the balance sheet had not been disputed, no one had been punished for its publication: did this mean false balance sheets were not criminal?[81] Both the responsibilities of managers and the legal status of misrepresentation would be made a little clearer in the aftermath of a monumental crash which was just around the corner.

1866 AND ALL THAT

The concession of limited liability in the mid 1850s did not lead to a sudden boom in company formations. Though the number of registrations grew, from 306 in 1858 to 512 in 1862, many of these were small, experimental, and ultimately abortive enterprises.[82] But 1863 saw a major bull market in the City, fed by the surfeit of capital seeking new outlets as a result of the American Civil War, prompting speculative formations. In 1863, 760 limited companies were registered, 975 in 1864, and 1,014 in 1865.[83] Among the most fashionable investments were finance companies, modelled on France's Crédit Mobilier, monster organizations which mobilized large sums of capital for an eclectic range of often highly speculative undertakings.[84] Unknown in the City before 1863, there were fifty of them by 1866.[85] The other key feature of the boom was the conversion of hundreds of private firms to limited companies, a move cautiously welcomed by the *Economist* as

[79] *Morning Post*, 19, 20 April 1865; *The Times*, 19, 20, 21 April 1865.
[80] *Daily News*, 21 April 1865; *Birmingham Daily Post*, 24 April 1865.
[81] *Morning Post*, 21 April 1865.
[82] D. Morier Evans, *Speculative Notes and Notes on Speculation, Ideal and Real* (1864; repr. New York, 1969), 228–9.
[83] Ibid. 230; H. A. Shannon, 'The First Five Thousand Limited Companies and their Duration', *Economic History*, 3 (1932), 421.
[84] David Kynaston, *The City of London: Volume 1, A World of Its Own, 1815–1890* (London, 1994), 220–1.
[85] Bishop Carleton Hunt, *The Development of the Business Corporation in England, 1800–1867* (Cambridge, MA, 1936), 147.

furnishing capitalists with a broader 'choice of good investments'.[86] However, not all the investments were good, and the financial journalist David Morier Evans claimed that the amount of 'jobbery' among the new promotions surpassed the bubble eras of 1824–25 and 1845.[87]

Fears about the soundness of many of the new ventures proved justified with the failure in early 1866 of a company which exemplified both of the central characteristics of the boom. The Joint-Stock Discount Company was formed in 1863 with a nominal capital of £2 million to take over the discount business of the broker James Freeling Wilkinson. Wilkinson was made managing director of the new concern, whose prospects seemed good. But unsupervised by his board, Wilkinson swiftly turned to finance, tying up the company's capital in a series of risky ventures. At the start of the year 'well-informed speculators' began dumping its shares, and in March its directors declared insolvency, prompting a slide in the shares of other finance companies.[88] As anxiety mounted, the press tried to pacify the market, claiming that the alarm 'has been carried to excess'.[89] This seemed true when speculative sellers began 'bearing' the shares of Overend, Gurney, and Co., the most respected discount house in the City. But when the share value dropped, pressure for repayment of deposits grew, and after the Bank of England declined to help, the unthinkable happened: Overend and Gurney suspended payment. The shock was immense and a full-blown panic followed on 'Black Friday', 11 May, which destroyed many of the new finance companies and banks; more than 200 joint stocks went bust in three months.[90]

Many culprits were fingered for the crisis: the Bank of England, short-sellers on the Stock Exchange, greedy investors.[91] But as the bankrupt concerns were wound up, it soon became clear that corrupt governance was also to blame, and shareholders proved more willing than in previous decades to pursue their managements into the criminal courts. Misappropriation of company money was the first offence to be tested. As with the Unity Bank, the powers vested in the Court of Chancery by the 1862 Companies Act proved instrumental. The first case concerned Wilkinson's Joint-Stock Discount Company, whose collapse in March had triggered the crisis. While the company's paper assets were more than sufficient to cover its liabilities of £3.9 million, there was significant doubt as to their real value. At a general meeting shortly after the failure, shareholders were told that the company's affairs were so complex and intertwined with other firms that it was impossible to say what the total loss would be. Throughout the meeting 'there were constant cries on the part of the proprietors that criminal proceedings should be instituted'.[92] Indeed, the scandalous nature of the company's transactions led the Master of the Rolls to reject the directors' request that the company be wound up

[86] *Economist*, 10 December 1864.
[87] Evans, *Speculative Notes*, 78–9.
[88] *The Times*, 1 February, 8, 12 March 1866.
[89] Ibid. 30 April 1866.
[90] Hunt, *Business Corporation*, 154.
[91] *Money Market Review*, 12, 19 May 1866; *The Times*, 14 May 1866.
[92] *The Times*, 19 March 1866.

voluntarily, instead ordering a compulsory liquidation, with Robert Palmer Harding as official liquidator.[93]

During the liquidation it transpired that the previous August, Wilkinson had used the company's money to pay a private debt of £5,000 to the stockbrokers Capper, Escombe, and Lawson. In the company's accounts, Wilkinson recorded the transaction as a loan to the brokers, but when Capper was examined in Chancery he denied that he owed the company anything.[94] As a result of the discovery of such a blatant case of misappropriation, Harding felt it 'a public duty' to act. He secured the leave of the court to prosecute Wilkinson, who was arrested on charges of fraudulently taking company money, framed under the Larceny Act. When he appeared at the justice room of Mansion House, the proceedings attracted 'extraordinary interest', with the court 'crowded by gentlemen connected with banking and other commercial concerns'.[95] After three hearings, the Lord Mayor Thomas Gabriel decided that there was enough evidence to send Wilkinson for trial.[96] Convicted at the Old Bailey, he was sentenced to penal servitude for five years.[97]

The case was notable for three reasons. Wilkinson was the first victim of the crisis of 1866 in the criminal courts. He was the first senior figure in a joint-stock company to be convicted under the Larceny Act.[98] And his sentence was five times as long as that given to the worst of the British Bank offenders. The outcome landed like a bombshell on the City, indicating the extent to which company directors had considered themselves immune to prosecution. One paper observed that the verdict had 'fluttered the dovecots' of the Stock Exchange:

> It was not at all supposed he would be convicted.... People in the City laughed at the trial, and took it for granted the prisoner would 'get off'. Even now, when the astonishment has subsided, they say there must have been a sufferer by the Company amongst the Jurors. So lowered is our commercial morality, that it seems incredible to business men a thief on a large scale should get any punishment.[99]

Wilkinson and his company were widely held up as emblems of the excesses of the last few years, and his conviction was favourably received by the press, with hopes expressed that it would correct 'the lax notions of right and wrong' prevalent among company managements.[100]

However, some noted that while the sentence was 'just recompense for his conduct in squandering the property of the shareholders', this was not the offence for

[93] *Daily News*, 19 March 1866. Harding's firm had filled the same role in the Royal British Bank liquidation: Garry D. Carnegie, 'Sir Robert Palmer Harding', *ODNB*.

[94] *The Times*, 10 November 1866.

[95] Ibid.; *Morning Post*, 10 November 1866.

[96] *The Times*, 15, 24 November 1866.

[97] *Reg. v. Wilkinson* (1867), *The Times*, 10, 11 January 1867.

[98] Edward Greenland, manager of the Leeds Banking Company which had collapsed in 1864, was convicted in October 1866 and sentenced to fifteen months' imprisonment with hard labour. Though he faced charges under the Larceny Act, he was actually convicted for perjury in relation to false returns of the bank's notes and bills to the Commissioner of Stamps. *Reg. v. Greenland* (1866), *Leeds Mercury*, 26 October 1866.

[99] *Bury and Norwich Post*, 15 January 1867.

[100] *Standard*, 12 January 1867; *London Review*, 12 January 1867.

which Wilkinson was convicted.[101] Even the judge, Baron Gillery Pigott, had seemed more concerned in his sentencing speech with Wilkinson's general mismanagement of the company than with the misappropriation of the £5,000.[102] This disjunction raised doubts about how far the outcome would really clarify the law. It also provided fuel for a concerted campaign in the City to secure Wilkinson's early release—it was widely felt that he had been unfairly punished as an example.[103] Such arguments cut little ice with the Home Office, but when it subsequently emerged that the evidence on which Wilkinson had been convicted was false—the money he was accused of taking was in fact borrowed by the stockbrokers, as he had always insisted—he received a free pardon in July 1868, eighteen months into his sentence.[104]

Despite this, three subsequent prosecutions based on sounder evidence established misappropriation by managers as within the ambit of the criminal law. The new power given to Chancery to authorize prosecutions was deployed in the case of the Oriental Commercial Bank. One of the casualties of May 1866, it was wound up under the supervision of the court. During the liquidation, it emerged that there had been much blurring of the boundaries between the bank's money and that of its manager, Demetrio Pappa, and on the application of the creditors, Vice-Chancellor William James authorized his prosecution. His defalcations amounted to £10,000 and he owed the bank a further £6,000, but he was prosecuted for a single transaction in which he used £800 subscribed by a share applicant to pay off a private debt. Though the jury recommended him to mercy on account of his previous good character, the Recorder Russell Gurney—no relation of the Gurney bankers—sentenced him to five years' penal servitude.[105] A private shareholder prosecuted Samuel Greenway Finney, manager of the English Joint-Stock Bank which failed the day after Overend and Gurney, under the Larceny Act for appropriating the bank's money and failing to enter the transactions in the company's books. At the Old Bailey in July 1869, Finney pleaded guilty to the appropriation of £666, his counsel appealing for mercy on account of his advanced years and large family. But Gurney decreed that this was an offence which 'must be checked by punishment' and sentenced him to twelve months' imprisonment.[106] A third prosecution showed that the 1861 Bankruptcy Act could also be used against joint-stock company personnel if they petitioned for personal bankruptcy. William Shipman, the London manager of the Agra and Masterman's Bank which had collapsed in June 1866, passed his examination but his discharge was opposed by his largest creditors, the bank's directors. The court decided that Shipman's secret partnership with one of the bank's customers, in which they used the bank's money to gamble in loans and shares, racking up losses of over £70,000, consti-

101 *Standard*, 12 January 1867; *Sheffield and Rotherham Independent*, 14, 15 January 1867.
102 *The Times*, 11 January 1867.
103 Ibid. 15 April, 27 May 1867.
104 Ibid. 22 March 1867, 7 July 1868.
105 *Reg. v. Pappa* (1870), *The Times*, 7 January, 6, 7 May 1870.
106 *Reg. v. Finney* (1869), *The Times*, 15 July 1869; *Morning Post*, 15 July 1869.

tuted 'rash and hazardous speculation', and he was sentenced to twelve months in Whitecross Street Prison.[107]

The string of prosecutions represented a significant break with the previous business culture of avoiding recourse to the law in dispute resolution. It was encouraged partly by the growing size of joint-stock constituencies and the consequent attenuation of social ties between directors, shareholders, and creditors. It was also a result of the formalization of winding-up practices and the establishment of procedures for bringing criminal actions. While trials in Queen's Bench were heard before special juries of bankers, merchants, and esquires, thus preserving a sense in which the commercial community was settling its own disputes, fraud cases were more often decided before ordinary juries in the Central Criminal Court: a clearer shift away from previous habits of self-regulation.[108] Fraudulent misappropriation by clerks and other lower officials had long been successfully punished by the criminal law, but making managers and managing directors criminally liable for these offences had hitherto proven more difficult.[109] The successful prosecutions demonstrate a new willingness of the criminal courts to regulate behaviour in the joint-stock economy in the interests of shareholders and creditors. Nevertheless, embezzlement was not the chief scandal of the 1866 crash. The biggest company to fall, Overend and Gurney, highlighted another, more serious, type of fraud: misrepresentations and concealments in prospectuses that induced investors to place their trust in insolvent firms.

Of all the failures of 1866, Overend and Gurney's was the one which caused the most astonishment. 'Men who heard the news in their counting-houses and offices refused to believe it, but rushed forth and pressed their way through the dense masses congregated in the streets around, in order to *see* that the doors were really closed'.[110] Until 1865 a private firm, its successful flotation in July of that year with a nominal capital of £5 million was heralded as 'the greatest triumph which limited liability has yet achieved'.[111] The shares had been hugely popular with investors:

[107] *Re William Shipman* (1869), *The Times*, 21 April 1869; *Birmingham Daily Post*, 21 April 1869. However, Shipman was released after having served less than half of his sentence due to ill health: *Pall Mall Gazette*, 15 October 1869.

[108] The self-regulation thesis is advanced in Sarah Wilson, 'Law Morality and Regulation: Victorian Experiences of Financial Crime', *British Journal of Criminology*, 46 (2006), 1085–8. Though there were still property (and gender) qualifications for common juries, a familiar nineteenth-century complaint was that educated men were rarely to be found on them: David Bentley, *English Criminal Justice in the Nineteenth Century* (London, 1998), ch. 10.

[109] This was particularly true of banks. Despite the change in the law in 1840 to facilitate actions against company officials who were also shareholders, such prosecutions remained difficult. In 1855, the directors of the Shropshire Banking Company refrained from prosecuting their manager and cashier, suspected of embezzling up to £160,000, in the belief that as shareholders they were not amenable to the criminal law. In 1856, the directors of the Gloucestershire Banking Company prosecuted a branch manager for embezzling £3,250, but Judge William Wightman argued that as a shareholder in the bank, 'great difficulty must arise in charging him with embezzling his own property', and the case collapsed: *Reg. v. Evans* (1856), *Bristol Mercury*, 9 August 1856. See also *Berrow's Worcester Journal*, 17 February 1855.

[110] *Money Market Review*, 19 May 1866.

[111] *Bankers Magazine*, quoted in Paul Barnes, 'A Victorian Financial Crisis: The Scandalous Implications of the Case of Overend Gurney', in Judith Rowbotham and Kim Stevenson (eds), *Criminal Conversations: Victorian Crimes, Social Panic, and Moral Outrage* (Columbus, OH, 2005), 59.

100,000 were issued, but applications were received for over twice this amount.[112] However, the liquidators' report issued a month after its collapse showed that, far from taking on a sound firm, the limited company had purchased a business drowning in bad debts—paying half a million pounds for it. The purchase was effected by two deeds of transfer, but only one of these was mentioned in the company's prospectus; the second, private deed transferred the private firm's debts to the company, and this was kept from the shareholders. Though it was impossible yet to tell exactly how much the liquidation would realize, the liquidators predicted that a large deficiency was inevitable. On the publication of the report, the market price of the company's shares dropped to less than nothing. Despite the fact that Overend and Gurney was a limited company, only £15 was paid up per £50 share, leaving shareholders facing an overhanging liability of up to £35 per share. What had seemed valuable assets were now passports to bankruptcy.[113]

This crushing additional liability focused shareholders' minds on money not justice. The announcement in August of a £10 call per share was the catalyst for a prolonged three-cornered contest between creditors, shareholders, and directors to fix liability for the company's debts.[114] In response to the announcement, a faction of shareholders formed a defence association to contest the call citing fraudulent misrepresentation by the directors.[115] By the middle of October, only about a fifth of calls had been paid. The liquidators secured a Chancery order compelling payment, but the shareholders took their resistance to the courts.[116] Recent verdicts had suggested that judges and juries were coming to regard directorial misrepresentation in prospectuses as reasonable grounds for negating shareholder liability, so their chances of success seemed fair.[117]

The case was decided in February 1867 by Vice-Chancellor Richard Malins, a former Conservative MP. He had harsh words for the directors. 'If the public had been told by the prospectus what those who issued it knew, not a single share would have been taken'. They had defrauded their shareholders—'allowing another to act in the belief of a fact which one knew to be untrue was a fraud'—and had it been a question of deciding between the shareholders and the directors, he would have granted relief. But the shareholders sought relief from their liabilities to the

[112] W. F. Finlason, *A Report of the Case of the Queen v. Gurney and others, in the Court of Queen's Bench* (London, 1870), 47.

[113] *The Times*, 8 June 1866; *Money Market Review*, 9 June 1866.

[114] *The Times*, 23, 26 July, 18 August 1866.

[115] Ibid. 29 August, 10 September 1866.

[116] Ibid. 18, 19 September, 19, 23 October 1866. Only 30 per cent of the shareholders (676 of 2219) actually joined the association, but the underwhelming response to the call suggests that many more passively supported it: *Daily News*, 11 February 1867; *The Times*, 21 January 1868.

[117] Several cases were settled in favour of shareholders in 1865–66: *Re Scottish and Universal Finance Bank, Ship's Case* (1865) 46 ER 486, *The Times*, 17 February 1865; *Kisch v. Central Railway Co. of Venezuela* (1865) 46 ER 584, *The Times*, 22 July 1865; *Re Russian (Vyksounsky) Ironworks Company* (1866) 14 LT (NS) 659, *The Times*, 18 July 1866; *Glamorganshire Iron and Coal Co. v. Irvine* (1866) 176 ER 861, *The Times*, 15 August 1866. For more on this trend, see Michael Lobban, 'The Politics of English Law in the Nineteenth Century', in Paul Brand and Joshua Getzler (eds), *Judges and Judging in the History of the Common Law and Civil Law: From Antiquity to Modern Times* (Cambridge, 2012), 129–31.

company's creditors, which were not negated by the fraud. Both the shareholders and the creditors were innocent victims, but the creditors 'were somewhat more innocent than the shareholders'. The creditors, who had no hand in the management of the company, looked to the shareholders' register to know who they were trusting, and removing names from this list retrospectively would deliver 'a fatal blow' to the principle of limited liability.[118] The courts thus took a similar course to that negotiated in the wake of 1845's railway mania: after initially supporting shareholder claims, they moved decisively in favour of enforcing debts, in the name of buttressing the joint-stock economy.[119] The creditors eventually received twenty shillings in the pound, plus interest, after shareholders paid calls of £25 per share beyond the £15 already paid up.[120]

THE PROSECUTION MANIA

Thoroughly routed in their tussle with creditors, shareholders now turned their attention to their directors. Could the fraudulent prospectuses which had lured shareholders to their doom be made criminally punishable? It was a question which divided legal authorities. When a select committee was appointed to investigate company law in March 1867, witnesses who discussed criminality gave conflicting evidence.[121] Charles Wordsworth QC, an expert on companies, told the committee that directors issuing false prospectuses were criminally liable for a misdemeanour under the Larceny Act, a piece of legislation which was 'of considerable importance', but which was 'not sufficiently known'.[122] But Henry Thring, who had drafted much legislation for the government since the early 1850s including the Companies Acts, took a narrower view of the law.[123] He thought that 'fraud is only criminal now when it is committed for particular objects and for particular purposes. For instance, it is not criminal to puff a company in any degree of extravagance whatever, however fraudulent it may be in the ordinary sense of the term'. When asked whether he thought misrepresentations in prospectuses should be criminal, he became evasive: 'I should have no doubt about its being a fraud, but whether you make it criminal or not is another question.' He was pressed twice more, but deflected the questions.[124] So, the Companies Act which followed later that year was silent on the issue of criminal liability, instead seeking to improve civil remedies. Section 38 enabled shareholders to sue if a

[118] *Re Overend and Gurney, ex p. Oakes and Peek* (1867), LR 3 Eq. 576, *Daily News*, 11 February 1867. The shareholders appealed against the decision, but lost in the House of Lords: *Oakes v. Turquand* (1867) LR 2 HL 325, *The Times*, 16 August 1867.

[119] For more on this, see Chapter 4, and R. W. Kostal, *Law and English Railway Capitalism, 1825–1875* (rev. repr., Oxford, 1997), ch. 2.

[120] Barnes, 'Victorian Financial Crisis', 61.

[121] For more on the committee, see James Taylor, *Creating Capitalism: Joint-Stock Enterprise in British Politics and Culture, 1800–1870* (Woodbridge, 2006), 188–96.

[122] *Report from the Select Committee on Limited Liability Acts*, PP 1867 X. 15.

[123] C. P. Ilbert, rev. H. C. G. Matthew, 'Henry Thring', *ODNB*.

[124] *Select Committee on Limited Liability Acts*, 127–8.

prospectus failed to specify the dates of, and names of parties to, all contracts entered into by the company.[125]

The status of the false prospectus—and of false representations more generally—in criminal law was thrashed out over the course of 1869, with Lord Mayor James Lawrence, recently elected Liberal MP for Lambeth—faced with a succession of actions by shareholders in the failed companies of 1866. Leading the way was an Overend and Gurney shareholder named Adam Thom. A Scottish lawyer and a deeply religious man who had been a judge in Canada, he had settled in London just as Overend and Gurney was being floated.[126] Claiming that prosecution was rendered necessary because the commercial community had closed ranks behind the directors (it was 'the only mode of purifying the air of the mercantile firmament'), he put together a case against them with the aid of his solicitor George Lewis, who had represented the Unity Bank shareholders.[127] Just before Christmas 1868, Lawrence granted summonses against the directors.[128]

All eyes were on Mansion House on New Year's Day, 1869 when the six directors, John Gurney, Henry Gurney, and Robert Birkbeck—the vendors of the old business—and Harry Gordon, Henry Barclay, and William Rennie, appeared to answer the charges. Leading the prosecution, Lewis faced an intimidating group of defence lawyers including William Ballantine, William Sleigh, Hardinge Giffard, Harry Poland, and Montagu Williams. But Lewis, still only 35, was fast forming the reputation for devastating effectiveness which would see him become one of the most famous lawyers of the late Victorian era.[129] He opened by alleging that 'a more stupendous fraud than that which had been committed by the defendants never disgraced this country'. The directors had conspired to induce Thom and others to become shareholders in an insolvent business by concealing the truth of the old firm's parlous financial condition. The number of defendants, lawyers, and witnesses necessitated a switch to the larger Queen's Bench courtroom after two days, but Lewis's mastery of the details of the intricate case was apparent to all. Central to the prosecution's case was evidence provided by the accountant Oswald Howell, an 'arithmetical sprite' who seemingly knew Overend and Gurney's books—which were hauled every morning to the courtroom in two or three wagons—by heart. Though the press noted that the audience was 'of a much superior class to that usually found in courts of justice', it had 'little or no sympathy with the defendants'. Telling points against them were met with 'ill-suppressed murmurs of disapprobation or by ironical laughter'. At the end of the month Lawrence stated that there was sufficient evidence to commit the defendants for trial. There was little doubt where the public's sympathies lay, with Lawrence's decision greeted

125 30 & 31 Vict. c. 131, s. 38. Sections 34–6 introduced new criminal offences designed to protect share warrants against forgery and other infringements.

126 Geoffrey Elliott, *The Mystery of Overend and Gurney: A Financial Scandal in Victorian London* (London, 2006), 197–9.

127 Adam Thom, *Overend and Gurney Prosecution: in its Relation to the Public as Distinguished from the Defendants* (London, 1869), 7.

128 *The Times*, 11 March 1868; *Pall Mall Gazette*, 19 December 1868.

129 John Juxon, *Lewis and Lewis* (London, 1983).

by enthusiastic cheers both in and outside the courtroom.[130] The cheers resounded throughout the press. Some, like the Liberal satirical magazine *Fun* (see Figure 6.1), saw it as a reassertion of the class blindness of British justice. The thoughts of others, like the more conservative *Punch* (see Figure 6.2), were with the ruined shareholders, for whom the committal represented a small measure of vengeance.

When the prosecution began, some had recognized that, if successful, it could encourage actions in other companies whose shareholders had been deceived, and so it proved.[131] Though smaller than Overend and Gurney, the Merchants' Company was similar to its larger rival in many respects. Like the famous discount house, it was formed in 1865 as a conversion from a private firm, Messrs. Lane, Hankey, and Co., to whose partners it paid £62,500 for the goodwill of the business. Like Overend and Gurney, the new limited company had a short lifespan, failing in November 1866, with the shareholders subsequently alleging that the old firm was hopelessly insolvent when it was floated. Richard Lane, Horace Chapman (son of one of the partners of Overend, Gurney and Co. before it was floated), and former Indian army officer Frederick Helbert, were partners in the original firm and became directors in the new limited company.[132] During the Overend and Gurney hearings, they were summonsed before the Lord Mayor at the behest of a shareholder. The charges concerned both the company's prospectus and its initial balance sheet, and were framed on the law of conspiracy and the Larceny Act.[133] Later that month a different shareholder launched a parallel action against Lane together with James Childs, another director. This concerned the company's call circular of May 1866 which stated that the company had 'made no losses', but that it was calling money as a precaution in view of the straitened financial climate. The prosecution claimed that the directors in fact were concealing substantial losses, trying to prop up a failing firm.[134]

The greater complexity of the first prosecution meant that the Lord Mayor was able to decide on the Lane and Childs case first, three weeks after his Overend and Gurney verdict. While the directors probably thought that the company might eventually get out of difficulty, 'he did not think they were justified in issuing that circular, because the affairs of the company were clearly known to them, that it had made losses'. It was therefore his duty to commit the defendants for trial, 'and it would remain for another tribunal to determine how far the view he had taken of the matter was correct or otherwise'.[135]

But Lawrence's view of the case proved to be the minority one. At the opening of the March Sessions of the Central Criminal Court, prosecuting barrister

[130] *The Times*, 2, 4, 18, 28 January 1869; Montagu Williams, *Later Leaves: Being the Further Reminiscences of Montagu Williams, QC* (London, 1891), 11.
[131] *Wrexham Advertiser*, 26 December 1868.
[132] *Daily News*, 5 October 1866.
[133] Mansion House Justice Room, Court Register, November 1868–November 1869, f. 44 (26 January 1869), London Metropolitan Archives, CLA/004/04/030.
[134] *The Times*, 19, 29 January 1869.
[135] Ibid. 20 February 1869.

EVEN-HANDED JUSTICE.

"NOW THEN, YOU RESPECTABLE GENTLEMEN, COME INTO THE DOCK WITH THESE OTHER ROGUES!"

Figure 6.1 'Even-Handed Justice', *Fun*, 13 February 1869

William Seymour applied for permission to drop the case. Having gone through the company's books and consulted with accountants, he had concluded that there was nothing false in the call circular as to the use of the word 'losses'. There had been no losses in trade: the company's main shortfalls at this stage were caused by unpaid calls and forfeited shares, but even these were not

COMMITTED FOR TRIAL.

Ruined Shareholder. "YES, THEY ARE COMMITTED FOR TRIAL; BUT WE, MY CHILD, TO *HARD LABOUR FOR LIFE!*"

Figure 6.2 'Committed for Trial', *Punch*, 6 February 1869

really 'losses'. Forfeited shares could be regarded as a profit to the company, which got the use of the money paid on them and could reissue them. As for unpaid calls, the company was justified in hoping that they might be paid in the future. Seymour had therefore told his client that he could not expect a conviction, and advised him to drop the case. The Recorder Russell Gurney agreed: even if losses had been made, which was doubtful, there was no evidence that the defendants had wilfully made the statement knowing it to be untrue, and as there was no chance of a conviction, he allowed the prosecution to drop.[136]

This very public rejection of his decision to send the case to trial surely influenced how Lawrence acted in the other Merchants' Company prosecution, which was still pending. He decided against committing the directors for trial, basing his decision on a moral and legal distinction. A prospectus might be morally false—by creating a misleading impression through the suppression of material facts—without being legally false, and it was his job to decide the legal question. The prospectus's main sin was that it only referred to the commission business of the firm, and not the struggling trading arm of its business. This omission would have tipped off the careful investor that all was not well—Lawrence stated that the prospectus would never have deceived him—and was therefore insufficient grounds for a criminal prosecution.[137] Lawrence was clearly retreating from the interpretation of the law underpinning his decision to commit the Overend and Gurney directors for trial, given that the main case against them was that they had concealed the true state of the firm's finances, not that they had stated actual falsehoods.

A second probable factor behind Lawrence's decision was the claim by Lane's solicitor—George Lewis again—that the prosecution was nothing but a vehicle for extortion: 'two distinct and deliberate offers had been made to compromise the matter by the payment of small sums of money', which the defendants had rejected.[138] To be sure, the scent of extortion was apparent in other shareholder prosecutions around this time, causing Lawrence to complain that his court was being used for illegitimate purposes, and that respectable names had been besmirched for no good reason.[139] This may have encouraged him to treat shareholder allegations with a little more caution. So, when the directors and manager of the English Joint-Stock Bank were summonsed for publishing a false balance sheet and making false entries in the company's books, Lawrence dismissed the case against the directors but sent the manager, Samuel Finney, to trial on charges of embezzlement, on which, as we have already seen, he was convicted.[140]

By now, the *Standard* had lost patience with prosecuting shareholders, and after Lawrence's decision in the English Joint-Stock Bank case wrote with some satisfaction that the 'mania for company prosecutions has received another check'. The paper hoped that shareholders 'who have been clamouring for vengeance' would now realize that criminal proceedings would be costly and abortive.[141] Indeed, a further case towards the end of the year confirmed that the scope of the law was narrowing. In November, the managing directors of yet another of the banking

[136] Ibid. 2 March 1869.
[137] Ibid. 1 May 1869.
[138] Ibid. 12 April 1869.
[139] The prosecution of the directors and manager of the Hercules Insurance Company, casually abandoned in favour of a civil suit, prompted these comments: ibid. 15 May 1869; *Lloyd's Weekly Newspaper*, 16 May 1869. In September an action against the directors of the Albert Life Assurance Company was discredited when it emerged that the prosecutor was a 'wrecker' hired to damage the company: *The Times*, 20, 27 September, 18 October 1869.
[140] *The Times*, 8 May, 8 June 1869.
[141] *Standard*, 8 June 1869.

casualties of 1866 appeared before Lawrence at Mansion House. Again there were echoes of Overend and Gurney. In August 1865, Barned's Banking Company (Limited) was established to buy out a private bank, James Barned and Co., which had traded in Liverpool for over half a century. The private bank, though once profitable, had run into severe difficulties, but this was not known to the shareholders of the new company, who paid £160,000 for the firm. The company declared a dividend of 6 per cent in February 1866 but suspended payment weeks later. The private bank was owned by uncle and nephew Charles and Lewin Barned Mozley, prominent in Liverpool trade and politics; Charles had become Liverpool's first Jewish mayor in 1863. The prosecutor, a London shareholder, charged the Mozleys with issuing a false prospectus, in a prosecution framed under both the Larceny Act and the law of conspiracy. Lewis was the prosecuting solicitor once more, and though these kinds of charges were no longer a novelty, the hearing 'excited very great interest'.[142]

But the case collapsed when Harmood Walcot Banner, a respected Liverpool accountant and one of the bank's liquidators, described the Mozleys, who had been ruined by the bank's failure, as 'honourable men' who believed they were solvent at the time of the transfer, and carried it out 'in strict honour'.[143] After Banner's evidence, Lewis had to admit that 'however indiscreet or imprudent the transfer of the business might have been', he was satisfied that 'the defendants had acted without fraud in the formation and conduct of the business'. With Lawrence's blessing, he withdrew all charges.[144] For all present—prosecution, defence, and judge—the case revolved around the intentions of the Mozleys. This interpretation drove a wedge between deception and recklessness on one hand and criminality on the other. A director could be as reckless as he liked with his shareholders' money—and as deceptive as he liked in communicating what he was doing—provided he was gambling to win. Criminality was only incurred if the director intended his shareholders to lose.

The public mood was shifting decisively against litigious shareholders. *The Times* had received several letters complaining of the flood of criminal and civil actions which was driving capital abroad and hindering economic recovery. 'Who would now be a director... in these days of prosecution at the Mansion-house and persecution by the Court of Chancery', one correspondent wondered. The new villains of the piece were the 'needy lawyer' and the 'briefless barrister' who harassed directors at the behest of 'penniless' shareholders. It was time to shield directors from malicious prosecutions by extending to them the protection already enjoyed by private trustees under the Larceny Act, that prosecutions had to be authorized by the Attorney General.[145] It was in this climate of growing hostility to shareholders that the trial of the Overend and Gurney directors took place at the end of the year.

[142] *The Times*, 5 November 1869.
[143] Geoffrey Tweedale, 'Sir John Sutherland Harmood-Banner', *ODNB*.
[144] *The Times*, 10 December 1869.
[145] Ibid. 13 December 1869.

THE FINAL ACT

The prosecution was privately financed, and Thom's resources were finite. Having failed to raise sufficient funds for his 'national battle' after an appeal to the public, he applied to Henry Bruce, Home Secretary since the election of Gladstone's Liberals in December 1868, for the government to take over the prosecution and its costs.[146] Bruce declined and suddenly the future of the prosecution was in doubt.[147] When the matter was raised in the Commons, Bruce explained that it had been discussed by the Cabinet, which decided that nothing about the case justified departure from the rule that injured parties should conduct their own prosecutions.[148] The only exception Bruce knew of was the Royal British Bank, which he somewhat enigmatically stated was 'not so much ... a precedent to be followed as an example to be avoided'.[149] Bruce hoped that the matter would rest there, but several members tried to force the government to perform a last-minute U-turn. A protracted debate ensued during which first Bruce, then the Attorney General Sir Robert Collier, and finally Gladstone himself, defended the Cabinet's decision. Gladstone echoed Bruce in arguing that such prosecutions were best left to the victims, unless they were too poor to act themselves, but this was certainly not the case in this instance. Indeed, it was the status and behaviour of the victims which provided Gladstone's killer argument for non-intervention. Rejecting the contention that not to prosecute would be a blow to commercial morality, he flipped the argument, claiming that a government prosecution would have calamitous effects on 'the future prudence and self-restraint of a generation too greedy of money and too ready to adopt one of the most doubtful means of making money—that of placing their investments in concerns of which they know nothing at all, with the view of making large and easy gains, of reaping the fruits of industry without its toil'. This was not a worthy cause for the British taxpayer to support.[150] Thom was therefore left to finance the prosecution himself.

The trial, further delayed by its removal at the behest of the defendants to the Court of Queen's Bench so that it could be heard by a special jury, finally took place in December. With Lewis—a solicitor—unable to conduct the prosecution, Thom had hired the eccentric radical Irish barrister and mystic Edward Kenealy to present his case.[151] He was not held in high esteem by his peers, with recklessness, a poor mastery of detail, and a tendency to prolixity among his many shortcomings.[152] Ranged against Kenealy in an unequal battle was the finest legal talent

[146] Ibid. 2 February 1869.

[147] Ibid. 25 June, 7 July 1869.

[148] Gladstone's terse note of the Cabinet meeting reads: 'Thom's applicn for public aid in prosecuting Gurney. Declined.' *The Gladstone Diaries*, ed. M. R. D. Foot and H. C. G. Matthew, 14 vols (Oxford, 1968–94), vii. 85.

[149] Hansard, 3s, 197: 822 (30 June 1869).

[150] Ibid. 975–95 (1 July 1869). Gladstone was pleased with his performance, noting in his diary, 'H of C. 4½-8 and 9¼-1¾: spoke on Gurney Prosecution principally. One of my least bad.' *Gladstone Diaries*, vii. 89.

[151] J. A. Hamilton, rev. Rohan McWilliam, 'Edward Vaughan Hyde Kenealy', *ODNB*.

[152] Elliott, *Overend and Gurney*, 215–16.

money could buy, including the Solicitor General Sir John Coleridge, and Sir John Karslake, Attorney General in the previous Conservative administration, together with Ballantine, Giffard, and Poland.[153] The acquittal of the defendants after a nine-day trial is usually attributed to Kenealy's inept performance, or to the inability of Victorian law to touch City insiders.[154] But the outcome was chiefly the result of an essentially sound, if somewhat narrow, interpretation of the law by the judge, Chief Justice Cockburn, expounded in his summing up to the jury.[155]

The prosecution was based on section 84 of the Larceny Act, the law of obtaining money by false pretences, and conspiracy, but central to Cockburn's reasoning were principles derived from common law and equity. Exaggerated praise did not render a person liable in contractual disputes—only entirely false representations could do this—and it was all the more important to observe this rule in criminal actions. But rather than making false representations, the prospectus, 'as succinct and jejune a prospectus as one ever saw', made no representation at all as to the firm's assets. All it did was fail to mention the existence of the second deed transferring the private firm's debts to the company, and it was an accepted principle in equity that non-disclosure did not amount to fraud.[156] Parties claiming ignorance had to show not only that they did not have information, but that they could not with due diligence have obtained it. Given how few shareholders had bothered to look at the deed which was made available, reasoned Cockburn, it was unlikely that drawing attention to the other deed would have stopped many of them investing.[157] By alleging sins of omission rather than commission, the prosecution was on shaky ground: as the chief legal reporter for *The Times* later noted, '[i]t was the first attempt to found a criminal prosecution on mere silence and supposed suppression'.[158]

Above all, argued Cockburn, there was no evidence of guilty intent. Despite the fact that the private firm had suffered massive losses and was technically insolvent, its 'enormous earning power' remained intact, as suggested by its turnover of £160 million in the nine months of its life as a limited company. The plan to save the firm by going public was an entirely reasonable one. If the directors had sold their shares and realized a profit, this might be evidence that the company was a bubble, but 'their not selling them may fairly lead to the opposite inference'. Cockburn's exculpation of the directors was possibly influenced by his own experiences of the joint-stock economy, which had been an important source of income for him. As a barrister in the 1840s, he had built up a lucrative railway practice based on the

[153] The defendants' costs were £1,000 a day: *Leeds Mercury*, 1 January 1870.
[154] Elliott, *Overend and Gurney*, 215–18; Juxon, *Lewis and Lewis*, 85–7; Wilson, 'Law Morality and Regulation', 1086–7; *Reynolds's Newspaper*, 2 January 1870.
[155] A point underlined afterwards in the legal press: *Law Times*, 25 December 1869, 1 January 1870.
[156] P. S. Atiyah, *The Rise and Fall of Freedom of Contract* (Oxford, 1979), 469.
[157] *Reg. v. Gurney* (1869) 11 Cox 414, *The Times*, 23 December 1869. For useful commentary, see Finlason, *Queen v. Gurney*.
[158] Finlason, *Queen v. Gurney*, vii.

high volume of promotions, extensions, and amalgamations in the boom years.[159] In the process, he seemed to have developed a greater affinity with directors than shareholders. Though he did criticize the partners of the old firm for 'turning aside from the safe and settled path of business' and plunging their capital in 'the wildest speculations and the rashest enterprises', this was a delusion shared by the victims of the flotation, and Cockburn turned the moral point on the shareholders. 'There can be no doubt that the spirit of speculation and gambling has taken deep root in the minds of all classes of the community', and those who used to be satisfied with modest profits now gambled their fortunes chasing enormous gains. If Overend and Gurney's fate taught investors that great gains meant great risks, and that it was 'unsafe to embark in enterprises of which they cannot comprehend the scope, the management of which they cannot really control', then it would have done some good.[160]

The special jury of merchants and bankers was in tune with Cockburn's view of the case, and took less than ten minutes to acquit. Bizarre scenes followed: as soon as the foreman announced the verdict, wild cheers broke out, which Cockburn could not control, and which eventually became deafening, at which point they were taken up by the crowds outside the courtroom who were awaiting the verdict. Hearing this only encouraged those inside to renew their cheering. It was a strange inversion of the 'howls of execration' heard in the same courtroom in January when the defendants were committed for trial.[161] This reversal of attitudes was the final reason for the prosecution's failure. Actions against directors were initially viewed sympathetically, but as the number of cases multiplied, and as the motives of the prosecutors were increasingly called into question, shareholders lost the moral high ground. With economic recovery sluggish, the glut of criminal actions came to be seen in a negative light, and interpretations of the law tightened, with guilty intent reasserted as the crux of any successful prosecution.[162]

CONCLUSION

A superficial glance at criminal prosecutions in the early 1860s seems to reveal an unfairly skewed justice system. Light-fingered clerks like Pullinger received draconian sentences while crooked directors like Morrison easily evaded the clutches of the law. But these outcomes were chiefly a function of a system in which private prosecutions were the norm, and whereas boards could use company funds to punish employees, defrauded shareholders usually prioritized civil redress over criminal actions. The government saw little need to interfere with this situation, but this was not evidence of class bias, at least not in the way that is usually

[159] The money helped to launch his parliamentary career in 1847. *Bristol Mercury*, 22 November 1880; *Standard*, 22 November 1880.

[160] *The Times*, 23 December 1869.

[161] Ibid.

[162] It was not the shareholders' final defeat, for they subsequently failed even to secure civil redress from the directors: *Peek v. Gurney* (1871) LR 13 Eq. 79; *Peek v. Gurney* (1873), LR 6 HL 377.

suggested. Government did occasionally intervene to conduct prosecutions of fraudsters, but only when the victims were working-class. Intervention was justified chiefly to buttress the culture of thrift which government was trying to promote through measures such as the POSB. And the fact that fixing criminal responsibility even in primitive financial institutions like savings banks, operating out of local school rooms, and effectively managed by a single individual, proved so difficult cannot have encouraged the government to try its luck in the more complex joint-stock sector.

However, private prosecutions were beginning to fill the gap. Looser social ties between executives and their constituents in the large metropolitan financial institutions meant that when things went wrong, investors who in the past might have resorted to informal means to resolve conflicts now looked to the law for redress. They found a champion in George Lewis, a tenacious and brilliant solicitor who specialized in cases of alleged fraud. Moreover, reforms to the Companies Acts permitted prosecutions out of company assets, making criminal proceedings more feasible than hitherto. Consequently, the years following the 1866 commercial crisis saw a spate of attempted prosecutions. If magistrates had acted as strict gatekeepers in previous crises, insisting that shareholders apply other remedies, they now responded to the public mood and committed many cases for trial.

In the higher courts, however, the two main types of offence uncovered after the crisis—embezzlement and misrepresentation—were treated in very different ways. The former offence was successfully punished in a number of cases. But no one was imprisoned for misrepresentations in company prospectuses and balance sheets, the devices which had enticed so many shareholders. This was not because of a class-biased law, but because of dominant moral interpretations of the crisis. For judges and politicians alike, the main moral issue after 1866 was not the behaviour of directors, but the behaviour of shareholders whose greed for large profits had fuelled the boom, and who after the bust were doing everything in their power to resist their liabilities to creditors. The principal legal question to be resolved, then, was not whether fraud left directors liable to criminal prosecution, but whether it entitled shareholders to shed their financial liabilities. This question was resolved against the shareholders. Only after this reverse did shareholders change tack and launch criminal proceedings against their directors. Early cases were committed for trial, and these encouraged shareholders in other companies to follow suit. That several of these were seemingly instituted to try to force directors to make civil redress, combined with fears about the damaging effects of the glut of prosecutions on trust, sparked a backlash against shareholders. There was a distinct narrowing of definitions of what constituted fraudulent misrepresentation. Omission of material particulars was deemed not to be a criminal offence, with principles derived from commercial law in the civil courts invoked to support this stance. And whereas in 1858 the British Bank directors had been convicted of misrepresentation even though they did not mean to ruin their shareholders, now the 'honest' intentions of directors were considered ample proof of their innocence.

This outcome, together with the fact that the government resolutely resisted initiating or funding any prosecutions throughout the crisis, might suggest that the nation had retreated from the criminalization of company fraud. But the measures introduced in 1857 and 1861 to facilitate prosecutions had been put to use rather than becoming dead letters, complementing the existing laws against conspiracy and false pretences which also underpinned several actions. In fact, the 1860s saw more attempted prosecutions of company managements than any previous decade. And far from representing a high-water mark in the battle against fraud, this trend was to intensify in the final decades of the century.

PART THREE

ENFORCEMENT

7

Offences Against the State: The 1870s

The 1860s ended with the rout of shareholders in the financial institutions whose collapse in 1866 had prompted one of the century's worst economic crises. Though their attempts to prosecute their directors had initially been popular, they ultimately failed because their motives were discredited, and because their actions were thought to be exacerbating the climate of mistrust which was preventing economic recovery. By the end of 1869, the message from the courts seemed to be that the criminal law only had a marginal role to play in policing joint-stock disputes. Yet victims of fraud continued to bring their grievances before the courts, and the higher frequency of prosecutions witnessed in the late 1860s was maintained in the new decade. Like the earlier trials, most revolved around that most contested of documents, the prospectus. But whereas the issue in 1869 had been disclosure, the issue was now somewhat more fundamental: could directors be held responsible for a prospectus which lured people to invest in a bubble? Whilst the trials met with mixed results, the successes indicated a growing acceptance of private criminal prosecutions as a valid element in the regulatory mix. But this was not all. Sparked by the publicity given to some particularly bad cases in the middle of the decade, concerns about commercial morality strengthened arguments for the establishment of a public prosecutor. Such proposals were to receive a cautious but receptive response from paternalists in Disraeli's Conservative government.

A SYSTEM OF PUFFING

In January 1870, Stephen Dummere, a Cheapside tea dealer, was approached by William Henry White, a surveyor for the Manchester Insurance and Banking Company. White wanted to rent office space on the first floor of Dummere's premises, and gave W. H. Albus, a director of the company, as a reference. Albus informed Dummere that White 'had given the company every satisfaction', and so Dummere let the offices to White. What Dummere did not know was that this was the latest in the regular relocations of the Manchester Insurance and Banking Company, which had begun life just a year earlier, in January 1869, in Southport. Five months later it had moved to Manchester, and in November, to City Road, London. The choice of address in Cheapside was not coincidental. Practically opposite were the offices of the Manchester Assurance Company, a respectable and long-established firm. The company was able to capitalize on the confusion between the two, drumming up a large amount of business.[1]

But when the company started resisting legitimate claims on fire insurance policies, its customers turned to the law for help. The man they approached was George Lewis, now established, thanks to his activities in the 1860s, as the 'go-to' solicitor for company fraud cases. The victims, mostly small tradesmen, could not afford to pay Lewis, but his father, James Lewis, had been renowned for his kindness towards poorer clients (he had been dubbed 'the Poor Man's Lawyer'), and his son continued this tradition, noting that he took on the case 'purely as a matter of charity towards the poor people who had been defrauded, there being no public officer to bring the case before the Court'.[2] In June, Lewis had White arrested on charges of publishing a false prospectus, and he appeared before Lord Mayor Robert Besley. Lewis read at length from the prospectus; the details were so bizarre that Besley interrupted at one point to ask Lewis whether he was quoting a page of *Punch*. It certainly offered much more than most of its rivals. As well as an inclusive attitude towards lives—all were eligible 'from one month old to 85 years'—the company also provided banking facilities, complete with chequebooks. It also promised to grant free emigration tickets on every paid-up share. Criticizing other companies for burying their profits in reserve funds, it returned its profits to policyholders every six months, but these could be called upon in the event of the company encountering difficulties. This, however, was unlikely: insurers had 'the security of a large capital subscribed by a numerous proprietary'; the money was invested in mines and plantations held in the West Indies. Furthermore, the directors, who included both White and Albus, were all experienced businessmen who had a large stake in the company.[3]

But this was a tissue of lies, Lewis claimed. White and Albus were the same person, Albus being the Latin form of White. Usually, White signed the policy in front of the customer, with the signature of Albus already on the document. But one insurer, a Bermondsey cabinetmaker, testified that he saw White sign both names on the policy. When he asked why this was, White told him that he had been authorized by Albus to sign on his behalf. The customer now had his doubts, and when asked to pay the 6s premium, he pointed to a stool in his shop and, as a joke, said that he would give the stool and 1s. White hesitated, but then agreed to these unusual terms. Other witnesses who had seen inside the company's offices testified that this was not a real place of business: no board meetings were held; no clerks were employed; one witness had seen chequebooks but no money, apart from 'some farthings in a bowl'. It was an empty shell of a company: the directors listed in the prospectus were mostly inventions, and besides White, there were just a handful of canvassers paid to pound the streets finding customers.[4] One thing that should have warned the policyholders was the poor spelling in some of the policies: examples included 'St. Luke's' being spelt 'Look's', and 'marine' rendered as 'marian'. Besley

1 *The Times*, 8 June 1870.
2 John Juxon, *Lewis and Lewis* (London, 1983), 20; *The Times*, 8 June 1870.
3 *The Times*, 8 June 1870.
4 Ibid.; *Pall Mall Gazette*, 8 June 1870.

'could hardly trust himself to comment upon the credulity of the public and the extent to which people practised upon it', and if the case had come to light a generation earlier, it is easy to imagine the Lord Mayor would have been satisfied with giving the case some publicity as a warning to the gullible.[5] But now he not only committed White for trial, but took up Lewis's suggestion that as the prosecution was 'in the public interest', it be conducted by the City Solicitor. It was, he thought, 'a desirable course in a case where the persons defrauded were, as a body, so poor'.[6]

When White's case came to the Old Bailey in July, he faced twenty-four counts relating to the prospectus, framed under section 84 of the Larceny Act, and the law of obtaining money by false pretences. Quite apart from the scale of the two enterprises, the case differed from the Overend and Gurney trial in that the charges of fraud rested not on non-disclosure, but on the statement of material falsehoods: namely, that the directors listed were fictitious, as were the surgeon and arbitrator, there was no large subscribed capital, and the company did not offer 'every possible advantage' to those wanting to insure. The company 'had no existence save for the purposes of fraud and...was a fictitious company'.[7] However, the principles of freedom of contract which had underpinned Chief Justice Cockburn's perspective in the Overend and Gurney trial were shared by the judge in this case, Justice John Byles. Though he had authored a popular volume, *Sophisms of Free Trade*, criticizing the overly dogmatic commitment to political economy, these views did not always translate into his legal judgements, and he was unconvinced that misrepresentation should be policed by the criminal law.[8] The previous year, he had directed the jury to acquit a man who had taken a deposit from an employee after claiming he 'had a good business' when in fact he was a bankrupt. Byles decreed that making a false representation of the value of a business might be 'grossly fraudulent', and might form the basis of a civil action, but could not sustain a criminal charge of obtaining money by false pretences.[9] And now he displayed very little sympathy for White's victims, observing that the prospectus 'was calculated to excite the suspicions of prudent people, but, unhappily, the majority of the people were not prudent'. Yet the defence's main arguments—that the non-existence of Albus and the fraudulent nature of the company were not proven—were brushed aside by the jury, who reached an instant verdict of guilty. The prosecution now noted that White had defrauded 'many hundreds of poor people', and Byles sentenced him to five years' penal servitude.[10]

Some were contemptuous of White's 'poor little attempt at imposition'.[11] But while this was a world away from the high finance milieu of Overend and Gurney, the case was recognized as significant because of the principles at stake, and it

5 *The Times*, 16 June 1870.

6 Ibid. 23 June 1870.

7 Indictment Nos. 105–6, William White (11 July 1870), TNA, CRIM 4/779.

8 P. S. Atiyah, *The Rise and Fall of Freedom of Contract* (Oxford, 1979), 380–3; Gareth H. Jones and Vivienne Jones, 'Sir John Barnard Byles', *ODNB*.

9 *Reg. v. Williamson* (1869) 21 LT 444.

10 *Reg. v. White* (1870), *The Times*, 14 July 1870; *Pall Mall Gazette*, 15 July 1870; *OBP*, July 1870, William Henry White (t18700711-570).

11 *Leeds Mercury*, 1 July 1870.

'excited great interest in the City'.[12] Though the victims had been criticized both by the Lord Mayor and Judge Byles, the outcome suggested that perhaps customers were better able than shareholders to mobilize the criminal law in their favour. But a second case, coincidentally in White's old stamping ground, suggested that shareholders were also able to score victories against directors who issued false prospectuses.

Three days before White's arrest, two men of gentlemanly bearing appeared at Manchester police court. Thomas Gibson and Arthur Yeomans had issued prospectuses soliciting subscriptions in the North Caradon Mining Company. Now they were charged with obtaining money by false pretences from Nathan Horsley, a Hartlepool shipowner, who had been persuaded by the prospectuses to send a cheque for £200. The men were in the employ of Edwin Harvey Wadge, a third conspirator currently in Paris. When they were arrested, the police found an incriminating letter from Wadge about the Cornish mine, instructing Gibson to 'keep the thing before eight or ten newspapers at the same time, because we must run off a few hundreds as quickly as possible. The moment I get another £100 I shall take nice offices here and go about the French thing. I'll put £4,000 in your pocket, old fellow.' A police inspector was sent to Cornwall to look at the site of the mine. He found other mines, including the South, East, and West Caradon Mines, all of which were said to be prosperous. But none of the locals he spoke to knew anything about a North Caradon Mine, and when he visited the estate of the Rilla Mill, which is where the men actually held a licence to mine, all he found was 'an old wheel-pit, which had been filled up for many years, and which was overgrown with furze and ferns'. After three hearings, the magistrate Francis Headlam concluded that there was sufficient evidence to commit the pair for trial.[13]

When the case came to trial at the Manchester Assizes in August 1870, the absent Wadge again loomed large. A mining agent who had been declared an outlaw after failing to attend his bankruptcy examination three years previously, Wadge had used Gibson, his former clerk, to conduct his schemes while in exile.[14] Wadge had sent frequent letters to Gibson instructing him how to promote the North Caradon Company which, fortunately for the prosecution, meant an exhaustive paper trail, extensive extracts from which were read out in court. Wadge had told Gibson to apply for a licence, form a company on the cost-book principle, use his name and one or two others ('any names would do'), and distribute circulars to likely dupes ('Be careful to write only to distant ones, and beware not to send to those who are unfriendly to us, for it will open their eyes and stir them up'). A different circular was sent to investors known to have lost money in previous speculations—including a number of clergymen—encouraging them to 'make another throw'. In total, Gibson issued five thousand circulars. Wadge drew up the prospectus and sent it to Gibson, and a 'flashy report' on the wonderful prospects of the mine was sent to the *Mining Journal.*

[12] *The Times*, 23 June 1870; *Standard*, 14 July 1870.
[13] *The Times*, 4 June 1870; *Northern Echo*, 6 June 1870; *Manchester Times*, 11, 18 June 1870.
[14] *Manchester Times*, 30 March 1867.

Wadge instructed Gibson to advertise heavily in the country press, the advertisements paid for by shares. 'Whether the shares turn out good or not it will make a magnificent foundation for our second thing'. These strategies proved successful. Gibson's cashbook showed that £2,054 in share subscriptions had been received. After deducting the expenses of £208, the remaining £1,816 was divided between the two men. 'Not one penny was devoted to carrying on mining operations,' the prosecution claimed.[15]

Gibson needed a good lawyer, and he hired John Torr, an eloquent Northern Circuit barrister always in demand 'for actions in which a bold front and a ready tongue were required'.[16] First, Torr tried to muddy the moral waters, suggesting that the prosecutor Horsley was an inveterate speculator 'in a hurry to get rich'. But his main gambit was to freely admit that what his client had done was dishonest, but consistent with wider standards of commercial immorality. If the jury found Gibson guilty of getting up a bubble company,

> he did not know how many would escape among themselves in that great city at the present moment. He was aware of the danger of what he was saying, but he would not shrink from his duty. He appealed to them whether this was not going on in the highest of circles, whether the whole country was not ringing with it within the last few years, and yet no notice was taken of it... Was not business carried on with a system of puffing—called falsehood, if they liked; and if when these men issued this prospectus they had some hope that the venture would succeed, they were not to be convicted of swindling, although they might have put some gloss upon the affair.... [P]rospectuses... had always been exaggerated, from Holloway's Pills downwards, and that could not be looked upon as anything beyond a little over-colouring, which might be wrong morally, but was not an offence to answer in a criminal court.

If there had been any hope, albeit remote, that the mine could have turned out profitable, they could not convict, for 'success justified all things' in this age.[17]

Was such an interpretation consistent with the law? In his summing up on the second day of the trial, Baron Anthony Cleasby, known as a conscientious and cautious judge, and a Conservative in politics, gave a detailed summary of the state of the law: though commenting in passing on the 'credulous' people who fell for the scheme, he did not get sidetracked into discussing the moral culpability of investors.[18] The first question facing the jury was whether the mining company was real or not. If the men took ground with the genuine intention of starting a mine, the jury could not convict 'merely from the fact of their giving a coloured gloss to it'. In other words, Torr was correct that an exaggerated prospectus by itself was not enough to convict them. But if the evidence showed that there was no intention to start a mine, and that Wadge and Gibson promoted the scheme purely for their personal enrichment, the jury faced a second question, for it was not enough to

[15] *Reg. v. Gibson* (1870), *Manchester Times*, 13 August 1870.

[16] *Manchester Times*, 16 March 1878.

[17] Ibid. 13, 20 August 1870.

[18] He was three times a failed parliamentary candidate: G. C. Boase, rev. Hugh Mooney, 'Sir Anthony Cleasby', *ODNB*.

show that there was a fraudulent scheme by which money had been obtained. Only if there was a statement of fact known to be false by the person making it, on the strength of which money had been obtained, could the jury convict. For Cleasby, there was sufficient evidence of this: the prospectus and advertisements had stated that mining operations were in active progress, and that the results were favourable: 'That was a distinct statement, which was not simply puffing as it were, but a distinct statement of fact, inducing people to suppose that the thing was a reality', whereas in fact no mining had been done and no metals found.[19]

With this strong steer, the jury found Gibson guilty of obtaining money by false pretences, but acquitted Yeomans as they accepted his defence that he was only a paid clerk who did not share in the profits and was simply following instructions from Gibson. Sentencing Gibson, Cleasby told him that the documents found in his possession revealed 'a scheme of unparalleled audacity'. He had shown no mercy to any of his victims, sending them 'friendly cozening' letters to try to milk them further. Cleasby therefore decided to give the severest punishment he could by law: five years' penal servitude.[20]

The Manchester authorities did not forget Wadge. In 1873, he returned to England, trading as a mining agent in London under an assumed name. Word got back to Manchester and an inspector was sent to the capital to arrest him. Swiftly committed for trial on charges of conspiracy and false pretences, like Gibson, he hired Torr to defend him.[21] The barrister had little choice but to try the same defence he had used for Gibson, admitting that Wadge had 'overpuffed and overdescribed a mining speculation', but claiming that this was not a criminal offence. The jury took just five minutes to convict, and Baron Charles Pollock sentenced him to five years' penal servitude.[22]

However, the law had definite limits. Prospectuses had to contain clear-cut falsehoods in order to sustain criminal actions. A useful contrast to the North Caradon case is afforded by the Lady Constance Mining Company. The company's affairs were examined in 1875 in Manchester police court before Headlam, the magistrate who had committed Gibson for trial. Formed for working mines in the North Wales mountains, it had attracted several thousand pounds from the public but had yielded no ore. A London dentist who had lost £200 launched criminal proceedings against four of the directors, but after an extensive investigation, Headlam dismissed the case. He agreed that the shareholders had been defrauded; nevertheless, he did not believe that the offence could be dealt with in a criminal court. 'From the evidence there is no doubt there were mines on the Halkyn Mountain, some of which were paying while some were not. Some of the evidence shows that there were prospects of getting more ore out of this mine. Consequently it cannot be said that the mine was utterly worthless.' Thus the men went free.[23]

[19] *Manchester Times*, 20 August 1870.

[20] Ibid.

[21] *Bradford Observer*, 29 November 1873; *Freeman's Journal*, 2 December 1873; *Royal Cornwall Gazette*, 6 December 1873.

[22] *Reg. v. Wadge* (1873), *Birmingham Daily Post*, 10 December 1873; *Huddersfield Daily Chronicle*, 10 December 1873; *The Times*, 12 December 1873.

[23] *Manchester Times*, 24 December 1875.

The Lady Constance venture occupied the grey area between legitimate and illegitimate enterprise, but irregularities in real companies actually doing business rarely troubled the criminal courts in the early 1870s, even when considered scandalous. In 1872, the declining dividends paid by the once-prosperous Metropolitan Railway Company prompted shareholders to appoint two new directors with a mandate to investigate the company's books. The pair's report brought the company to crisis point. It outlined a series of abuses, chief of which was the fact that the directors had purposely under-reported the company's enormous legal costs and other liabilities in its balance sheets in order to boost the flagging dividend. This was considered deplorable but not fraudulent. The press criticized the 'futile juggling' indulged in by the directors to pay these 'delusive dividends', but did not even discuss the possibility of criminal repercussions; nor did the shareholders explore this option. The directors were guilty of 'neglect' and 'mismanagement', but ultimately there was no intent to lure shareholders to their ruin—the line was intended to be profitable—so there was no fraud.[24]

Even so, in the early 1870s the criminal law was becoming accepted as having some role to play in the regulation of the joint-stock economy. Company fraud trials were no longer the rarity they had been before the late 1860s. After Wadge's conviction in 1873, *Freeman's Journal* was delighted to see this 'gifted projector . . . the last of the Montague Tiggs', end up in prison, 'wherein so many bold designs and so much misapplied energy find their grave'.[25] This final piece of moralizing hints at the shift in expectations that was beginning to occur. It was no longer assumed that company fraud was beyond the law, and bubble-blowing company promoters were beginning to join embezzling managers in prison. And for both groups, escape abroad was no longer an automatic route to safety: when a new extradition act was passed in 1870, the list of crimes covered included embezzlement, larceny, obtaining money by false pretences, and any act of fraud by company directors or officers made criminal by any act of parliament.[26] But, as the cases discussed above indicate, the insistence on proving guilty intent meant that the law could only reach those who intended their shareholders to lose.

THE WAY WE LIVE NOW

Drawing the line here was thought necessary to protect businessmen acting in good faith from malicious or otherwise unjustified criminal litigation. But did this give too much latitude for unethical behaviour? When Baron Pollock sentenced Wadge, he had underlined the need for a stiff punishment in order to defend commercial morality: 'in a large commercial centre of what was the greatest country in the world for honest commercial enterprise, it was of the highest importance that integrity and uprightness in the enterprises of commerce should be kept up'.[27] But

[24] *The Times*, 16 August, 10 October 1872; *Economist*, 12 October 1872.
[25] *Freeman's Journal*, 11 December 1873.
[26] 33 & 34 Vict. c. 52, first schedule.
[27] *Birmingham Daily Post*, 10 December 1873; *Huddersfield Daily Chronicle*, 10 December 1873; *The Times*, 12 December 1873.

confidence in Britain's superiority in matters of business ethics, an article of faith among many, and reiterated by Pollock, was slipping. Indeed, aggravated by the prolonged economic slump which began in 1873, the decade saw a genuine crisis of confidence in the state of the nation's commercial morality which went far deeper than the usual moralizing about the market. As Martin Wiener notes, success in conquering 'the external criminality of the streets'—crime rates were falling from the 1860s—together with the waning of the moral certitudes linking crime with questions of character which had characterized early nineteenth-century thought, turned middle-class attention inward in the late Victorian period, 'from the public house to the counting house'.[28] Awareness that respectable veneers might conceal wickedness had never been more acute.

Lord Mayors of London sometimes used their position to comment on commercial standards, and on reaching the end of his term in 1874, Sir Andrew Lusk, a self-made man, long-time chairman of the Imperial Bank, and a Liberal MP, struck an unusually sombre note.[29] Son of a strict Scottish Presbyterian, he had been brought up with strong religious principles, and these were offended by the marked proliferation of criminal activity he detected during his year in office. The increase was not in 'vulgar crimes', however—these had fallen—but in 'crimes by persons of education', and he was 'afraid that the many cases connected with commercial and other companies which he had noticed during his tenure of office there did not say much for the morality of the times in which he lived'.[30] A number of cases involving dubious promotions had come to him over the year. Five directors of the Peat Coal and Charcoal Company were charged with conspiring to defraud their shareholders. The company raised about £35,000 in subscriptions from the public, but unbeknownst to the investors, the directors paid over £12,000 of this to the Société Générale, the only five members of which were the five men charged. The Société Générale, not to be confused with the French company of the same name, was to float the Peat Coal Company, but as its paid-up capital was only £45, the prosecution claimed that it was nothing more than 'a sort of conduit pipe to draw off the cash of other companies'.[31] Around the same time, three of the directors of the Ruby Consolidated Mining Company, Edward Hartmont, Edward Del Banco, and Leonard Heyneman, were summoned before Lusk. A shareholder who had lost £500 in the scheme accused them of issuing a false prospectus containing statements which they knew to be untrue. By these false pretences, the shareholders were induced to pay £285,000 for Nevada silver mines which the men had purchased for just £40,000.[32] A third case appeared towards the end of Lusk's term, when six directors of the Eupion Fuel and Gas Company were accused of conspiring to defraud the Committee of the London

[28] Martin J. Wiener, *Reconstructing the Criminal: Culture, Law, and Policy in England, 1830–1914* (Cambridge, 1990), 244.

[29] Charles Welch and Anita McConnell, 'Sir Andrew Lusk', *ODNB*.

[30] *Daily News*, 9 November 1874.

[31] *The Times*, 2 July 1874.

[32] Ibid. 10 July 1874.

Stock Exchange by 'rigging' the market in the company's shares. If the scheme had worked, it would have netted the group a quarter of a million pounds.[33]

Meanwhile, in the civil courts, judicial condemnations of the behaviour of promoters and directors were becoming commonplace.[34] One of the most controversial figures was Baron Albert Grant. Born Abraham Gottheimer, son of a Central European Jewish pedlar, he entered the world of finance in his twenties, forming the Mercantile Discount Company in 1859, then becoming involved in the boom of the mid 1860s. The majority of his flotations led to legal tussles involving accusations of fraud, and though he buttressed his position by securing election to parliament as a Conservative and doing high-profile charitable work, the civil actions against him began to mount in the 1870s.[35]

One of these concerned his Lisbon Steam Tramways Company. The prospectus had stated that £309,000 was required to construct the tramway, but failed to disclose that £45,000 of this was to be paid to Grant, with further secret payments to the directors, the owner of the concession, and the contractors. Furthermore, Grant had engaged in share-rigging to manufacture a premium before allotment, and paid journalists to write favourable notices. Despite these efforts, the company was a failure, and soon after, the secret commissions were discovered. A shareholder managed to recover his investment in an action based on section 38 of the 1867 Companies Act, and with ninety similar actions pending from other shareholders in the company, Grant appealed against the judgement, arguing that what he did was common practice in the City.[36] The Court of Appeal upheld the original verdict, with Lord Chief Justice Sir Alexander Cockburn, the presiding judge in the Overend and Gurney trial in 1869, disputing Grant's justification of share rigging. 'The fact that the practice was usual does not affect its morality', he told Grant. Hyping the shares to induce others to buy them, only for them to become worthless, was not bona fide dealing, but was 'really getting money by means of false pretences'.[37]

Grant is widely believed to be one of the chief inspirations for the brash, bullying, and bent financier Augustus Melmotte who stalks the pages of the decade's most powerful indictment of commercial morality, Anthony Trollope's *The Way We Live Now*. Serialized through most of 1874 and 1875, it is an attack on deception in all its forms, from the puffing of worthless books for favours, to fraudulent company promotion by corrupt financiers. Though possessing an unsavoury past, Melmotte is welcomed into society because he lives splendidly and the cash-

[33] Ibid. 9 October 1874.

[34] Vice-Chancellor Malins, who, it should be remembered, had decided on the Overend and Gurney civil case, said that the dealings of the National Bank of Ireland and the Imperial Land Company of Marseilles, involving two Irish Liberal MPs, were 'more dishonourable than anything which he had ever met with in his professional career': *Re Imperial Land Company of Marseilles* (1870), *The Times*, 21 March 1870.

[35] P. L. Cottrell, 'Grant (Gottheimer), Albert (Abraham) Zachariah', in D. J. Jeremy (ed.), *Dictionary of Business Biography*, 623–9; see also Richard Groom, 'The Conduct of Parliamentary Elections in Kidderminster, 1832–1880', PhD thesis, Coventry University, 2010, ch. 6.

[36] *Twycross v. Grant* (1876), *The Times*, 12, 13, 14 July 1876.

[37] *Twycross v. Grant* (1877) 36 LT 812, *The Times*, 18 May, 4 June 1877.

strapped aristocracy think he can make them rich. They therefore become his tools in the flotation of a huge US railway bubble.[38] In his *Autobiography*, Trollope later confessed the didactic purpose which lay behind his novel. Modern society, he feared, believed that if dishonesty lived in palaces, gave dinners, and dealt in millions, 'then dishonesty is not disgraceful, and the man dishonest after such a fashion is not a low scoundrel'.[39] Certainly, Grant's rise had illustrated the tolerance of dishonesty among social elites. The Conservative Party leadership was under no illusions as to Grant's nature, Edward Stanley, the 15th Earl of Derby, recording in his diary in 1874 that he was 'a disreputable speculator, who has more than once narrowly escaped prosecution for fraud'. Yet his scandalous career was inconvenient rather than fatal to his ambitions: Derby noted the following year that Grant's strategic moves—purchasing and renovating Leicester Square and donating it to the public; buying up a Liberal paper, the *Echo*, and turning it into a Conservative organ—were making things difficult for the party. 'He has done too many dirty acts to be whitewashed: and too many that are useful to be neglected.'[40]

Consequently, although it received mixed reviews at the time—it may not have made comfortable reading for some—Trollope's novel clearly struck a nerve. Several newspaper editorials published around this time could have been lifted from its pages. *The Times*, for example, identified

> increasing audacity, increasing greed, increasing fraud, increasing impunity... the country in general is now regarded as a prey upon which any number of vultures, scenting it from afar, may safely light and securely gorge themselves... what we are noticing is notorious and universal. There are scores of persons now going about with hardly a blemish on their characters, and revelling in the profits of this traffic.[41]

Another London paper claimed that 'the City of London is yearly becoming more and more a sink of iniquity, that robberies are daily more openly plotted, that the standard of commercial morality is assimilating itself to that of a pirate's den, and that men of wealth fish for the money of the poor and the unwary with absolute impunity'.[42] The *Irish Times* thought that the large numbers of companies wound up in the past few years included some of 'the most iniquitous frauds ever contemplated by professional swindlers'. The shareholders had been ruined, but the promoters were 'now monied men, holding their heads high, and living luxuriantly'.[43]

At the heart of all these pronouncements was the growing conviction that public opinion—the traditional regulator of commercial behaviour—was failing to curb sharp practice. It had long been believed that publicity would flush fraudsters out of the system in a self-regulating market. But as the market for shares grew more impersonal and face-to-face relations became less important, the

[38] Anthony Trollope, *The Way We Live Now* (London, 1876).

[39] Anthony Trollope, *An Autobiography* (Oxford, 1950; repr. 1980), 355.

[40] Diary entries for 28 January 1874 and 27 June 1875, *A Selection from the Diaries of Edward Henry Stanley, 15th Earl of Derby (1826–93)*, ed. John Vincent (London, 1994), 160, 227.

[41] *The Times*, 11 August 1875.

[42] An unnamed 'metropolitan journal', repr. in the *Star*, 3 December 1874.

[43] *Irish Times*, 10 March 1875.

effectiveness of these traditional extra-legal mechanisms declined.[44] If dishonesty and disgrace had become disconnected, one inference could be that external interventions were needed to enforce standards. The criminal trial therefore started to seem like a possible solution, and some began looking to the government to put it in motion. Thus, Cockburn's words in *Twycross v. Grant* were seized upon in parliament. If share-rigging amounted to obtaining money by false pretences, was it not the government's job to take legal proceedings against City operators suspected of the practice? This was the question put to the Conservative Attorney General, Sir John Holker, by Sir Edward Watkin, railway director and Liberal MP. Holker doubted that Cockburn had meant that share-rigging was actually criminal, and denied that it was any part of an Attorney General's duty to hunt out City corruption.[45] But the question did not go away, and four days later Home Secretary Richard Cross was asked whether he planned to appoint a public prosecutor to 'deal with the delinquencies of the rich as effectually as the police deal with those of the poor'.[46]

Cross used a recently appointed royal commission on the workings of the Stock Exchange as an excuse to avoid giving an opinion on the matter. But this was not mere stonewalling, for Disraeli's Conservative administration, in power since 1874, was showing an active interest in re-evaluating the laws regulating the financial sector. In addition to the royal commission on the Stock Exchange, a select committee on foreign loans had reported in 1875, and in May 1877, a committee was appointed to inquire into the Companies Acts of 1862 and 1867.[47] The committee started gathering evidence soon after these questions on criminal law in the Commons, and fraud was a prominent theme throughout. Proposals for corporate governance reforms to redress the balance of power between directors and shareholders were discussed at length. Yet the committee members could agree on practically nothing, with the result that no less than nine different committeemen put forward their own resolutions, representing in effect nine different reports. These resolutions ranged from interventionist measures such as limiting the borrowing powers of companies, giving the Registrar authority to vet company constitutions, and reintroducing the compulsory publication of balance sheets, to deregulatory proposals such as repealing section 38 of the 1867 act. The official report by necessity left out most of the contentious topics and, just one page long, was regarded as something of a non-event, receiving only a desultory discussion in the Commons. During this, Viscount Sandon, the President of the Board of Trade, made the government's adherence to traditional views on the responsibilities of shareholders very clear, viewing 'with horror the danger of too much interference'. Reforms to company law signalled to 'ignorant people' that 'the state was taking the whole responsibility on its own shoulders of seeing that commercial

44 R. B. Ferguson, 'Commercial Expectations and the Guarantee of the Law: Sales Transactions in Mid-Nineteenth Century England', in G. R. Rubin and David Sugarman (eds), *Law, Economy and Society, 1750–1914: Essays in the History of English Law* (Abingdon, 1984), 207.

45 Hansard, 3s, 234: 1435–8 (7 June 1877).

46 Sir George Campbell, Hansard, 3s, 234: 1581–2 (11 June 1877).

47 This was moved by George Gregory, a backbench Conservative, and agreed to by Edward Stanhope, Parliamentary Secretary to the Board of Trade: ibid. 180 (1 May 1877).

undertakings were sound, and that they need not trouble themselves about the matter'.[48]

Nevertheless, if the path to company law reform was blocked, there was an alternative, suggested by the evidence of Sir George Jessel, one of the most senior witnesses before the committee. Solicitor General under Gladstone until 1873, he then succeeded Lord Romilly as Master of the Rolls. From his vantage point in the Chancery Division of the new High Court of Justice, Jessel had gained an unrivalled insight into fraudulent business practice, and was consequently pessimistic about the state of commercial morality.[49] He had little time for the project of prevention, however. Reintroducing legislative safeguards such as publication of accounts was pointless (he had 'an utter distrust of these pieces of paper, called balance sheets'), because '[y]ou cannot make people honest by Act of Parliament'. The way to tackle fraud was to punish it when it was exposed. There was no need to create new criminal laws, for the existing law was sufficient: directors could be punished as fraudulent trustees, and while promoters were not trustees in law, they could be prosecuted under the law of false pretences, or the law of conspiracy, which was 'quite wide enough to reach them'. The problem lay in setting these laws in motion: 'no one [was] willing to incur the enormous expense and trouble of instituting prosecutions under these acts', and he could not blame ruined shareholders for shirking this role. The 1862 act gave Chancery judges the power to order prosecutions, which Jessel had recently used when it was discovered that the managing director of the Bronfloyd Mining Company had falsified its accounts. But such prosecutions were paid for out of company assets, so it was quite rare for the victims to support them. The answer was the appointment of a public prosecutor to take on the responsibility for—and crucially the cost of—such actions.[50]

Jessel exaggerated when he claimed that no one was willing to institute criminal proceedings, but recent events had underlined the fragility of these actions. Of the fraud cases committed to trial by Lusk during his time as Lord Mayor, only one ended satisfactorily, with the conviction and imprisonment of four of the Eupion directors in July 1876 after several long delays.[51] The other two cases were compromised, however. The second time the Peat Coal Company directors appeared at Mansion House, the shareholders' solicitor George Lewis announced that the directors had agreed to terms in a Chancery suit, so there was no need for the shareholders to persist with the criminal prosecution. Lusk was furious that such an egregious fraud had been compromised in this manner, but could not compel the prosecution to continue, so the directors walked free.[52] The motives of Henry Askew, the prosecutor in the Ruby Mines case, were also questioned, the defence lawyers alleging

[48] Ibid. 239: 1705–12 (10 May 1878).

[49] Following the Supreme Court of Judicature Acts of 1873 and 1875, the Court of Chancery was replaced by the Chancery Division of the High Court of Justice.

[50] *Report from the Select Committee on the Companies Acts, 1862 and 1867*, PP 1877 VIII. 125–36. The managing director was sentenced to eighteen months' hard labour: *Reg. v. Balcombe* (1877), *Western Mail*, 9, 11 May 1877; *Cheshire Observer*, 12 May 1877.

[51] *Reg. v. Aspinall* (1876) 2 QBD 59, *The Times*, 18 February, 4 July 1876.

[52] *The Times*, 9, 14 July 1874; *Graphic*, 18 July 1874.

that his main aim was to force compensation from the directors, but this did not stop Lusk committing Hartmont and Heyneman for trial after a thorough series of hearings.[53] Nevertheless, it was subsequently reported that Askew 'appeared to have remained dormant in the matter, and the solicitor in the case seemed to have retired from it'. Either Askew had had second thoughts about the costs of the prosecution, or the allegations against him were true and he had been bought off.[54]

These outcomes demonstrated that shareholders often viewed criminal prosecutions as adjuncts to civil actions, a means to encourage directors to come to terms. They were less interested in pursuing such prosecutions in the name of upholding public justice or commercial morality. The abandonment of the Ruby Mines prosecution exasperated Lusk, and converted him to the idea of a public prosecutor to avoid future miscarriages of justice.[55] Unexpected voices were joining the chorus. *The Times*, usually sceptical about wholesale interferences in joint-stock governance, thought that the fraudulent practices discussed before the committee on company law provided ample evidence to justify the establishment of a public prosecutor.[56] The Committee of the Stock Exchange also thought that rather than legislative restrictions on 'the free current of business' in the securities market, the best way to check fraudulent practices was 'to simplify the present cumbrous and costly civil and criminal procedure, and thus to afford the ready means of bringing wrong-doers within the reach of the law'.[57] Given the Committee's long-standing preference for self-regulation, its rejection of restrictions on its activities was predictable, yet this made its advocacy of criminal penalties all the more surprising.[58] In the mid 1870s, then, criminal sanctions for rogue directors and promoters won widespread acceptance as an alternative to a tightening of company law which would hamper honest boards and lull shareholder vigilance.

Jessel had pointed out that there was no need to wait for parliament to approve the principle of a public prosecutor, for the Solicitor to the Treasury, Augustus Stephenson, already responsible for prosecuting coinage offences and fraudulent bankruptcies, could carry out prosecutions on an ad hoc basis.[59] In fact, this is what the government had already started to do.[60] In January 1876, Richard Oakley,

[53] *The Times*, 6, 19 August 1874.

[54] Ibid. 1 January 1877. For more on Hartmont, see Michael Lobban, 'Commercial Morality and the Common Law: or, Paying the Price of Fraud in the Later Nineteenth Century', in Margot Finn, Michael Lobban, and Jenny Bourne Taylor (eds), *Legitimacy and Illegitimacy in Nineteenth-Century Law, Literature, and History* (Basingstoke, 2010), 119–47.

[55] *The Times*, 1 January 1877.

[56] Ibid. 14 September 1877.

[57] *Report from the Select Committee on Loans to Foreign States*, PP 1875 XI. 247.

[58] Ferguson, 'Commercial Expectations', 196.

[59] *Select Committee on the Companies Acts, 1862 and 1867*, 131–7. For the development of the Treasury Solicitor's prosecutorial functions, see J. Ll. J. Edwards, *The Law Officers of the Crown* (London, 1964), 371–3; David Bentley, *English Criminal Justice in the Nineteenth Century* (London, 1998), 84.

[60] One legal scholar, writing about a Treasury prosecution for homicide in 1870, argues that press coverage was instrumental in prompting the government to act. Public outcry was undoubtedly a factor in some of the fraud cases discussed below, but the government had not previously responded to pressure in this way; it was testing the legal waters by selecting cases which it thought it could win. Richard W. Ireland, 'Sanctity, Superstition and the Death of Sarah Jacob', in Anthony Musson and Chantal Stebbings (eds), *Making Legal History: Approaches and Methodology* (Cambridge, 2012), 299–300.

manager and proprietor of the Co-Operative Credit Bank, was arrested on the sworn informations of his accountant and one of his branch managers. This was not a joint-stock company: indeed, Oakley had drawn business from joint-stock banks by claiming that as his firm was not encumbered with the costly paraphernalia of the corporation, he could pay interest rates of 18 per cent. Savers pumped £50,000 into his bank's sixty branches before it collapsed. Halfway through the hearings before the Lord Mayor, the Treasury Solicitor took over the prosecution on the grounds that the case was 'of too much importance to be left in private hands'.[61] Under the Treasury's guidance, Oakley was successfully convicted of obtaining money by false pretences and sentenced to five years' penal servitude.[62] As with the prosecutions earlier in the decade, the extreme credulity of the depositors did not negate the legitimacy of the prosecution in the views of commentators, with the sentence welcomed as 'wholesome' and tending 'to sober a dangerous class of persons'.[63] But the question remained whether the government would take on more complex joint-stock frauds.

THE TREASURY PROSECUTES

The answer was an emphatic yes. Bubble companies seemed to offer the best chances of success, though it turned out that one man's bubble was another man's struggling business. In December 1877, following lengthy police surveillance, the Treasury prosecuted Alfred de Lara, manager of the Fine Art Publishing Company. The prosecution alleged this was not a bona fide business, but a scam for obtaining deposits, fees, and artwork from gullible lady artists. After a thorough examination at Bow Street police court, however, the magistrate Sir James Ingham dissented. The books showed that de Lara had carried on a legitimate business for a considerable time, and when he reached the end of his resources he had, like many struggling tradesmen before him, resorted to 'certain devices'. But these devices would not sustain a criminal charge, and so Ingham discharged the defendant.[64]

Other attempts proved more successful. One case underlined that criminal prosecutions offered the government an alternative to controversial reforms to company law. In early 1878 the Reverend William Blake, a Norfolk rector, won a civil suit against the Albion Life Assurance Society, recouping the £60 he had paid for a policy four years previously. The odd sequence of events which led Blake to take out the policy was exposed during the trial. Responding to an advertisement in the *Standard* offering commission-free, low-interest loans on personal security, Blake was offered the £1,500 he needed to purchase a living by a London-based civil engineer, Henry Howard.[65] The loan came with a condition: that Blake insure his

[61] *Morning Post*, 26 February 1876; *Liverpool Mercury*, 26 February 1876.
[62] *Reg. v. Oakley* (1876), *The Times*, 14 August 1876.
[63] *The Times*, 25 March, 14 August 1876.
[64] *Daily News*, 18 January 1878; *The Times*, 18 January 1878.
[65] *Standard*, 24 September 1874.

life for the same sum with an insurance office of Howard's choice—the Albion—as collateral security. But this turned out to be one of many requirements: before the loan was granted, Blake had to agree to a whole raft of unreasonable terms, including making out a bill of sale on his furniture, finding two sureties to guarantee the loan, and signing a bond for the full £1,500. He refused, and was left with an insurance policy he did not want, and no loan. Blake would not walk away, however, and his solicitor tracked down other customers with similar experiences. It transpired that Howard and the Albion were in league. Howard, operating under a variety of identities including his real name, Thomas Wood, induced customers to take policies with the company to obtain loans. But the loans were never granted, and were never intended to be granted.[66]

The case did not end with Blake's recovery of his £60. One of the members of the jury wrote to the press after the trial claiming that the government was indirectly to blame for the fraud. While the 1870 Life Assurance Companies Act, passed in response to abuses exposed in the late 1860s, obliged companies to register their balance sheets with the Board of Trade, these returns were not vetted by the Board.[67] Evidence that the Albion was a fraud could have been ascertained from its returns, but they were 'unhappily buried, in Parliamentary Blue-books', published year after year 'without one word of comment or warning'. If the Board had acted, Blake and many others would not have been defrauded.[68] The question was taken up in parliament by Sir Joseph Pease, the Liberal industrialist and banker, who asked whether the government would in future supervise insurance company accounts more carefully.[69] The President of the Board of Trade, Sir Charles Adderley, categorically denied that government had a responsibility to vet or monitor company returns.[70] Pease's request was evidence of the ratchet-like logic of investor protections, and government was wary of going any further down this path. But there was an alternative.

Four days after Pease's question, five men connected with the Albion appeared at Bow Street police court on warrants obtained by the Treasury.[71] Harry Poland, leading the prosecution, explained that after disclosures made during the civil trial 'it became the duty of the Crown to take up the prosecution of the case, which was one of vast importance to the country'.[72] Keeping Thomas Wood, aka Howard, company in the dock were George Thompson and James Northcott, the director

[66] *Blake v. Albion Life Assurance Society* (1878) 4 CPD 94, *Daily News*, 4 February 1878; *Lloyd's Weekly Newspaper*, 10 February 1878; *Standard*, 7 March 1878; *The Times*, 11 March 1878.

[67] 33 & 34 Vict. c. 61, ss. 5–10. The main scandal was the collapse of the Albert Life Assurance Company in 1869: Timothy Alborn, 'The First Fund Managers: Life Insurance Bonuses in Victorian Britain', in Nancy Henry and Cannon Schmitt (eds), *Victorian Investments: New Perspectives on Finance and Culture* (Bloomington, IN, 2009), 71–3.

[68] *Daily News*, 13 March 1878.

[69] Hansard, 3s, 238: 1590–2 (19 March 1878).

[70] Ibid. 239: 519–20 (4 April 1878).

[71] *Morning Post*, 25 March 1878; *The Times*, 25 March 1878.

[72] *Pall Mall Gazette*, 29 March 1878; *Morning Post*, 29 March 1878; *The Times*, 29 March 1878. Poland was Senior Treasury Counsel at the Old Bailey until 1889: Ernest Bowen-Rowlands, *Seventy-Two Years at the Bar: A Memoir* (London, 1924), 1.

and manager of the Albion, together with William Shaw and Thomas Slinker, Wood's clerks. Three further clerks—all brothers of Shaw—were subsequently arrested. The hearings continued through April and into early May, with Sir James Ingham eventually committing all eight men for trial.[73]

The case was tried before Justice Henry Hawkins at the Old Bailey towards the end of May. The defendants faced two sets of charges: one for obtaining money under false pretences, the second for conspiracy to defraud. The false pretences concerned the nature of the Albion and of the money-lending business: both, the prosecution claimed, were shams. The conspiracy rested on the links between the two arms of the operation.[74] Proving this in a court of law necessitated presenting a substantial amount of evidence, leading to an epic trial lasting ten days; nearly as long as the Royal British Bank trial a generation earlier. Although the Albion was registered under the Companies Act, it was, the prosecution claimed, 'not a real business at all': it had no capital, no insurance fund, no securities, no solicitor; it incurred no legal expenses. In 1863, Thompson and five others contributed £50 each to establish the company. Of this, £100 was spent on Chancery Lane offices and furniture, leaving a capital of just £200, though the nominal capital was advertised as £50,000. No shares were held by the outside public, allowing the company to announce attractive but meaningless dividends of 6 per cent. When the company failed, it had just £1,700 to meet all its liabilities. Wood's loan office was also a sham, the prosecution claimed, because if he had intended to lend money, he would have made sure to inform borrowers of the securities required before they paid their premiums. Wood was the main beneficiary: entitled to an enormous 50 per cent commission on all policies secured, he netted a useful income of around £2,000 a year, Thompson and Northcott receiving smaller sums.[75]

The defence's main task was to present the Albion as a legitimate business, and they showed that the company did in fact pay out on insurance policies to the tune of £32,000 during its lifetime, and that it sometimes declined applications. This was surely not the behaviour of a fraudulent office? Thompson and Northcott's counsels claimed that their clients knew nothing of Wood's unethical behaviour, and could not be held liable. The prosecution countered that paying out on policies was not proof of honesty, but was simply necessary in order to perpetuate the fraud. Moreover, it was impossible for Thompson and Northcott to claim ignorance of the moneylender's activities because of the number of letters of complaint the Albion received from his victims. The defence had nonetheless sowed doubt in the minds of the jury. After more than two hours' deliberation, they returned to ask Hawkins 'what would constitute false pretences on the part of an insurance company'. Hawkins explained 'that they must not look at the question of this society as an incorporated society, but at the acts of the prisoners as individuals'. After further deliberation, the jury found Wood, Northcott, Thompson, and William Shaw guilty of conspiracy and obtaining money by false pretences; Slinker was guilty of conspiracy only; Shaw's

[73] *The Times*, 13 May 1878.
[74] Indictment No 81, Thomas Wood (27 May 1878), TNA, CRIM 4/889.
[75] *Reg. v. Wood* (1878), *The Times*, 30 May, 6 June 1878.

brothers were pronounced innocent tools in the hands of the others, and acquitted. Hawkins concurred with this verdict, calling it 'a most cruel fraud'. Known as a harsh judge—his nickname was 'Hanging Hawkins'—he thought it his duty to pass a deterrent sentence, and he gave the three principal offenders five years' penal servitude apiece, Shaw and Slinker receiving lesser sentences.[76]

Though difficult to prove in court, the Albion was ultimately judged to be a sham business. The government also took the bold step of prosecuting frauds perpetrated in a legitimate business. In 1877, the affairs of the Artisans, Labourers, and General Dwellings Company were in crisis. Founded in 1866 as part of the 'five per cent philanthropy' movement which provided low-cost, high-quality housing to the working classes whilst also generating profits for investors, the company seemed to be highly successful.[77] But in the background rumbled concerns over the company's financial management, prompting the resignation of three of the company's biggest patrons, including the Earl of Shaftesbury.[78] Trouble came to a head at the company's annual general meeting in March 1877. One of the auditors objected to the 6 per cent dividend recommended by the board as unwarranted by the company's earnings. The directors replied that it was 'a matter of good policy' to keep the dividend at 6 per cent, 'so that they might induce capitalists to come and help them to complete their undertakings'. While the meeting adopted the board's report, the auditor resigned, and the shareholders appointed a committee, chaired by the Liberal MP Evelyn Ashley, Shaftesbury's son, to investigate the company's financial condition.[79] Within a month, three members of the company appeared in the dock of Bow Street police court charged by the committee with conspiring to defraud the shareholders of £30,000.

The men were Dr John Baxter Langley, chairman of the board, the unfortunately named William Swindlehurst, manager and secretary, and Edward Saffery, the company's estate agent.[80] The 'irrepressible' Baxter Langley was the most prominent of the three.[81] A radical, he had been variously a newspaper editor, author, lawyer, surgeon, parliamentary candidate, and a campaigner on issues ranging from trade unions to the contagious diseases acts. Although the shareholders' committee had uncovered a host of irregularities, the main charge of the prosecution, conducted by the omnipresent George Lewis, was that the three had purchased estates cheaply then sold them to the company at inflated prices, pocketing the difference.[82] After beginning legal proceedings, the committee secured an audience with Home Secretary Cross to request help. The fact that the shareholders were so well connected—several sat in parliament, and among their ranks was the leading

[76] *The Times*, 10 June 1878; Herbert Stephen, rev. P. R. Glazebrook, 'Henry Hawkins', *ODNB*.

[77] John Nelson Tarn, *Five Per Cent Philanthropy: An Account of Housing in Urban Areas between 1840 and 1914* (Cambridge, 1973).

[78] The bone of contention was the board's refusal to circulate a report on the company's financial position: *The Times*, 4 January 1876.

[79] *Lloyd's Weekly Newspaper*, 4 March 1877; *The Times*, 5 June 1877.

[80] *The Times*, 4, 19 July 1877.

[81] *Musical Standard*, 28 November 1868.

[82] *The Times*, 4 July 1877.

banker Nathan Mayer Rothschild—probably greased the wheels. Following further enquiries, Cross ordered the Treasury Solicitor to take up the prosecution, and soon afterwards, magistrate James Vaughan committed the defendants for trial.[83]

As in the Albion case, the Old Bailey trial before Commissioner Robert Kerr in October was not straightforward. This time, the prosecution, led by Attorney General Holker, looked like being derailed by legal technicalities. All three defendants were charged with conspiracy to defraud the company; Baxter Langley and Swindlehurst were also charged under the Larceny Act with appropriating the company's money for their own use. The charges under the Larceny Act could not be sustained, argued the defence, led by Sir Henry James, Gladstone's former Attorney General, because legally speaking, the money the men were said to have misappropriated did not belong to the company, but to Saffery, who had acquired it legally. Nor was there evidence of conspiracy or false pretences, because there was no written contract or agreement between the men to divide the money among themselves. The strategy only half worked: Kerr agreed to reserve the first point regarding the Larceny Act for further consideration, but not the second, so the case would go to a jury.[84]

James's other main gambit was to admit the immorality of what the men had done, but to draw a distinction between immorality and illegality, and to claim that such practices were widespread. James conceded that the men 'had acted most improperly, and he, as their counsel, would not attempt to defend such conduct; that they had shown an absence of honourable and proper moral feeling in accepting this bribe, bonus, commission, or whatever it might be termed', but this practice was not illegal. Indeed, it 'was a known truth that half the transactions in the City of London were oiled by this giving of presents'.[85] But as the North Caradon trial had demonstrated a few years earlier, this was a risky strategy, all the more so when the judge was a High Church Scotsman of 'naturally deep and sincere religious feeling'.[86] Famed for the bluntness of his addresses to the jury, Kerr dismissed most of the defence's arguments.[87] The case, Kerr told the jury, was straightforward. If Saffery had kept the profits he made on the sales, there would have been no criminal case. But Saffery did not keep the profits: most of them made their way to Baxter Langley and Swindlehurst. The jury had to decide whether there had been an understanding between the men to share in the profits. It did not matter if the agreement was not in writing, nor did it matter that the property had subsequently risen in value—a fact which the defence had laboured. If there was an understanding between them, this constituted evidence of a conspiracy to injure the company. The jury found all three defendants guilty, though recommended Saffery to mercy.[88]

[83] *Daily Gazette*, 26 July 1877; *Standard*, 4 August 1877; *The Times*, 16 August 1877. Another director was charged with conspiracy, but absconded and was not found.

[84] *Reg. v. Baxter Langley* (1877), *The Times*, 24, 26 October 1877; *Daily News*, 26 October 1877.

[85] *The Times*, 26 October 1877.

[86] G. Pitt-Lewis, *Commissioner Kerr: An Individuality* (London, 1903), 7.

[87] He once reportedly gave a summing-up of just twelve words: 'Gentlemen of the jury, the man stole the ducks. Consider your verdict.' Nic Madge, 'Summing Up: A Judge's Perspective', *Criminal Law Review* (September 2006), 823.

[88] *Daily News*, 26 October 1877; *The Times*, 26 October 1877. Holker decided not to press for judgement on the Larceny counts, which would have meant going to the Court of Criminal Appeal.

Baxter Langley was 'astounded' by the verdict as he had no inkling that directors could be criminally prosecuted for 'receiving money from a person who had made a profit'. But Kerr, like his fellow Scotsman Campbell in the Royal British Bank trial twenty years earlier, stressed the need for law to intervene to tackle commercial immorality. The alleged ubiquity of the offences in the City was no excuse: rather, if this were true, it was all the more necessary for the court, 'which has no reason for public existence unless as a guardian of public morality—to mark its sense of these acts by passing sentence of sufficient severity, not to punish, but to deter others'. Notorious for his 'terrible sentences', Kerr decided that as this was the first time a case of this nature had been tried, he would pass 'a comparatively mild sentence', on the understanding that future cases would not be dealt with so leniently. Baxter Langley and Swindlehurst were given eighteen months' hard labour, Saffery received twelve months.[89] Half a century after the exposure of the payment of secret commissions to the Arigna Iron and Coal Company directors, the practice had finally been criminalized.

Twice the government had successfully intervened to prosecute the managements of companies engaged in fraudulent activities. The convictions were hailed partly for their social effects—the *Morning Post* welcomed the Artisans conviction because it was 'indispensable that the law should be administered equally to the rich and to the poor'—but chiefly for their anticipated economic effects.[90] No more was the market conceptualized as self-healing, as it had been in the evangelical economics fashionable earlier in the century. It was harder to see failure as having a purgative effect when permissive company law enabled irresponsible entrepreneurs to endlessly reinvent themselves using the vehicle of the limited company. Frauds undermined confidence and led to economic stagnation, and the external intervention of the law was required to restore confidence by punishing those who abused public trust. Discussing the Artisans case, the *Huddersfield Daily Chronicle* was explicit on this point. Letting the Baxter Langleys go unpunished

> would soon work a panic of incalculable disaster. Every sovereign buttoned up in the pocket instead of being invested, is a loss not only to the individual but to the productive power of capital; yet wide spread nefariousness in handling investments would lead to an extensive buttoning up of pockets, and the consequent stagnation of the tributaries which flow into the aggregate ocean of wealth.[91]

Similarly, the Albion conviction was welcomed for its economic benefits. Insurance frauds undermined trust and discouraged thrift and frugality, and whatever undermined thrift, wrote the *Derby Mercury*, 'strikes at the foundation of individual virtue and public prosperity'. The prosecution was therefore welcomed as an

[89] *Daily News*, 27 October 1877; *The Times*, 27 October 1877; Edmund D. Purcell, *Forty Years at the Criminal Bar* (London, 1916), 298. Baxter Langley's sentence was partially remitted in December 1878 by the action of the Home Secretary, acting on medical advice. Though he staged a recovery, living for another thirteen years, his public career was over, and he spent the remainder of his life in obscurity. *The Times*, 16 December 1878; *Reynolds's Newspaper*, 28 February 1892.

[90] *Morning Post*, 27 October 1877.

[91] *Huddersfield Daily Chronicle*, 29 October 1877. For similar sentiments, see *Preston Guardian*, 27 October 1877; *Western Mail*, 27 October 1877; *Era*, 28 October 1877.

essential intervention to enforce honesty in financial transactions.[92] Had the prisoners been acquitted, wrote *The Times*, 'ingenious frauds of this character would have received an encouragement which is not at all needed'.[93]

The onus for achieving these positive outcomes was beginning to fall on the state, and Disraeli's government proved willing to subsidize the victims of fraud in order to uphold 'individual virtue and public prosperity'. Doing so was not cheap. The cost of the Artisans prosecution was £1,225; the Albion cost £2,150. This meant that the total expense of criminal prosecutions for the year exceeded the original estimate by £2,000.[94] Despite this, there was appetite for even more prosecutions. For the *Standard*, the 'chief lesson' of the Albion case was the pressing need for a public prosecutor. For years the victims had suffered in silence, too embarrassed and too scared to act, but had there been a public prosecutor, the victims would have come to him at once, and the company's operations would have been ended much sooner. 'To trust, as at present, to the public to protect themselves is to lean upon a broken reed.'[95] Less than ten years after Gladstone's government had resisted intervening in the Overend and Gurney prosecution, company fraud, it seemed, was now firmly established as a public issue, the deterrence of which was a legitimate government function.[96] This was confirmed by events at the end of the decade.

A PUBLIC PROSECUTOR

In the autumn of 1878, scenes not witnessed in Scotland since the crisis of 1857 were played out on the streets of the nation's cities. On Wednesday 2 October the City of Glasgow Bank announced its suspension, news which was greeted with 'unmingled astonishment'. No bank was held in higher esteem among Scottish investors—even the Solicitor General for Scotland, Sir John Macdonald, held its shares—and while gossip as to the bank's stability had been circulating in the week before the stoppage, most discounted this as rumour 'invented for Stock Exchange purposes'. Indeed, such was confidence in the bank that its £100 shares had been changing hands for up to £243 days before its collapse, making them nearly as valuable as Bank of England stock. The morning of the suspension, crowds gathered outside the bank's head office and some of the larger branches, unwilling to believe that the doors would not open. Police were on hand to keep order, but the crowds lingered through the day, hoping that 'some scrap of information favourable

[92] *Derby Mercury*, 19 June 1878. See also *Daily News*, 10 June 1878.

[93] *The Times*, 10 June 1878. See also *Hampshire Telegraph and Sussex Chronicle*, 12 June 1878.

[94] *An Estimate of the Sums Required to be Voted for the Service of the Year Ending 31st March 1879, in Addition to the Sums Already Provided in the Estimates Presented in the Session of 1878*, PP 1878–79 XLVIII. 17.

[95] *Standard*, 10 June 1878. See also *Illustrated Police News*, 15 June 1878.

[96] The prosecutions of company directors represented a tiny percentage of overall Treasury prosecutions, but were among the most noteworthy and expensive. A return in 1881 showed that the Treasury conducted 1,745 prosecutions between 1877 and 1880, the large majority (1,144) of which were coin prosecutions: *Return of all Prosecutions and other Proceedings in the Nature of Prosecutions Conducted by the Solicitor to the Treasury during the last Three Years, 1877–80*, PP 1881 LXXVI. 121.

to their interests might be obtained'. Though the other Scottish banks had agreed to accept City of Glasgow bank notes in an attempt to stave off the kind of panic seen in 1857, mistrust spread through the sector. Banks across the country were 'besieged'; several customers were observed waddling home 'laden with the gold which they had withdrawn'. Rumours of suspension were rife; the Glasgow Stock Exchange opened with 'a serious panic' the morning of the failure, while shares on the Edinburgh and London exchanges also dropped.[97] The Earl of Derby recorded in his diary the general sense of anxiety and insecurity, noting that 'other failures are feared'.[98] But over the coming weeks only two other joint-stock banks suspended—the Caledonian Bank, which later reopened, and the West of England and South Wales District Bank.[99] If the City of Glasgow Bank had not fallen as part of a general banking crisis, why exactly had it failed?

The press was not slow to speculate, and rumours of reckless lending were rife.[100] Yet it was hard to reconcile this with the reputation of the board, which was made up of respected capitalists and gentry from Glasgow and Edinburgh: Robert Salmond, an Ayrshire laird, Henry Inglis, a landed proprietor, John Innes Wright, an East Indian merchant, William Taylor, a Glasgow magistrate and member of a large grain firm, John Stewart, an Edinburgh merchant, Lewis Potter, a shipping magnate, and Robert Stronach, who was also the manager. All were prominent in Scottish society; several were philanthropists and public benefactors; some were well-known Sabbatarians—Potter even refused to read Monday newspapers.[101] Even so, the bank had a spicy history, having encountered more than its share of trouble in its forty-year existence. Suspending payments during the 1857 crisis with losses of over £700,000, it subsequently staged a miraculous recovery, developing a reputation as a dynamic, buccaneering institution. Some of its shareholders and customers would mock officials of the older Scottish banks for being 'old-wifish' and 'slow of movement'.[102] By the late 1870s, it boasted a paid-up capital of £1 million, a reserve fund of half a million, and deposits of over £8 million. It had 133 branches—more than any other bank in Scotland—and had been paying dividends of 12 per cent to its 1,200 shareholders.[103]

The meaninglessness of these figures was revealed a fortnight after the failure when the bank's accountants issued their preliminary report. Its finances bore little relation to the picture painted in the last balance sheet, issued four months earlier. The bank had loaned its entire capital and reserve several times over to just three large firms. Rather than pull the plug on these overdrawn accounts and admit its losses, it had

[97] *Leeds Mercury*, 2 October 1878; *Pall Mall Gazette*, 2 October 1878; *The Times*, 3, 4, 5, 16 October 1878; *Aberdeen Weekly Journal*, 2, 3 October 1878; J. H. A. Macdonald, *Life Jottings of an Old Edinburgh Citizen* (London, 1915), 373–5.

[98] Entry for 3 October 1878, *Diaries of Edward Henry Stanley*, 42.

[99] For more on the latter, see Chapter 8.

[100] *Aberdeen Weekly Journal*, 3 October 1878; *The Times*, 4 October 1878.

[101] *The Times*, 21 October 1878; *Aberdeen Weekly Journal*, 22 October 1878; *Freeman's Journal*, 3 February 1879.

[102] Richard Saville, *Bank of Scotland: A History, 1695–1995* (Edinburgh, 1996), 421.

[103] *Aberdeen Weekly Journal*, 2 October 1878; *The Times*, 3 October 1878. Leo Rosenblum, 'The Failure of the City of Glasgow Bank', *Accounting Review*, 8 (1933), 285.

continued lending, concealing the losses in its accounts, until the deception had reached epic proportions: the deficiency was now over £5 million, and the shareholders faced massive calls to cover the bank's liabilities to depositors, for the bank had unlimited liability.[104] The report, widely reproduced in full in the press, was every bit as shocking as the original news of the bank's collapse.[105] The main topic of conversation not only in Scotland, but in the City of London, it was widely recognized as 'one of the most startling revelations of fraud which had ever been made'.[106]

Unlike the frauds of George Hudson a generation earlier, the morality of the case was presented in black-and-white terms. Criticisms of profit-hunting shareholders were muted, with *Reynolds*'s an isolated voice in reproaching middle-class shareholders 'who worship in the temple of Mammon', and expected huge dividends for doing nothing.[107] The collapse was more commonly regarded as a 'national calamity'; the shareholders were viewed as akin to victims of a natural disaster, and were recipients of organized charity, ranging from a benefit performance by the famous actor Henry Irving, to a huge relief fund—one the first national funds dedicated to shareholders in a private company—which eventually raised £388,000.[108] Rather than giving moral lessons in the perils of greed, the press called for immediate retribution, despite the fact that several of the directors were advanced in years (Salmond was 74, Potter 72), and Potter was known to be very ill.[109] In doing so, it followed the lead of the business community, which united in condemning what the directors had done. The case was considered 'so utterly black and scandalous that men can hardly trust themselves to characterize it', and 'even the strongly-nerved in the commercial community stood aghast'. The balance sheets 'went far beyond the common temptation of reckoning as good what ought to have been abandoned as hopelessly bad debts; they seem to have invented securities which never had an existence, and to have suppressed liabilities that were only too real'.[110] The wealthy former banker Lord Overstone thought the case 'completely eclipsed' the Western Bank case for 'recklessness, trickery, and roguery', and predicted that 'some of the Directors will find their way to hard labour at Portland or Dartmoor'.[111] Likewise, the press called for the directors to be prosecuted in order to restore confidence in Scottish banking, and to repair national honour.[112]

[104] *The Times*, 19 October 1878; *Freeman's Journal*, 21 October 1878.

[105] S. G. Checkland, *Scottish Banking: A History, 1695–1973* (Glasgow, 1975), 470–1; *Western Mail*, 19 October 1878; *Bristol Mercury and Daily Post*, 21 October 1878.

[106] *The Times*, 21 October 1878; *Aberdeen Weekly Journal*, 22 October 1878.

[107] *Reynolds's Newspaper*, 20 October 1878.

[108] *The Times*, 19, 25 October 1878; *Standard*, 21 October 1878; E. A. French, *Unlimited Liability: The Case of the City of Glasgow Bank* (London, 1985), 19.

[109] *Bristol Mercury and Daily Post*, 21 October 1878; *Freeman's Journal*, 21 October 1878; *Western Mail*, 19 October 1878.

[110] *The Times*, 21, 25 October 1878. The scale of the misrepresentations is charted in Anon., *The Great Trial of the Seven City of Glasgow Bank Directors for Using and Uttering False Balance Sheets* (London, 1879), 8–10.

[111] Overstone to G. W. Norman, *The Correspondence of Lord Overstone*, ed. D. P. O'Brien, 3 vols (Cambridge, 1971), iii. 1316.

[112] *The Times*, 19 October 1878; *Aberdeen Weekly Journal*, 22 October 1878.

But prosecution was far from a foregone conclusion. The Larceny Act did not apply to Scotland, so it was unclear whether the directors could be held criminally liable for misrepresentation.[113] Even making false returns to the government of the bullion held against notes issued was a civil rather than a criminal offence, and one for which the bank, rather than the directors personally, were liable.[114] Moreover, the shell-shocked shareholders were unlikely to initiate criminal proceedings, and while Scotland, unlike England, had a public prosecutor in the form of the Lord Advocate, this officer had no track record of pursuing company fraud cases.[115] Nevertheless, the government acted decisively. Just twenty-four hours after the report's publication the Crown authorities in Scotland ordered the arrest of the seven directors, who were charged with 'falsehood, fraud, and wilful imposition'.[116] Within two weeks they were committed for trial.[117] A measure of how far expectations of government had changed since the Overend and Gurney scandal just a decade previously was the fact that the arrests did much to 'calm public excitement' and 'restore confidence by giving bank shareholders and depositors some guarantee that in other cases similar malpractices are not being pursued or can be practised with impunity'.[118]

Their trial in Edinburgh's High Court in January 1879 was a major news story which occupied the graphic reporters of the day: seeing the directors of such a large enterprise in the dock was still something of a novelty (see Figure 7.1). Accused of the 'wicked and felonious fabrication of balance sheets... with intent to defraud', the defendants also faced charges of theft and embezzlement.[119] The embezzlement charges, founded on the idea that obtaining a loan on inadequate security was a criminal offence, were particularly controversial and early in the trial the judge, Lord Justice Clerk James Moncreiff, said that the prosecution faced a difficult task proving them. Sure enough, halfway into the trial, after presenting evidence solely on misrepresentation, Lord Advocate William Watson withdrew the embezzlement and theft charges. It was strongly suspected that this had been the intention all along, and that the charges had been framed in order to deny the defendants bail, preventing them from absconding before the trial. The upshot was that the directors were ultimately tried for the same offence as the Royal British Bank directors a generation ago.[120]

[113] *Standard*, 19 October 1878; *Aberdeen Weekly Journal*, 22 October 1878.

[114] Chancellor Sir Stafford Northcote thought this was wrong, writing to Cross 'we must make false returns punishable': letter of 17 November 1878, ff. 146–7, British Library, Cross Papers, Add.51265.

[115] As seen in Chapter 5, the Lord Advocate declined to prosecute following the Western Bank of Scotland failure. In 1866, the directors of the Edinburgh and Glasgow Railway Company asked the Lord Advocate to prosecute the chairman of the North British Railway Company for falsification of accounts, but to no avail: *The Times*, 8 November 1866; *Leeds Mercury*, 21 November 1866.

[116] *The Times*, 21 October 1878; *Aberdeen Weekly Journal*, 21 October 1878; William Wallace (ed.), *Trial of the City of Glasgow Bank Directors* (London, 1905), 10.

[117] *The Times*, 4 November 1878.

[118] Ibid. 22 October 1878.

[119] Anon., *Great Trial*, 8.

[120] *Reg. v. Stewart* (1878), *The Times*, 20, 22, 28 January 1879; *Glasgow Herald*, 1 February 1879. Charges of fraud and deception were not sufficient to deny defendants bail, but embezzlement and theft were.

Figure 7.1 'Not Guilty, My Lord': The City of Glasgow Bank Directors in the Dock, *Report of the Trial of the Directors of the City of Glasgow Bank* (Edinburgh, 1879), between pp. 28–9

How would Moncreiff view the alleged misrepresentations of the defendants? As a Whig and a strong free trader, who once told the Edinburgh Chamber of Commerce that 'the true secret of national prosperity is to leave trade as unfettered as you can—leave it to its natural career', would he be cautious about applying the criminal law to company directors?[121] Clearly not. In his charge to the jury

[121] Wilson Harvey Bain, 'The Life and Achievements of James, First Baron Moncreiff, 1811 to 1895', MLitt thesis, University of Glasgow, 1977, 225–6.

he explained that there had to be evidence of fraudulent intent before they could convict, and proving intent could indeed be the sticking point in fraud trials. But he drew a distinction between intent to ruin the bank and its shareholders—as in the case of a bubble scheme—and intent to deceive the shareholders and the public as to the true condition of the bank. Moncreiff dismissed the idea that the directors conspired to ruin the bank for their own gain. They held their shares to the end, and there was no evidence that they were trying to flee a sinking ship. However, Moncreiff told the jury that the second type of dishonest intent was just as serious a crime, at least in its effects, thus undermining the main prop of the men's defence: that they had merely sought to keep the bank afloat until better times came.

> So far from being a defence, that was exactly the offence and motive described in the indictment... they hazarded exactly the interests which would have been imperilled if they had been actuated by the strongest and most malignant motive. The men who were induced to buy shares were ruined precisely as they would have been if that had been the result intended by the directors.[122]

This view of the law was informed by a strict sense of commercial morality which trumped any argument for laissez faire. Descended from eight generations of clergymen, and a man of strong Presbyterian views, Moncreiff told the jury that 'there was one thing a director was bound to have, and that was in every case honesty, and neither the interests of the shareholders nor the chance of recovering the debt... justified or excused him in making a deliberate statement which he knew to be false'.[123] After this, the jury unanimously found Stronach, the manager, and Potter, the longest-serving director, guilty on all counts. But for the other five, the evidence was less clear-cut, so they were acquitted of falsifying the balance sheets themselves, merely of publishing them knowing to be false, and by a majority only rather than unanimously.[124] In his sentencing, Moncreiff absolved Stronach and Potter of 'corrupt' personal motives, noting that if they had been convicted on the counts of theft or embezzlement, the sentence would be much harsher. He gave the pair eighteen months' imprisonment, without penal servitude. The other five had been found guilty of a lesser crime, and four of them had already been imprisoned for three months awaiting trial, so he sentenced them to eight months each. The prisoners were deeply affected by the outcome, particularly Stronach, 'who cried bitterly'. Hooting crowds followed them on their short journey in the police van to Calton Jail.[125]

The press recognized the trial, which at eleven days was the longest in the history of Scotland's criminal courts, as a landmark in Scottish law.[126] The *Glasgow*

[122] *The Times*, 1 February 1879; *Report of the Trial of the Directors of the City of Glasgow Bank* (Edinburgh, 1879), 234–55.

[123] Bain, 'Life and Achievements', viii.

[124] *The Times*, 1 February 1879. Majority verdicts were permitted in Scottish law.

[125] Ibid. 3 February 1879. One of the former directors, James Nicol Fleming, who absconded shortly after the bank's collapse, was caught and tried in 1882 for the same offences. He was convicted and sentenced to eight months: *Glasgow Herald*, 4 July 1882.

[126] *Daily News*, 1 February 1879.

Herald welcomed the fact that the trial had established the falsification of balance sheets as a criminal as well as a civil offence, and hoped that the outcome would be 'well pondered' by all directors.[127] Many commentators thought the trial would perform an important regulatory role, setting new standards of honesty in the economy and reinvigorating commercial morality. The guilty verdict placed a new obligation on directors to tell the truth about their company's affairs. Each of the defendants had probably reassured himself that 'he was only doing what thousands of other men had done before him', but this illusion had been 'rudely dispelled by the stern finding of the jury'.[128] The outcome would prove 'a safeguard for good faith in banking', on which 'we are so much dependent for the stability of trade'.[129] The lesson was certainly heeded: the punishments meted out by Moncreiff were 'the first and only sentences for fraud in Scottish clearing bank history'.[130]

The Glasgow Bank scandal put the Conservative government's stance on company law under strain, generating renewed demands for regulatory overhaul. The most popular solution was—as in previous crises—public auditors appointed by government.[131] Chancellor Sir Stafford Northcote responded by introducing a bill with two main aims. The first was to adjust the liability regime in joint-stock banks. Banks had been reluctant to take advantage of the legalization of limited liability in 1858, partly because they would have to keep large sums of capital idle to reassure depositors. But the City of Glasgow Bank failure highlighted the catastrophic effects which could follow from unlimited liability, with the shareholders ultimately facing calls of £2,750 per share to meet the bank's liabilities. The bill therefore introduced a system of reserve liability designed to allow banks to restrict their liability whilst retaining the confidence of depositors.[132] The second main purpose of the bill was to provide for annual audits by auditors appointed at the general meeting.[133] This fell far short of the public audit urged by reformers, for the auditors did not have to be qualified professionals. Even the government doubted that it would have much effect. Home Secretary Cross told the House that the audit clause would have prevented the City of Glasgow Bank fraud, but in the next breath admitted that if banks were dishonest, 'it would be difficult for any audit to defeat them'.[134] Certainly, members on both sides of the House were convinced of the futility of legislative interventions in corporate governance.[135] Liberal frontbencher William Forster believed that directors could

[127] *Glasgow Herald*, 1 February 1879.

[128] *Leeds Mercury*, 1 February 1879; *Birmingham Daily Post*, 1 February 1879.

[129] *Dundee Courier and Argus*, 3 February 1879. For similar views, see *Daily Gazette*, 1 February 1879; *Freeman's Journal*, 1 February 1879; *Sheffield and Rotherham Independent*, 3 February 1879.

[130] Checkland, *Scottish Banking*, 473.

[131] Stephen P. Walker, 'More Sherry and Sandwiches? Incrementalism and the Regulation of Late Victorian Bank Auditing', *Accounting History* 3 (1998), 41.

[132] Graeme G. Acheson and John D. Turner, 'The Death Blow to Unlimited Liability in Victorian Britain: The City of Glasgow Failure', *Explorations in Economic History*, 45 (2008), 251–2.

[133] Hansard, 3s, 245: 799–800 (21 April 1879); 42 & 43 Vict. c. 76.

[134] Ibid. 248: 1562 (29 July 1879).

[135] Ibid. 988–9 (22 July 1879).

easily avoid the 'searching examination' intended by the act, but did not call for more rigorous legislation on the grounds that it was impossible for the legislature 'to do the work of the shareholders', whose job it really was to secure a meaningful audit.[136] But once again, innovations in criminal law offered an alternative to reforming company law, and a second government measure passed in the same session, though neglected by historians of the company, was far more significant in its ramifications for the joint-stock economy.

Leading lawyers such as Lord Brougham and Lord Chief Justices Campbell and Cockburn had repeatedly highlighted the many defects of the system of private prosecution in England before commissions and committees in 1845, 1854–56, and 1874.[137] But disagreement on what a system of public prosecution should look like—whether it should be modelled on the Scottish or Irish codes or based on new principles—together with fierce opposition on the grounds of cost, meant that little progress was made.[138] Impetus for reform increased in the 1870s, with fresh bills prepared on the subject, and the Judicature Commission, appointed to investigate the entire legal system of the country, gave its unanimous approval to the idea of a public prosecutor in 1874, with one member stating that crimes were offences 'not against the individual who may have been injured... but against the Community or State'.[139] But still there was no breakthrough. What helped to push past this impasse was the widespread eagerness to see company frauds punished. Whilst the new police forces had gradually taken on a de facto public prosecutorial role, they focused on public disorder offences rather than complicated financial cases which they did not have the expertise to deal with, and scandals ranging as far back as the Independent West Middlesex case in 1841 had begun to win converts to the idea of a public prosecutor to tackle the crimes of the wealthy.[140] As we have seen, Disraeli's government authorized prosecutions in several high-profile fraud cases in England by the Treasury Solicitor, although it seemed cautious about going further. It had prepared a bill to establish a public prosecutor, yet this was held back in 1877 and 1878, with Cross warning the House that it would not be a cheap measure.[141] But the City of Glasgow Bank case advertised the benefits of a

[136] Ibid. 249: 857 (12 August 1879); Walker, 'Sherry and Sandwiches', 35, 48.

[137] Edwards, *Law Officers*, 339–59; Keith Smith, 'The Trial: Adversarial Characteristics and Responsibilities; Pre-trial and Trial Procedures', in *The Oxford History of the Laws of England*, 13 vols (Oxford, 2003–), xiii. 63–5; Paul Rock, 'Victims, Prosecutors and the State in the Nineteenth Century England and Wales', *Criminal Justice*, 4 (2004), 336–7.

[138] Before the 1870s, there had been only one bill before parliament on the subject, in 1854, which had been withdrawn: Edwards, *Law Officers*, 349.

[139] The words are Cockburn's: *Judicature Commission: Fifth and Final Report of the Commissioners*, PP 1874 XXIV. p. xix.

[140] For the growing prosecutorial functions of the police, see Douglas Hay and Francis Snyder, 'Using the Criminal Law, 1750–1850: Policing, Private Prosecution, and the State', in Douglas Hay and Francis Snyder (eds), *Policing and Prosecution in Britain, 1750–1850* (Oxford, 1989), 39; Smith, 'The Trial', 63, 67. Back in the 1860s, the *Pall Mall Gazette* argued that a public prosecutor was necessary in order to secure justice in cases of 'complicated commercial frauds': *Pall Mall Gazette*, 2 January 1869.

[141] Hansard, 3s, 229: 1189–90 (25 May 1876), 233: 1077 (13 April 1877), 235: 1519–20 (19 July 1877), 242: 1526 (8 August 1878).

public prosecutor, the press noting that Scottish law, in contrast to its English equivalent, had been 'prompt and effective', and provided the opportunity for the government to act. It introduced its bill early in the 1879 session.[142]

More limited than earlier schemes of public prosecution, cost nonetheless remained a sticking point, with Liberals grumbling that there was no way of knowing whether the bill would commit parliament 'to an annual expenditure of £5,000 or £100,000'.[143] However, commercial fraud was the main battlefield in the debate, cited by both advocates and opponents of the bill. Some Liberals and Conservatives questioned whether recent frauds had demonstrated the need for public prosecutions. The Conservative John Floyer thought that it was 'prejudicial to the English character... to imitate the example of various foreign countries, and teach people to look to Government for everything. If people would not look after their own property, it was not right that they should be able to ask the Government to do it for them.' Mitchell Henry, a Gladstonian Liberal, echoed the line his leader took in 1869, disagreeing with those 'who seem to think that everybody should be protected in speculations into which they may enter by holding the terror of the law over the persons who commit some trifling breach of commercial law'.[144] Nonetheless, both Cross and Holker sold the measure to the Commons as a way of tackling 'cases of remarkable fraud', and a majority of members welcomed rather than feared this.[145] James Whitwell, a Liberal, saw the act's ability to bring 'commercial delinquents' to justice as a major selling point; his fellow Liberal John Barran thought that the mercantile community as well as the public more generally would see the benefits of the measure.[146] Indeed, the Associated Chambers of Commerce passed a resolution expressing its support of the bill, while local chambers of commerce also petitioned parliament in support.[147] Buoyed too by widespread support in the press, the bill passed its stages easily and received Royal Assent in July.[148]

CONCLUSION

Reg. v. Gurney had seemed to establish two things: that misrepresentation was not a crime provided it was done with 'honest' intentions; and second, that the government would not prosecute commercial frauds in the interests of defrauded shareholders. But both positions were overturned in the 1870s, with a host of successful prosecutions based on misrepresentation by directors, several of which were conducted on an ad hoc basis by the government, which formalized its involvement in criminal prosecutions in 1879.

142 *Sheffield and Rotherham Independent*, 3 February 1879; see also *Standard*, 1 February 1879.

143 Benjamin Williams, Hansard, 3s, 244: 966–7 (14 March 1879).

144 Hansard, 3s, 244: 984, 988 (14 March 1879).

145 Ibid. 976, 980 (14 March 1879).

146 Ibid. 983, 992 (14 March 1879). Similar sentiments were expressed by William Rathbone (Liberal) and James Bulwer (Conservative): 968–9.

147 *Bristol Mercury and Daily Post*, 6 March 1879; *The Times*, 19 April 1879.

148 *The Times*, 17 March 1879; *Glasgow Herald*, 17 March 1879; *Leeds Mercury*, 29 May 1879; 42 & 43 Vict. c. 22.

Why had this reversal taken place? To some extent it was a consequence of a gradual reconceptualization of corporate fraud, from a private to a public offence.[149] This was partly a function of the growing size of companies: with increasing fields of operation, dishonest companies could wreak havoc among far wider constituencies than just their shareholders. More importantly, it was a result of the changing status of corporate property. Company shares now represented many millions of pounds of national wealth, but were highly vulnerable to fraud. In theory, protection was provided by the private governance mechanisms established in company constitutions which enabled shareholders to hold management to account. But the limits of shareholder power were becoming clearer, and the result was a depoliticization of the role of shareholders within their companies. They became less expected to hold their directors to account, and the state was called upon to fill the regulatory vacuum. Mid-Victorian governments had resisted this, but the 1870s saw a transition from Gladstonian liberalism to 'Tory democracy' which was significant. Admittedly, Conservative Ministers were just as sceptical as their Liberal predecessors about tightening company law: the unhappy example of the 1844 Companies Act was still remembered. Focusing on the lack of company law reform, historians have concluded that the late Victorian response to fraud was completely inadequate. But this only tells half the story. Ministers found an alternative solution in the criminal law. Home Secretary Cross was an advocate of what his biographer calls 'responsive government', and an unremarked aspect of this was his readiness to intervene to ensure the prosecution of fraudulent entrepreneurs, using the criminal law to enforce honesty in business. Taking these initial experiments further, his support for the principle of public prosecution was instrumental in the legislative innovation of 1879.[150]

By the late Victorian period, evangelical views of crises as purging the system were falling completely out of favour, replaced by a vision of the economy as a mechanism which required outside intervention by the law if it was to operate efficiently. This vision was consistent with a different strand of religious thought, particularly prominent in Presbyterianism, which expected high standards of commercial morality from businessmen, and which saw wealth and status as no shield to the discipline of the law. These attitudes can be traced through Peter Laurie's firm stance on metropolitan frauds in the 1840s, Chief Justice Campbell's views on business laxity in the 1840s and 1850s, Lusk's public pronouncements on commercial morality in the mid 1870s, and finally Moncreiff's insistence on boardroom honesty in the City of Glasgow Bank trial. By these means a stern view of the responsibilities of directors was gradually imported into English law from north of the border.

As we have seen, where scholars have examined criminal law, the verdict has tended to be that punishments given to company fraudsters were too light to have

[149] Jane Garnett, 'Commercial Ethics: A Victorian Perspective on the Practice of Theory', in Christopher Cowton and Roger Crisp (eds), *Business Ethics: Perspectives on the Practice of Theory* (Oxford, 1998), 128.

[150] Five years previously, he had commented privately that he did 'not think that we can let this matter sleep any longer'. Dennis J. Mitchell, *Cross and Tory Democracy: A Political Biography of Richard Assheton Cross* (New York, 1991), 6, 77–8, 147.

any significant impact, and merely illustrate the hypocrisy of Victorian criminal justice, which treated clerks and workers more harshly than privileged defendants. It is true that commentators were sometimes disappointed: the short sentences handed down by Moncreiff to the City of Glasgow directors were almost 'direct incitements to fraud'; Kerr was also criticized for taking the status of the conspirators too much into account when sentencing in the Artisans case.[151] However, such judgements are wide of the mark. Both judges exercised moderation more because of the novelty of the prosecutions than because of the class of the offenders. And while the criminal justice system as a whole saw a move towards lighter sentencing from the early 1870s, this was certainly not reflected in the tough punishments doled out in 'bubble' cases, as evinced by the five-year sentences for White, Gibson, Wadge, Oakley, Wood, Northcott, and Thompson.[152] In cases of misrepresentation caused by the desire to keep a legitimate concern afloat, the directors went down with the shareholders and as a result, the moral boundary lines between 'the plunderer and the victim' were not sufficiently clear-cut to warrant swingeing sentences.[153] There is also a danger in anachronism when interpreting punishments: given the ignominy and shame that were widely believed to accompany a criminal conviction, contemporaries often supported lighter sentences. The Earl of Derby noted of the City of Glasgow Bank directors that having held high positions, 'the social ruin & disgrace of the sentence is in itself punishment enough'.[154] The eighteen months given to Baxter Langley and Swindlehurst were variously described in the press as 'terrible', 'severe and degrading', and 'erring neither on the side of excessive leniency nor excessive severity'.[155] Even the class warriors at *Reynolds's Newspaper* supported these 'severe' but 'justified' sentences.[156] Thus even short sentences were widely seen as a potentially valuable device for regulating the economy.

But questions remained. The judgement in the City of Glasgow case set the bar for the ethical standards expected of directors very high. Would this be confirmed by subsequent judgements, or would the precedent be renounced, as had happened after the Royal British Bank prosecution in 1858? Second, the misrepresentations of the City of Glasgow directors were sins of commission rather than omission, in contrast to the Overend and Gurney case. It was uncertain whether failures to disclose could be criminalized in the same way. Finally, although parliament had authorized the establishment of a new office for public prosecutions, due to come into operation in January 1880, it remained to be seen whether it would fulfil the considerable hopes of reformers.

151 *Standard*, 3 February 1879; *Freeman's Journal*, 29 October 1877.

152 Wiener, *Reconstructing the Criminal*, 258–60.

153 *The Times*, 4 February 1879.

154 Entry for 2 February 1879, *Diaries of Edward Henry Stanley*, 95.

155 *Belfast News-Letter*, 29 October 1877; *Morning Post*, 27 October 1877; *Hampshire Telegraph and Sussex Chronicle*, 31 October 1877.

156 *Reynolds's Newspaper*, 28 October 1877.

8

A Mixed Economy of Prosecutions: The 1880s

At 9.35 a.m. on Tuesday 27 April 1880, George Leonard, a Bristol colliery proprietor, strode into the courtroom at the Old Bailey. He was followed at intervals by six others: Alexander Allen, a wealthy Clifton gentleman; two former barristers: Joseph Coates, now a parliamentary agent, and Hereford George, now a clergyman; two bankers: Clement Lucas and John Gilbert; and Jerom Murch, a Unitarian minister, philanthropist, and four-time mayor of Bath.[1] Between them, they represented a cross-section of the south-west's civic elite, but they were on trial for publishing false balance sheets as directors and manager of the West of England and South Wales District Bank.

In many ways this looked like a re-run of the City of Glasgow Bank trial fifteen months earlier. The West of England was a large, long-standing, and widely trusted institution. Formed in 1834, it had a paid-up capital of £750,000 and its accounts showed a reserve fund of over £150,000. From its Bristol base, its influence spread across the region, opening forty-two branches. Its fortunate shareholders, who numbered nearly 2,000, had often received double-digit dividends, together with generous bonuses, and despite the economic downturn in the mid 1870s, the bank still paid an annual 8 per cent.[2] But, as at the Scottish bank, these dividends concealed a darker reality. The company had built a portfolio of bad debts, and towering above the rest was a catastrophic account with Booker and Co., a Cardiff tinplate works. By 1869 the overdraft had reached £400,000, but the bank continued to lend money and the total debt subsequently passed the half-million pound mark. Several banks experienced runs following the City of Glasgow Bank's sudden collapse, and the West of England Bank's lack of liquidity meant that it could only briefly hold out, suspending payment in December 1878.[3] Few could quite believe it—it ranked as the worst commercial disaster that had ever struck Bristol—and once the iron shutters had been pulled down at head office for the last time, thousands came to see for themselves, 'evidently determined to have ocular... proof of the fact'.[4]

Just as the directors of the Glasgow Bank had chased their losses and concealed them from the shareholders, so the directors of the West of England Bank had 'committed the same error on a smaller scale'.[5] The similarities between the cases

[1] *Bristol Mercury and Daily Post*, 28 April 1880; Alex Kolaczkowski, 'Jerom Murch', *ODNB*.
[2] *The Times*, 9 December 1878.
[3] Michael Collins, 'The Banking Crisis of 1878', *Economic History Review*, 42 (1989), 504–27.
[4] *The Times*, 10 December 1878; *Bristol Mercury and Daily Post*, 10 December 1878.
[5] *The Times*, 21 December 1878.

were enough to persuade the Conservative government, while the bill establishing a public prosecutor was still progressing through parliament, to instigate a criminal prosecution, following correspondence between some of the shareholders and Home Secretary Cross.[6] As in the Scottish case, the prosecution rested on the balance sheets issued immediately prior to the bank's failure, though, as it took place in England, it was framed under the Larceny Act, and the law of conspiracy. The trial was a lengthy and complex one—the books and papers produced were said to weigh several tons—and after the first day, proceedings had to be switched to the Court of Queen's Bench because the Old Bailey proved too cramped.[7] The trial lasted nearly as long as the Glasgow case—eight days—and was notable for the number of leading counsel involved: Sir John Holker and Sir Hardinge Giffard, the law officers in the outgoing Conservative administration, for the prosecution, and Sir Henry James, Charles Russell, Farrer Herschell, Edward Clarke, and John Day, among others, for the defence.[8] But there was a crucial difference—the judge. Lord Chief Justice Cockburn, who had argued so strongly for the acquittal of the Overend and Gurney directors, presided, and this proved to be significant.[9]

When presenting the case for the prosecution, Holker, recognized by contemporaries as 'a powerful advocate' who was always scrupulously fair to his opponents, admitted that the defendants had not gained at the expense of their shareholders, and that they had sincerely hoped that the bad debts would come good.[10] But he 'cared not what their object or motive might have been', for the fact was, they had committed 'a gross piece of deception'. The balance sheets for 1876 and 1877 had continued to list the value of the mortgage on the Booker works at its 1872 level of £450,000, without taking into account the rapid depreciation in its value: in 1879 the bank's liquidators had tried unsuccessfully to sell the works for just £80,000. The men 'had no right to put forward incorrect statements...The proper thing for them to do was to tell the truth and nothing but the truth. The only protection the public had was that balance sheets should tell the truth.'[11] But clashes between Holker and Cockburn revealed conflicting interpretations of the law: the friction between the two was apparent from an early stage, and Cockburn 'appeared very soon to form an opinion in favour of the defendants'.[12] The judge harried Holker during the latter's final address to the jury, and when the Attorney General signalled that he wanted to read a passage

[6] *Bristol Mercury and Daily Post*, 31 May 1879. Cross's Cabinet colleague Sir Stafford Northcote had slightly less sympathy for the shareholders, expressing amusement at local plans to relieve failed speculators by getting up a lottery: letter of 8 January 1879, ff. 153–4, British Library, Cross Papers, Add.51265.

[7] *Morning Post*, 24 April 1880.

[8] Edward Clarke, *The Story of My Life* (New York, 1919), 172.

[9] Also perhaps significant was the fact that the prosecution was instigated by a Conservative Home Secretary and conducted by Conservative law officers, whereas the accused, among whom was Murch, a Liberal, were defended by several leading Liberal lawyers, and that the judge, was also a Liberal. The political dimension did not become overt during the trial but may have influenced proceedings.

[10] Clarke, *Story of My Life*, 127.

[11] *Bristol Mercury and Daily Post*, 31 May 1879, 28 April 1880.

[12] Clarke, *Story of My Life*, 173.

from Lord Justice Clerk Moncreiff's summing up in the Glasgow case, Cockburn lost his temper, turning to the jury and telling them 'You must take your law from me, and not from any other Judge'. He only grudgingly allowed Holker to read the section in which Moncreiff said that the directors' intention to keep the bank afloat was no defence against lying.[13]

Cockburn indicated just how far he differed from Moncreiff's interpretation of the law in his summing up the next day. He began by belittling the offences the directors were charged with. The real grievance of the shareholders and creditors against the directors was their rash speculations which had caused the bank's collapse. 'That is the substance of the complaint; we are here only dealing with its shadow.' But the substance of the complaint, the mismanagement, could not be punished criminally—at most, it made the directors civilly liable. Cockburn doubted whether what remained—falsification of balance sheets—could sustain a criminal charge. He first queried whether what the directors had done really counted as falsification. 'If the board had made a fictitious entry of something which they knew to be valueless, or which did not exist, that would have been a false entry.' But they merely failed to allow for the depreciation of the value of assets caused by trade depression, and listed their former values, which they might one day recover. Furthermore, even if the accounts were taken to be false, intention to defraud was also necessary, but there 'could scarcely have been any intention on their part to defraud', because they were trying to keep the bank going in the interests of shareholders and creditors. Cockburn was here rowing vigorously away from Moncreiff's views. For the Lord Chief Justice, truth-telling was *not* an absolute duty of a director: to have revealed the bank's real state would have produced 'an immediate depreciation of the property of the shareholders, and it was in the interests of the shareholders that the facts should be kept as it were in abeyance, and not at once disclosed, so as to alarm the public. It would be of no advantage to the shareholders to be told that their shares were worthless.' After such a strong steer from the judge, the jury took just fifteen minutes to acquit all the defendants, a decision received with loud applause.[14]

It might seem odd that the outcome of this trial was so different to that of its Scottish analogue the previous year. In part, it was a result of the much longer interval between collapse and trial: in those sixteen months, passions had clearly cooled, and economic recovery to some extent vindicated the board's valuation of its assets: in the first quarter of 1880, the Booker company actually turned a small profit. But more than that, it was a product of the great fluidity in interpretations of the law. Newspapers were nearly uniform in their approval of the verdict. 'Men must not be sent to prison because they are not good bankers', asserted *The Times*.[15] The bank's balance sheets, most agreed, were 'honest errors' or 'sanguine forecasts', rather than deliberate frauds.[16] The press had no difficulty distinguishing

13 *Daily News*, 5 May 1880; *The Times*, 5 May 1880.
14 *Reg. v. Murch* (1880), *The Times*, 6 May 1880.
15 Ibid.
16 Ibid.; *Manchester Times*, 8 May 1880.

this case from the City of Glasgow failure, but in doing so, displayed collective amnesia about the facts of the Scottish case. Intent to defraud was lacking, it was confidently asserted, because none of the West of England directors profited personally by their actions—indeed some were ruined by them—and they all stuck by the 'sinking ship'.[17] Whatever errors of judgement they committed, all was done in the interests of the shareholders.[18] Yet most of this could have equally been said of the Scottish bank's directors who, though initially facing charges of embezzlement and theft, were only tried for the false balance sheets.

The *Standard* demonstrated a better memory than its peers, arguing that the two cases differed 'rather in degree than in kind'. It thought that the outcome would 'rather tend to confuse the mind as to what the duty of a bank director really is'. The defence had argued that 'deceiving the shareholders for their own benefit is not deceiving them', and that assets of no current worth could be listed at a value which they previously held, or at which they might have in the future, which the paper thought a 'startling theory'.[19] To be sure, the verdict removed the clear marker which had seemingly been laid down by the outcome of the City of Glasgow Bank trial, and re-imposed what had been the accepted view of intent to defraud in the 1860s: if a director did not set out to ruin his shareholders, he could not be held criminally liable for fraud. Although the City of Glasgow Bank directors were convicted of publishing false balance sheets, it is likely that the widespread belief that they had 'taken from the till' had helped the jury to reach a guilty verdict, true also of the Royal British Bank case. Where this element was lacking—as in the West of England case—convictions were unlikely. Thus the state of the law was left in a very confused state as the new office of Director of Public Prosecutions was established, and the resulting difficulty of securing convictions was soon brought home to the unfortunate office holder.

A WILFUL FALSITY IS A FRAUD

Disraeli's Conservative ministry had proved increasingly willing to instigate fraud prosecutions in the late 1870s, but it was far from certain that this trend would continue following the return of Gladstone's Liberals in April 1880, given the vehemence of Gladstone's views on such actions, outlined during the Overend and Gurney debate in 1869.[20] Yet responsibility for future prosecutions now rested chiefly with the new Director of Public Prosecutions (DPP), whose office came

[17] *Bristol Mercury and Daily Post*, 6 May 1880; *Birmingham Daily Post*, 6 May 1880; *Daily News*, 6 May 1880.

[18] *Morning Post*, 6 May 1880; *Ipswich Journal*, 11 May 1880.

[19] *Standard*, 6 May 1880. The paper's Conservative politics might have been a factor in its more critical stance on what Murch, a leading Liberal, and his fellow directors had done, though under the editorship of William Mudford, it was not zealously partisan: Dennis Griffiths, *Plant Here the Standard* (London, 1996).

[20] See Chapter 6.

into being in January 1880.[21] The first Director, John Maule QC, had been Recorder of Leeds for twenty years, was well respected locally, and was known to government, having sat on the Royal Commission on the Jamaican atrocities in 1865.[22] The appointment was well received in legal circles, some commentators predicting that the new office, with Maule at the helm, would 'revolutionize' the nation's criminal justice system.[23] But it would have to be a revolution on a shoe-string. The Conservatives established the new office cautiously and with the emphasis on economy. In a December 1879 letter to the chairmen of quarter sessions in England and Wales, Cross had stressed that it was 'not intended that the new system should supplant, but only supplement, the system at present in use. In the great majority of cases there will be no need for the interference of the Director of Public Prosecutions.' In January 1880, Holker drew up rules for Maule to follow which stated that the DPP would only prosecute in cases which he judged to be 'of importance or difficulty, or in which special circumstances seem to him to render his action necessary to secure the due prosecution of an offender'.[24]

The Conservatives were keen to keep expenses to a minimum. The DPP's salary of £2,000 was considered modest for the responsibilities entailed, being little more than county court judges received 'for their mostly common-place labours'. The act empowered the government to employ up to six assistants to help the DPP, but it started by appointing just one, on a salary of £1,000, together with three clerks, and the total annual cost of the office was around £4,000.[25] The government's economy-mindedness seems to have jeopardized the health of the staff: in May, one concerned MP told the Commons that he had heard that the DPP 'had been lodged in such an unhealthy office that he had been laid up with typhoid fever, as well as one of his assistants'. The government spokesman thought it was not as bad as all that, but accepted there were 'sanitary defects in the office' and 'another more suitable place had been provided'.[26]

However, these obstacles did not prevent Maule from instigating company prosecutions, the first coming in May 1880. Following his intervention, no less than thirteen men connected with the Northern Counties of England Fire Insurance Company, including several prominent Lancashire industrialists, were brought before Francis Headlam at Manchester police court on charges of publishing false accounts and conspiring to defraud the company's shareholders and creditors.[27]

[21] Though the Attorney General retained ultimate responsibility for prosecutions, which he exercised in major cases: see Chapter 10.

[22] *Leeds Mercury*, 24 December 1879, 23 October 1889.

[23] *York Herald*, 26 December 1879; *Pall Mall Gazette*, 27 December 1879.

[24] *Report of the Committee Appointed to Inquire into the Office of Public Prosecutor*, PP 1884 XXIII. 38–9.

[25] 42 & 43 Vict. c. 22, ss. 2–3; *Birmingham Daily Post*, 29 December 1879; *Committee Appointed to Inquire into the Office of Public Prosecutor*, vi.

[26] Hansard, 3s, 252: 854 (31 May 1880). Additionally, there seemed to be considerable confusion in government as to whether the DPP was ultimately responsible to the Home Secretary or the Attorney General, suggesting that the new office may not have been a high priority for ministers. Ibid. 265: 604 (20 August 1881), 266: 785–6 (16 February 1882).

[27] *Manchester Times*, 29 May 1880; *Leeds Mercury*, 29 May 1880.

The company was formed in 1876 with a nominal capital of £100,000, but only 1,100 of the company's 20,000 shares were taken, the majority by the directors, while customers were also slow to come forward. To try to kick-start demand, the company twice ramped up the nominal capital, first to £250,000 then to £1million, issuing balance sheets which conjured profits by leaving off large items from the debit side and anticipating payments. These moves failed to stave off collapse, which came at the end of 1879 once the company's tiny capital was exhausted and claims started falling due.[28] Despite the professionalization of audit in the late nineteenth century—the Institute of Chartered Accountants in England and Wales (ICAEW) had formed in 1880, and by 1886 over three-quarters of publicly quoted companies were audited by accountants—the case highlighted once more the uselessness of audits when auditors were the creatures of the board.[29] The company's auditor, George Nesbitt, was a member of the Manchester Institute of Accountants, but had helped the directors to conceal the true state of the company's finances.[30] After extensive hearings, Headlam committed all bar one of the men for trial at Manchester Assizes.[31]

The defendants were probably relieved when they discovered that the judge was to be Lord Justice George Bramwell. A vigorous supporter of general limited liability in the 1850s, his faith in individualism has been described as 'fanatical' and 'simplistic', with his political and economic philosophy resting on the sanctity of freedom of contract and dislike of 'grandmotherly protection'.[32] His legal judgements were often coloured by these extreme views, and it would have been no surprise to see him invoke the principle of *caveat emptor* in favour of the defendants. Yet although the prosecution, led by up-and-coming Irish advocate Charles Russell, suffered some blows, with charges against four of the twelve defendants having to be withdrawn during the eight days of the trial, it was bolstered by Bramwell's summing up. He started by observing that it was vital that the public be protected from commercial frauds, because the damage they did was 'almost beyond calculation'. Citing the City of Glasgow Bank case, he noted that 'a pitched battle between two armies would produce probably less misery than that abominable fraud did'. He derided the gambit employed by the defence counsels: admitting that their clients were bad directors, but not fraudulent ones. The question was not whether they were bad directors, but whether they had lied. Like Moncreiff, and unlike Cockburn, Bramwell thought that '[a] wilful falsity was a fraud. It did not matter how good or how pure, or how right-minded the intention might be...If

[28] *Manchester Times*, 17 July 1880; *Daily News*, 23 July 1880.

[29] Derek Matthews, *A History of Auditing: The Changing Audit Process in Britain from the Nineteenth Century to the Present Day* (London, 2006), 11. For a particularly sceptical view, see T. A. Lee, F. Clarke, and G. Dean, 'The Dominant Senior Manager and the Reasonably Careful, Skilful, and Cautious Auditor', *Critical Perspectives on Accounting*, 19 (2008), 677–711.

[30] Roy Chandler, John Richard Edwards, and Malcolm Anderson, 'Disciplinary Action against Members of the Founding Bodies of the ICAEW', *Accounting, Auditing & Accountability Journal*, 21 (2008), 831–2.

[31] *Leeds Mercury*, 26 June 1880.

[32] P. S. Atiyah, *The Rise and Fall of Freedom of Contract* (Oxford, 1979), 374–80; Edward Manson, *The Builders of our Law during the Reign of Queen Victoria* (London, 1895), 137.

they wilfully told untruths they were guilty of a fraud. No man had a right to tell a falsehood to another, even though he thought it would be for his benefit.' Bramwell denied that the scheme was a bubble, believing that the defendants 'hoped to make it a good thing'. But this did not excuse the steps they took to prop it up.[33]

The jury acquitted two of the defendants, but found the other six guilty of conspiracy to defraud.[34] Bramwell's sentencing speech, delivered in a crammed courtroom with hundreds outside unable to gain a seat, underlined what had been suggested in the late 1870s: the criminalization of fraud was not in conflict with economic individualism and permissive company law; it was a natural and necessary adjunct to it. This advocate of freedom of contract placed great importance on the legal enforcement of honesty in the boardroom in the absence of adequate supervision from shareholders. The right of men to associate freely together in commercial enterprises was essential to the country's prosperity, but 'persons who embark their money in such undertakings cannot judge for themselves; they have to trust to those who are responsible for the management for the proper conduct of the undertakings, and mutual confidence of men in one another is shaken by cases such as this'. Bramwell decided to be lenient owing to the high characters the men received, the jury's recommendation to mercy for five of the six, and because they had not appropriated the company's money. He therefore sentenced the four directors to six months' imprisonment apiece without hard labour; Nesbitt received twelve months, while James Crabtree, the manager who was considered the main mover behind the company, was given eighteen months with hard labour.[35]

If the men had misrepresented their company to the public, the press could be accused of the same thing in the editorials which followed the verdict. Eager to draw a clear distinction between this case and the West of England Bank trial a few weeks earlier, editorials ignored Bramwell's assertion that the Northern Counties was not a bubble, painting it in the darkest colours: 'here we have a deliberate system of fraud coolly carried on from the first', wrote the *Era*.[36] 'It was a tissue of lies from beginning to end', asserted *The Times*.[37] It was an 'organized fraud', a 'fraudulent scheme' with a 'well-baited hook', a 'bogus' company, and a 'hollow and rotten investment'.[38] But once again, the *Standard* grasped what was really going on. Admitting the differences between the two cases—unlike the West of England Bank, the Northern Counties was short-lived and never turned a profit—it recognized that central to both cases was the question of lying, and in what circumstances it was justified. It praised Bramwell's reassertion of the duty of truth-

[33] *Reg. v. Mills* (1880), *Daily News*, 22 July 1880.

[34] *The Times*, 22 July 1880. The men also faced other indictments under the Larceny Act but the prosecution did not press these, satisfied with the conviction for conspiracy.

[35] Ibid. 23 July 1880; *Daily News*, 23 July 1880.

[36] *Era*, 25 July 1880.

[37] *The Times*, 23 July 1880.

[38] *Daily News*, 23 July 1880; *Manchester Times*, 24 July 1880; *Huddersfield Chronicle*, 24 July 1880.

telling, but contrasted this with Cockburn's very different view that lying could be justified provided the intentions were pure. This divergence was 'sufficiently striking to induce a suspicion that the law as to the abstract duties of directors of companies is not yet uniformly interpreted even by the judges themselves'.[39] This point was to be underlined by three further cases, which framed the responsibilities of directors much more loosely.

A SERIES OF REVERSES

Maule's first foray into the prosecution of company frauds was successful, and he did have other victories. He initiated prosecutions which saw the conviction in 1883 of the promoters behind the London General Cab Company and the London Finance Bank, and in 1884 of the management of a cluster of interlinked insurance companies and benefit societies including the Permanent Life, Fire Insurance and Loan Company, which preyed on working people in the capital. In neither case were the companies in question registered, and none of the defendants could afford legal representation.[40] But when he took on legitimately registered companies whose directors could afford lawyers, he was less successful. In September 1881, what seemed like a strong case came to the Old Bailey. John Anderson Reist was accused of obtaining money by false pretences. He had advertised in the London papers offering employment in 'first-class established' companies to capable gentlemen, on condition that a large sum be invested in advance, usually in the shares of the company in question.[41] In one case, an Essex rector was persuaded to take a £500 stake in the Patent Safety Saloon Boat Company in return for his son being made secretary at £250 a year. At the office, the son wrote letters and filled registers but saw little business transacted, and was only paid a small weekly advance on his salary. Several other victims testified to having paid for similar positions in other Reist companies, including Major Thomas Lund, a retired artillery officer, and a former mayor of Nottingham. The prosecuting barrister, Montagu Williams, admitted that it was perhaps surprising that 'a man of the world' like Lund should have been taken in, but stressed that Reist was 'as specious an individual as could well be found', who possessed 'a most impressive and delusive manner of speech'. Other victims, like the Essex clergyman, were 'unversed in the ways and wiles of the crowded city' and were helpless against schemers like Reist. There were 'no legitimate businesses bringing in any profits at all', and the money was therefore obtained fraudulently.[42]

However, the prisoner's defence counsel Edward Clarke argued that the charges fell because the companies were 'regularly constituted and incorporated'; Reist

[39] *Standard*, 23 July 1880.
[40] *Reg. v. Gordon* (1883), *The Times*, 31 January 1883; *Reg. v. Miller* (1884), *The Times*, 7 March 1884, 29 November 1883.
[41] See, for example, *Standard*, 20 July 1880.
[42] *Reg. v. Reist* (1881), *The Times*, 17 September 1881.

may have exaggerated the value of his business, but this was not the same as a false statement of a definite fact. In support, he cited Justice John Byles's 1869 ruling in *Reg. v. Williamson* that misrepresentation of a business's worth, even if 'grossly fraudulent', did not incur criminal liability.[43] The judge, Recorder Thomas Chambers, was happy to defer to Byles, not solely on narrow legal grounds, but for wider moral reasons. He believed that the 'doctrine of *caveat emptor* ought to prevail more largely', and feared what the end result might be if the criminal law were 'extended to cases in which too much flattery and *couleur de rose* were imported into the description of a business'. He was sorry for the victims, but thought they should be pursuing civil suits, and therefore directed the jury to acquit.[44]

This was the first blow to the DPP. The second came just a few months after, and concerned the 'notorious' Harry Stanley, who seemed to be just the kind of dubious company promoter the DPP was intended to take on.[45] Through the 1870s Stanley registered a series of joint-stock companies, often for fire insurance, all of which had two things in common: first, their short lifespans; second, their employment of Stanley—sometimes known as 'Count Stanley'—as manager at generous salaries.[46] Following complaints from several women inveigled into one of his schemes, George Lewis secured a warrant for his arrest, whilst lobbying Maule to take over the prosecution at the public expense.[47] Stanley fled to South Africa, but when he returned to London two years later, he was arrested and his papers seized, with Maule agreeing to authorize a public prosecution.[48] The charges, framed under the Larceny Act, concerned the prospectuses of the Government Security Fire Insurance Company, registered in 1875. The prospectuses boasted that the first share issue had been fully taken up, and that the company was doing a large and profitable business. But 2,500 shares were held by a William Smith, who could not be traced (because he did not exist, claimed the prosecution); 436 shares stood in the name of company officers and their nominees, some of them children, and they had been paid for with promissory notes payable in three or five years' time. A further 1,816 shares were held by newspaper proprietors, who accepted fully paid-up shares in return for printing the company's advertisements. There were only forty-six ordinary shareholders, who had between them paid just £359—the only part of the supposed capital which had been paid for. The prospectuses claimed that the company had insured property worth £1million, but £873,000 of this came from one policy taken out, prosecutor Harry Poland sarcastically explained, by Stanley 'upon certain bonds for their safety during the very perilous journey between Dover and Calais', for which he had paid ten guineas. Poland claimed that the entry was made in the books 'for the purpose of gulling the public', though the other £127,000 was made up of genuine business. Stanley left the company in 1877; it struggled on for a few months, but went into liquidation before the end

[43] *Reg. v. Williamson* (1869) 21 LT 444. The case is discussed at greater length in Chapter 7.
[44] *The Times*, 17 September 1881; *Bristol Mercury and Daily Post*, 19 September 1881.
[45] *The Times*, 28 July 1880.
[46] *Hull Packet*, 25 October 1878; *Leeds Mercury*, 8 November 1878; *Standard*, 29 July 1880.
[47] *Daily News*, 27 February 1880; *Star*, 2 March 1880.
[48] *Freeman's Journal*, 16 January 1882; *Hull Packet*, 20 January 1882; *Standard*, 23 January 1882.

of the year. The company's total receipts—shares, debentures, and premiums—had been £3,170. Of this, Stanley took over half—£1,843—in salary and preliminary expenses. On this evidence, Stanley was committed for trial.[49]

The trial took place over two days in March 1882. Once again Chambers was the judge, though this time he was less directive. The prosecution, led by John Day, produced a host of witnesses who had lost out as a result of their transactions with the company, including shareholders, a debenture holder, company employees, and a newspaper proprietor. But Stanley, who conducted his own defence, skilfully deflected blame for the company's failure onto the mismanagement of his successors, who should have been the ones standing in the dock. He ably cross-examined the witnesses, inducing the company's liquidator to admit that 'as a fact there were people holding shares representing 33,000*l.* or thereabouts—the statement is correct by the books—the statement "Amount of insurances effected upwards of one million" is true by the books'. Stanley thus contended that there was no case to go to the jury. Chambers ruled that 'although there was a sense in which the shares were taken up, whether they were taken up in a *bona fide* sense was a question for the Jury'. But clearly impressed by Stanley's performance, the jury immediately acquitted him of all charges.[50]

Another setback was to follow, this time in the north-east. When the liquidator of the Northern Counties Bank failed to persuade Justice Joseph Chitty to authorize the criminal prosecution of those responsible for its failure, he wrote to the DPP asking him to step in and take on the case.[51] The bank was a small institution serving Newcastle and its environs; its depositors were mostly miners and small tradesmen who, because the bank's assets were so reduced, stood to salvage no more than five shillings in the pound.[52] The DPP considered the case bad enough to intervene, and in September 1883, the bank's manager William Ogilvie, together with two of its biggest debtors, George Bell and George Hutchinson, were summoned to Newcastle police court.[53] Bell and Hutchinson had accumulated overdrafts totalling £17,000, with little security, and Ogilvie falsified dates and sums in the bank's account books in order to give the men time to pay the money back, 'as interference would have resulted in loss to the bank'. Ogilvie admitted falsifying documents presented to the board to make it seem the pair owed less than they really did, but other offences, such as destroying documents and issuing false balance sheets, he claimed he did with the full co-operation of the directors. The main plank of his defence was that guilty intent was lacking. 'Right or wrong, commercially or morally speaking, all that Ogilvie did he did honestly, for what he thought the best interests of all parties.' Moreover, he had not put any of the bank's money

[49] *The Times*, 24 January, 14 February 1882.

[50] *Reg. v. Stanley* (1882), *Daily News*, 6 March 1882, *OBP*, February 1882, Harry Clench Stanley (t18820227-330).

[51] Chitty refused on the grounds that the majority of the creditors opposed the proposal: *Birmingham Daily Post*, 7 March 1883; *Manchester Times*, 10 March 1883.

[52] *Newcastle Courant*, 13 October 1882, 2 March 1883; *Leeds Mercury*, 26 February 1883; *Birmingham Daily Post*, 7 March 1883; *Manchester Times*, 10 March 1883.

[53] *North-Eastern Daily Gazette*, 19 May, 24 September 1883; *The Times*, 25 September 1883.

in his own pocket, whereas most of the directors had overdrawn accounts when the bank collapsed. The magistrate allowed Hutchinson and Bell to go free, but thought that Ogilvie had a case to answer.[54] The manager was tried before Justice William Field and a special jury at Newcastle Assizes in January 1884. The prosecution accused Ogilvie of making and publishing false balance sheets and falsifying the bank's books, with intent to deceive and defraud the shareholders. But at the end of the two-day trial the jury accepted Ogilvie's version of events and acquitted him of all charges.[55]

This series of cases highlighted a lack of consistency among judges and juries. A legal guide to the responsibilities of company directors published in 1884 noted the differences between Moncreiff and Cockburn, but 'conceived that the law stands as... laid down by Lord Justice Clerk'.[56] Yet while judges did sometimes follow Moncreiff in holding truth-telling as a sacred duty of management, in several other cases the law was applied in a less rigorous manner giving those accused of fraud several 'outs'. Following these reverses, Maule understandably became more selective in deciding which cases to take up, a reticence which was to prove his undoing.

THE BALLET GIRL

Establishing the office of public prosecutions created a crisis of expectations. As we have seen, Maule was not idle, but the public expected more, not just in fraud cases, but across the spectrum of criminal activity. Cross's warning in 1879 that most cases would continue to be prosecuted by private parties and that the new official would only get involved in exceptional cases was not heeded. The limited remit of the post (subtly reflected in the name 'director of public prosecutions', rather than 'public prosecutor') was ignored by critics, all of whom referred to Maule as the 'public prosecutor', and lambasted him for not doing enough to justify his salary. As early as August 1881, politicians on both sides of the House seized the opportunity provided by the annual vote on the law charges to make their dissatisfaction known. The Conservative barrister Charles Warton complained that 'up to the present time the Public Prosecutor had, practically, done nothing', and asked 'whether the Government really did believe in a Public Prosecutor or not'. The Liberal solicitor Henry Fowler said 'There was a Public Prosecutor, but no public prosecutions', and suggested that the office looked very much like a 'sinecure'.[57] These votes became an annual ritual in which Maule's perceived inactivity was lamented, and the government forced to remind critics of the limited remit of the post.[58] Judges added to the heat, some-

[54] *Newcastle Courant*, 19 October, 2 November 1883.

[55] *Reg. v. Ogilvie* (1884), *The Times*, 18, 19 January 1884.

[56] Henry Hurrell and Clarendon G. Hyde, *The Law of Directors and Officers of Joint Stock Companies* (London, 1884), 120.

[57] Hansard, 3s, 264: 1047–52 (5 August 1881).

[58] In these debates, Conservatives often blamed the government while Liberals usually focused their attacks on Maule. See, for example, ibid. 282: 1403–14 (2 August 1883).

times making public attacks on Maule for ignoring important cases or taking on 'trifling' ones.[59] One of the DPP's chief critics was the Liberal barrister and MP Sir George Campbell, nephew of former Chief Justice and Lord Chancellor John Campbell, who in early 1883 asked Attorney General Sir Henry James whether the government were in earnest in 'really making the prosecution of serious offences a public and not a private function?'[60] James had to explain that a genuine 'public prosecutor' could only be maintained at much greater expense: there was a trade-off between justice and cost, and the public had to decide how much money it was willing to spend on securing justice. Vague promises that he and Home Secretary William Harcourt would 'endeavour to make the best arrangements in their power' were as far as he was willing to go.[61]

But the government was soon forced to go much further, all because of the plight of a poor ballet girl. Charlotte Blackman had been seduced by Dudley Stanhope, son of the Earl of Harrington, and had given birth to a child. In August 1881, he executed a deed for the support of the child via his solicitor, the omnipresent George Lewis, by which £150 was to be paid to Blackman in three instalments. Deciding to start a new life in Liverpool, Blackman wanted access to the next cash instalment ahead of time, and so in December 1881, she unwisely approached Peter Taylor of the National Advance Bank, the Strand, for a loan of £15, on the security of the deed. When she defaulted on the first repayment, Taylor and his solicitor Edwyn Boynes applied to Lewis, as executor of the deed, for a much larger sum, including costs and interest. Lewis repaid the amount originally advanced but declined to pay any more. The men issued a writ against Blackman, and obtained a judgement against her for over £40. Lewis, learning of this 'false judgement', applied for a summons against Taylor and Boynes for conspiracy to commit fraud.[62]

Lewis had taken up Blackman's cause out of charity, but wanted the DPP to take it off his hands, and wrote to Maule in August 1882, stressing that 'in the public interest, it is very important that such frauds upon poor people should be punished'. Perhaps influenced by the fact that Lewis had entangled him in the failed prosecution of Harry Stanley earlier that year, Maule declined. An increasingly tetchy correspondence ensued over the following weeks between Lewis and Ernest Sparks, Maule's assistant director, with Lewis claiming that before the office of DPP was created, the Treasury Solicitor was always willing to take on cases such as this, and threatening to forward the correspondence to the Home Secretary. Lewis continued with the prosecution, and succeeded in having Taylor and Boynes committed for trial. When a true bill was returned against the pair at the Old Bailey, the grand jury censured the DPP for his inaction. This made Attorney General James take notice, but Maule stuck to his guns, assuring him that

59 See comments of Justice Henry Hawkins, reported in *Morning Post*, 29 November 1882. His intervention was debated in parliament: Hansard, 3s, 275: 474–5, 496–7 (1 December 1882).

60 G. Le G. Norgate, rev. David Steele, 'Sir George Campbell', *ODNB*.

61 Hansard, 3s, 276: 829–30 (26 February 1883). See also ibid. 273: 857–9 (4 August 1882).

62 *The Times*, 9 April 1883; *Liverpool Mercury*, 26 May 1883; *Standard*, 29 May 1883.

the case 'presented no difficulties of fact or in law', and so was not one in which he could act.[63]

Further embarrassment came when the trial took place in April 1883 at the Court of Queen's Bench. In his summing up, Lord Chief Justice John Coleridge said that he did not think the DPP would have exceeded his powers by prosecuting, and if he were mistaken, 'the sooner interference in such a case was made to come within the Public Prosecutor's functions the better'. These sentiments were echoed by the jury when they delivered their verdict of guilty, and the pair were sentenced to twelve months' imprisonment apiece.[64] Coleridge's words were seized upon by the press; what had been a vague sense of discontent crystallized into a full-blown scandal, with Maule the ungallant villain of the piece. Underneath the headline 'NO MONEY, NO LAW', *Reynolds's Newspaper* said that the case showed 'how the law lends itself, not to the protection, but to the oppression of the poor'.[65] It was not just the radical press which was incensed. 'If solitary and well-nigh friendless women are not entitled to all the protection the law can give to save them from the scoundrels who seek to prey upon their helplessness and inexperience, it is difficult to say what class of persons are,' wrote the Liberal *Bristol Mercury*.[66] The DPP became a target of the satirists. *Funny Folks* featured a comic strip called 'Pro Bono Public Prosecutor' in which Harcourt and James, after many failed attempts, only succeed in spurring Maule into action when they hint at an abolition of his office.[67] *Punch* carried a grotesque cartoon depicting the DPP as a broken automaton which Lewis was trying and failing to wind up (see Figure 8.1).[68]

When the correspondence between Lewis and the DPP's office was laid before the Commons the following month—exposing Maule's repeated refusal to have anything to do with the case—the scandal escalated.[69] Many papers echoed the *Liverpool Mercury*'s question, 'What is the precise use of the Director of Public Prosecutions?'[70] Realizing that the avalanche of criticism would not go away, Harcourt appointed a departmental committee to inquire into 'the present action and position of the Director of Public Prosecutions'. The committee consisted of

[63] *Copy of Correspondence between the Director of Public Prosecutions and Mr. George Lewis in reference to the case of the Queen v. Taylor and Boynes*, PP 1883 LV. The issue was also raised in the Commons: Hansard, 3s, 274: 1117–18 (9 November 1882).

[64] *Reg. v. Taylor* (1883) 15 Cox 265, *The Times*, 14, 19, 20 April 1883; *Daily News*, 29 May 1883; *Standard*, 29 May 1883.

[65] *Reynolds's Newspaper*, 15 April 1883.

[66] *Bristol Mercury and Daily Post*, 13 April 1883. See also *Daily News*, 11 April 1883; *Birmingham Daily Post*, 12 April 1883.

[67] *Funny Folks*, 21 April 1883.

[68] Historians have tended to take these criticisms at face value. Smith, for example, dubs the 'ultra-cautious' Maule the 'Director of a Few Public Prosecutions': Keith Smith, 'The Trial: Adversarial Characteristics and Responsibilities; Pre-trial and Trial Procedures', in *The Oxford History of the Laws of England*, 13 vols (Oxford, 2003–), xiii. 67–8.

[69] *Copy of Correspondence between the Director of Public Prosecutions and Mr. George Lewis.*

[70] *Liverpool Mercury*, 26 May 1883. See also *Standard*, 25, 29 May 1883; *Western Mail*, 26 May 1883; *Daily News*, 29 May 1883; *Leeds Mercury*, 29 May 1883; *Birmingham Daily Post*, 30 May 1883; *Lloyd's Weekly Newspaper*, 3 June 1883.

SOMETHING WRONG WITH THE MECHANISM.

Mr. George Lewis trying to Wind-up the Public Prosecutor.

Figure 8.1 'Something Wrong with the Mechanism', *Punch*, 21 April 1883

Harcourt, James, the Solicitor General Sir Farrer Herschell, and five others, including three of the DPP's most outspoken critics—the Conservatives Henry Holland and John Gorst, and the Liberal Henry Fowler. Between June and August 1883, the committee interviewed Maule, his assistant Sparks, Treasury Solicitor Augustus Stephenson, and the barrister Harry Poland, who conducted many public prosecutions.

Maule defended himself robustly, insisting that at all times he had acted within the guidelines laid down for him in 1880. Indeed, statistics presented to the committee exploded the myth of the do-nothing DPP. In the three years before the establishment of the office, the Treasury Solicitor was conducting a growing number of prosecutions, from 318 in 1877 to 459 in 1879, the majority of which were for Mint and bankruptcy offences. That increase continued in the 1880s, with 581 prosecutions in 1880 and 592 in 1881, though there was a slight dip with 567 in 1882. Of these prosecutions, a significant proportion was initiated by the DPP's office: 35 per cent in 1880, rising to 42 per cent in 1882.[71] Maule denied that there were many valid prosecutions which he failed to take up, grumbling about the endless stream of applications 'from people who know nothing about what they are writing about' and who demanded he prosecute offences which did not even come under the criminal law.[72] As a result, the DPP turned away two-thirds of the 2,324 applications made to him between January 1880 and March 1883, arguing that in most cases, 'the ordinary machinery for conducting prosecutions is quite sufficient'.[73] Of course, one of these rejected applications was the Blackman case, and inevitably he was asked about it. Disdainfully noting that 'the public mind is attracted by a certain class of cases', he said it was his job to focus on crimes which involved 'very large and important interests like a great fraud—a joint stock bank case, for instance, by which many people have been ruined'.[74]

However, it was an administrative oddity of the new system that was to seal Maule's fate. Although the public tended to believe that the DPP had sole responsibility for public prosecutions, the Treasury Solicitor, who had conducted these prosecutions before 1880, in fact retained a significant role. While the DPP initiated prosecutions, he did not conduct them; this was left, as before 1880, to the Treasury Solicitor. Stephenson, who had filled this role since 1875, drew the committee's attention to the duplication of work this system necessarily entailed, and called for the amalgamation of the offices. Careful not to criticize Maule personally, he nonetheless argued that the public prosecutor's office was 'a fifth wheel to the coach, and is really a hindrance to the work'.[75]

The committee was persuaded and Stephenson's recommendation formed the centrepiece of the report, issued in June 1884. The initiation and management of prosecutions would be united under the Treasury Solicitor, who would also have the title of DPP. The regulations governing his actions should be redrawn to allow him greater freedom of action; in particular, the limitations of 'difficulty', 'importance', and 'special circumstances' in Holker's original rules should be omitted. Finally, the new system would be supplemented by a requirement that chief constables in boroughs and counties report all indictable offences in their district to the DPP, highlighting any cases requiring intervention to secure justice. The committee predicted that their recommendations would create a win-win situation—more prosecutions at a lower cost.[76]

[71] *Committee Appointed to Inquire into the Office of Public Prosecutor*, 10.

[72] Ibid. 2–3. Sparks, his assistant, also suggested that they had to deal with lots of timewasters, and gave a vivid picture of the office: 'It is a very curious place to be in, because there are all sorts of people coming in; there are madmen, and all sorts of people.' Ibid. 26.

[73] Convictions had been secured in 69 per cent of the cases taken up: *Return of the Proceedings of the Director of Public Prosecutions*, PP 1883 LV.

[74] *Committee Appointed to Inquire into the Office of Public Prosecutor*, 3–4.

[75] Ibid. 10. One legal scholar describes Stephenson's testimony as 'a naked "take-over" bid': J. Ll. J. Edwards, *The Law Officers of the Crown* (London, 1964), 368.

[76] *Committee Appointed to Inquire into the Office of Public Prosecutor*, v–vii.

While the proposals did not go far enough for many critics, who urged the government to recognize the prosecution of *all* criminal offences as a legitimate and necessary function of the state, most newspapers welcomed them as a significant step in the right direction.[77] The government moved quickly and obtained the passage of the Prosecution of Offences Act, implementing the committee's recommendations, that session.[78] Maule was pensioned off, and Stephenson became the DPP with immediate effect.[79] Would this bring about the change so earnestly desired by reformers?

PRIVATE DUTIES

On his first day as DPP, Stephenson wrote to Home Secretary Harcourt explaining that he would trial the existing regulations under which his predecessor had acted until the end of the year, by which time he expected to have identified the defects in the system and be able to advise what changes were needed. In January 1885, Stephenson's report revealed that he did not envisage a major change in approach; indeed, his stance was indistinguishable from that of his predecessor. 'It is much easier to spend public money than to save it', he observed, and with a section of public opinion looking to the DPP to prosecute every case which came before him, 'the Director, unless his hands are strengthened by the regulations in the interests of economy, will not only have every inducement to spend the public money, but will have great difficulty in resisting the pressure of private persons seeking to save their pockets at the public cost'.[80] So the new regulations, redrafted by James in April 1885, did not represent a radical departure from past practice.[81] Although the stipulation in the old regulations that the DPP would only act in cases 'of importance or difficulty', or when 'special circumstances' applied, had been regarded by the committee as too restrictive, very similar wording was used in the new regulations. While they went further than the 1880 rules by introducing the 'public interest' as a justification for action, they also restated the previous limitations.[82] As one legal historian has recently noted, as a clarification of the grounds for intervention, the new regulations were 'a signal failure'.[83]

The principal influence on Stephenson's policy was the memory of the repeated reverses his predecessor had experienced in the courts. Both economy and morality

[77] *Daily News*, 9 June 1884. For similar comments, see *Standard*, 7 June 1884; *The Times*, 7 June 1884; *Liverpool Mercury*, 9 June 1884; *Leeds Mercury*, 9 June 1884; *Morning Post*, 7 June 1884. Even some Scottish commentators were positive: *Glasgow Herald*, 11 June 1884.

[78] 47 & 48 Vict. c. 58.

[79] Hansard, 3s, 292: 80–2 (7 August 1884).

[80] *Copy of Return Showing the Working of the Regulations made in 1886 for Carrying out the Prosecution of Offences Acts, 1879 and 1884*, PP 1887 LXVII. 2–4.

[81] The political instability of these months meant that the regulations could not be formally approved by parliament until June 1886.

[82] *Draft of Regulations Framed under the Prosecution of Offences Acts, 1879 and 1884*, PP 1886 LIII. 2.

[83] Smith, 'The Trial', 69. They were sufficiently vague to not be revised again until 1946: Joshua Rozenberg, *The Case for the Crown: The Inside Story of the Director of Public Prosecutions* (Wellingborough, 1987), 22.

guided Stephenson's policy: he chose to act only in cases where the chances of conviction were very high, offering value for money to the taxpayer, and when the victims were poor and unable to deploy the law themselves. Thus, under Stephenson there was no shortage of state prosecutions of company fraud cases, but nearly all of them fell into one of two categories. First were bogus companies, the main victims of which were either those who were persuaded to pay money up front for phoney positions of employment, or customers who contracted for services they never received.[84] Maule's decision to prosecute John Reist for an employment scam had not been vindicated at the Old Bailey, but Stephenson had more success in this field. In 1885 a gang of four accountants and commission agents were convicted of promoting a string of businesses including the International Fish Dinner Company with fraudulent intent, and were sentenced to between twelve and fifteen months' hard labour.[85] The following year, William Dormer, an accountant who had formed a bogus bank, the London and North British, offering work to needy clerks, was convicted. Dormer collected £406 from eleven victims before he was brought to justice. He received five years' penal servitude, while his assistant was imprisoned for eighteen months with hard labour.[86] The same year saw the conviction of the manager and solicitor of the Legal and General Mercantile Creditors' Protection Association—a debt-collecting society which kept the debts once they were collected. Both men received twelve months' imprisonment with hard labour.[87] In 1888, three men behind a string of sham insurance companies, including the 'Property' and the 'John Bull', who had received small premiums from thousands of investors since the mid 1870s, were convicted, receiving sentences of between twelve and twenty-two months' hard labour.[88]

The second type of action concerned irregularities by the employees of financial institutions for the working classes. So, in 1884, Richard Pexton and Christopher Firby, a borough coal inspector and a whitesmith who served as treasurer and secretary of the Hull Rechabite Loan Society, were convicted of conspiring to defraud its depositors by concealing the firm's insolvency, and were sentenced to nine months' imprisonment.[89] The following year the Bristol-based Colston Benefit

[84] The former scam was particularly widespread in the mid 1880s when unemployment was a particular problem. Though there are no official unemployment statistics, figures from trade unions show that the years 1884–87 were especially difficult: Chris Cook, *Britain in the Nineteenth Century, 1815–1914* (London, 1999), 208.

[85] *Reg. v. Hughlings* (1884), *The Times*, 16 January 1885; *OBP*, December 1884, Frederick Pope, Harry Hughlings, Edward Errington, James Pryor, Caleb Titcomb (t18841229-164).

[86] *Reg. v. Dormer* (1886), *The Times*, 13 May 1886.

[87] *Reg. v. Edwards* (1886), *The Times*, 19 April 1886.

[88] *Reg. v. Corbett* (1888), *The Times*, 6 January 1888, *Standard*, 20 January 1888. Most of these prosecutions were relatively low profile, but where they did attract press attention, they were usually well received, few complaining that taxpayers' money was being used to bail out the foolish. The *Daily News*, for example, thought it 'incredible' that anyone would have subscribed to the International Fish Dinner Company, and wished the public 'would exercise a little care', but wrote that the Treasury had 'most properly undertaken' the case: *Daily News*, 16 January 1885.

[89] *Reg. v. Pexton* (1884), *Hull Packet*, 15 August, 21 November 1884, *Leeds Mercury*, 15 August, 22 November 1884, *Newcastle Weekly Courant*, 21 November 1884. The firm, a registered friendly society, had liabilities beyond assets of over £12,000 when it failed.

Building Society collapsed and it was discovered during the winding up that George Morris, the secretary, had embezzled over £3,000. The DPP took over the prosecution which had been initiated by the liquidator and Morris was sentenced to five years' penal servitude.[90] In 1887, John McEwen, manager of the Jarrow Permanent Building Society and the Jarrow branch of the North-Eastern Banking Company, was convicted of embezzling over £10,000 from the two institutions and was sentenced to ten years' penal servitude.[91] The following year, William Phillips, secretary of the Atlas Building Society and a well-known Bristol auctioneer, was prosecuted for the misappropriation which led to the society's collapse, receiving twelve months' hard labour.[92]

Stephenson selected his cases extremely well, and prosecutorial failures in fraud cases were a rarity in his first five years as DPP.[93] But like Maule, his approach was predicated on a belief in a 'mixed economy' of prosecutions. His job was to complement, not supersede, private prosecutions, and, as his assistant Hamilton Cuffe stressed, dispensing legal advice to applicants was an important part of his role. After receiving guidance, Cuffe claimed, victims of crime were often happy to prosecute a case themselves, 'though until the advice was given they apparently considered this to be beyond their powers'.[94] Some victims did certainly prove willing to act, with the result that the 1880s saw a genuine mixed economy of prosecutions across the joint-stock economy. Bogus companies of the type successfully prosecuted by Stephenson were the subject of several successful private prosecutions.[95] Lies in prospectuses were also privately prosecuted under the law of false pretences and conspiracy. In 1881, shareholders combined to bring Ledru Rollin Reynolds, promoter of the Silver Valley Mines Company, to court. Their charge was that despite the claims of the 'alluring' prospectus, the Cornish mines in question were fictional. Reynolds pleaded guilty and was sentenced at the Old Bailey to two years with hard labour.[96] In 1889 the shareholders of the short-lived Hull Tallow Refining Company successfully proved that it was a vehicle for the fraudulent conversion of a business belonging to a bankrupt tallow chandler. The three promoters, one of whom had been a parliamentary candidate in the Home Rule interest, pleaded guilty at the Old Bailey, and were sentenced to between six and eighteen months' hard labour.[97]

[90] *Reg. v. Morris* (1885), *Bristol Mercury and Daily Post*, 6 August, 29 October 1885.

[91] *Reg. v. McEwen* (1887), *York Herald*, 5 November 1887, *Northern Echo*, 5 November 1887.

[92] *Reg. v. Phillips* (1888), *Bristol Mercury and Daily Post*, 8, 9, 10, 11 August 1888.

[93] A rare reverse was the 1885 action against John Jones, the elderly promoter and secretary of several London building societies, for embezzlement. After Jones's committal, the DPP seemed to have had a change of heart, and no evidence was presented at the trial: *Reg. v. Jones* (1885), *The Times*, 11, 18 July 1885, *OBP*, September 1885, John Jones (t18850914-833).

[94] *Return Showing the Working of the Regulations made in 1886*, 29–30.

[95] See for example *Reg. v. Humphreys* (1884), *Standard*, 15, 18 December 1884, 20 January 1885; *Reg. v. Bernard* (1888), *The Times*, 4 June 1888; *Pall Mall Gazette*, 22 June 1888; *OBP*, July 1888, John Bernard and James Monteith (t18880702-644).

[96] *Reg. v. Reynolds* (1881), *The Times*, 16 September 1881.

[97] *Reg. v. Jones* (1889), *Daily News*, 13 March, 13 April 1889, *Sheffield and Rotherham Independent*, 17 September 1892.

False balance sheets formed the basis of other convictions. In 1884, the liquidator of the Yorkshire stone merchants C. H. Denham and Co. prosecuted the managing director Charles Denham for issuing false balance sheets which had for many years exaggerated the profits made in order to keep the company's shares at a large premium. Convicted at Leeds Assizes, Justice Mathew sentenced him to twelve months with hard labour.[98] The following year a shareholder of the Castle Crag Steamship Company successfully prosecuted the managing directors Robert Tomlinson and George Thompson for inserting false entries into one of the company's balance sheets to conceal expenses incurred following the loss of the company's ship. Justice Manisty sentenced the men to three months each at Liverpool Assizes.[99]

Nonetheless, the long-recognized weaknesses of private prosecutions—corruption and compromise—were still evident. As soon as Ledru Reynolds, the Cornish mine promoter, had been released after serving his two-year term, a retired actor named John Allen had him arrested claiming that he had lost £700 in Reynolds's fraudulent Industrial Bank. Over the course of the next few hearings, Reynolds's lawyer repeatedly alleged that Allen had instituted the action solely to secure the return of his money, and had offered to drop proceedings if reimbursed. Though Allen emphatically denied this, the fact that the case was subsequently abandoned suggested that money may well have changed hands.[100] Later in the decade, two subscribers obtained the committal of two directors of the Lewthwaite Company, one of whom was the Irish peer Lord Clarence Graves, for misrepresenting the value of a patent in the company's prospectus. But when the case came on at Queen's Bench, the prosecutors abandoned it after friends of the defendants agreed to reimburse them.[101] Other prosecutions were brought without any evidence to justify the charges or with vindictive motives, incurring stern condemnations from magistrates: in 1882 at Clerkenwell police court, John Hosack threw out a summons against the managing director of the Photographic Artists' Co-operative Supply Association after four hearings. Hosack said that the case should never have been brought into a criminal court: there was no evidence of fraud and, contrary to the prosecution's allegations, the company was not insolvent, but was still trading successfully.[102]

A more fundamental problem with the mixed economy of prosecutions was its seeming inability to combat the bigger City scandals.[103] Although many were fixated on the idea that the economy was trapped in depression in the 1880s,

[98] *Reg. v. Denham* (1884), *Leeds Mercury*, 7, 8 August 1884.

[99] *Reg. v. Tomlinson* (1885), *Liverpool Mercury*, 22 June, 6, 7 August 1885.

[100] *Morning Post*, 12, 22 September, 20 October 1883; *Standard* 27 October 1883.

[101] *Reg. v. Graves* (1887) *The Times*, 18, 24, 27 February 1886, 20 January 1887.

[102] *Standard*, 20 September, 5 October 1882; *Morning Post*, 9, 16 November 1882.

[103] Michie argues that the City enjoyed a relatively positive public profile in the later 1880s and into the early 1890s, until it was tarnished by the gold-mining scandals of the mid 1890s, but as shown below, City scandals attracted much attention in parliament and the press in these years. Ranald C. Michie, *Guilty Money: The City of London in Victorian and Edwardian Culture, 1815–1914* (London, 2009), ch. 4.

standards of living were in fact rising faster than at any previous point in the century, and this was reflected in a large increase in the number of joint-stock company formations.[104] Average annual UK company registrations in the 1860s had been 705, and 1,016 for the 1870s, before shooting up to 1,858 in the 1880s. By 1890, the Companies Registrar believed there were 13,323 registered companies in operation in the UK.[105] While these numbers are partly explained by the growing fashion among small businesses to register as private companies in order to obtain the benefits of limited liability, many of the new registrations were large enterprises, and the numbers represent striking evidence of the growing importance of limited companies to the national economy.[106] These companies needed to attract capital from a wider pool of investors, and so there was a greater use of low denomination shares of £1 or less from the late 1870s.[107] A further incitement to investment was the development of what contemporaries called the 'new financial journalism': writing designed to make economic topics more accessible and entertaining to financial neophytes.[108] The drive was led by the *Financial News* (established in 1884) and the *Financial Times* (1888), and was supported by the proliferation of popular investment manuals such as Francis Pixley's *The Shareholder's Handbook* (1884) and Percy Campbell's *Stock Exchange: True Principles of Steady Successful Speculation and Investment* (1885).[109]

Investors needed all the help they could get, for nobody could fail to note the instability of the new promotions. The percentage of companies dissolving within three years of formation reached 25.6 per cent by 1875–83.[110] The Royal Commission appointed in 1886 to investigate the trade depression observed that the limited liability acts had 'created a class of "promoters", whose interest lies rather in the creation of an industrial undertaking and the speedy sale of its shares at a premium than

[104] L. C. B. Seaman, *Victorian England: Aspects of English and Imperial History, 1837–1901* (London, 1973), 269.

[105] *Returns of the Names, Objects or Business, Places where Business is or was Conducted, Date of Registration, &c, and the Total Amount of Calls Received of all Joint Stock Companies Formed since the 1st day of January 1889 to the 31st day of December 1889, and also the Number of Shareholders in Each of the said Companies at the Date of the Last Return,* PP 1890 LXVIII. 190–2.

[106] Timothy Guinnane et al., 'Putting the Corporation in its Place', *Enterprise and Society*, 8 (2007), 703–5.

[107] H. A. Shannon, 'The Limited Companies of 1866–1883', *Economic History Review*, 4 (1933), 296; J. B. Jefferys, 'The Denomination and Character of Shares, 1855–1885', *Economic History Review*, 16 (1946), 45–55; P. L. Cottrell, *Industrial Finance, 1830–1914* (London, 1980), 81. Though note that Cottrell disputes the extent of the transition to low denomination shares.

[108] That said, the earlier Victorian financial press could be spicier than is sometimes represented: James Taylor, 'Watchdogs or Apologists? Financial Journalism and Company Fraud in Early Victorian Britain', *Historical Research*, 85 (2012), 632–50.

[109] Dilwyn Porter, 'City Editors and the Modern Investing Public: Establishing the Integrity of the New Financial Journalism in Late Nineteenth-Century London', *Media History*, 4 (1998), 49–60; David C. Itzkowitz, 'Fair Enterprise or Extravagant Speculation: Investment, Speculation, and Gambling in Victorian England', *Victorian Studies*, 45 (2002), 121–47.

[110] Though the figure for 1856–65 was not dramatically lower, at 22.3 per cent, the far greater number of companies in the later period meant that the overall number of failures, and the number of investors involved, was of course much higher, and they were more visible: Shannon, 'Companies of 1866–1883', 302.

in its permanent prosperity'.[111] The new wave of investors, armed with their newspapers, manuals, and circulars, little suspected that these media could be the means of their ruin.[112] Abbott, Page, and Co. were a firm of stockbrokers who through the 1880s advertised a monthly share list giving share tips which, if followed, could net investors profits of up to 1,000 per cent.[113] The firm was in fact a front for a serial company promoter named John Neil, and the share lists were devices to channel funds to a series of unsuccessful mining companies he established with his confederates. Thanks to blanket advertising and paid-for press 'puffs', uninformed investors plunged their life's savings into the schemes tipped in the circulars. Neil frequently appeared at Mansion House, but was always able to 'square' his prosecutors, and bagged an estimated quarter of a million pounds before finally absconding in late 1887.[114] While Neil found it expedient to absent himself, other fraudulent promoters acted more brazenly. Harry Marks, editor of the *Financial News*, used his paper to expose financial frauds and corruption, but also to promote his own dubious schemes, such as the Rae-Transvaal Gold Mining Company in 1887. The paper recommended its shares thirty-three times early that year, as a result of which over £45,000 was subscribed, but only £138 was spent on prospecting equipment, no gold was found, the company was dissolved a year later, the shareholders losing everything. Far from facing prosecution, the following year he was elected to the London County Council, and in the 1890s became a Conservative MP.[115]

As a result, although the 1880s saw more company fraud prosecutions than in any previous decade, there was still a pervasive belief that the City was being inadequately policed. After a brief honeymoon period after the 1884 shake-up at the DPP's office, the old frustrations soon returned. In March 1887, the Liberal MP Henry Fowler requested a parliamentary return showing how the DPP's new regulations had been implemented, with the numbers of applications and prosecutions undertaken.[116] This return, initially intended as a one-off, subsequently became an annual event. But if critics in and out of parliament were trying to pull the DPP in the direction of greater activity, his masters, particularly after the return of the Conservatives under Lord Salisbury in 1886, were dragging him in the opposite direction, towards greater economy. In July 1887 the Treasury appointed a committee to consider cutting costs at the Treasury Solicitor's department. Due to a series of amalgamations, of which the DPP's office was just one, the department now boasted forty-nine staff with an annual wage bill of over £21,000. The committee's

[111] *Final Report of the Royal Commission Appointed to Inquire into the Depression of Trade and Industry*, PP 1886 XXIII. p. xviii.

[112] The diffusion of bogus financial newspapers is discussed at length in *Statist*, 6 September 1890.

[113] For one of their many advertisements, see *Standard*, 24 January 1880.

[114] *Statist*, 10 March 1888; *Standard*, 9 November 1887.

[115] Paul Johnson, 'Civilizing Mammon: Laws, Morals and the City in Nineteenth-Century England', in Peter Burke, Brian Harrison, and Paul Slack (eds), *Civil Histories: Essays Presented to Sir Keith Thomas* (Oxford, 2000), 314–15.

[116] Hansard, 3s, 312: 525 (17 March 1887).

report concluded that the department was overstaffed and that economies were needed.[117] In his August 1888 return to parliament, Stephenson therefore focused on the question of efficiency, including statistics showing a 'gradual but perceptible decrease' in the costs of his office since 1884.[118] But this was the last thing many of his critics wanted to hear!

This tension between economy and justice was brought out into the open in 1888 by the *Statist*, a respected financial journal established in the late 1870s. In July the editor wrote to Stephenson drawing his attention to the 'bogus companies and trusts' of Neil's Abbott-Page Group, which had defrauded thousands of investors of 'hundreds of thousands of pounds'. Cuffe replied on behalf of Stephenson that the case had been passed on to the City Solicitor, but the editor was not satisfied, pointing out that it was 'of such vast public importance, and of so complex a nature' that it needed to be taken up by a public department. Stephenson stood firm, but the journal gained its revenge by publishing its correspondence with him under the heading 'To Parliament', on the eve of the annual vote on the law charges in November, included in which was, of course, Stephenson's salary.[119]

Publication had the desired effect. Edward Pickersgill, a radical Liberal MP, moved to reduce Stephenson's salary to call attention to his inactivity. He claimed that as 'City men' were implicated in the Abbott-Page case, it was not prudent to leave it in the hands of the City Solicitor; it was the DPP's duty to investigate alleged frauds on this scale.[120] Pickersgill's motion triggered a fierce debate on the role of the state in policing the joint-stock economy. Supporting the motion was Sir George Campbell, whose economic justification for taking a firmer line on fraud presented stock market investment as central to the nation's prosperity and conflated the shareholder and the public interest. The effect of fraud (which 'honeycombed' the country) was 'to prevent prudence and saving amongst the community'. Large investors could take care of themselves, but it was 'totally impossible' for the 'smaller men' to protect themselves against fraud. Other nations, such as France, punished company fraud more reliably, and as a result had stronger cultures of saving. Ignoring France's example would damage England economically, by debarring small investors from placing their savings in industrial enterprises. He challenged the government directly: 'Did the Government mean to say that it was not the duty of the Director of Public Prosecutions to prosecute mercantile and financial frauds which were directed against the public interest?'[121]

While governments had been prosecuting individual cases of financial fraud for over a decade, they were unwilling to accept blanket responsibility for them. So, instead of highlighting the many successful prosecutions that had taken place,

[117] *Report of Committee Appointed by the Treasury to Inquire into the System of Conducting the Legal Business of the Government*, PP 1888 LXXX, pp. iii-vi.

[118] *Return of Working of Regulations for carrying out Prosecution of Offences Acts*, 4–5.

[119] *Statist*, 10 November 1888. The paper had started printing articles against the group on 30 July 1887. It later asked 'Have we a Public Prosecutor in fact, or have we only one in name?... In Scotland and on the Continent they manage things very differently.' Ibid. 17 November 1888.

[120] Hansard, 3s, 330: 972–5 (12 November 1888).

[121] Ibid. 1001–2.

ministers adopted a defensive stance, resisting any principle which would bind them to open-ended expenses. Home Secretary Henry Matthews argued that 'the case of a bogus company was one in which no direct duty to prosecute lay on the Public Prosecutor'.[122] W. H. Smith, First Lord of the Treasury, explained that individuals who were defrauded 'were bound, as citizens, to defend themselves and prosecute those who had done them wrong'. It was immoral for people to expect high rates of interest from investments, and also to expect that 'if there was anything wrong behind these investments, that there would be a public watch-dog, so to speak, to pounce down on the individual who offered the inducements'.[123] This line was shared by the Liberal front bench. Sir Henry James, twice Attorney General under Gladstone, dusted down the Grand Old Man's line on company prosecutions:

> He remembered one of the most convincing arguments was used in that House by... [Gladstone], who, when he was asked to countenance a public prosecution in the case of Overend, Gurney, and Co., declined to do so, because it would have been giving aid to speculators, and saying to persons who wanted to get high dividends—'You are not to trust to your own intelligence.' He protested against the teaching that when a man could not get back his money from a public company he should be able to go to the Public Prosecutor and so commence a prosecution.[124]

With Liberal support, the government was able to see off Pickersgill's motion by 180 votes to 90, though these numbers indicated that there was a significant minority willing to contemplate nationalizing the costs of protecting middle-class investors.

Taken at face value, these speeches from the front benches seemed to represent a renunciation of the idea that the state should be trying to combat City fraud. Reinforcing this impression was the failure earlier that year of a bill to reform the Companies Acts. The bill, prepared by the government, and running to over a hundred pages, embodied the recommendations of the Royal Commission on the Depression, and would, among much else, have reintroduced the legal requirements for publication of balance sheets and compulsory audits, introduced new measures making the registration process more rigorous, and obliged directors to take a substantial stake in their companies.[125] Hopes were raised that 'Parliament, which brought the professional company-promoter into existence, will at last interpose to curtail his power of mischief'.[126] But the bill made slow progress, only reaching the Lords in June 1888, and, meeting stiff opposition there, the government allowed it to drop, cited by historians as proof that Salisbury's government was not serious about tackling abuses in the joint-stock economy.[127]

But appearances were deceptive, for the government was genuinely concerned about the problem of fraud. In April 1888, as the bill was making its laboured way

122 Ibid. 980.
123 Ibid. 1002–3.
124 Ibid. 999.
125 *A Bill to Consolidate and Amend the Companies' Acts*, PP 1888 II.
126 *The Times*, 12 January 1888.
127 Cottrell, *Industrial Finance*, 64–6.

through the Commons, Salisbury wrote to government representatives abroad for information on the formation, regulation, and dissolution of joint-stock companies in these countries, to feed into the process of reform. Reports from twenty-three countries were received, but it was data on domestic companies which proved more influential.[128] In May, Joseph Chamberlain asked Sir Michael Hicks-Beach, President of the Board of Trade, for a return of company liquidations carried out in Chancery since 1862.[129] Whilst occupying this post in Gladstone's ministry, Chamberlain had brought in a Bankruptcy Act (1883) establishing the office of Official Receiver, appointed by the Board of Trade, responsible for publicly investigating the conduct of debtors, and reporting on cases of fraud to the court.[130] Though he did not spell it out, Chamberlain's agenda was to investigate the possibility of extending this system to the joint-stock economy. The information was printed in December 1888 and revealed a sorry situation: of the companies in Chancery, 22 per cent had been in liquidation for over ten years; a further 20 per cent had been in the court for over five years. The costs, where ascertainable, were enormous.[131] The system pleased no one but the lawyers who operated it.[132]

After the failure of the 1888 Companies Bill, the government decided to prioritize reforming the dissolution of companies, and the result was a bill introduced by Hicks-Beach in February 1890 to extend the provisions of the Bankruptcy Act to companies. This was one of three pieces of company legislation passed during the session, together with the Companies (Memorandum of Association) Act and a private bill, the Directors Liability Act.[133] Historians have tended to treat the last of these, designed to stiffen the civil liabilities of directors and promoters, as the most important.[134] However, the Companies (Winding-Up) Act had the greater significance. It had a dual function, aiming to satisfy both the commercial community which had long demanded quicker and cheaper liquidation, and the wider public interest, by securing greater publicity in the winding-up process and thus deterring fraud. 'The principle upon which the Bill is based is that a man who undertakes to manage other people's affairs should have the same sense of responsibility as in managing his own', Hicks-Beach explained. Offences by individuals which were punished in bankruptcy were ignored in winding up because there were currently 'no officials charged with the impartial and independent duty of investigation or the punishment of fraud'.[135] The bill changed this by shifting the

[128] *Reports from Her Majesty's Representatives Abroad respecting the Formation, Regulation, and Dissolution of Public Companies in Foreign Countries*, PP 1889 LXXVII.

[129] Hansard, 3s, 325: 1230 (3 May 1888), 326: 530–1 (17 May 1888).

[130] 46 & 47 Vict. c. 52. See Fiona M. Tolmie, *Corporate and Personal Insolvency Law* (2nd edn, London, 2003), 11; Barbara Weiss, *The Hell of the English: Bankruptcy and the Victorian Novel* (Cranbury, NJ, 1986), 46.

[131] *Return of all Companies which have been Ordered to be wound up, under the Provisions of the Companies Acts, Compulsorily or under the Supervision of the Court, since the Commencement of the Companies Act, 1862*, PP 1888 LXXX.

[132] *Economist*, 20 December 1879.

[133] 53 & 54 Vict. cc. 62–4.

[134] For a recent example, see Rob McQueen, *A Social History of Company Law: Great Britain and the Australian Colonies, 1854–1920* (Farnham, 2009), 250–2.

[135] Hansard, 3s, 341: 1401–2 (27 February 1890).

liquidation of companies out of Chancery and back into Bankruptcy. When a compulsory winding-up order was granted, the Official Receiver in Bankruptcy would become the provisional liquidator. He would convene separate meetings of the company's creditors and contributories (the shareholders) to give them the option of appointing a liquidator of their own, or confirming him as liquidator. After this, the Official Receiver would submit a preliminary report to the court confirming the causes of failure, and whether further inquiry into the promotion, career, or failure of the company was required. On the basis of this report, the court could oblige anyone connected with the company to be publicly examined; it was also able to order promoters, directors, or officers to repay any sums misapplied by them. Finally, the Official Receiver was empowered to make further reports to the court stating whether fraud had been committed by anyone associated with the company.[136] As a result, Hicks-Beach hoped that as well as improving the amount of salvage, the measure would also reduce 'the number of wrecks'.[137] Objections to the bill, which applied to England and Wales only, largely revolved around technicalities rather than principles, and it enjoyed a relatively smooth passage through parliament, receiving royal assent in August.[138]

The bill was recognized as a significant anti-fraud measure. Welcomed by the Association of Chambers of Commerce at their annual meeting in March, it also garnered a positive response from the press.[139] The *Standard* hailed the government's 'laudable determination to deal with, and, if possible, to put an end to, the scandals to which the extension and multiplication of joint-stock companies have given birth'. The bill dealt with an 'abuse which the commercial community are practically agreed in regarding as of crying urgency'.[140] *The Times* noted that, together with the Directors' Liability Bill, the measure was creating 'quite a little scare among company promoters and directors of a certain class'. While it thought that nothing parliament could do would make winding up a company as straightforward as dealing with an individual's bankrupt estate, it welcomed introducing the Official Receiver into the joint-stock sector. It was now made somebody's responsibility to investigate, and public examinations presented 'a delicious opportunity for laying bare the secret history of the promotion of a bubble company'.[141] The *Economist*, though slightly cooler, still welcomed the bill as 'a decided step in the right direction' which would 'guard the public against the wiles and machinations of unscrupulous promoters . . . and the host of harpies who now batten upon over-credulous investors'.[142] But few predicted just what a major impact the act would have.

[136] 53 & 54 Vict. c. 63, ss. 2, 4, 6–10, 31.

[137] Hansard, 3s, 341: 1401 (27 February 1890).

[138] The only real controversy concerned whether the provisions of the bill should extend to voluntary winding-up under supervision of the court (i.e. the half-way house between voluntary and compulsory liquidation): ibid. 347: 847–57 (25 July 1890). Scotland was included when the winding-up laws were next revised in 1908: 8 Edw. VII c. 69, part iv.

[139] *Sheffield and Rotherham Independent*, 26 March 1890.

[140] *Standard*, 27, 28 February 1890.

[141] *The Times*, 19 June 1890.

[142] *Economist*, 22 February 1890.

CONCLUSION

The establishment of the DPP in 1880 raised hopes that the state would take a more active role in prosecuting company frauds. And indeed, Maule, the first holder of the new office, built on the tentative steps taken in this direction by the Treasury in the late 1870s, initiating a series of prosecutions in the early 1880s. But his approach was based on the assumption, prevalent on both Liberal and Conservative front benches, that his role was to supplement, not supplant, private actions; a mixed economy of prosecutions. This vision was not shared by many commentators who now saw a clear distinction between the civil law as the means by which individuals could gain financial recompense, and the criminal law, by which a community would dispense justice. This disjunction between the two versions of the law was exacerbated by the boom in company promotions—the annual number of new registrations practically doubled between 1878 and 1883 from 886 to 1,766.[143] Even if the *proportion* of fraudulent enterprises had not increased (and many suspected that it had), the overall *number* of dubious schemes had, and the number of disappointed investors likewise. So, although frequency of company fraud prosecutions was increasing, it was not doing so quickly enough for many critics. What these critics did not acknowledge was one of the chief reasons for Maule's caution: the unsettled state of the criminal law as applied to companies. In the late 1870s and early 1880s, judges were making contradictory statements on the law, and juries were sometimes returning unpredictable verdicts, which meant that several of the cases taken up by Maule failed to yield convictions. But Maule's resulting caution led to a scandal which prompted his replacement and the absorption of the DPP's office by the Treasury Solicitor.

Learning from Maule's failures, Stephenson built an impressive conviction rate on a larger volume of prosecutions than his predecessor had managed, indicating that the courts were becoming less narrow in their application of criminal responsibility, in the most egregious cases at least. But, like Maule, Stephenson believed in a mixed economy of prosecutions, leaving much to the private sector. This faith in the ability of victims of company fraud to prosecute the perpetrators was, to some extent, well founded. Creditors and shareholders—frequently aided by the ubiquitous George Lewis—were often prepared to instigate proceedings, and obtained convictions in a number of cases involving both real and sham companies. As a result, the 1880s saw more company promoters, directors, and managers in the criminal courts than any previous decade. Yet this did not satisfy critics who focused on the cases not taken up rather than acknowledging the successes which were occurring: it seemed that every conviction created the expectation of further convictions. Under pressure from MPs demanding that they nationalize the cost of all prosecutions, Conservative ministers felt compelled to make speeches retreating from the principle of subsidizing *any* such prosecutions. But the activities of the DPP belied these claims. Moreover, a reform of the process of company liquidation laid the groundwork for a significant extension of the scope of the criminal law in the final decade of the century.

[143] *Returns of Number of Shareholders*, 190–1.

9

Regulating the City: The 1890s

The Winding-up Act of 1890 had not directly addressed the issue of criminal prosecutions, and its supporters believed that it would improve commercial morality chiefly through the publicity generated by public examinations, and through the powers given to the Official Receiver to enforce repayment by promoters and directors of monies misapplied. However, the act had unexpected repercussions in the criminal courts. The extent of sharp practice revealed in winding-up proceedings in the first year of the act's operation in 1891 shocked the Board of Trade which, towards the end of the year, took an important decision. Rather than leaving criminal prosecutions to be funded out of company assets, as stipulated by the Companies Act of 1862, the Board decided to assimilate the Winding-up Act with the Prosecution of Public Offences Act of 1879. The Board corresponded with Augustus Stephenson in late 1891 and agreed a system whereby the Board would bring cases requiring prosecution to the DPP, to ensure that such proceedings could be conducted at public expense.[1] The following year, Stephenson confirmed that 'prosecutions of fraudulent promoters or directors of companies, when the winding-up of such company shall be under an Order of Court . . . will in future be undertaken by the Director at the instance or on the application of the Board of Trade', provided there was sufficient evidence to warrant prosecution.[2] Whereas the burden of deciding whether to prosecute had previously fallen on the DPP alone, now the decision was shared, effective machinery now existing by which cases of possible fraud were sifted, examined, and presented to the DPP. The impact on the criminalization of fraud was immediate.

Nevertheless, while the new system was welcomed by the business community and the public alike, it was vulnerable on a number of fronts. Lawyers and accountants were resentful of growing incursions by the state into the profitable territory of 'winders'—their term for company liquidations—and lobbied to reinstate winding-up as a private process.[3] The Treasury was concerned about the potential expenses and obligations incurred by the new office and tried to curb its extension. The legitimacy of the public examinations which were a central feature of the new system was questioned in the courts. And most fundamentally of all,

[1] *Report of the Inter-Departmental Committee Appointed to Inquire into the Limits of the Action of the Board of Trade as Regards the Liquidation of Companies under the Companies (Winding-up) Act, 1890*, PP 1893–94 LXXXI. 12.

[2] *Return Showing the Working of the Regulations made in 1886 for Carrying out the Prosecution of Offences Acts, 1879 and 1884*, PP 1892 LXV. 22.

[3] *Statist*, 8 March 1890.

judges were still divided on where the boundaries lay between criminal and civil liability for fraud. Could directors be convicted even when they did not directly benefit financially, or was criminality inseparable from personal profit? Was knowledge of a lie enough to prove criminality, or did guilty intent have to be proven? And could behaviour widely regarded as common practice in the City—the payment of secret commissions, the casual blurring between company money and managers' money, omissions of material facts in prospectuses—really be made the subject of successful criminal prosecutions? This tumultuous decade would see all these questions answered.

AN ENGLISHMAN, AN IRISHMAN, AND A SCOTSMAN

As had been the case with the act establishing the DPP in 1879, the Winding-up Act left many of the important administrative details to be decided later by the relevant government department. The Board of Trade had to create and staff a new Department of Companies Liquidation, and the Board was heavily influenced by its experience with the Bankruptcy Department, which it had formed following Chamberlain's 1883 Bankruptcy Act. Thus, the first set of rules for the new department was modelled on the rules for the Bankruptcy Department, and it was staffed by personnel from this department. Charles Stewart, appointed Official Receiver for Winding up in the High Court, had been an Assistant Official Receiver in Bankruptcy.[4] John Smith, Inspector-General in Bankruptcy, became the first Inspector-General in Companies Liquidation. Smith's job was to act as the conduit between the President of the Board of Trade and the Official Receiver, directing the Official Receiver's actions, and supervising the administration of the act.[5] Finally, Sir Roland Vaughan Williams of the Bankruptcy Court was appointed Judge of Chancery Division, which is where winding-up cases were first heard.[6] Vaughan Williams had long been considered an expert on bankruptcy. He first published *The Law and Practice of Bankruptcy* in 1870, which was still in print in the 1890s and beyond, reaching its thirteenth edition in 1925.[7]

Vaughan Williams, Smith, and Stewart shared a highly moral vision of the new law. For them, it was not simply an administrative tool facilitating the efficient distribution of assets after company failure; it was a means of improving the moral tenor of business. Smith, in particular, saw his role in these terms. A Scotsman of considerable business experience, having been a chartered accountant, a banker in Bombay, a Yorkshire wholesaler, and finally a director of the London and Yorkshire

[4] Outside London, the existing Official Receivers in Bankruptcy attached to the County Courts had their roles enlarged to become Official Receivers under the new act.

[5] *Inter-Departmental Committee*, 1.

[6] Victor M. Batzel, '"The General Scope of the Act": A Study of Law, Moralism, and Administration in England, 1844–1910', *Canadian Journal of History*, 22 (1987), 356–7.

[7] P. A. Landon and Steve Hedley, 'Sir Roland Lomax Bowdler Vaughan Williams', *ODNB*. He was uncle of the famous composer.

Bank, his first annual report to the Board of Trade was a statement of intent.[8] Rather than confining himself to an anodyne summary of the numbers of firms wound up and their assets and liabilities, he lobbed a grenade into the debate on joint-stock companies. He estimated that the 874 companies wound up in 1891 had total losses of over £20 million, which represented 'a heavy tax... upon the industries or savings of the community'. The average lifespan of the 119 companies compulsorily wound up under the court was just three years; many had existed less than a year. Smith did not believe that normal commercial fluctuations or misfortune were to blame. Rather, he argued that 'under the Companies Acts, a wide field has been opened up for the prosecution of objects of a more or less fraudulent character'.[9]

In Judge Vaughan Williams and Official Receiver Stewart, Smith had willing allies. Vaughan Williams shared Smith's 'sense of moral outrage', as one historian puts it, at ethical shortcomings in business, and proved very willing to order the public examinations which uncovered much of the dirt on which Smith based his pessimistic conclusions.[10] In 1891, he approved the examination of 123 promoters, directors, and officers involved in seventeen companies, rising to 146 the following year. The examinations were ably conducted by Official Receiver Stewart, an Irishman with experience of law and accountancy; his interrogatory skill meant that the examinations threw 'a flood of light upon the mysteries of company promotion'.[11] Even when public examinations were not ordered, Stewart's diligence and skill as a liquidator (he was described as being 'full of Irish energy and grasp of affairs', his maxim was 'Do everything at once'), soon won the trust and respect of creditors and shareholders.[12] The determination of these three men to take fraud seriously led to two major prosecutions in the first year of the new act's operation.

The first of these arose out of the Argentinean depression of 1890 which triggered the Barings Crisis in November.[13] Though Barings was the highest-profile victim, the crisis also hit other British banks, including the English Bank of the River Plate. The crisis brought this flourishing concern, which had divided close to £200,000 a year, to insolvency. In August 1891, the bank's creditors secured a compulsory winding-up order. Stewart's inquiries focused on the managing director, Arthur Smithers, who had founded the bank in 1881, and ran its affairs with little supervision from his fellow directors. Smithers was heavily indebted to the bank, owing nearly £60,000 in advances authorized by the board. But unbeknownst to the directors, for years Smithers had been in the habit of using the office current cash account for his own purposes, being careful to replace the missing money

[8] Batzel, 'General Scope', 354.

[9] *First Report by the Board of Trade under Section 29 of the Companies (Winding-up) Act, 1890*, PP 1893–94 LXXXI. 3–13.

[10] Batzel, 'General Scope', 357.

[11] *First Report by the Board of Trade*, 4.

[12] *The Times*, 5 September 1932.

[13] David Kynaston, *The City of London: Volume 1, A World of Its Own, 1815–1890* (London, 1994), ch. 21.

before the annual audit each September. When the bank broke, he owed more than £7,000, and could not repay it as he had lost it in Argentine securities.[14] Stewart passed his findings on to Stephenson, who decided to prosecute Smithers under the Larceny Act for fraudulent misappropriation, and after a thorough examination in Mansion House, he was committed for trial at the Old Bailey.[15]

Smithers' fate hung on conflicting interpretations of intent. The defence, led by former Attorney General for the Liberals Sir Charles Russell, did not dispute the fact that Smithers had taken the money. But Smithers had believed that he would be able to repay the money, and intended to repay it; therefore even though he took the money without authority, there was no fraudulent intent. Russell 'hoped that the broad line of demarcation between conduct which was reprehensible and that which was criminal would never be effaced by the verdict of a Jury'.[16] The jury disagreed with where Russell had drawn the line, however, and found Smithers guilty.[17] Justice Sir Lewis Cave, a judge with extensive experience of business cases, approved of the verdict.[18] Smithers knew he had no right to take the money, and that this might result in the owners losing the money, so 'it would have been a scandal if the jury had found any other verdict than what they did find—a scandal anywhere, but especially in this city... the centre of the commercial activity in the world'. Cave felt obliged to pass a sentence which he trusted 'will be a lesson to persons of your advantages and opportunities, to teach them that if they misappropriate moneys, or, in other words, steal moneys entrusted to them for speculation, they must expect a very severe sentence'. He therefore consigned Smithers to four years' penal servitude, an outcome well received by the press, which had given the case extensive coverage.[19]

Smithers's misappropriations had been uncovered by the Official Receiver's investigations. By the time he had been sentenced, a second trial was pending, the first to illustrate the benefits of the public examination of company officials which the Winding-up Act permitted.[20] Thomas Gilbert, a stockbroker, company promoter, and newspaper proprietor who divided his time between Paris and London, established the Gold Queen (Mining) Company with a nominal capital of £180,000 in £1 shares in early 1888. As promoter, director, and secretary of the company, he packed the board with compliant 'guinea-pig' directors, including a deaf vice-admiral who later admitted that he could not hear what was said at board meetings, and never asked questions.[21] The company paid Gilbert £165,000 for

[14] *The Times*, 17, 30 October 1891, 20 January 1892.

[15] Ibid. 17 October, 21 November 1891.

[16] *Reg v. Smithers* (1892), *The Times*, 20, 21 January 1892, *Standard*, 21 January 1892.

[17] *The Times*, 21 January 1892.

[18] He edited several texts on commercial law: J. M. Rigg, rev. Hugh Mooney, 'Sir Lewis William Cave', *ODNB*.

[19] *The Times*, 22 January 1892; *Standard*, 22 January 1892; *Pall Mall Gazette*, 22 January 1892; *Penny Illustrated Paper*, 30 January 1892. The 1891 Penal Servitude Act had lowered the minimum sentence from five to three years: 54 & 55 Vict. c. 69 s. 1.

[20] *The Times*, 14 December 1891.

[21] 'Guinea-pig' was the common name for 'gentlemen of more rank than means, who hire themselves out as directors of companies, and who have a guinea and a copious lunch when they attend board meetings': [John Doran], 'High-Class Slang', *Temple Bar*, 31 (February 1871), 320–1.

mining property in Colorado which Gilbert had arranged to purchase from his son-in-law for $24,000. Gilbert received £5,000 in cash, the remaining £160,000 in shares, but did not follow through with the purchase.[22] Gilbert was publicly examined in the Bankruptcy Court by Stewart. At the second examination in October 1891, Gilbert cheerfully admitted that he had no title to the mines when he sold them to the company, but claimed that this was 'a mistake'. He was probably surprised therefore when, on leaving the building after his examination, he was arrested on a warrant obtained by the Treasury.[23] The following day he appeared at Guildhall police court. The charges related not to his title to the mines, but to his embezzlement of some of the subscription money, and falsification of the company's books. The Gold Queen's principal investor had been Anthony Gibbs, a Bristol gentleman. He had sent Gilbert five cheques totalling £5,000, but the company's accounts did not show the largest two cheques, for £2,000 apiece, because Gilbert had paid them into his own account. On the third hearing, he was committed for trial at the Old Bailey.[24]

The crux of Gilbert's defence when his trial took place in May 1892 was that the 4,000 shares Gibbs had bought with the two cheques had been Gilbert's vendor's shares, not the company's shares, and that he had therefore been entitled to dispose of them as he wished, without accounting for them in the company's books. The prosecution, led by Sir Edward Clarke, Conservative Solicitor General, disagreed: the claim that these were vendor's shares was 'contradicted by all the documents', and the case 'practically rested upon documents'. The money belonged to the company, had come to Gilbert as secretary, and had not been accounted for by him. The jury found Gilbert guilty, and the Recorder Sir Charles Hall (who had succeeded Sir Thomas Chambers in February) sentenced him to three years' penal servitude.[25] The verdicts and heavy sentences in these two cases showed that courts were willing to enforce the distinction between company money and personal money which the managements of some companies were prone to blur. That they both concerned real City firms rather than ephemeral bubble companies suggested that the legal apparatus established by the act of 1890 was able to catch bigger fish than had mostly been the case in the previous decade. An even bigger fish was about to swim into view, but would the net secure him?

BOTTOMLEY'S SWINDLE

For a man who had spent his formative years in an orphanage, Horatio Bottomley had achieved a lot before his thirtieth birthday. After obtaining experience of the law as a shorthand writer, in his mid-twenties he moved into publishing, and in

[22] *The Times*, 11 July, 23, 24, 30 October, 6 November 1891, 9 May 1892; *First Report by the Board of Trade*, 20–1.

[23] *The Times*, 23 October 1891.

[24] Ibid. 6 November 1891.

[25] *Reg. v. Gilbert* (1892), *The Times*, 9 May 1892.

1887, after three years of expansion and amalgamation, his firm MacRae, Curtice and Co. landed a major coup when it acquired the contract for the publication of Hansard, the record of the nation's parliamentary debates. The next stage in Bottomley's empire-building was the merger of his company with four other leading publishing firms which, the prospectus boasted, would establish a 'powerful combination of practically all departments of the printing and publishing trades'.[26] The new company, the Hansard Publishing Union, was launched with a capital of £375,000 in April 1889. Bottomley, as managing director, assembled an impressive board chaired by Sir Henry Isaacs, a Liberal alderman destined to become Lord Mayor of London later that year.[27] The Hansard name proved a lure to the public and the flotation was massively over-subscribed. Bottomley quickly capitalized on the enthusiasm for shares by orchestrating a further share issue of £125,000 to finance the purchase of paper mills and printing works in Devon and Surrey, and investors were treated to a first-year dividend of 12 per cent, financed by a loan of £50,000 from the Debenture Corporation. In July 1890, the Union made a further share issue, doubling the company's capital to £1million, but this was not so successful, with suspicions about the company's soundness beginning to spread. Bottomley had overreached. The £50,000 loan fell due at the end of 1890, but the company could not pay, so the Debenture Corporation seized the company's premises and petitioned for compulsory winding-up, which was granted in May 1891, the same month that Bottomley filed for personal bankruptcy.[28] Though some Stock Exchange insiders had referred to the company as 'Bottomley's Swindle', the crash came as a surprise to many.[29] As the roguish journalist Frank Harris, who knew Bottomley, later noted: 'The failure came too soon, the ruin was too big; it shocked business people.'[30]

The press was quick to smell fraud and demanded retribution: the *Saturday Review* thought that 'the attention of some one in authority should be speedily turned' to Bottomley's affairs, while the *St James's Gazette* complained about official inaction and claimed that '[n]obody quite knows what the exact functions of the "Public Prosecutor" are'.[31] But the first step was for Official Receiver Stewart to probe the company's affairs, and the public examination of the directors and officers took place through the second half of the year.[32] The press kept up the pressure for a prosecution, Henry Labouchere earning himself a libel writ at the end of the year when his paper *Truth* carried a poem making various accusations against 'Bottomley's wild scheme', accompanied by an illustration of the promoter as a beadle

[26] *Pall Mall Gazette*, 6 April 1889.

[27] These events are covered in more detail in Julian Symons, *Horatio Bottomley* (London, 1955), chs. 1–2; Alan Hyman, *The Rise and Fall of Horatio Bottomley* (London, 1972), ch.3.

[28] *The Times*, 31 January 1891, 3 March 1892; *Morning Post*, 2 May 1891; *Pall Mall Gazette*, 13 May 1891.

[29] Hyman, *Horatio Bottomley*, 34.

[30] Frank Harris, *My Life and Loves*, 4 vols (n.p., 1922), ii. 423.

[31] *Saturday Review of Politics, Literature, Science and Art*, 18 April 1891; *St James's Gazette*, 14 April 1891.

[32] *The Times*, 9 June, 22, 23 July, 3 November, 3 December 1891.

welcoming his victims into the workhouse.[33] After Stewart issued his report on the case, Stephenson decided to act, and in March 1892, Bottomley, together with three others—Sir Henry Isaacs, who had by now resigned as alderman, his brother and business partner Joseph, and Bottomley's brother-in-law Charles Dollman, a furrier's clerk and an undischarged bankrupt—were summonsed to Bow Street magistrates. Unlike his fellow defendants, Bottomley decided to conduct his own defence, which only intensified press interest in the unfolding drama. He performed 'with such coolness' that sketch artists were dispatched to the courtroom to capture the scene for readers who could not get enough of the case (see Figure 9.1).[34] After eleven days of hearings, the four were committed for trial.[35] By now, Bottomley was almost a celebrity, and in the interval caused by the trial's relocation to the Court of Queen's Bench, he published *Horatio Bottomley: Hys Booke*, which promised 'The True Story of the Hansard Union'.[36] Serialized in the *Western Mail* as 'THE BOOK

Figure 9.1 'The Hansard Union Prosecution at Bow Street Police-Court', *Illustrated London News*, 12 March 1892

[33] *Truth*, 'Christmas Number, 1891', and 3 December 1891.
[34] *Penny Illustrated Paper*, 9 April 1892.
[35] *The Times*, 1 March, 7 April 1892.
[36] Horatio Bottomley, *Horatio Bottomley: Hys Booke* (London, 1892), 6, 57.

OF THE SEASON', Bottomley claimed it had sold 10,000 copies by the time of the trial.[37] It displayed the boldness and gift for self-promotion which were to stand Bottomley in such good stead during the trial, which began at the end of January 1893 before the respected but capricious judge, Sir Henry Hawkins.[38]

There was an extensive set of counts, twenty-one in all, charging various permutations of the four defendants with a series of crimes under the law of conspiracy and the Larceny Act. But at the heart of the prosecution's case were secret profits totalling nearly £150,000 Bottomley had obtained from the company, first at the time of the original flotation, and again with the purchase of the paper mills and printing works. Bottomley executed the sales in the names of 'dummies', concealing both the fact that he was the vendor of the properties, and that he was making exorbitant profits on the deals. In the original flotation, the nominee was James Phillips, a stockbroker's clerk; the second time it was Dollman. 'It is said to be usual to put forward a dummy to mask the vendor; but is it honest?' asked Sir Charles Russell, who led the prosecution.[39] He did not deny the right of men to buy and sell to make a profit, 'but if you are once in a fiduciary position with regard to the buying company, law, honour, and justice forbid you to take advantage of that position for the purpose of exacting a largely increased value from the company'. If the shareholders had known Bottomley was acting as buyer and seller, they would not have subscribed. The other defendants knew about these transactions, and helped Bottomley to conceal them.[40]

After nearly a fortnight of complex financial evidence and legal argument, the prosecution concluded. Now it was Bottomley's turn. While his fellow defendants paid for strong legal teams, Bottomley, who turned 33 during the trial, again chose to defend himself, and he proved a skilled advocate, combining a mastery of legal and business detail with a genius for manipulating emotions, achieved by identifying villains and martyrs. In his alternative narrative of events, there were two villains: the first was Stewart, the Official Receiver. He exploited the prosecution's reliance on Stewart's evidence, pointing out that none of the Hansard Union's auditors, accountants, or directors had been called to give evidence. He was thus able to paint himself as victim of a cruel vendetta by a state functionary, who was attempting to advance his career at an innocent man's expense. The second villain was the Debenture Corporation, which had hastened to close down the Hansard Union when it defaulted. Bottomley was fortunate that Jabez Spencer Balfour, chairman of the Corporation, had recently fled the country after his business empire had collapsed, and Bottomley harped on this fact. The Hansard Union, he claimed, 'had not failed, but had been wrecked' by Balfour's Corporation. Bottomley was the martyr, the scapegoat for the sins of the age, 'when the air both at home and abroad was dense with frauds'. Rather than quitting his company when

37 *Western Mail*, 15 November 1892; *Bristol Mercury and Daily Post*, 28 April 1893.

38 For a vivid portrait of his unpredictability, see Edmund D. Purcell, *Forty Years at the Criminal Bar* (London, 1916), 59–65.

39 Russell was Attorney General since the Liberals' resumption of power the previous August.

40 *Reg. v. Bottomley* (1893), *The Times*, 31 January, 1 February 1893.

it got into difficulties, he had stood by his post and done his duty. This is what had caused his bankruptcy, 'in which he gloried'.[41]

Events further played into Bottomley's hands when the trial was interrupted for two months by the illness of a juror. When it resumed, Russell was absent, called away to Paris to take part in an international fisheries arbitration.[42] This meant that the Solicitor General, Sir John Rigby, a Chancery lawyer with no experience of criminal trials, took over the prosecution.[43] Hawkins did not like Rigby and delighted in pointing out his blunders. More important than personality, however, was Hawkins's interpretation of the law. Before his elevation to the bench, Hawkins had defended businessmen charged with fraud, unsuccessfully in the case of Sir John Dean Paul in 1855, and successfully in the case of several of the Overend and Gurney directors in 1869. And despite a reputation for severity which had earned him the nickname 'Hanging Hawkins', he was a Liberal with a rather narrow view of the criminal law as applied to directors, reminiscent of that of former Lord Chief Justice Cockburn.[44] Hawkins decided that no case had been made out against Sir Henry since it had been shown that he had not received 'a single farthing of the profits of the promotion of the original company or from the purchases . . . Whether a man gets anything is to my mind very material in a criminal case.'[45] Rigby countered that Sir Henry was accused of complicity in Bottomley's fraud, and not benefiting financially was no proof of innocence, but Hawkins directed the jury to acquit Sir Henry. Shortly afterwards, and despite protests from Rigby, Hawkins reached a similar determination in the case against Joseph.[46]

This left only Bottomley and Dollman to face charges of conspiracy, and in his final summing up, Hawkins nailed his colours firmly to the mast. Having obtained, so Bottomley later claimed, a copy of *Hys Booke* during the trial, Hawkins accepted Bottomley's account as truth, and felt that he had been unfairly dealt with.[47] Hawkins rejected the assertion that the Hansard Union was established solely to line Bottomley's pockets, observing that it was 'a very sensible and very rational scheme; the objects seemed to be good'. The properties acquired by the company were apparently thriving and genuine businesses. Using another man as a nominee to facilitate the transfer of the properties was not against the law, nor was taking secret profits. No evidence had been produced to show that the properties were not worth what the company paid. Nor did the evidence sustain the charge that Bottomley misled either the directors or the shareholders. The directors had ample opportunity to check the contracts, but they chose not to, while the prospectus fully satisfied the requirements of the law. Hawkins had sympathy for arguments that the law ought to be changed to make directors criminally liable for negligence, and to increase the disclosure requirements for prospectuses. But he insisted that

[41] *The Times*, 15, 16 February 1893.
[42] Ibid. 6 April 1893.
[43] J. B. Atlay and Patrick Polden, 'Sir John Rigby', *ODNB*.
[44] Herbert Stephen, rev. P. R. Glazebrook, 'Henry Hawkins', *ODNB*.
[45] *The Times*, 19 April 1893.
[46] Ibid. 21, 26 April 1893.
[47] *Bristol Mercury and Daily Post*, 28 April 1893.

they had to deal with the law 'as we find it, and must not strain it'. He thought that the law had been strained in this case, and the prosecution had shown signs of personal animus. After a trial lasting twenty-four days, the jury took about as many minutes to acquit both defendants.[48] According to Bottomley, not long after the trial Hawkins invited him to his private rooms to congratulate him, and told him that with his gifts for rhetoric and the law he should train for the bar; later, he delivered Bottomley his wig and his case notes as mementos of the trial.[49] The former Solicitor General Sir Edward Clarke, who had defended Sir Henry Isaacs and so might be considered unlikely to complain at the outcome, thought that the trial showed off Hawkins' 'worst characteristics', singling it out as a low point in the judge's 'career of public disservice'.[50]

Bottomley had charmed Hawkins; he also mesmerized several press observers, who predicted future success for this 'man of rare resources'.[51] Rather than question the verdict, editorials unleashed a torrent of criticism on the government for the way it had conducted the case: the charges were 'hastily framed'; the prosecution had been 'bungled'.[52] Some papers claimed that the suit, which cost a total of £6,136, should never have been taken up at all.[53] The *Daily Telegraph* insisted that before such cases were brought into court—and enormous expenses incurred—the government had to be sure that it was right.[54] The *St James's Gazette* went further, calling the prosecution 'a foolish failure'. The government's law officers should have known that 'they could not substantiate the vague and "fishing" charges'. With little sense of irony, given it had led the cry for criminal action back in 1891, it claimed that the Treasury 'has been partly led into its error, on this occasion, by the press'.[55] The *Yorkshire Herald* was a lonely voice highlighting journalistic hypocrisy, observing with both justice and understatement that had the DPP refused to act, he 'would doubtless have been reproached'.[56] Clearly, Stephenson could not win!

When delivering its verdict, the jury had echoed Hawkins's comments on the necessity of stiffening the legal responsibilities of guinea-pig directors.[57] But the government firmly rebuffed calls for a re-examination of company law. It was not desirable, President of the Board of Trade Anthony Mundella argued, 'to institute a general inquiry into the working of the Companies Acts until fuller experience has been gained of the effect of the very drastic provisions contained in the Act

[48] *The Times*, 27 April 1893; *Daily News*, 27 April 1893.

[49] Hyman, *Horatio Bottomley*, 55; Symons, *Horatio Bottomley*, 35–6. Symons notes that the story is uncorroborated, but that Bottomley displayed the wig and notes to guests at his Pall Mall residence.

[50] Edward Clarke, *The Story of My Life* (New York, 1919), 135.

[51] *Dundee Courier and Argus*, 27 April 1893. For similar praise, see *Western Mail*, 27 April 1893; *Liverpool Mercury*, 27 April 1893.

[52] *Birmingham Daily Post*, 27 April 1893; *Sheffield and Rotherham Independent*, 27 April 1893.

[53] *Return Showing the Working of the Regulations made in 1886 for Carrying out the Prosecution of Offences Acts, 1879 and 1884*, PP 1894 LXXI. 10.

[54] Repr. in *Yorkshire Herald*, 28 April 1893.

[55] *St James's Gazette*, 27 April 1893.

[56] *Yorkshire Herald*, 28 April 1893.

[57] *The Times*, 27 April 1893.

passed so recently as 1890'.[58] But would the humiliating failure of the Bottomley trial discourage future prosecutions? The previous chapter showed how the failed prosecutions of the early 1880s sapped official will to take on major cases of fraud, and it has been claimed that this happened in the 1890s, with the verdict serving 'as a tonic to other company promoters'.[59] Indeed, Russell and Rigby were left licking their wounds after their bruising experience, with Rigby's experience so traumatic 'that it is freely said the Solicitor-General hopes it will not be repeated'.[60] But while Bottomley was allowed to continue his dubious company flotations unmolested, the case had no wider impact on the machinery of the law, which was already in the midst of dealing with an even bigger scandal.

THE BALFOUR GROUP

On a Friday morning in early September 1892, a notice was fixed to the doors of the London and General Bank that payments were suspended. The notice attracted only 'a small crowd', and the press reassured readers that this was a relatively insignificant institution.[61] But the stoppage was of much greater importance than was first apparent. *The Times* noted somewhat enigmatically that the bank's chairman, whom it did not name, was a director of sixteen other companies. This was Jabez Spencer Balfour, leading nonconformist, temperance campaigner, and Liberal MP for Burnley. The London and General had been established in 1882 to provide banking facilities for Balfour's main venture, the Liberator Permanent Building and Investment Society. Founded in 1868, and exploiting Balfour's religious and political contacts to the full, the Liberator had developed into the nation's biggest building society, with 30,000 depositors and shareholders, most of them working- and lower middle-class. But the bank's failure caused it in turn to suspend, and by the end of the week, two more Balfour companies had fallen.[62] First was the building firm J. W. Hobbs and Co., quickly followed by the House and Land Investment Trust.[63] With the Liberator's management maintaining a 'studied silence', some of the society's creditors seized the initiative, securing a compulsory winding-up order at the start of October.[64]

Stewart gathered the largest depositors and shareholders together at the end of the month to hear his preliminary report. His revelations were shocking. Of the £3.4 million the company had loaned on mortgage, £3.2 million had gone to just three companies, all part of the Balfour Group: J. W. Hobbs and Co. (£2.1 million), the

[58] Hansard, 4s, 12: 924–5 (15 May 1893). See also ibid. 11: 1495–6 (28 April 1893).

[59] Symons, *Horatio Bottomley*, 35–6.

[60] *Yorkshire Herald*, 29 April 1893.

[61] *Pall Mall Gazette*, 2 September 1892; *The Times*, 3 September 1892; *Morning Post*, 3 September 1892.

[62] *Pall Mall Gazette*, 3 September 1892; *Morning Post*, 3 September 1892.

[63] *Leeds Mercury*, 10 September 1892; *The Times*, 10 September 1892. Panic spread beyond the Balfour group, with several building societies and banks facing runs: *Leeds Mercury*, 12 September 1892; *The Times*, 14, 15, 16, 17, 20 September 1892.

[64] *The Times*, 15, 17, 19, 20 September, 5 October 1892.

House and Land Investment Trust (£0.6 million), and the Real Estates Company (£0.5 million), which had joined the other two in liquidation earlier that month. A fourth Balfour company, G. Newman and Co., had owed nearly £250,000, but this debt was transferred to the Real Estates Company shortly before the crash. The prospects of shareholders and depositors could not have been much grimmer.[65] Public opinion was scandalized. One nonconformist minister remarked that the Liberator had not been a building society in any true sense for years 'but rather a *huge speculating concern*', paying big dividends regardless of earnings, and '*doing business under false pretences*'.[66] Furious investors demanded criminal prosecutions, though Stephenson informed them that before he could take any action, the Official Receiver had to complete his investigation, which was likely to be a lengthy process.[67]

Nevertheless, rapid progress was made in relation to one corner of Balfour's empire owing to the talkativeness of a key witness. George Kentish was the confidential clerk and brother-in-law of James W. Hobbs, a well-known Croydon builder, former mayor of the town, and managing director of the company which bore his name. Kentish spilled the beans on a series of scams in which he had aided his employer. In one, Hobbs inflated his expense account with the Liberator by means of forged bills of exchange in the names of Hobbs's creditors. The money thus obtained from the Liberator was used to pay off Hobbs's personal debts to Granville Wright, solicitor and financial manager of the Balfour Group companies. Another con came in 1886 when Hobbs's firm was converted to a limited company. One of the debts absorbed by the company was £2,405 owed to a milliner named Mrs Hobbs, the wife of Hobbs's cousin. But the debt was fictitious: Mrs Hobbs received a series of cheques from the company in payment of the 'debt'; each cheque she paid into her account, and within a day or two, wrote a cheque for the same amount to Hobbs. While digging into these transactions, Stewart found fraud at a second building company, involving Wright and George Newman, chairman of G. Newman and Co. The worst example came in 1889 when Newman borrowed £36,000 from the Liberator to purchase land near the Albert Hall. Only £24,500 was actually spent, the remaining £11,500 was pocketed by Newman and Wright, and concealed through false entries in the books.[68] Hobbs, Wright, and Newman were all arrested and appeared at Bow Street magistrates before James Vaughan in a series of hearings which laid bare the illegal transactions. The evidence against the men was strong, and on Thursday 23 February 1893, the same day that William Caseley, a Brighton valet in his fifties who had lost his life's savings in the Liberator companies, blew out his brains with a revolver, Vaughan committed the three for trial.[69]

[65] *Birmingham Daily Post*, 1 November 1892; *The Times*, 1 November 1892.

[66] J. Stockwell Watts, *The Truth about the 'Liberator' Building Society: Respectfully Addressed to the Thirty Thousand Shareholders and Depositors* (2nd edn, London, 1892), 4, 9.

[67] *The Times*, 1, 2, 12 November 1892.

[68] Ibid. 13, 17, 21 December 1892, 27 January, 18 February, 18 March 1893.

[69] Ibid. 24, 25 February 1893. His was not the only suicide prompted by the failure: David McKie, *Jabez: The Rise and Fall of a Victorian Rogue* (rev. repr., London, 2005), 264.

The men were tried at the Old Bailey during the two-month hiatus in the Hansard Union trial, with Hawkins again presiding. There were three separate, consecutive trials, dealing with the various charges of forgery, misappropriation, and falsification of books. All three essentially revolved around the sanctity of joint-stock property and whether management were permitted to use it for their own purposes. The prosecution, led by Sir Charles Mathews, the feted criminal advocate, showed how the men used the building companies at the heart of the transactions 'as a sieve to pass the money obtained from the Liberator Society into their own pockets'.[70] The defence team had little scope to question the facts of the transactions, so had to cast the men's motives in the best possible light, vilify the chief witness Kentish—a self-confessed forger—and invoke the principle of *caveat emptor*. But in each case, Hawkins brought the questions back to basic business principles: it was clear that, unlike in the Bottomley trial, he did not think that the law had to be strained to reach what the men had done. On the forgery counts, Hawkins accused the defence of muddying the waters: the case was in fact simple. The men were patently guilty of forgery, and all the jury had to decide was whether they did it with guilty intent. On the fake debts to Mrs Hobbs, Hawkins deprecated the practice of inserting pretended liabilities into contracts, which was clearly done to defraud innocent investors. The Albert Hall land deal, unlike Bottomley's secret commissions, clearly came under the criminal law: 'if a man represented that he wanted 100*l.* to acquire a property, and he only required 25*l.*, there was no man in the wide world who knew anything of the law who would not say that the balance of 75*l.* was obtained by false pretences'. Under this guidance, the jury reached guilty verdicts in all three cases.[71]

In sentencing, Hawkins invoked the widely reported suffering of the Liberator's victims—'those poor people whose sad losses had left them beggars in their old age, and who were now absolutely ruined by the loss of all the little treasure which they had put by for their declining years'—in order to justify retributive sentences. There were no mitigating circumstances: the three were guilty of 'deliberate, continuous, and systematic fraud'. He therefore sentenced Hobbs and Wright to twelve years' penal servitude for the forgeries and five years' penal servitude for the other offences, to run concurrently. He gave Newman five years' penal servitude.[72]

While the outcome was welcomed by the press, the widespread view was that justice would only be done when Balfour himself—'the devil-fish' who preyed on the savings of innocent investors—was punished (see Figure 9.2).[73] But this seemed unlikely to happen any time soon: days after the arrests in December 1892 he had caught a steamer bound for Argentina. Warrants for Balfour's apprehension were issued the following February, but he had chosen his bolt-hole

[70] *Reg. v. Wright* (1893), *The Times*, 27 March 1893.

[71] *The Times*, 23, 24, 28 March 1893; *Daily News*, 28 March 1893.

[72] *The Times*, 28 March 1893; *Daily News*, 28 March 1893.

[73] *Birmingham Daily Post*, 29 March 1893; *The Times* 28 March 1893; *Daily News*, 28 March 1893.

THE DEVIL-FISH OF TO-DAY.

Figure 9.2 'The Devil-fish of To-day', *Review of Reviews*, November 1893, 550

wisely: though an extradition treaty had been negotiated three years earlier, this had never been ratified by the Argentinean parliament, and Britain had recently failed to secure the return of other wanted criminals from the territory.[74] Talks with the Argentine authorities yielded no results, and the Liberal government faced mounting public criticism, made worse by the lack of proceedings against any other Balfour Group directors, despite exhaustive public examinations

[74] McKie, *Jabez*, 125.

between February and August 1893.[75] As frustrations mounted, the government was accused first of incompetence in allowing Balfour to escape, then of sluggishness in pursing his extradition, and finally, in some quarters at least, of corruption, with suspicions mounting that Balfour had friends in the Liberal administration who were shielding him.[76] The waxworks museum Madame Tussaud's swiftly capitalized on public opinion. One of its chief attractions in May 1893 was a model of Balfour: if the man himself could not be found, then his effigy was the next best thing.[77] Strategically positioned just outside the Chamber of Horrors, 'Balfour' attracted much attention. A widely reported incident occurred in August, when an 'old man, whose whole get-up spoke of better days, was seen to walk to the effigy...shake his withered, palsied fist in its cruel face, and totter out of the building'.[78]

Public criticism of the government was a little unfair. When Balfour absconded, there was not the evidence against him to justify an arrest. The mass of papers involved made progress slow, and the failure of the Hansard Union prosecution in 1893 must have weighed particularly heavily with all concerned as a reminder that charges had to be carefully framed.[79] Even when evidence had been amassed against other Balfour Group directors, the authorities naturally wanted to delay their trial until Balfour himself had been obtained: trying the men together would maximize the chances of convictions. After a long legal struggle, the government finally managed to secure Balfour's extradition, and he was greeted by large crowds at Southampton docks in May 1895.[80] His committal for trial was completed shortly before the Liberal Government fell.[81] That autumn all eyes turned to Queen's Bench when his trial took place before Sir Gainsford Bruce and a special jury (see Figure 9.3). He was joined in the dock by four of his fellow directors, George Brock, George Dibley, Morrell Theobald, and Major John Wright—Granville Wright's brother.[82]

Bruce, a lifelong Conservative who had briefly sat in the Commons, and had spoken in favour of the Directors' Liability Bill in 1890, had a reputation as 'a sound and careful lawyer' before he was raised to the Bench. 'By no means a brilliant man', he was rather of 'modest and simple nature', and was averse to 'moralizing

[75] Though a pair of banker brothers, Richard and Albert Benham were convicted of obtaining advances totalling £49,000 as customers of the London and General Bank by means of forged securities. They were sentenced to penal servitude for fourteen and five years respectively: *The Times*, 4 July 1893.

[76] Hansard, 4s, 19: 268–9 (1 December 1893), 24: 1187 (24 May 1894), 25: 19 (31 May 1894), 428 (5 June 1894), 29: 78–89 (20 August 1894), 31: 573–94 (7 March 1895).

[77] *Morning Post*, 6 May 1893; *Judy*, 31 May 1893.

[78] *Standard*, 8 August 1893; *Aberdeen Weekly Journal*, 18 August 1893; *Newcastle Weekly Courant*, 19 August 1893.

[79] A point made by Sir John Rigby, now Attorney General, in the Commons: Hansard, 45, 29: 78–89 (20 August 1894).

[80] David Rock, 'Victorian Globalization in Microcosm: The Rise and Fall of Jabez Spencer Balfour', in Fernando López-Alves and Diane E. Johnson (eds), *Globalization and Uncertainty in Latin America* (New York, 2007), 38–42.

[81] *The Times*, 7, 24 May 1895.

[82] A sixth defendant, Frank Moses Coldwells MP, died of heart failure before the trial, after complaining that 'he was being slowly killed by worry': ibid. 31 July 1895.

Figure 9.3 'The Alleged Liberator Companies' Frauds: The Trial of Jabez Balfour', *Illustrated London News*, 23 November 1895

at large or of making cheap jokes, or of playing to the gallery'.[83] In short, he could not have been more different to Hawkins, and with Balfour declining to emulate Bottomley by presenting his own defence, the trial was a more sober affair. The first indictment charged Balfour, Brock, Dibley, and Theobald, as directors of the Lands

[83] Ibid. 26 February 1912; Hansard, 3s, 345: 1271 (18 June 1890).

Allotment Company, with issuing false balance sheets between 1887 and 1892 to induce people to become shareholders. From 1880 the company made no profits, but to sustain repeated new share issues, the balance sheets showed 'vast sums' in earnings and large dividends were declared.[84] By these means, explained Sir Richard Webster, the Conservative Attorney General who led the prosecution, 'a constant stream of money flowed in from the public', which 'for many years averted the inevitable smash'. The paper profits were manufactured by collusion between the directors, who pretended to buy properties from each other at imaginary prices in bogus transactions. In reality, the directors were paying out with one hand as dividend what they were receiving with the other as capital.[85]

The defence lawyers, seeing what had worked so well in the Hansard case, attempted to vilify the Official Receiver who, 'with a staff of clerks and experts, since 1893 had been ransacking tons of books for the purpose of "piecing" together these charges'. They also claimed that paying dividends from capital was ordinary City practice. Bills incorporating railways always carried a provision sanctioning the payment of dividends out of capital during construction. 'Was not a building society always constructing?' But their main strategy was to play pass-the-parcel with responsibility, exploiting the weakened accountability inherent in the joint-stock form. So, the jury were told that Theobald had not taken an active part in the direction of the company from the late 1880s, and deferred to the judgement of the rest of the board. Brock had joined the Liberator as a clerk in 1868, and though he subsequently became a director, he did not dare challenge long-standing policy. Dibley was an innocent who was manipulated by the other defendants. He did not know what was going on, trusting those who kept the books, which he did not look at himself. Even Balfour's counsel, John O'Connor, joined in this game. The idea that Balfour was the 'life and soul' of these companies was a press invention; increasingly preoccupied with his parliamentary ambitions, he was less involved in their management than the other directors, who bore chief responsibility for the failure. But these efforts went largely unrewarded, with the jury finding Balfour, Brock, and Theobald guilty on all counts, though they were divided on Dibley.[86]

The following day the second indictment was tried before a fresh jury. This time, Balfour was the only defendant, and the charge was that Balfour and Granville Wright made a secret profit on the sale of Whitehall Court, a set of model dwellings on the Thames Embankment. The property was bought by Hobbs and Co. in 1886 from its indebted developer for £57,500, then sold to the House and Land Investment Trust, of which Balfour was the chairman and Wright the solicitor, for £77,500. The £20,000 difference was divided between the two men, and as in the Hansard Union case, a dummy was used as an intermediary. This time it was Octavius Greig, a Devonshire fish farmer related to Wright, who was paid £100 for use of his name. Webster contended that the deal contravened section 81 of the Larceny Act on the fraudulent appropriation of company property, because Balfour

[84] The company's capital was pumped up from just £15,000 in 1867 to £1.25m by 1888.
[85] *Reg. v. Balfour* (1895), *The Times*, 26 October, 20, 21 November 1895.
[86] *The Times*, 12, 13, 14, 15, 20, 21 November 1895; *Morning Post*, 21 November 1895.

had converted the House and Land Investment Trust's money to his own purposes.[87] The elephant in the room was the Hansard Union case, in which similar secret profits were made. O'Connor tried to quote from Hawkins's charge to the jury, but Bruce scolded him; it was confusing the issue to cite opinions based on the facts in another case. O'Connor went on to claim that the commission had been paid as a reward to Balfour for negotiating such a good deal, having driven the property developer down from his initial asking price of £100,000 to nearly half that figure. The whole transaction, O'Connor claimed, was 'honest, open, and above board'; using an intermediary such as Greig was 'a common practice as old as the hills'.[88] However, Bruce's summing up left very little scope for an acquittal. He found it difficult to see how the deal could have been made with honest intent. The evidence contradicted the defence's claim that the commission was known to all parties. A false statement was inserted into the minutes to conceal it, while Balfour stated shortly after the transactions took place that not a penny of commission was paid to anyone. Though this was a special jury, it had little difficulty agreeing with Bruce's stern view, taking just half an hour to return a guilty verdict.[89] The outcome could hardly have differed more from the Hansard Union debacle two and a half years earlier.[90]

Bruce, his aversion to moralizing notwithstanding, dwelled upon the effects of the men's crimes on the company's many victims, and told Balfour that he had 'carried out with great ingenuity in your management of these companies a long series of frauds which have been the means of obtaining thousands, nay, millions, of pounds' from innocent and thrifty people. He was merciful to Brock and Theobald. The former was under Balfour's spell, and had suffered massive losses when the companies collapsed; the latter had resigned from the companies at the start of 1892 and 'urged his co-directors to return to the path of honesty'. He therefore sentenced them to nine and four months' imprisonment with hard labour respectively. He showed no such leniency to Balfour, though. Whilst acknowledging that remorse must form 'no small part' of his punishment, it was his duty to pass 'a severe and exemplary sentence'. He therefore sentenced Balfour to seven years' penal servitude for the offences in each of the two indictments, to run consecutively, not concurrently.[91]

The devil-fish had finally got his comeuppance. But what was the wider significance of these high-profile trials? In part, they played a social function. The victims

[87] *The Times*, 22, 28 November 1895.

[88] Ibid. 27, 28 November 1895.

[89] Ibid. 28 November 1895. An act of 1870 had supplemented the existing stipulation that jury members be bankers, merchants, or esquires with a new property qualification: James Oldham, 'Special Juries in England: Nineteenth-Century Usage and Reform', *Journal of Legal History*, 8 (1987), 159.

[90] Webster dropped the remaining indictments involving the Liberator and the Building Securities Company: Dibley's health was so poor that he could not face a second trial for the time being, while the evidence against Wright was considered weak: ibid. 29 November 1895; *Dundee Courier & Argus*, 29 November 1895.

[91] *The Times*, 29 November 1895; *Dundee Courier & Argus*, 29 November 1895. Balfour was released in April 1906, having served ten and a half years of his sentence, earning maximum remission for good behaviour: Duncan Bythell, 'Jabez Spencer Balfour', *ODNB*; McKie, *Jabez*, 236.

were mostly small investors, many of them working-class. If Bottomley's more affluent investors could afford the loss, Balfour's could not, and far from being 'rash investors' paying 'the penalties of speculation', they were thrifty and humble people whose only sin was trusting the guarantees of their social superiors.[92] In both sets of Balfour Group trials, the judges drew attention to their plight, arguing that it necessitated harsh punishment. The press fully backed this retributive justice with reference to the status of the victims.[93] Indeed public sympathy for them was such that shortly after the failure, a relief fund was established, which eventually raised over £140,000.[94] Whereas Bottomley's acquittal had been greeted with applause, Balfour's conviction was met with 'an indecent display of exultation from the mob who crowded around the Law Court steps'.[95] The hefty sentences meted out to him, and to his colleagues two years earlier, were a way of demonstrating to the angry mob that well-born fraudsters would be treated the same as common criminals.

But there was an economic dimension too which was even more important. For some, the Balfour trial was the means by which honest business, embodied by the commercial men of the special jury, could express its condemnation of dishonest business, stigmatizing certain practices as beyond the pale. The *Liverpool Mercury* said that the jury, 'as every-day business men', brought 'commonsense and worldly experience' to the examination of 'the dry facts of financial administration' on which the cases hinged, and returned the only verdict possible.[96] The *Hampshire Telegraph* commented: 'The jury found—and every honest man will rejoice that they have done so—that juggling with balance-sheets and issuing false reports . . . is a fraud which merits punishment.'[97] The *Morning Post* ridiculed the defence's suggestion that what the directors had done was 'an everyday transaction in the commercial life of the business men of London'.[98]

Yet this is exactly what some commentators claimed after the trial. The *Bristol Mercury*, for example, told its readers that 'exactly the same frauds for which Jabez Balfour has been sent to penal servitude are being perpetrated almost daily . . . the line between honesty and dishonesty is very thinly drawn'.[99] If such frauds were in fact rife, what were the chances that the outcome would act as a deterrent to others? *Freeman's Journal* was pessimistic, arguing that what the case demonstrated above all else was 'the absolute worthlessness' of safeguards like balance sheets and audits.

[92] Anon., *The Story of the Liberator Crash: With some Account of the Life and Character of Jabez Spencer Balfour*, 'Westminster Gazette' Popular No. 5 (November 1893), 37.

[93] *Morning Post*, 28 March 1893; *The Times*, 28 March 1893; *Daily News*, 28 March 1893; *Liverpool Mercury*, 28 March 1893; *Freeman's Journal*, 29 March 1893; *Standard*, 21 November 1895; *Birmingham Daily Post*, 21 November 1895; *Lloyd's Weekly Newspaper*, 24 November 1895; *Bristol Mercury and Daily Post*, 29 November 1895.

[94] *The Times*, 19, 30 December 1892, 10 October 1908.

[95] *Glasgow Herald*, 29 November 1895.

[96] *Liverpool Mercury*, 21 November 1895.

[97] *Hampshire Telegraph and Sussex Chronicle*, 23 November 1895. See also *Manchester Times*, 22 November 1895.

[98] *Morning Post*, 21 November 1895.

[99] *Bristol Mercury and Daily Post*, 29 November 1895. See also *The Times*, 29 November 1895.

Shareholders could only protect themselves by being sceptical about glowing statements, and satisfying themselves with modest profits.[100] Though common earlier in the century, such harping on the lessons for investors was unusual by 1895, for a significant shift had occurred. Whereas in the evangelical world view it was the economic catastrophe itself which was welcomed as teaching prudence and purifying the commercial atmosphere, now it was the criminal trial which was regarded as having the cleansing effect. Faith in the self-regulating economy had weakened and by the 1890s, the criminal trial—an external event triggered by state functionaries—had taken on a key role in the regulation of the economy. 'That the denouement of the Liberator trials will purify our commercial atmosphere there is reason to hope and to believe,' wrote the *Standard*.[101] The *Yorkshire Herald* thought that 'the air will be clearer' after the trial.[102] According to this new outlook, it was company directors, not shareholders, who had lessons to learn. 'The moral effect of the trial will be very great', reasoned the *North-Eastern Daily Gazette*. 'More than ever we believe the claims of the maxim "Honesty is the best policy" are being recognized in business circles and in the everyday transactions of mercantile life.'[103] This judgement was reiterated ad infinitum in press reports.[104] The criminal law was now fully accepted as a legitimate tool in the fight against fraud. More than this, criminal prosecutions were essential in the context of a permissive company law. 'The facilities for creating public companies, the ready means they afford for drawing money from investors, make it essential to secure honesty in their administration', wrote the *Daily News*. Balfour's fate would 'long stand as a terrible but salutary warning to financial adventurers'.[105]

The fact that the collapse of the Liberator Group had led to the successful prosecution of half a dozen such adventurers was testimony to how far the legal machinery had developed. The *Glasgow Herald* praised 'the rigorous spirit in which the existing Company Law is being administered by the English Courts', and argued that the Larceny Act was proving a powerful weapon against fraudulent directors.[106] Criticisms of the outgoing Liberal government melted away, with its conduct of the Balfour affair now held up as one of its few genuine achievements. The cost may have been immense—over £14,000—'but the case was one of such importance to a commercial country that no one will grudge the outlay', wrote *The*

[100] *Freeman's Journal*, 29 November 1895.

[101] *Standard*, 29 November 1895. It saw the criminal judgement as part of a harder line being taken against fraud across the board. It welcomed recent civil judgements, including one by Vaughan Williams, which made auditors civilly liable for fraud in the same way as any other company officer under the terms of the 1890 Winding-up Act: *Re Kingston Cotton Mill Company (Limited)*, *The Times*, 4 November 1895.

[102] *Yorkshire Herald*, 29 November 1895.

[103] *North-Eastern Daily Gazette*, 29 November 1895.

[104] *Manchester Times*, 22, 29 November 1895; *Leeds Mercury*, 29 November 1895; *Yorkshire Herald*, 29 November 1895; *Pall Mall Gazette*, 29 November 1895; *Glasgow Herald*, 29 November 1895; *Leicester Chronicle and Leicestershire Mercury*, 30 November 1895; *Lloyd's Weekly Newspaper*, 1 December 1895.

[105] *Daily News*, 29 November 1895.

[106] *Glasgow Herald*, 21 November 1895. See also *Standard*, 21 November 1895.

Times.[107] The outcome seemed to reveal a legal system more robust in its treatment of fraudsters than ever before. But the new winding-up law which had provided the means by which the Liberator frauds were investigated and prosecuted had some powerful enemies, and even before 1895 a backlash was developing against it, jeopardizing its ability to yield similar results in the future.

THE NEW SYSTEM UNDER ATTACK

The Winding-up Act stipulated that in cases of compulsory liquidation, the Official Receiver would be made provisional liquidator, and the company's creditors and shareholders would have the option of continuing him as liquidator or appointing an outside liquidator. While it was widely predicted that creditors and shareholders would prefer to appoint their own liquidators rather than rely on a state functionary, this was not the case, and in 1891 he was continued in 85 per cent of cases, rising to 93 per cent the following year.[108] This created an unexpectedly heavy workload for the new Department of Companies Liquidation, reflected in rapidly increasing costs. Predicted to cost under £5,000 in 1890, it was in fact costing £15,000 by the end of 1892.[109] In addition, public examinations generated much 'extremely arduous' work for the department.[110] So in November 1892, the Board of Trade wrote to the Treasury asking for an increase in staff.

This sparked an interdepartmental row. In January 1893, the Financial Secretary to the Treasury John T. Hibbert replied, expressing concern at this rapid bureaucratic expansion. He claimed that the bill's framers had not envisaged such extensive interference in the nation's joint-stock business by a public department. His objections were partly financial. Though recognizing that the fees generated by the department covered its expenses, he feared that the necessity of maintaining a large permanent staff would jeopardize public funds in the future if the number of liquidations fell away. He also thought that the activity of the department would leave it politically exposed whenever the results of liquidation were disappointing. And there were ideological objections. Hibbert accepted that government should prosecute those 'guilty of commercial misconduct which affects large classes of the community, and may injure public credit', and could legitimately manage company property in the short term until creditors and shareholders had organized their own affairs. But going any further was to engage in illegitimate competition with those who made a living from company liquidation.[111]

Hibbert's intervention sparked the appointment of an interdepartmental committee, containing representatives from the Board of Trade, the Treasury, and the

[107] *Return Showing the Working of the Regulations made in 1886 for Carrying out the Prosecution of Offences Acts, 1879 and 1884*, PP 1897 LXXIII. 65; *The Times*, 21 November 1895.

[108] *Inter-Departmental Committee*, vii.

[109] Ibid. x.

[110] *Second General Annual Report by the Board of Trade under section 29 of the Companies (Winding-up) Act, 1890*, PP 1893–94 LXXXI. 22.

[111] *Inter-Departmental Committee*, x.

law, to decide how the act should be administered. Sitting in the first half of 1893, during the Bottomley and first Balfour Group trials, witnesses included Smith, Stewart, Vaughan Williams, and Hamilton Cuffe, Stephenson's deputy, who was to succeed him as DPP in October 1894.[112] Also interviewed were two representatives from the Incorporated Law Society, and one from the Institute of Chartered Accountants; in addition, the committee received a letter from the Association of Chambers of Commerce.

The law and accountancy witnesses lobbied hard for retrenchment. They presented Stewart as an over-ambitious and selfish man who used his position to unfairly influence creditors and shareholders and to grab business which rightfully belonged to private liquidators.[113] They thought that the processes of investigation and realization of assets should be entirely divided, arguing that Board of Trade could obtain the information it needed without burdening itself with the unnecessary task of administration.[114] Ultimately, if this separation jeopardized criminal prosecutions, this was no great loss. Frederick Whinney, Fellow of the Institute of Chartered Accountants, who had been winding up companies for forty years, thought that little was gained by such prosecutions: 'I was acquainted with the Royal British Bank prosecution. Then there was the prosecution of Overend Gurney and the City of Glasgow Bank; but whether anybody has been the better for them or not is a grave question.'[115]

Smith, Stewart, and Vaughan Williams presented a united front against these proposals, insisting upon the importance of the public exposure and criminal prosecution of fraud. Vaughan Williams argued that under the old system 'an enormous quantity of fraud remained unexposed'. The official administration of insolvent estates was beginning to effect a change, and abandoning this would harm 'the true commercial interests of the country'.[116] All three insisted on keeping the functions of investigation and administration together as only those who had administered the estate could effectively investigate it. Stewart explained how the realization of assets helped investigation: 'the mere collection for unpaid calls helps you; I apply to a contributory for unpaid calls, the contributory states that I was induced by fraud to subscribe for shares. That continually occurs, and he gives me particulars.' When an outside liquidator was appointed, the minute books, ledgers, letter books, and all other documents were immediately passed to him. The Official Receiver could apply to the court for access, but having to compete with the liquidator inevitably made investigation more difficult. Furthermore, being in control of liquidation made it clear to company officials that the Official Receiver was 'master of the situation', and this was important in investigations. In the Hobbs and Wright case, for example, Stewart doubted that he could have got Kentish to talk had he not also been liquidator. Finally, the liquidation work generated the

[112] Cuffe was second son of the third Earl of Desart, an Irish peer, and succeeded to the title in 1898 on the death of his older brother. A barrister, he had been an Assistant Solicitor to the Treasury since 1878: *The Times*, 5 November 1934.

[113] *Inter-Departmental Committee*, 24–5.

[114] Ibid. 68.

[115] Ibid. 26. His reservations were shared by one of the legal witnesses: 70.

[116] Ibid. 54.

fees which currently paid for his staff; without these fees, he feared his office would be 'starved' of staff by the Treasury.[117]

Crucially, the business community championed their case. The secretary of the Association of Chambers of Commerce wrote to the committee supporting the actions of the Official Receiver's office, stating that 'much public good will result from their investigations and prosecutions, and they would therefore desire that the Receivers should not be hampered or restricted in the performance of these duties'. It thought it unlikely that the prosecutions would have taken place if the Receivers had not been in charge of the winding-up proceedings, and the 'deterrent effect' these prosecutions produced was enhancing commercial morality.[118]

The committee's report, issued in July 1893, was a ringing endorsement of the way the act had been operated by Smith, Stewart, and Vaughan Williams. It dismissed the objections of the lawyers and accountants. Uncoupling the duties of investigation and administration would cause 'delay, friction, increase of cost, and loss of efficiency'. It had found that the permanent officials had been working 'from 10 to 12 hours a day for months at a stretch', and that the clerks had had to work 1,900 hours overtime in connection with the Balfour Group alone. It therefore recommended augmenting the Official Receiver's staff. 'If the work has to be done, it must be done efficiently, and adequate salaries must be given to the men who are to do it.'[119] The recommendations were quickly implemented, with Stewart promoted to the role of 'Senior Official Receiver', and two additional Official Receivers added above the three existing Assistant Official Receivers.[120] By 1895, the annual cost of the office had swollen to over £34,000.[121]

The new system had weathered a combined attack on it from lawyers, accountants, and the Treasury, and had emerged stronger. But it was to face further tests. The first was posed by company directors wanting to conceal their affairs from the official gaze by securing voluntary liquidations outside the court. The most effective way of achieving this was to inflate the amount of vendors' capital—often fictitious—vesting the controlling stake in a company in its management, making a vote in favour of voluntary liquidation at the general meeting a formality. Whereas the amount of vendors' capital in companies being voluntarily liquidated was £10.9 million in 1892, by 1899 this had grown to £40.4 million, outstripping the publicly subscribed capital of £31.9 million.[122] Directors could also thwart

[117] Ibid. 10–16.

[118] Ibid. 40.

[119] Ibid. v–ix.

[120] *Second General Annual Report by the Board of Trade*, v. Though when Stewart resigned in 1895 to take up the post of Clerk of the London County Council, he was replaced by George Barnes, one of the two Official Receivers appointed in 1893, and the number of Official Receivers was reduced from three to two: *Fifth General Annual Report by the Board of Trade under section 29 of the Companies (Winding-up) Act, 1890*, PP 1896 LXXVI. p. iv.

[121] *Fourth General Annual Report by the Board of Trade under section 29 of the Companies (Winding-up) Act, 1890*, PP 1895 LXXXVIII. p. iii.

[122] *Seventh General Annual Report by the Board of Trade under section 29 of the Companies (Winding-up) Act, 1890*, PP 1898 LXXXIV. 5; *Ninth General Annual Report by the Board of Trade under section 29 of the Companies (Winding-up) Act, 1890*, PP 1900 LXXVIII. 5; *Eleventh General Annual Report by the Board of Trade*, PP 1902 XCIII. 12.

creditors' attempts to obtain a compulsory winding-up order by charging the company's remaining assets to friendly debenture holders. Consequently, while the 119 compulsory liquidations in 1891 represented 13.6 per cent of total liquidations for that year, the percentage subsequently stabilized at a lower level: between 1895 and 1914 it never exceeded 8.5 per cent and was usually around 6–7 per cent.[123]

Moreover, the legality of public examination was challenged in the courts. The first three years of the act's operation saw a rapid extension of the system. The number of companies investigated in this way rose from seventeen to forty-one between 1891 and 1893, and the number of directors, managers, and officials questioned nearly doubled, from 123 to 241. This expansion was facilitated by Vaughan Williams' construction of the act, which gave him wide latitude to order examinations if the Official Receiver's report disclosed matters he thought desirable to bring to the notice of the court.[124] However, subsequent legal rulings left the validity of this interpretation in some doubt.[125] The Board of Trade's law officers took the question to the House of Lords for a final and definitive interpretation of the law, but the House of Lords ruling, in March 1896, was very restrictive. The Lord Chancellor, Hardinge Giffard, now ennobled as the Earl of Halsbury, judged that an order for a public examination could only be made on a report directly alleging fraud against named individuals, and that such examinations must be limited to the parties charged with fraud.[126]

Historians have concluded that the new act was ultimately a flop. Becoming 'not a weapon but an administrative instrument', the act yielded disappointing results and Smith's crusade against business immorality had failed by his retirement in 1904.[127] But even if the ambitious Smith did not achieve everything he wanted, his office still accomplished much more than these criticisms would suggest. That the annual number of compulsory liquidations only dropped below triple digits in five of the twenty-five years between 1891 and 1915—involving a total of 2,941 companies—demonstrates that this was a significant break with the past, a systematic intervention in the affairs of a wide range of businesses by a state department which necessitated a considerable bureaucratic effort. While the bulk of these compulsory liquidations occurred at the High Court, many—usually between a quarter and a third—took place in the county courts, showing that it was not only metropolitan concerns that were being regulated.

It has been claimed that the House of Lords' decision on public examinations 'removed from the crusaders their most effective weapon', implying that examinations came to an abrupt end as a result of the verdict.[128] This is misleading: the

[123] Calculated from statistics in Smith's annual reports.

[124] *Re Great Kruger Gold Mining Co.* (1892) 3 Ch. 307; *Re Trust and Investment Corporation of South Africa* (1892) 3 Ch. 332.

[125] The relevant cases are summarized in *Fourth General Annual Report by the Board of Trade*, 28–30.

[126] *Re English and Scottish Mercantile Investment Trust, ex p. Barnes* (1896), AC 146 HL; *Fifth General Annual Report by the Board of Trade*, 15–19.

[127] Batzel, 'General Scope', 364; V. Markham Lester, *Victorian Insolvency: Bankruptcy, Imprisonment for Debt, and Company Winding-up in Nineteenth-Century England* (Oxford, 1995), 228–39.

[128] Batzel, 'General Scope', 361.

ruling curbed rather than killed public examinations, which continued to take place in significant numbers through to the Great War. While in 1897, there were public examinations of just twenty-six individuals in ten companies—the lowest figures yet recorded—the following year this had bounced back to 100 individuals in twenty-seven companies. The five years from 1898 to 1902 saw an annual average of public examinations for sixty-five individuals involved in twenty-one companies: lower than the early days of the act, but enough to act as a valuable means of investigating and publicizing corporate immorality. Moreover, the House of Lords ruling did not undermine criminal prosecutions. Smith observed that 'if the enforcement of the criminal law against fraud is regarded as the chief object of the act, it cannot be said that the judgment in question has materially affected the result', because the evidence on which prosecutions were sustained usually came from other sources. Public examinations, Smith explained, were chiefly useful for shedding light on 'irregularities' in company promotion and management which were not actually criminal, thus providing warnings for the investing public 'as to the nature of the risks to be guarded against'.[129]

A SECOND PROSECUTION MANIA

For Smith, what posed a bigger threat to criminal prosecutions than the limitation of public examination was the inadequacy of the existing criminal sanctions against the variety of frauds perpetrated by wily promoters and directors. His annual reports usually contained wish lists of extensions to the law. He advocated revising section 84 of the Larceny Act on the publication of fraudulent statements to include fraudulent omissions of fact, not just false statements of fact, and wanted to extend it to promoters who were not also members of the company. He thought that the principles of the Debtors Act, 1869, could be applied to company directors, so that certain crimes would entail a presumed intent to defraud 'unless a jury is satisfied to the contrary'. He thought that the principle of criminal negligence should be introduced into company law. Whereas the law of conspiracy had been used to obtain convictions where statutory provisions were inadequate, it could not be used where frauds were committed by one person, highlighting the need for reform.[130] Smith's superiors at the Board of Trade agreed on the need for a fresh investigation into company law, Permanent Secretary Sir Courtenay Boyle noting that limited liability had led to some serious abuses and that legislation was required 'in the interests both of the investing and of the trading public'.[131] So a departmental committee was appointed in November 1894 with Lord Horace Davey in the

[129] *Sixth General Annual Report by the Board of Trade under section 29 of the Companies (Winding-up) Act, 1890*, PP 1897 LXXX. 16.

[130] *Third General Annual Report by the Board of Trade under section 29 of the Companies (Winding-up) Act, 1890*, PP 1894 LXXVII. 30; *Fourth General Annual Report by the Board of Trade*, 26; *Seventh General Annual Report by the Board of Trade*, 25; *Eleventh General Annual Report by the Board of Trade*, 7; 32 & 33 Vict. c. 62, s. 11.

[131] *Third General Annual Report by the Board of Trade*, v-vi.

chair. But while both Smith and Vaughan Williams were given seats, the committee regarded amendment of the criminal law as outside its brief, and in any case legislation did not ensue until 1900.[132]

Legislative intervention proved unnecessary, however, for the existing law—in new hands—proved sufficiently rigorous to secure the convictions of an unprecedented number and variety of fraudulent businessmen, with certain forms of behaviour designated criminal much more firmly than hitherto. It would have been understandable had the courts in these years simply regurgitated the tried and tested doctrines of freedom of contract and *caveat emptor*—few relevant cases were published in the law reports, while handbooks on the legal responsibilities of directors only cited the most famous cases of yesteryear.[133] But by the later 1890s the courts were rejecting the narrow construction of the law favoured by the previous generation of judges like Cockburn (1802–80), Chambers (1814–91), and Hawkins (who resigned in 1898 aged 81). Surveying late Victorian civil litigation, P. S. Atiyah detects a tentative retreat from earlier positions on misrepresentation, with a 'new morality' placing more responsibility on sellers not to mislead contracting parties.[134] This more expansive interpretation of legal duties in turn influenced the outlook of a younger generation of criminal judges, including Bruce, born in 1834, Sir Charles Hall (1843), and Sir Forrest Fulton (1846), Common Serjeant from 1892. These men felt unconstrained by established legal principles: Hall, for example, 'had had very little, if any, training and experience in Criminal Courts' before he became Recorder in 1892, making up for his deficiencies 'by a recourse to common-sense methods'.[135] With the change in personnel, old orthodoxies began to fall away. There was an obvious tension between the views of Hawkins in the Hansard Union case and Bruce in the House and Land Investment Trust case, which left it uncertain whether the receipt of secret commissions was a criminal offence or not. But Bruce's take on the law was the one which won out. Balfour appealed against his conviction on the Whitehall Court deal, his lawyers citing Hawkins's judgement. Justice Alfred Wills was sceptical, claiming that if a director represented 'to a company that some one else is a vendor when he himself is the real vendor, and when by doing so he gets a large profit for himself, I should be very loth indeed to acquiesce in the view that that was not a

[132] *Report of the Departmental Committee Appointed by the Board of Trade to Inquire what Amendments are necessary in the Acts relating to Joint Stock Companies Incorporated with Limited Liability under the Companies Acts, 1862 to 1890*, PP 1895 LXXXVIII. pp. vi–vii. For more on the Companies Act, 1900, see Epilogue.

[133] The third edition of one such text, published in 1896, mentioned only three criminal trials—Overend and Gurney, the City of Glasgow Bank, and the West of England Bank, the most recent of which was by that point sixteen years old: Henry Hurrell and Clarendon G. Hyde, *The Law of Directors and Officers of Joint Stock Companies* (3rd edn, London, 1896), 176–82. As late as 1913, a text purporting to explain the law on prospectuses only mentioned two criminal trials: *Reg. v. Gurney* and *Reg. v. Aspinall*, the latter being over forty years old: Frederick Edward Farrer, *The Law Relating to Prospectuses Simply and Exhaustively Stated for Lawyers and Laymen* (London, 1913), 149–50.

[134] P. S. Atiyah, *The Rise and Fall of Freedom of Contract* (Oxford, 1979), 771–2.

[135] Purcell, *Forty Years*, 106–7. Before his appointment as Recorder, he had been Attorney General to the Prince of Wales: J. M. Rigg, rev. Catherine Pease-Watkin, 'Sir Charles Hall', *ODNB*.

fraud'. The Court of Appeal accordingly dismissed the application in February 1896.[136]

This left the way clear for secret commissions to be punished in other cases. When the National Bank of Wales took over a local bank in Bangor in 1890, Henry Collins, the general manager, and two directors paid themselves commissions totalling £30,000, and did not enter the transaction in the company's books. When the Metropolitan Bank of England and Wales later took over the firm, it discovered the secret commissions, and reported them to the DPP. The three men were arrested and charged under the Larceny Act with misappropriating the £30,000. At the Old Bailey trial, Recorder Hall took a dim view of the commissions. 'Money was pocketed belonging to the bank without a shade of excuse, and this was managed in such a way as might have remained undiscovered for many years longer'. The two directors pleaded guilty, and the jury convicted Collins. Hall sentenced Collins, whom he saw as the instigator of the plot, to four years' penal servitude; the others received fifteen and eight months' hard labour respectively.[137]

Other legal reverses in the first half of the decade were overcome in the second. The collapse of the Portsea Island Building Society in 1891 after a run on its deposits was followed by criminal proceedings against its secretary Thomas Wills for the theft of £16,000, and against five directors together with Wills for publishing false balance sheets.[138] Wills pleaded guilty to the theft and was sentenced to five years' penal servitude, but in 1893, after a ten-day trial in Queen's Bench before Hawkins on the false balance sheet charges, the jury could not reach a verdict against the directors.[139] Instead of seeking a retrial, the government abandoned the case which, at £7,259, had cost the government even more than the Hansard Union prosecution earlier that year.[140] When asked why this was, Attorney General Russell explained that a retrial was unlikely to produce a different verdict, citing the fact that 'none of the directors or officials had corruptly put...money into their pockets' as the main issue splitting the jury.[141]

Nevertheless, absence of personal gain was no obstacle to obtaining convictions in several other false balance sheet cases later in the decade. In 1899, the DPP took on Edward Beall, a notorious company promoter, known in the City as the 'Black Prince'.[142] He had boosted one of his ventures, the London and Scottish Banking and Discount Corporation, by publishing balance sheets showing fictitious profits

[136] *The Times*, 21 December 1895; *Standard*, 22 February 1896.

[137] *Reg. v. Collins* (1897), *The Times*, 20 November 1897, 15 January 1898, *Standard*, 15 January 1898, *North-Eastern Daily Gazette*, 8 February 1898; *Return Showing the Working of the Regulations made in 1886 for Carrying out the Prosecution of Offences Acts, 1879 and 1884*, PP 1898 LXXIII. 24–5.

[138] *Morning Post*, 15 December 1891; *The Times*, 11 March, 2 April 1892.

[139] *Reg. v. Townsend* (1893), *The Times*, 23 June 1893, *Standard* 23 June 1893.

[140] *Return Showing the Working of the Regulations* (1894), 10, 26–7.

[141] Hansard, 4s, 17: 1109–11 (13 September 1893).

[142] Dilwyn Porter, '"Speciousness is the Bucketeer's Watchword and Outrageous Effrontery his Capital": Financial Bucket Shops in the City of London, *c.* 1880–1939', in John Benson and Laura Ugolini (eds), *Cultures of Selling: Perspectives on Consumption and Society since 1700* (Aldershot, 2006), 115.

and declaring 7 per cent dividends. £30,000 was obtained from the public in share payments; some depositors were also lured. Beall was tried with three of his fellow directors for several offences, including circulating false statements under section 84 of the Larceny Act. Although the three directors were not accused of benefiting personally, Justice Arthur Channell presented the law to the jury in such a way that emphasized the duty of directors to tell the truth, regardless of whether they profited from misstatements or not. 'The alleged intent to defraud did not mean an intent to put the money into their own pockets. It was not of the essence of the offence that they should themselves profit by the consequences of the misstatements, but what was necessary to be proved was that they made the misstatements and made them knowingly.' The jury convicted three of the quartet; Beall received four years' penal servitude; his colleagues received eighteen and twelve months' imprisonment in the second division respectively.[143] Other convictions were achieved on a similar basis. George Birt, managing director and chairman of the Millwall Dock Company, was accused in 1899 of issuing false balance sheets with intent to defraud. Birt had done this in order to keep the company afloat for as long as possible rather than to conceal defalcations, but the prosecuting barrister, Charles Mathews, argued that 'It would be a very bad day for the commercial morality of this country when only a man who intended to enrich himself personally could be charged with fraud'. Birt was convicted and sentenced to nine months' hard labour.[144]

The Birt case was a private prosecution, brought by Birt's fellow directors who regretted allowing him unsupervised control for a quarter of a century. It was not an isolated example, for the 1890s continued to see a mixed economy of prosecutions. Even companies which were privately wound up could yield successful criminal actions, for misappropriation in the case of Bark and Jobson (Limited), a Liverpool pawnbroking firm, and for obtaining money by false pretences in the case of the Coolgardie Mint and Iron King Gold Mines.[145] This mixed economy was still very much official policy. In a Commons debate on the activities of the DPP in 1897, Attorney General Webster argued for a restricted view of his responsibilities. He drew what was by now a familiar distinction between cases in which the victims were poor and those in which they were rich, arguing that this distinction should continue to inform the DPP's decisions: 'In bad cases of crime affecting poor people the Public Prosecutor ought not to hesitate about taking action, but it was a different matter when pressure was brought to bear upon him to conduct cases affecting wealthy people who ought themselves to act as prosecutors'.[146]

[143] *Reg. v. Beall* (1899), *The Times*, 2, 20 November 1899. The Prison Act, 1898 divided prisoners not sentenced to penal servitude or hard labour into three divisions: 61 & 62 Vict. c. 41, s. 6.

[144] Although the jury only found him guilty of intent to deceive rather than to defraud, Justice Ridley still recognized this as a serious offence: *Reg. v. Birt* (1899), *The Times*, 20 February, 23 March, 15 May 1899.

[145] *Reg. v. Bark* (1896), *Liverpool Mercury*, 3, 4 December 1896; *Reg. v. Kirby* (1899), *The Times*, 20 September 1898, 24 March, 5 July 1899; *Standard*, 16 January 1900. Nevertheless, private prosecutions remained vulnerable to compromise: *Reg. v. Fauvel* (1897), *The Times*, 25 November 1897.

[146] Hansard, 4s, 48: 1353–8 (30 April 1897).

Without a doubt both Stephenson and Cuffe, who took over the job in 1894, proved consistently anxious to protect the culture of working-class self-help, as evinced by the long succession of building society prosecutions through the decade. Embezzling secretaries in the Cardiff Building Society (1890), the Berwick Equitable Benefit Building Society (1893), the Lancaster and County Building Society (1894), the Bayswater and Kensington Building Society (1895), and the Richmond Permanent Benefit Building Society (1897), among many others, all found themselves on the wrong end of crown prosecutions, receiving sentences of between eighteen months and seven years.[147] By contrast, Stephenson and Cuffe did not always take up the company cases referred to them by the Inspector General, and Cuffe went on record stating that more prosecutions should be funded from the estates of the companies themselves.[148] Nevertheless, closely aided by senior metropolitan police officers who were gradually gaining expertise in complex financial cases, the DPP was showing an increased willingness to spend money defending the interests of middle- as well as working-class investors.[149]

This was caused by a significant culture shift, which saw a decline in the negative attitudes which had dogged speculation in company shares through the century. There is much cultural evidence suggesting that—contrary to historians who argue that positive attitudes to speculation were dominant by mid-century and were what prompted the concession of limited liability in 1855—the decisive shift took place somewhat later in the century. It was partly driven by numbers. In 1864 there had been 209,126 railway shareholders; just a generation later, in 1887, this number had risen to 546,438, meaning that one in 67 people in the UK held railway stock.[150] A 1901 estimate of the number of shareholders outside the railway sector produced a figure of 445,000.[151] These numbers alone had a normalizing effect. Moreover, the meaning of speculation changed as chaos and manipulation were replaced by regularity and rules in representations of the 'science of the market'.[152] At mid-century, popular fiction had highlighted the destruction wrought by the intrusion of share-dealing into the home—the most sacred space in the Victorian worldview. Describing the collapse of the railway bubble in 1845, one novelist wrote of 'the whispering fear with which each new disaster was communicated from partner to partner, from husband to wife, from father to son...the tidings that might in a single hour hurl down their children from affluence to beggary'.[153]

[147] *Western Mail*, 26 March 1890; *Aberdeen Weekly Journal*, 14 October 1893; *The Times*, 7 March 1894; *Return Showing the Working of the Regulations made in 1886 for Carrying out the Prosecution of Offences Acts, 1879 and 1884*, PP 1896 LXIX. 15; *Return Showing the Working of the Regulations* (1898), 20–1.

[148] Smith usually noted when the DPP had failed to take up cases in his annual reports. See, for example, *Sixth General Annual Report by the Board of Trade*, 17.

[149] Basil Thomson, *The Story of Scotland Yard* (London, 1935), 250–1.

[150] J. B. Jefferys, 'Trends in Business Organisation in Great Britain since 1856', PhD thesis, London University, 1938, 386; *Economist*, 22 January 1887.

[151] Ranald Michie, *The London Stock Exchange: A History* (Oxford, 2001), 72.

[152] Alex Preda, *Framing Finance: The Boundaries of Markets and Modern Capitalism* (Chicago, IL, 2009), 90.

[153] Robert Bell, *The Ladder of Gold: An English Story*, 3 vols (London, 1850), i. 226–7.

By the end of the century, fiction was presenting this intrusion in comic terms. In a fictional interlude in an 1887 essay on the City, John Hopkins describes a family dinner interrupted by the arrival of a telegram for the daughter. She tears open the envelope and exclaims: 'Confound it, I am bearing Mooners Deferred, and I'll be shot if they have not got up one!' Her brother chides her for not taking his advice to bull Egyptians, but mother butts in: 'I don't care so much for your tips', she says, 'I lost a century in Preference Puffers by operating on your tip.' The daughter asks what her father would do. The father solemnly replies: 'I counsel you to always snatch a profit and to cut a loss.'[154] Certainly, speculation did not suddenly shed all its negative connotations in popular fiction, and the familiar themes were still in place—bogus promotions, guinea-pig directors, and sudden panics. But what was missing was the overarching opprobrium formerly attached to speculation. Rather than being the road to hell, speculation was now presented as 'a cure for the blues' for bored gentlemen seeking new pastimes.[155]

As joint-stock companies came to be seen as vital to the nation's economic fortunes, and 'speculation' became rebranded as 'investment', public disapproval of swindled investors softened. This was in evidence from the proliferation of relief funds for defrauded shareholders in the later years of the century. The speculators ruined by the collapse of a fraudulent company, previously condemned as fools blinded by greed, were now more likely to be seen more as blameless victims of natural disasters. With investors viewed as deserving recipients of charity, it became easier to justify using taxpayers' money to protect them. The traditional response—exhorting shareholders to insist upon better standards of corporate governance—seemed like a busted flush by the 1890s, as the dice were loaded so completely in favour of directors. *The Times*, for example, shed its traditional hostility to company law reform, admitting that 'the ordinary Englishman needs protection when he goes into the City to do business with the astute gentry who construct ephemeral companies'.[156] The *Economist*, a bastion of shareholder vigilance in Walter Bagehot's day, was also won over to the cause of greater state protection.[157] One type of safeguard the state could offer was the criminal prosecution, and denying middle-class shareholders what was freely extended to working-class investors in building societies and friendly societies on a point of principle began to seem perverse.

So, the final years of the century witnessed a veritable glut of state prosecutions, and crucially, the judges in these trials were receptive to the idea that shareholders needed protecting. Despite the fact that the question of fraud had always cut across political lines, it is noticeable that many of the judges in the big trials of the 1890s—Bruce, Hall, Fulton—were Conservative, while several of their predecessors who

[154] John Baker Hopkins, 'Catch 'Em Alive, Oh!', *Tinsley's Magazine*, 40 (January 1887), 64–5.
[155] Bracebridge Hemyng, 'The Hypochondriac; or, a Cure for the Blues', in *'The Stockbroker's Wife' and other Sensational Tales of the Stock Exchange* (London, 1885).
[156] *The Times*, 20 November 1894.
[157] *Economist*, 25 January 1890, 15 July 1893, 17 November 1894, 24 December 1898.

had shown less enthusiasm for such prosecutions—Cockburn, Chambers, Hawkins—were rather traditional Liberals. This was another manifestation of a recurring theme: throughout the century, Conservatives had seemed more comfortable extending a paternalist hand of protection to naïve investors than Whigs and Liberals: it could be seen in the contrast between William Venables and Peter Laurie as Lord Mayors; later, between the stances of the Gladstone and Disraeli ministries. And Cuffe, who ordered far more company prosecutions than either of his predecessors, was also a Conservative.[158]

Promoters who foisted worthless companies on the public were targeted more vigorously than before, with false prospectuses brought firmly within the criminal law. In 1896, the West Australian (Gold District) Trading Corporation was formed to take over the business of a syndicate supplying the rapidly growing mining community of the region. The prospectus stated that the syndicate had a large number of active and profitable depots and agencies in Western Australia, that it had already shipped £60,000 of goods, and that it had made double its capital in profits, justifying a dividend of 100 per cent. None of this was true; both concerns were promoted by Louis Goodman, a London dentist, whose main aim was to 'pump and dump' the corporation's shares. The scheme worked, with the £1 shares rocketing on the stock market, peaking at £102 10s before collapsing. Goodman, together with the corporation's general manager, Herbert Squier, made at least £25,000. When the pair were brought to trial, Goodman pleaded guilty to charges of obtaining money by false pretences, Squier to a conspiracy charge. Justice William Grantham—another Conservative—believed that the plan was 'not originally conceived in fraud' but became fraudulent, and so sentenced Goodman, who had already spent five months in prison awaiting trial, to eighteen months' hard labour, and Squier to six months.[159]

Even promoters who eschewed prospectuses could be reached by the law. The Alliance Financial Corporation's main mode of attracting investment was the 'widow's letter', sent out to potential investors purporting to be from a widow anxious to realize her dead husband's assets, including shares in the corporation, which she was willing to sell at a loss. Included was the name and address of the secretary to the corporation, Samuel Capon, and when the investors contacted Capon, he confirmed the widow's story, and suggested that the shares would pay up to 35 per cent that year. The corporation was also regularly puffed in the *Financial World* newspaper, edited by Henry Cooke, and owned by John Grunell, the managing director of the corporation. Those who subscribed received no dividends or invitations to general meetings, because the corporation did no business. Altogether

[158] It is difficult to push this too far, however, since the Fraudulent Trustees' Act was drafted by a Liberal Attorney General, and the judges in the key Royal British Bank and City of Glasgow Bank trials were Whigs. Nevertheless, the two most important late nineteenth-century legislative innovations—the establishment of the DPP and the 1890 Winding-up Act—were both the work of Conservative administrations.

[159] *Reg. v. Goodman* (1899), *The Times*, 18, 20, 21 April 1899; *Return Showing the Working of the Regulations made in 1886 for Carrying out the Prosecution of Offences Acts, 1879 and 1884*, PP 1899 LXXIX. 24–6.

Grunell, the mastermind of the scheme, obtained about £15,000 from the public. He pleaded guilty to conspiracy to defraud and obtaining money by false pretences; Capon and Cooke were found guilty of conspiracy. Common Serjeant Sir Forrest Fulton sentenced Grunell to four years' penal servitude; the others to nine and ten months' hard labour each.[160] Louis Lupton was another who shunned prospectuses but was nevertheless prosecuted. Lupton, otherwise known as James Turner, used his paper, the *City Times*, to promote the Lydenberg Consolidated Mines (Limited), netting £21,000 from investors. The company transacted no business and spent nothing on mining operations. Lupton was found guilty of obtaining money by false pretences and of conspiracy along with two of his subordinates. He was sentenced to five years' penal servitude; the two others to twelve months' hard labour each.[161] The popular press thought that the verdict 'should result in the City of London being swept clean of the "spiders" who spend their time in trapping unwary "flies" '.[162]

Courts were keen to enforce the sanctity of shareholders' property. For many years a leading light in Liverpool shipping, William Tapscott promoted and managed a string of companies for purchasing and operating steamships. Despite receiving a generous salary and a commission on gross earnings, he got into the habit of using company money for his own purposes, including share speculations, eventually draining them of £36,000. He transferred money backwards and forwards between the companies at audit time to conceal the defalcations, until in April 1897 he became bankrupt. The Official Receiver discovered the financial juggling and the DPP prosecuted Tapscott for misappropriation under the Larceny Act. His defence was that the transferrals were made not to deceive the shareholders, but to prevent discredit from falling on any of the companies, and to tide them over their difficulties, which he expected would be temporary. These arguments did not wash with Justice Edward Ridley. In his summing up, he told the jury that although the companies had overlapping proprietorships, Tapscott 'had no right to use the money of one for the purposes of the other. If that principle were to obtain in commercial matters there would indeed be a door opened through which it would be possible for a man to reach wide opportunities of committing fraud.' The jury convicted, and Ridley gave him three years' penal servitude, a sentence which visibly 'staggered' the defendant.[163]

[160] *Reg. v. Grunell* (1895), *The Times*, 12, 21 August, 26 November 1895, *Standard*, 26 November 1895; *Return Showing the Working of the Regulations* (1896), 18–19.

[161] *Reg. v. Lupton* (1898), *The Times*, 2, 6, 8 August 1898, *Standard*, 6, 8 August 1898.

[162] *Reynolds's Newspaper*, 14 August 1898; *Penny Illustrated Paper*, 13 August 1898. Women, usually flies, were turning spiders, but the law was able to catch them too. Martha Bowman, described as 'a most plausible swindler', registered the Artistic Dress Company as a limited company in November 1894. It promised dressmaking work to girls, but no legitimate business was done, and it existed simply to extract up-front premiums from the victims. Bowman was given eighteen months' hard labour; her male accomplice got twelve months: *Reg. v. Bowman* (1896), *The Times*, 13 January 1896, *Illustrated Police News*, 18 January 1896; *Lloyd's Weekly Newspaper*, 17 November 1895; *Return Showing the Working of the Regulations* (1896), 21–2.

[163] *Reg. v. Tapscott* (1897), *Liverpool Mercury*, 11, 13 December 1897, *The Times*, 13 December 1897.

Nasty shocks were felt elsewhere too, with the authorities proving willing to tackle new threats to investors. From the 1880s, among the novel facilities catering to the growing appetite for stock market speculation were the 'bucket shops' of the City of London. These were operated by 'outside brokers'—not members of the Stock Exchange and therefore not bound by any of its rules—who used addresses in the Square Mile to appear respectable and lure investors.[164] They specialized in obtaining lists of small shareholders from company files lodged at the Registry, then bombarding them 'with literature of a most alluring type'. Not all outside brokers were fraudulent, but their activities became increasingly mired in scandal towards the end of the century.

The 'bucketeers' were initially allowed to operate unmolested. But from the mid 1890s, the problem had become so bad that the authorities began to use the criminal law to clamp down on their activities. The Court of Aldermen authorized the City Solicitor Homewood Crawford to initiate bucket shop prosecutions from 1894, evincing the City's determination to clean up commercial operations in the Square Mile.[165] After some smaller cases resulted in convictions, Crawford began targeting larger ventures, and in 1897 secured multiple convictions in two major bucket shop trials.[166] Herbert Krahn, a Russian stockbroker and undischarged bankrupt, set up a network of short-lived firms described by Common Serjeant Fulton as 'a gigantic system of fraud'. Altogether, £8,500 was traced back to Krahn, who pleaded guilty to obtaining money by false pretences and received four years' penal servitude; his two accomplices receiving nine and twelve months' hard labour.[167] Five men were involved in an even bigger operation. In various permutations, and using multiple aliases, they ran a series of fraudulent schemes promising vast riches. Their chief project was a bucket shop which claimed to have discovered the secret of gambling on the stock exchange so that losses were impossible and gains practically unlimited. This scheme alone drew £10,500 from the public in three years, and they got many thousands more from their other ventures. In what was described as 'the most complicated and difficult [case] that the City police have had to deal with for years', with over a hundred witnesses interviewed, all five were convicted, receiving sentences of between nine months and seven years.[168] The DPP also got involved, prosecuting bucket shop operators such as Edward Morgan, promoter of the Bourse Finance Association and United Founders' Association. These invited payments from members of the public to cover the purchase of shares, but the shares were never bought and the investors lost their money. Morgan and a subordinate were found guilty of conspiracy,

[164] Porter, 'Speciousness'; Sidney Theodore Felstead, *Sir Richard Muir: A Memoir of a Public Prosecutor* (London, 1927), 161.

[165] Felstead, *Sir Richard Muir*, 162. Crawford was elected City Solicitor in 1885.

[166] Two young men were convicted of bucket shop operations, receiving eighteen and twelve months' hard labour respectively in separate trials: *Reg. v. Meeking* (1895), *The Times*, 13 December 1894, 10 January 1895; *Reg. v. Bentley* (1896), 20 May 1896, *Standard*, 8 May 1896.

[167] *Reg. v. Krahn* (1897), *Daily News*, 15 September 1897, *Lloyd's Weekly Newspaper*, 28 November 1897, *The Times*, 29 November, 15 December 1897, *Reynolds's Newspaper*, 19 December 1897.

[168] *Reg. v. Tarrant* (1897), *The Times*, 26 July, 22 October, 3, 5, 6 November 1897, *Lloyd's Weekly Newspaper*, 7 November 1897.

the former receiving five years' penal servitude, the latter fourteen months' hard labour.[169]

Cuffe believed that the need to uphold commercial morality gave him a mandate to take up prosecutions even when these were against the wishes of the victims. When the Mineral Estates Corporation went into liquidation in 1897, it was discovered that its managing director George Tippett had fraudulently discounted bills in London on a large scale, representing them as bona fide bills accepted against ores and minerals supplied, whereas they were simply accommodation bills. The bank which had discounted most of the bills did not want to prosecute, however. 'From a banker's point of view I resent the prosecution simply because it may affect the pocket,' the manager explained. Cuffe understood the manager's position, but it 'was one which could not be adopted by a public official in the wider interest of commercial morality and fair dealing', and so decided to prosecute. Tippett pleaded guilty to obtaining credit from banks by false pretences, and the Recorder Sir Charles Hall, endorsing Cuffe's decision, sentenced Tippett to nine months' imprisonment.[170]

It sometimes seemed that the more the state did to clamp down on company fraud, the more the public came to expect from the state, leading to a permanent tone of dissatisfaction in media coverage. After the successful conviction of Lupton and his confederates in 1898, for example, the *Pall Mall Gazette* observed that he was not the only 'promoting rogue' active in the City, and thought that 'more activity on the part of the authorities is necessary if the public are to be protected.' Nor was it any more satisfied with the decisive action that had recently been taken by the City Solicitor against the bucket shops, instead complaining that similar scams were still operated outside the Square Mile.[171] Nevertheless, the increased volume of prosecutions did lead to the unaccustomed phenomenon of good press for the DPP. Shortly before Stephenson's retirement, *The Times* wrote that what he had recently accomplished was 'sufficient to convince anyone that the public would suffer grievously if this much abused department did not exist'.[172] Cuffe, from September 1898 the Earl of Desart, came in for much praise for having raised the department 'from the state of obloquy into which it had fallen by reason of alleged sluggishness', earning particular credit for studying the 'dark ways' of 'fraudulent company mongers' and prosecuting several of them.[173] Accordingly, the controversy which had dogged the DPP in earlier years began to die down. In the late 1890s, while the office was occasionally discussed in parliament, the debates did not generate much heat, especially where his policy towards company

[169] *Reg. v. Morgan* (1897), *The Times*, 11 October, 27 November 1897, *Standard*, 18 October, 27 November 1897.

[170] *Reg. v. Tippett* (1899), *The Times*, 17 January 1899, *Standard*, 10 February 1899; *Return Showing the Working of the Regulations* (1899), 28–9.

[171] *Pall Mall Gazette*, 8 August 1898. Others were even more critical: see, for example, *Birmingham Daily Post*, 31 May 1900.

[172] It highlighted the cases of Hobbs, Wright, and Newman and the Portsea Island Building Society as frauds which would have gone unpunished but for the DPP: *The Times*, 19 May 1894.

[173] *Leicester Chronicle and the Leicestershire Mercury*, 24 September 1898.

frauds was concerned.[174] Even the judiciary, which had been quick to censure the DPP, now lauded him. At the conclusion of Balfour's trial, Bruce commented that 'the public were deeply indebted to the Public Prosecutor, the Official Receiver, and those who had assisted in the most difficult task of investigating these frauds... It was a matter of congratulation that the Public Prosecutor had not been deterred by the difficulties in the way.'[175] It was all testimony to how far the DPP's role had been transformed in the course of a few years.

CONCLUSION

Did all this activity actually improve commercial morality? Smith, the Inspector General, thought so. In 1900, he noted that the efforts of recently liquidated companies to obtain the public's money had 'met with a very meagre success' and ventured to suggest that this was in large part due to ten years' experience of the Winding-up Act. Public exposures had educated British investors, putting them on their guard against the strategies used to obtain their money. Gangs of 'unscrupulous and fraudulent promoters' who used to operate in darkness had now been uncovered, and 'many of these have been brought to justice and removed from the sphere of active enterprise, while others have found in the scanty response made by the public to their schemes, that the business is no longer of a profitable or attractive character'.[176] Of course, Smith was interested in presenting his efforts in the best possible light, and not everyone shared his optimism. At the end of 1898, Sir Charles Russell, Lord Chief Justice since 1894, used the occasion of Lord Mayor's Day to make a much-publicized speech claiming that company fraud was 'rampant', and was 'working insidiously to undermine and corrupt... public morality', comments which were widely quoted in the press as evidence that renewed legislative efforts were urgently needed to tackle fraud.[177]

While Russell had extensive experience of commercial immorality from both bar and bench, he was famous for striking a sombre note at public occasions, and was 'inclined to dwell more on perceived shortcomings than to emphasize achievements'.[178] Therefore it would be a mistake to allow his negativity to obscure what was achieved. It was in the 1890s that frauds connected to the promotion and management of joint-stock companies were decisively recognized as criminal offences, and a public, as opposed to a private, matter. The introduction of the DPP in 1880 had had a muted initial impact on the criminal prosecution of fraud largely due to a series of adverse verdicts in the first half of the

[174] See for example: Hansard, 4s, 48: 1353–8 (30 April 1897), 63: 861 (2 August 1898), 64: 139–44 (4 August 1898).

[175] *The Times*, 29 November 1895.

[176] *Tenth General Annual Report by the Board of Trade under section 29 of the Companies (Winding-up) Act, 1890*, PP 1901 LXIX. 7.

[177] *The Times*, 10 November 1898; *Daily News*, 10 November 1898; *Freeman's Journal*, 10 November 1898.

[178] J. C. Mathew, rev. Sinéad Agnew, 'Charles Arthur Russell', *ODNB*.

decade. Understaffed, overworked, and under constant pressure to provide value for money, the DPP learned to steer clear of the bigger financial cases. However, the Winding-up Act provided the bureaucratic machinery which made a more active stance viable. Although the neutrality of this machinery was challenged with some effect by Bottomley during the Hansard Union trial, it nevertheless provided a more objective basis on which to found prosecutions and further helped to depoliticize prosecutions by making them a joint decision between the Official Receiver, the Board of Trade, and the DPP, overseen by the Attorney General. None of this would have mattered if the courts refused to perceive criminality in lying prospectuses, false balance sheets, and secret commissions. But there was a profound shift in attitudes here. First to change were the police courts which no longer acted as gatekeepers restricting access to the criminal law as they had done for much of the century. By the 1890s magistrates only rarely refused to send substantiated cases of alleged fraud to trial. Once they reached trial, cases were handled by a younger generation of judges who, unlike their predecessors, recognized the limits of *caveat emptor*, and were more comfortable with the idea that the criminal law should regulate commercial transactions.

The criminalization of fraud was increasingly seen as essential, not only in the name of commercial morality, but of economic stability. The increased number of prosecutions was not a temporary experiment but established a new norm which came to be accepted by government, business, the courts, and the general public alike. There was to be no stepping back from two key principles: first, that certain transgressions by company directors, managers, and promoters were criminal, and second, that the state had a responsibility to prosecute at least some of them.

10

Epilogue: Following the Victorian Path

'The history of crime', argues V. A. C. Gatrell, 'is largely the history of how better-off people disciplined their inferiors'.[1] Certainly this is how most historians of crime in modern Britain have approached the subject, describing how the law was used to keep the labouring classes in line at a time of rapid social and economic change. This book, however, has been written in the belief that there is more to the criminal justice system than social control. Above all, it has sought to discover what happens when offences are committed against the middle classes *by* the middle classes.

Transgressions involving the promotion and management of joint-stock companies were not originally considered crimes. This was partly because these were seen as private disputes best resolved among the educated, affluent individuals involved. Early joint-stock companies grew out of the emerging civil society of the eighteenth-century town. The vigorous bourgeois culture which produced subscription associations and philosophical societies also spawned commercial enterprises. They were self-governing entities with constitutions and by-laws regulating the rights and responsibilities of members, the election of executives, and the resolution of disputes, and all were predicated on a notion of 'active citizenship'. They could only operate successfully if members oversaw their operations in an energetic and rational manner.[2] Early joint-stock companies little resembled the faceless corporations of more modern times, driven as they were by face-to-face interaction at general meetings, and trust based on personal knowledge and local reputation. When executives behaved improperly, it was up to the shareholder-partners to hold them to account: by voting them out of office, ostracizing them from the business community, or in extreme cases, suing them in courts of law or equity.

However, the collapse of the speculative boom of the mid 1820s placed this approach under strain for the first time. Shareholders uncovered practices so shocking in a number of metropolitan companies that, seemingly with the support of a scandalized public opinion, they took their grievances to the criminal courts. In the absence of any statutory provisions against company frauds, and with few precedents for such actions, magistrates and judges had a great deal of freedom to define the law according to their personal beliefs and political priorities.

[1] V. A. C. Gatrell, 'Crime, Authority and the Policeman-State', in F. M. L. Thompson (ed.), *The Cambridge Social History of Britain, 1750–1950*, 3 vols (Cambridge, 1990), iii. 245.

[2] Robin Pearson, 'Shareholder Democracies? English Stock Companies and the Politics of Corporate Governance during the Industrial Revolution', *English Historical Review*, 117 (2002), 864–5.

These men's approach to companies was partly a product of their material conditions. Their privileged backgrounds—very few judges rose from humble beginnings—together with their extreme wealth, led, it is often argued, to a concern with defending private property and a class bias.[3] These factors may have shaped their approach to the crimes of the labouring classes, but are less useful in helping us to understand how they dealt with conflicts within the business community. More salient, perhaps, is the fact that as a group, judges seem to have been conservative in their approach to personal finance. While several dabbled in canals, railways, and insurance companies, they usually kept their investments relatively small, showing a marked preference for the public funds.[4] There is evidence that at least some magistrates were similarly cautious in matters of investment.[5] This may have placed limits on the sympathy they extended to less cautious speculators: certainly this book has been peppered with tart observations on popular greed and gullibility from the bench. And, as R. Cocks notes, the nineteenth-century lawyer was supremely confident that he was 'capable of solving intricate commercial problems by using ideas culled from his experience of everyday life'.[6]

Moreover, in the early nineteenth-century way of thinking, the actions of speculators closely corresponded—more closely than those of directors—to existing definitions of crime and its causes. An 1839 Royal Commission on the County Constabulary claimed that crime was rarely caused by the pressure of destitution, but arose instead 'from the temptation of obtaining property with a less degree of labour than by regular industry'.[7] It was precisely this 'something for nothing' mentality which was thought to inspire the speculative manias which swept the nation every ten years. Prosecuting those who preyed on this weakness would simply encourage it; barring such speculators from pursuing criminal actions, on the other hand, would promote self-restraint and more circumspect behaviour in the future. Though it would be tenuous to push this link between speculation and criminality too far, it was sufficiently pronounced to muddy the moral waters in the legal tussles emanating from the joint-stock sector, ensuring that the criminal law remained dormant.

The moral scales began to shift around mid-century, however. The susceptibility of the joint-stock form to abuse was already very familiar—in this sense it is wrong to talk of the 'discovery' of company fraud in these years.[8] What happened was the problematization of company fraud, which in some respects mirrored,

[3] See, for example, Daniel Duman, *The Judicial Bench in England, 1727–1875: The Reshaping of a Professional Elite* (London, 1982), 100–4.

[4] Ibid. 138–9.

[5] Sir Peter Laurie's slow and steady approach to investment is discussed in Chapter 4.

[6] R. Cocks, 'Victorian Barristers, Judges and Taxation: A Study in the Expansion of Legal Work', in G. R. Rubin and David Sugarman (eds), *Law, Economy and Society, 1750–1914: Essays in the History of English Law* (Abingdon, 1984), 458. See also C. H. S. Fifoot, *Judge and Jurist in the Reign of Victoria* (London, 1959), 131.

[7] Cited in Gatrell, 'Crime, Authority and the Policeman-State', 251.

[8] As is claimed in Sarah Wilson, 'In Defence of Respectability: Financial Crime, the "High Art" Criminal and the Language of the Courtroom, 1850–1880', in Ian Inkster (ed.), *The Golden Age: Essays in British Social and Economic History, 1850–1870* (Aldershot, 2000).

albeit belatedly, the way that proletarian crime was reconceptualized as a 'problem' from the late eighteenth century. Gatrell has shown how crime became 'a vehicle for articulating mounting anxieties about...social change and the stability of social hierarchy' engendered by industrialization and urbanization. These fears 'invested crime with new meanings' and 'justified vastly accelerated action against it'—chiefly, the construction of the 'policeman-state'.[9] Though Gatrell conceptualizes this machinery of law as pointing exclusively at the working classes, it could also be turned on middle-class wrongdoers. Like proletarian criminals, fraudulent company directors also came to be viewed 'as one of the "enemies within" whom the mass society engendered': the main difference being whereas working-class criminals posed a threat to the social order, middle-class fraudsters jeopardized the new economic order.[10]

When companies had been relatively few in number, and when it was believed that shareholder-partners could regulate them effectively, their internal disputes were of little public interest. But by mid-century the inconvenient truth about companies was dawning. The ability of shareholders to keep their executives in check was shown to be distinctly limited when directors could so easily conceal losses, and use their gentlemanly status to inspire trust when it was least deserved. If there was dissent, they could crush it at general meetings by marshalling proxy votes.[11] Worse still, investors seemed almost pathologically incapable of learning from their mistakes. Shareholders struggled to resist the allure of unrealistically large dividends, while depositors fell for improbably high interest rates, and policyholders for impossibly low premiums: every new fraud which broke seemed to retell an age-old moral tale of gullibility and greed. Educating these investors seemed to be impossible, a conclusion reinforced by broader intellectual currents in the later years of the century. Central here were changing perceptions of human nature, specifically a declining faith in the rationality and capacity for self-control of the individual.[12] As Martin Wiener shows, this had implications for how the state treated criminals; it also had implications for how it treated speculators.

Politicians responded first, passing legislation in 1857 criminalizing a variety of frauds against investors: if they could not protect themselves, the law would have to do it for them. However, the statute was sufficiently open to interpretation for the outlook of judges—and juries—to remain crucial. What Michael Lobban says of the common law before 1850—that it was 'a flexible system of reasoning, with even its legal maxims and rules liable to reinterpretation and change in the light of new contexts'—is also true of the criminal law after 1850.[13] The courts could not initially agree on how far investors should be protected. How far did the principle

[9] Gatrell, 'Crime, Authority and the Policeman-State', 249.

[10] Ibid. 254.

[11] The decline in shareholder powers in the first half of the century is analyzed in depth in Mark Freeman, Robin Pearson, and James Taylor, *Shareholder Democracies? Corporate Governance in Britain and Ireland before 1850* (Chicago, IL, 2012).

[12] Martin J. Wiener, *Reconstructing the Criminal: Culture, Law, and Policy in England, 1830–1914* (Cambridge, 1990), 186–7.

[13] Michael Lobban, *The Common Law and English Jurisprudence, 1760–1850* (Oxford, 1991), 98.

of *caveat emptor* absolve promoters and directors from criminal liability? Was the duty to tell the truth absolute, or contingent on other factors? Charges to juries revealed significant differences between judges. Just as importantly, the structures for ensuring prosecutions took place at all were haphazard, relying as they did on private initiative. Though victims did put the new laws into motion, such actions were always vulnerable to compromise.

This situation changed decisively in the final twenty years of the century. First, there was an increasingly centralized approach to the prosecution of company fraud, embodied in the machinery established by acts of 1879 and 1890. Second, the cases this machinery was sending to the courts were being treated more consistently by judges, with a judicial consensus of sorts developing in the 1890s. The standards expected of directors became higher, and the duties expected of investors shrank. Admittedly, many cases never found their way into the courts. But to argue that this is evidence that the law was soft on fraud is to misunderstand the working of the criminal justice system. In her wide-ranging survey of late nineteenth-century metropolitan crime, Jennifer Davis concludes that 'prosecuted law-breaking represented only a tiny proportion of similar behaviour which... never reached the courts', for the formal sanction of the criminal prosecution supplemented rather than supplanted other possible sanctions, many of them informal.[14] These other sanctions continued to play an important role in the joint-stock economy as well. But what should not be overlooked is the construction of a disciplinary system of criminal law targeted at company management and enforced through a growing bureaucracy.

This story is not entirely incompatible with class-driven views of the law, because the laws were changed and the bureaucracy was developed chiefly to protect middle-class investors and buttress the market for shares. Corporate scandals threatened to destroy the trust required to sustain commercial transactions in an increasingly impersonal market: if dishonesty were tolerated and unpunished, confidence would crumble and the flow of capital through the economy would dry up. As the century wore on, then, the interests of investors and the wider 'public interest' became increasingly conflated. Whereas parliament was the first to act in defence of this public interest by changing the law in the 1850s, with the courts slower to respond, legal receptiveness to the needs of investors subsequently sharpened to the extent that, by the start of the twentieth century, judges were sometimes taking this interest more seriously than the politicians, as the next section demonstrates.

WRIGHT AND WRONG

During an ill-tempered debate in the Commons in February 1903, the Conservative Solicitor General Sir Edward Carson rose to defend Sir Robert Finlay, the

[14] Jennifer S. Davis, 'Prosecutions and their Context: The Use of the Criminal Law in Later Nineteenth-Century London', in Douglas Hay and Francis Snyder (eds), *Policing and Prosecution in Britain, 1750–1850* (Oxford, 1989), 400–1. As such, there was much continuity with the eighteenth century, when the vast majority of property crimes did not come before the courts: Peter King, *Crime, Justice, and Discretion in England, 1740–1820* (Oxford, 2000), 10.

Attorney General, from a vote of censure. Finlay faced criticism from his own benches as well as opposition Liberals for ordering the DPP, the Earl of Desart, not to prosecute Whitaker Wright, managing director of the London and Globe Finance Corporation, which had collapsed at the end of 1900 after losing its capital of £5 million and accumulating further debts of £3 million.[15] The winding-up process revealed that the corporation had been sustained by balance sheets concealing its insolvency. Assets were moved onto the corporation's books just before the annual balance sheet was drawn up, and removed afterwards. If its final balance sheet had been issued on 30 September rather than 5 December 1900, it would have disclosed a deficit of £1.6 million.[16] But Carson insisted that these subterfuges did not represent grounds for a criminal action:

> It is said that Mr. Whitaker Wright published a false balance-sheet. I believe that he did. I think that it is an admitted fact that this was done; but will any one get up and say that a man can be prosecuted because he publishes a false balance-sheet?... there ought not to be a vote of censure on the Attorney General because he does not prosecute under a law that does not exist.

Arthur Balfour, the Prime Minister, then stepped in. Though cloaked in diffidence based on self-professed lack of expertise in legal matters, his defence of Finlay was based on a clear view on the inability of the Larceny Act to sustain a prosecution. The 'phraseology of the statute' evidently applied only to fraudulent prospectuses, not balance sheets, and the government was thus powerless to act. The motion of censure was put to a vote and was defeated 166–115.[17]

The episode recalled the firm line taken by Gladstone's government in 1869 against proposals to bankroll the prosecution of Overend and Gurney's management. Indeed, it has been cited as evidence of the continuing failure of the criminal law to police commercial morality into the twentieth century.[18] Yet several differences between the two cases underline how far things had in fact changed between the middle years of Victoria's reign and its end. First, if some commentators saw no reason why taxpayers' money should be spent helping 'well-to-do speculators who hoped to earn a big profit'—echoing the reasons for Gladstone's decision in 1869—the firmness with which laws against misrepresentation had been enforced since then exploded the rationale for non-intervention advanced by the government in 1903.[19] Days after the vote, the campaigning journalist Arnold White pointed out that '[i]nnumerable convictions' for publishing false balance sheets had been achieved since the passage of the Larceny Act in 1861. Far from having

[15] Richard Davenport-Hines, 'Whitaker (James) Wright', *ODNB*.

[16] Sidney Theodore Felstead, *Sir Richard Muir: A Memoir of a Public Prosecutor* (London, 1927), 31.

[17] Hansard, 4s, 118: 347–81 (19 February 1903).

[18] Michael Lobban, 'Commercial Morality and the Common Law: or, Paying the Price of Fraud in the Later Nineteenth Century', in Margot Finn, Michael Lobban, and Jenny Bourne Taylor (eds), *Legitimacy and Illegitimacy in Nineteenth-Century Law, Literature, and History* (Basingstoke, 2010), 127.

[19] The words were those of 'W.P.', in a letter to *The Times*, 2 March 1903.

to delve back into 'ancient history' to find examples, there were many recent cases, including the conviction of George Birt, the managing director of the Millwall Dock Company, in 1899.[20] Embarrassingly for the government, the prosecution of Birt had been led by none other than Sir Edward Carson, and White invited the Solicitor General to reconcile his statements as prosecuting barrister in 1899 with those he had just made in the Commons.[21] Another correspondent accused Carson and Balfour of making 'an amazing blunder as to the law'. Balance sheets *were* punishable under the Larceny Act; the idea that it only applied to prospectuses was 'hopelessly unsound'. He did not have to go as far back as four years to find evidence to support his views. Less than twelve months ago, the DPP had secured the conviction of three men at Manchester Assizes for issuing false balance sheets in connection with the Patent Novelties Manufacturing Company, who received sentences of up to eighteen months.[22] It was thus impossible for the government to emulate Gladstone's stance in 1903 without appearing ridiculous.

Second, whereas the Overend and Gurney prosecution had to be bankrolled by a shareholder acting on his own initiative, Wright was eventually prosecuted by order of the High Court of Justice and the action was therefore funded out of the company's estate. Although the prosecution was opposed by a few shareholders and a number of creditors on the grounds of cost, Justice Henry Buckley—an expert on company law—overruled their objections.[23] He argued that his decision was 'not measured or limited or even concerned with pecuniary benefit to be obtained for the shareholders or creditors', the more important consideration being the defence of commercial morality.[24] The readiness of judges to make use of section 167 of the Companies Act of 1862 to authorize prosecutions thus provided an alternative recourse for the defrauded whenever the DPP failed to act.

Third, if the Overend and Gurney prosecution had been an ignominious failure, the action against Wright was a complete success. The trial, which took place at the King's Bench Division of the High Court in January 1904, revolved around the balance sheets which Carson and Balfour had insisted were beyond the reach of the criminal law. The defence argued that Wright was guilty only of a form of 'window-dressing' common in the City, but Justice John Bigham, a 'great commercial judge...with an intimate knowledge of City affairs', thought differently.[25] He told the jury that when the corporation became insolvent, it was the duty of the directors to tell the shareholders, rather than concealing the losses and engaging in secret speculations to try to redeem the corporation's fortunes. The jury convicted, and Bigham sentenced him to seven years' penal servitude. However, in a sensational coda to the case, Wright died before he could be taken to prison after swallowing a

[20] See Chapter 9.

[21] *The Times*, 26 February 1903; G. R. Searle, 'Arnold Henry White', *ODNB*.

[22] Letter from 'A Legal Correspondent', *The Times*, 2 March 1903. For the Manchester case, see *Rex v. Bradley* (1902), *Manchester Guardian*, 3 February, 30 April 1902.

[23] His textbook on company law, first published in 1873, reached its eleventh edition in his lifetime: D. E. C. Yale, 'Henry Burton Buckley', *ODNB*.

[24] *The Times*, 11 March 1903.

[25] Felstead, *Sir Richard Muir*, 35.

cyanide capsule he had secreted on his person, a scene which picture journalists relished conveying to their readers (see Figure 10.1).[26]

The outcome cast Finlay's refusal to prosecute in a poor light, and the government had to resist clamour for the resignation of both of its law officers.[27] But the reticence the government had shown in this case did not set a trend: far from it. Shortly after the conviction, the government effectively admitted its mistake by announcing that it would retrospectively pay all the costs of the trial.[28] Subsequent events showed that the political class had noted the perils of seeming too soft on the major fraudsters. Before the year was out, Carson found himself leading a state prosecution in the Old Bailey against the infamous City financier Ernest Terah Hooley and his colleague Henry Lawson for conspiracy to defraud shareholders in relation to the promotion of the Electric Tramways Company. Whilst Hooley was acquitted, Lawson was sentenced to twelve months with hard labour.[29] Before too long even Horatio Bottomley found himself back in a magistrate's court at the behest of the DPP on charges of conspiracy to defraud investors in relation to the Joint Stock Trust and Finance Corporation, though after extensive hearings the magistrates dismissed the case.[30]

If all fraud prosecutions had ended in acquittals, the political will to pump resources into them would have sagged. But in most cases magistrates, judges, and juries in the Edwardian period continued the trend begun in the late nineteenth century, eagerly applying statutory sanctions to enforce commercial morality.[31] The publication of false balance sheets was the subject of many prosecutions, and was considered a serious breach of trust between directors and shareholders. For example, the directors of Showell's Brewery, one of the great Birmingham breweries, were convicted in 1904 for fiddling the company's balance sheets to justify the desired dividend. Justice Alfred Wills told them that they had deliberately broken 'the utmost good faith which they owed to the shareholders'.[32] Complex cases of misappropriation were punished by the criminal law. In 1911, the director and secretary of the Anglo-Spanish Copper Company were convicted for establishing a secret banking account in the name of the company, into which was paid some of the money received from shareholders, which was then transferred to another company

[26] *Rex v. Wright* (1904), *The Times*, 27 January 1904, *Daily Express*, 27 January 1904. For a recent, relatively sympathetic, appraisal of Wright's career, see Jeremy Mouat, 'Whitaker Wright, Speculative Finance, and the London Mining Boom of the 1890s', in Raymond E. Dumett (ed.), *Mining Tycoons in the Age of Empire, 1870–1945: Entrepreneurship, High Finance, Politics and Territorial Expansion* (Farnham, 2009), 127–50.

[27] *Daily Express*, 28 January 1904; *Reynolds's Newspaper*, 31 January 1904.

[28] Hansard, 4s, 129: 160–1 (2 February 1904).

[29] *Rex v. Lawson* (1904), *The Times*, 19 December 1904.

[30] *The Times*, 13 March 1909. Bottomley's success was again attributed to his brilliant courtroom performance: Felstead, *Sir Richard Muir*, 182–4.

[31] The cited body of case law began to expand: the fourth edition of a legal guide, published in 1905, included references to *Rex v. Wright*, *Rex v. Lawson*, and *Reg. v. Stuart*, an 1893 case which established that a director could be convicted of embezzlement as a 'clerk or servant' under section 68 of the 1861 Larceny Act: Henry Hurrell and Clarendon G. Hyde, *The Law of Directors and Officers of Joint Stock Companies* (4th edn, London, 1905), 245–52.

[32] *Rex v. Showell* (1904), *The Times*, 12 January, 17 March 1904.

Page 6. THE DAILY ILLUSTRATED MIRROR. JAN. 27, 1904.

WHITAKER WRIGHT, SENTENCED TO SEVEN YEARS' PENAL SERVITUDE,—

As Mr. Whitaker Wright clutched at the rail of the staircase which led from the Court he staggered slightly. That was the last the public saw of him.

and misleading. It was—to borrow a phrase used by Mr. Justice Bigham—"a lie covered with the garb of truth."

Mr. Wright had lived in great splendour during his time of prosperity, and enjoyed all the adulation which is the attendant of financial success. Equally violent was the outcry against him when the great crash came, and the high-piled structure of his companies toppled over, involving thousands of shareholders in ruin.

There were loud demands for a prosecution. A committee was formed to achieve this object, but it met with many difficulties. The Public Prosecutor did not act, and on the matter being brought up in discussion in the House of Commons the law officers of the Crown stated that they saw no grounds for proceeding.

The words of Sir Robert Finlay, Attorney-General, were:—

"There is not, in the present state of the law, sufficient ground for proceeding against the people responsible for the balance-sheet of the London and Globe Finance Corporation with a prospect of success."

A PITIFUL CONTRAST.

Another means of testing the question was taken. A prosecution fund was subscribed, and submitted to Mr. Justice Buckley, who, after long consideration, gave leave to prosecute at the expense of the fund.

The next sensation was Mr. Wright's disappearance. He was sought vainly for some weeks, and was finally arrested on the 14th of last March on a French liner at New York.

Long and tedious negotiations for extradition followed: finally, last August, Wright was brought back to London—an aged and altered man, with grizzled beard and lined face. From the time of his flight till the condemnation yesterday his life must have been a terrible one, and some kind of pity, even if undeserved, involuntarily comes to anyone who thinks of the contrast between the heyday of his career and its dark close.

The whole of the case had been thrashed out in the eleven days' hearing; yesterday there remained nothing but the summing up of the judge and the jury's finding.

THE SUMMING UP.

Mr. Justice Bigham's tones in summing up were more than usually deliberate and solemn. A long and wearisome trial was ended, the Judge told the jury, and he had to congratulate them, as well as counsel, on the ability and clearness with which the case had been put before them.

The Judge then made another reference to the anonymous letters with which he had been "pestered," and advised the jury utterly to disregard any similar missives they might have received.

After analysing the twenty-six heads of the indictment, and stating the bearings of the two sections of the 1861 Larceny Act, under which they were framed, the Judge very gravely pointed out that the general charge against Mr. Wright was a serious one—a very serious one, he reiterated. Then he added impressively that unless the charge was proved beyond all reasonable doubt their verdict would be Not Guilty.

Nor, he continued, should the jury allow any words or demeanour of his, when he referred to certain transactions on which he had a decided opinion, to overmaster their own judgment. They were the tribunal as to all facts.

Having made a reference to the contention that the charge against Mr. Wright would have involved Lord Dufferin and Lord Loch, "now dead and gone," if they had been alive, and pointed out the obvious reply to this contention, the Judge proceeded to make a thorough examination of the indictments and the evidence, and his summing-up lasted altogether for three and a-half hours.

During the whole of it Mr. Whitaker Wright sat in his usual place, very attentive but without giving any indication of emotion. From time to time his hand grasped the small grey beard that he has grown since London and Globe days, but the action was suggestive rather of thought than of nervousness.

The jury retired shortly before two o'clock.

Mr. Whitaker Wright when sentence was passed upon him. A sketch in court by our special artist.

SCENE AT THE SENTENCE.

During the hour that followed the court became so crowded that many people preferred to give up their places and leave rather than undergo the strain of remaining packed in the extremity of discomfort.

When the jury slowly re-entered the box the silence that suddenly possessed the court was in tense contrast to the hubbub of discussion and speculation that had obtained a moment before.

Every eye was turned on Mr. Whitaker Wright, who had just stepped with a show of briskness to his seat, having been waiting in a room below the Bench.

Mr. Whitaker Wright, in his turn, looked anxiously towards the entering jury, as if trying to read from their faces what decision they had brought back with them.

There were some minutes of trying suspense before the Judge entered, and then the foreman

This is the Story of Whitaker Wright's Strange Career, His Bold and Speculative Life, His Success and Failure, His Trial, Verdict, Sentence and Death.

Mr. Whitaker Wright's remarkable trial and his equally remarkable career ended almost simultaneously yesterday.

Shortly after three o'clock in the afternoon the jury found the ex-financier guilty of fraud on all the twenty-six counts of the indictment; fifty minutes later Mr. Wright was lying dead in one of the ante-rooms of the Law Courts.

Apoplexy is given out as the cause of this dramatically sudden close of a career, extraordinary even in an age so prolific in glories of the kind. It is true that the strain of an ordeal like Mr. Wright has undergone may well have conquered an organisation more robust than his.

For though powerfully built and fresh-coloured he was too stout to be healthy, and, despite the remarkable stoicism he showed, it was quite evident that his calm only resulted from the exercise of that iron will which had been one of the discredited adventurer's chief commercial assets.

WHAT WILL THE INQUEST SHOW?

There are, however, other stories as to the manner in which Mr. Wright escaped the sentence of seven years' penal servitude that had just been passed upon him. It is suggested that he died, not through the strength of emotions acting on an enfeebled system, but by his own will, and the agency of poison. Nothing definite can yet be ascertained, but the inquest may lead to the revelation of a remarkable story.

During eleven days of the trial Mr. Wright had shown a cool and unembarrassed front in face of an indictment which might well have appalled a less resolute and stoical spirit.

He had been assailed by one of the finest intellects now engaged in advocacy. Mr. Rufus Isaacs had illuminated with his lucid and ingenious eloquence all the dark corners of the London and Globe trickery; and the record, when stated by this advocate, was almost in itself a passing of sentence. Even the great ability of Mr. Lawson Walton, the leader for the defence, could do little to help the prisoner against whom a charge of such gigantesque dishonesty, involving the ruin of hundreds of victims, was levelled.

THE LONDON AND GLOBE.

The history of the London and Globe would take volumes to tell in detail. Briefly, Mr. Wright, after making and losing small fortunes in America, came to England, and founded companies, which were amalgamated in 1897 as the London and Globe Finance Corporation, with a capital of £2,000,000. Two other companies were formed—the British America, with a capital of £1,500,000, and the Standard, with a similar capital. The capital of all the companies was £5,000,000—more than ten times the capital of the companies that had been their nucleus.

Lord Dufferin and Lord Loch were gained as directors; Mr. Wright was managing director; and the London and Globe boomed. Then came evil days. Shortness of money—much capital was locked up in the Waterloo and Baker-street Railway—led to difficulties.

To keep matters going Mr. Wright commenced a scheme of manipulation, which only a strong head can follow in all its windings; he so dealt with shares, and transferred great sums from one company to another, as to render the balance-sheets altogether false

While he was talking to his solicitor in the ante-room Mr. Whitaker Wright suddenly sprang from his chair. He took a few steps, then staggered, and fell back.

Figure 10.1 'Whitaker Wright, Sentenced to Seven Years' Penal Servitude', *Daily Illustrated Mirror*, 27 January 1904

run by the defendants. Justice Thomas Scrutton hoped the conviction would act as 'a warning that the arm of the law was long enough to reach the most complicated frauds and that punishment would follow dishonesty in company as well as in private matters'.[33]

Despite the fact that one-man companies had been recognized in law by the House of Lords decision in the case of *Salomon v. A. Salomon and Co.* in 1896, the criminal courts placed limits on the extent to which the corporate form could be exploited to defraud investors.[34] Frederick Grubb established an outside broking company, H. St. John Oliver and Partners, which in December 1912 received £894 from a Miss Miller for the purchase of Consols. Miller never received the Consols, or her money back, and Grubb was prosecuted for fraudulent misappropriation of property.[35] Convicted and sentenced to nine months' imprisonment in 1915, he appealed against the verdict. He did not contest the fact of fraudulent appropriation, but claimed that the money was entrusted not to him—Miller did not even know him—but to the company, and therefore he could not be convicted for the company's fraudulent conversion of it. However, the verdict was upheld by the Court of Criminal Appeal, Lord Chief Justice Rufus Isaacs ruling that a person was legally entrusted with property 'notwithstanding that the property is not delivered to him directly by the owner and that in fact the owner does not know of his existence'. Any other decision would mean that 'the interposition of a duly formed company as the person entrusted with the property' would shield any individual against any criminal penalty.[36]

What difference did the criminalization of fraud make? One thing it clearly did not do was eliminate fraudulent practices. Even the prospect of imprisonment was insufficient to deter those determined to defraud, for the potential gains were too enticing. And for those managing honest but failing businesses, the temptation to conceal losses in the hope of better times ahead was great, for if the deception worked, it was unlikely ever to be discovered. The prosecution of falsehoods in balance sheets did not necessarily prompt unimpeachable standards of disclosure across the joint-stock economy. Accounting historians have suggested that many statements in the early twentieth century were 'uninformative and misleading', though have acknowledged that corporate disclosures 'were not as poor as they might have been', and were better than other countries such as the US.[37] Whether this was because of the warning conveyed by criminal prosecutions is difficult to tell. But it is clear that the fraud trial was much more than an empty ritual. Major criminal prosecutions helped to restore confidence at key points of crisis, as we have seen with the City of Glasgow Bank and Liberator Group prosecutions in the

[33] *Rex v. Hogg* (1911), *The Times*, 26 April, 2 November 1911.

[34] *Salomon v. A. Salomon and Co.* (1896) AC 22. For more on this landmark case, see Paul Johnson, *Making the Market: Victorian Origins of Corporate Capitalism* (Cambridge, 2010), 153–9.

[35] This was under the 1901 Larceny Act, which revamped the provisions of the 1861 act against fraudulent misappropriation of property by individuals: 1 Edw. VII c. 10.

[36] *Rex v. Grubb* (1915), *The Times*, 23 March, 20 April, 11 May 1915.

[37] A. J. Arnold, '"Publishing Your Private Affairs to the World": Corporate Financial Disclosures in the UK, 1900–24', *Accounting, Business and Financial History*, 7 (1997), 161.

1870s and 1890s. The stream of smaller cases, taking place not only in London but at assizes throughout the country, had a cumulative impact, reinforcing societal values and standards and reminding company managements that acts of misappropriation and misrepresentation were not committed without risk, and that if prosecuted, they stood a good chance of imprisonment.

Fraud trials also affected popular perceptions of the efficacy of criminal justice, traceable in fictional portrayals of the careers of swindlers. Whereas mid-nineteenth-century novels had engineered resolutions by means of suicide, murder, accident, or occasionally repentance, by the end of the century the law was beginning to intrude into fictions as an agent of retribution. Headon Hill's 1896 novel *Guilty Gold: A Romance of Financial Fraud and City Crime* concerns the promotion of the Golden Kloof Mining Company, a non-existent South African gold mine, by Horace Vardon and his fellow City schemers. Fulfilling the demands of the melodramatic genre, Vardon resorts to murder when threatened with exposure and is hanged, but his co-conspirators are tried for fraud and imprisoned for between one and fourteen years, the sentence handed to Jabez Balfour the previous year.[38] The theme returns, albeit briefly, in Hill's later work, *The One Who Saw*, in which there is a passing reference to the Old Bailey trial of 'an absconding company promoter', who is convicted after a two-day trial.[39] Grace Pettman's 1912 novel, *A Study in Gold*, centres on the 'Napoleon of Finance' Caleb Otto-Smith, who runs an elaborate Ponzi scheme, using money from new subscribers to pay large dividends to existing shareholders. His schemes collapse, a warrant is issued for his arrest, he is apprehended on board a liner bound for New York, and is convicted.[40]

Reflecting the popular perception that not all those guilty of wrongdoing were prosecuted, several fictional fraudsters thrived rather than receiving their just desserts. In Hilaire Belloc's 1904 novel *Emmanuel Burden, Merchant*, I. Z. Barnett establishes the fraudulent Haymarket Bank, operating on Ponzi principles, which collapses ruining many. The failure brings him 'stigma' but he avoids prosecution, instead reinventing himself as promoter of foreign companies in the City, through which he grows rich.[41] The idea that dishonest men rose to the top is satirized in P. G. Wodehouse's *Psmith in the City*. Psmith describes the successful banker John Bickersdyke thus:

> As far as I can say without searching the Newgate Calendar, the man Bickersdyke's career seems to have been as follows. He was at school with my pater, went into the City, raked in a certain amount of doubloons—probably dishonestly—and is now a sort of Captain of Industry, manager of some bank or other, and about to stand for Parliament.[42]

[38] Ranald C. Michie, *Guilty Money: The City of London in Victorian and Edwardian Culture, 1815–1914* (London, 2009), 133–40.

[39] Headon Hill, *The One Who Saw* (London, 1905), 172–3, 184.

[40] Michie, *Guilty Money*, 194–201.

[41] Hilaire Belloc, *Emmanuel Burden, Merchant* (New York, 1904), 70–2; Michie, *Guilty Money*, 178–9.

[42] Michie, *Guilty Money*, 185.

Nevertheless, the Damocles sword of the law looms large in fictional representations. In H. G. Wells's 1909 work *Tono-Bungay*, Edward Ponderevo promotes a series of successful companies, including one to sell the worthless patent medicine which gives the novel its name. When his empire collapses, he is broken by examinations in bankruptcy ('They bait you—and bait you, and bait you. It's torture. The strain of it. You can't remember what you said. You're bound to contradict yourself. It's like Russia'). Knowing that his fraudulent practices, including paying spurious dividends, were about to be found out, and mindful of the fate of '[t]hat chap Wittaker Wright', he dodges arrest with his nephew by flying away in a newly invented airship, but dies before the authorities can track him down in France.[43]

It was widely accepted that the sterner stance of the criminal courts promoted a more honest business culture in the City. In a reversal of the situation in the 1820s, when commentators looked with envy at the ability of the criminal law to reach fraudsters in the US, now American pundits compared the British system favourably to their own. The *New York Post* presented Wright as a casualty of 'the severe English companies law', contrasting this outcome with the situation in the US, where 'our transgressors of the same moral law walk in free air, lavish their philanthropies, and are lauded from the pulpits as the exemplars of our youth'.[44] Wright's conviction showed that misrepresentation could be punished harshly by English criminal law; his suicide suggested the deep sense of shame these harsh penalties engendered. The moral functions performed by criminal prosecutions were hugely important. Convicted fraudsters were beyond the pale: the public weeding-out of such figures by means of the criminal trial served to reinforce Britain's self-perception as an honest, decent, moral nation. Much rested on the outcome of trials such as Wright's. 'The commercial morality of the City was at stake, the good name of the community was jeopardised; and so', the *Daily Express* concluded, 'it can only be a matter for national congratulation that a verdict of guilty was returned.'[45] Business historians tend to attribute the City's early twentieth-century reputation as a comparatively safe place to do business to a vigorous culture of self-regulation, but even they admit that '[i]t was important that the rogues were locked up, when something damaging could clearly be pinned on them'.[46]

FOLLOWING THE VICTORIAN PATH

Decisions made in the Victorian era continued to shape efforts to lock up the rogues long into the twentieth century. Wright had been convicted under the 1861 Larceny Act, and this law remained the means by which false balance sheets and prospectuses were prosecuted, though in Scotland, where the Larceny Act never applied,

[43] H. G. Wells, *Tono-Bungay: A Novel* (1909; repr. New York, 1916), 410–12.
[44] Repr. in *Financial News*, 28 January 1904.
[45] *Daily Express*, 27 January 1904.
[46] Leslie Hannah, 'Pioneering Modern Corporate Governance: A View from London in 1900', *Enterprise & Society*, 8 (2007), 666.

prosecutions needed to be based on the common law. The collapse in 1920 of the postwar speculative boom sparked a number of scandalous City failures, several of which were punished by means of the Larceny Act. The biggest scalp was that of financier Gerard Lee Bevan, chairman of the City Equitable Fire Insurance Company. In 1922, he was tried for issuing false balance sheets and a false prospectus. Like Wright, Bevan had bought in securities to appear in the balance sheet before selling them again immediately afterwards, to create the appearance that the company was doing better than it was. In the witness box, he had claimed that 'from his experience six out of ten balance-sheets published in the United Kingdom showed more cash at the date of the balance-sheet than the company was in the habit of holding during the major part of the year. Every big man knew perfectly well what was done.' But Justice Horace Avory slapped him down, expressing 'astonishment that any man who had been connected with the City of London during the last twenty years' could defend such dishonest 'window-dressing'. The jury convicted, and Avory sentenced him to seven years' penal servitude.[47]

The Larceny Act claimed many more victims in the 1920s, including the chairman, director, and auditor of Farrow's Bank, convicted in 1921 of issuing false balance sheets, and the promoter and two directors of the Chalk Fuel Power Gas and By-Products Corporation, imprisoned in 1928 for false prospectuses. In both cases, the defendants received sentences of up to four years.[48] By this time, the act had undergone some changes. The sections dealing with fraudulent appropriation and obtaining money by false pretences were hived off into a new Larceny Act in 1916, but the maximum penalties imposed remained unaltered, at seven and five years' penal servitude respectively.[49] It was under the terms of the 1916 act that Horatio Bottomley was finally brought to justice, when in 1922 he was sentenced to seven years' penal servitude for fraudulently misappropriating the funds of his Victory Bond Club.[50]

Not only was the Larceny Act still used, it was interpreted more expansively by judges in the twentieth century than in the nineteenth. Whereas in *Reg. v. Gurney*, Chief Justice Cockburn had ruled that the act could not cover frauds of omission, in the 1931 trial of Lord Kylsant, chairman and 'virtual dictator' of the Royal Mail Steam Packet Company, for issuing a false prospectus, Justice Robert Wright gave the jury a very different interpretation of the law, arguing that 'a document might be false, not because of what it stated, but because of what it did not state'. Kylsant was consequently convicted and imprisoned for twelve months.[51] The conviction

[47] *Rex v. Bevan* (1922), *The Times*, 2, 6 December 1922. For more on Bevan, see P. S. Manley, 'Gerard Lee Bevan and the City Equitable Companies', *Abacus*, 9 (1973), 107–15; Martin Vander Weyer, *Fortune's Spear: The Story of the Blue-Blooded Rogue Behind the Most Notorious City Scandal of the 1920s* (London, 2011).

[48] *Rex v. Farrow* (1921), *The Times*, 20 January, 22 June 1921; *Rex v. Eaton* (1928), *The Times*, 4 November 1927, 21 January 1928.

[49] 6 & 7 Geo. V c. 50, ss. 20, 32.

[50] *Rex v. Bottomley* (1922), *The Times*, 19, 30 May 1922; Julian Symons, *Horatio Bottomley* (London, 1955), ch. 18.

[51] *Rex v. Kylsant* (1931), *The Times*, 31 July, 5 November 1931; *The Royal Mail Case*, ed. Collin Brooks (1933; repr. New York, 1980). He was, however, acquitted on charges of issuing false balance sheets: John Richard Edwards, *A History of Financial Accounting* (London, 1989), 148–56.

was upheld on appeal, and later trials confirmed that omissions of material particulars were crimes if these omissions 'gave a reasonable person an impression which was untrue'.[52]

These interwar cases suggest another important point: the continuity in sentencing across the nineteenth and twentieth centuries. Not only did maximum sentences remain largely unchanged in the twentieth-century statute book, so judges' views on how to punish different crimes correlated closely with decisions made by their predecessors. In cases where the intent was deemed to be wicked, sentences of three years or more were passed; when a defendant's intentions were 'honest', when a conviction was based on new principles, or when a defendant was seen as the puppet of a bigger villain, sentences did not usually exceed eighteen months.

The Larceny Act continued to underpin prosecutions even after the Second World War, right up to its supersession in 1968 by the Theft Act.[53] Indeed, the charges relating to the issue of false balance sheets in the Fire, Auto, and Marine Insurance Company trial early that year were framed under its provisions. The company's founder, Emil Savundra, and its managing director, Stuart de Quincey Walker, were both convicted on these charges, and others of forgery, and sentenced to imprisonment for eight years and five years respectively.[54] Thus, somewhat remarkably, legal sanctions first implemented in the wake of the scandal caused by the Royal British Bank's failure in 1856 continued to regulate the corporate economy for two-thirds of the twentieth century.

Another central aspect of the nineteenth-century approach to the punishment of fraud also lived on in the twentieth: prosecutions based on the common law offence of conspiracy to defraud. The law of conspiracy had proved particularly useful for dealing with offences not adequately covered by statutes in the Victorian era, and many twentieth-century indictments against company fraudsters contained charges based on conspiracy alongside others founded on statutes. An example was the complex and convoluted trial lasting twenty-three days in 1922 concerning the promotion of the heavily over-capitalized Jubilee Cotton Mills. The chief defendant was Hooley once more. The gist of the case against him was that he promoted the company in order to offload its shares at large premiums on the public, who were lured by the declaration of a massive dividend of 33 per cent. These offences were covered by an indictment charging the defendants with conspiring together to cheat and defraud the purchasers of the shares. The jury convicted Hooley and three of his five co-defendants, and Hooley was sentenced to three years' penal servitude.[55] Such was the usefulness of the law of conspiracy

[52] See, for example, *Rex v. Bishirgian* (1936), a case involving a false prospectus issued by James and Shakspeare, Limited. The three defendants received sentences of up to twelve months: *The Times*, 22 February 1936.

[53] Theft Act, 1968 c. 60.

[54] *Reg. v. Savundra* (1968) 52 Cr. App. R 637, *The Times*, 17 January, 7, 8 March 1968; Richard Davenport-Hines, 'Emil Savundra', *ODNB*.

[55] Hooley was also convicted of obtaining money by false pretences, and of aiding and abetting one of his co-defendants to publish fraudulent statement: *Rex v. Hooley* (1922), *Manchester Guardian*, 7, 8, 10 April 1922.

to defraud that despite misgivings among some lawyers, it was specifically preserved in the Criminal Law Act of 1977.[56] Even critics, such as the Law Commission, acknowledged that '[t]he inexhaustible ingenuity of fraudsters... and the bewildering variety of methods they employ, mean that some frauds are difficult or impossible to prosecute for any offence other than conspiracy to defraud.'[57] Thus, when the law was recast once more by the Fraud Act, 2006, conspiracy to defraud was retained because of anxiety that its abolition might affect the ability to prosecute some of the most serious cases of fraud.[58] And so another key element of the nineteenth-century strategy for dealing with fraud continued to shape approaches long after Victoria's death.

This is not to argue that nineteenth-century law was found entirely sufficient in the twentieth. The law continued to develop in an ongoing process of innovation and extension, with new companies and fraud legislation introduced roughly every generation, in 1900–8, 1928–29, 1947–48, 1967–68, 1976, 1985, and 2006. But the idea of a rupture between nineteenth- and twentieth-century approaches to fraud is difficult to sustain. Rather than embarking on a new course in the twentieth century, legislators and lawyers travelled further down the path pioneered by their nineteenth-century predecessors. Twentieth-century innovations were predicated on the belief, formulated in the later years of Victoria's reign, that criminal sanctions had a crucial role to play in the regulation of business behaviour and commercial morality. While the century also saw alternative models of regulation—by stiff financial penalties, by terms of disqualification from boardrooms (first introduced in 1928), and self-regulation by the City—these all complemented rather than replaced criminal punishments.[59]

This process of legislative innovation began right at the start of the century, with the 1900 Companies Act, which embodied some of the recommendations of the 1894 Davey Committee.[60] Historians have focused on the act's disclosure and transparency requirements, in particular the closer regulation of the contents of prospectuses and the reintroduction of compulsory audits.[61] However, section 28 enhanced criminal sanctions, stipulating that anyone who 'wilfully makes a statement false in any material particular, knowing it to be false' in any return made under the act would be liable to a fine of up to £100, or imprisonment for up to two years.[62] This was significant because the offence rested on knowledge of falsehood rather than intent to defraud—the staple feature of earlier legislation. The

[56] Criminal Law Act 1977, c. 45, s. 5.2.

[57] *Fraud. Report on a Reference under section 3(1)(e) of the Law Commissions Act 1965*, PP 2001–02 Cm 5560, 56.

[58] Fraud Act 2006, c. 35, explanatory notes, s. 5.

[59] Boardroom bans could last up to five years: 18 & 19 Geo. V c. 45, s. 76. This was extended to fifteen years in 1985: Companies Act 1985, c. 6, s. 295.

[60] See Chapter 9.

[61] P. L. Cottrell, *Industrial Finance, 1830–1914* (London, 1980), 72–4; Rob McQueen, *A Social History of Company Law: Great Britain and the Australian Colonies, 1854–1920* (Farnham, 2009), 263–6.

[62] 63 & 64 Vict. c. 48, s. 28.

act did not make the annual presentation and registration of balance sheets compulsory, but the subsequent Companies Acts of 1907–8 did, and so the section became a useful adjunct to the Larceny Act in prosecutions for false statements.[63]

Subsequent waves of companies and fraud legislation, though making extensive use of fines like the 1900 act, were also vehicles for further incursions of the criminal law into the boardroom. The 1928 Companies Act introduced a host of new specific criminal offences for directors and officers of companies in liquidation which carried penalties of up to five years' penal servitude.[64] A more general offence in winding-up was also introduced—being party to carrying on a company with intent to defraud creditors, 'or for any fraudulent purpose'—punishable by up to twelve months imprisonment.[65] For companies still active, failing to keep 'proper books of account', or neglecting to present balance sheets at the general meeting, were both punishable by a six-month jail term.[66] 'Share pushing'—by means of door-to-door selling and by post—was also heavily regulated, and breaking these rules came with a six-month prison sentence for the first offence, twelve months for the second.[67] The main criminal innovation of the 1948 Companies Act related to false prospectuses. The aim was to shift the onus from the prosecution to prove guilty knowledge of false statements to the defence to prove ignorance of falsity.[68] Consequently, the act stipulated that where a prospectus contained 'any untrue statement', anyone authorizing its issue would be liable to two years' imprisonment unless he could prove 'either that the statement was immaterial or that he had reasonable ground to believe... that the statement was true'. A statement was deemed to be untrue if it was 'misleading in the form and context in which it is included'.[69] Stiffer penalties of up to seven years for publishing false statements were specified in the Theft Act of 1968, which replaced the Larceny Act, though here 'intent to deceive' did have to be proven. Nevertheless, the measure confirmed the expansive interpretation now adopted of falsity, the penalties applying to any statement which was 'misleading, false or deceptive in a material particular'.[70]

Later legislation continued to widen the ambit of criminal sanctions. So, under the 1976 Companies Act, officers making 'misleading, false or deceptive' statements to auditors whether orally or in writing could be punished by two years' imprisonment.[71] Moving into the era associated with City deregulation, the extension of the criminal law continued. The 1985 Companies Act made trading in a company's own shares punishable by up to two years' imprisonment, the same punishment set for insider borrowing by directors.[72] The punishment for carrying on a business for any fraudulent purpose, fixed at one year in 1928 and doubled to

[63] 7 Edw. VII c. 50, ss. 19.3, 21; 8 Edw. VII c. 69, s. 113.3.
[64] 18 & 19 Geo. V c. 45, ss. 73–5.
[65] Ibid. s. 75.
[66] Ibid. s. 39.
[67] Ibid. s. 92.
[68] *Report of the Committee on Company Law Amendment [Cmd. 6659]*, PP 1944–45 IV. 23.
[69] 11 & 12 Geo. VI c. 38, ss. 44, 46.
[70] Theft Act 1968, c. 60, s. 19.
[71] Companies Act 1976, c. 69, s. 19.
[72] Companies Act 1985, c. 6, ss. 143, 330, 342, schedule 24.

two years in 1948, was ramped up to seven years, and it now applied to all companies, not just those being wound up.[73] Another jump forward was made by the 2006 Fraud Act. 'Fraud' was not a statutory offence in the nineteenth century, nor was it in the twentieth. Only with the 2006 act did fraud itself become an offence, replacing the previous offences of deception stipulated in the Theft Act. The act aimed to replace the collection of over-specific and technical offences with the single offence of fraud, which could be committed in three ways, by false representation, by failing to disclose information, and by abuse of position. The act set a maximum prison sentence of ten years.[74]

As important as the laws themselves was the machinery by which they would be set in motion, and here there was also a process of building on nineteenth-century precedents rather than taking entirely new paths, with the DPP retaining chief responsibility for fraud prosecutions outside Scotland for most of the century. Whilst the Whitaker Wright episode had underlined the fact that the Attorney General held the last word in decisions to prosecute, the DPP conducted most cases without the interference of the law officers of the Crown, and thus policy on fraud prosecutions remained consistent across changes in ministry.[75] Nor did Desart's retirement in 1908 alter the situation. He was replaced by Sir Charles Mathews, senior counsel to the Treasury, a man with extensive experience of fraud cases.[76] Mathews was given more time to focus on criminal prosecutions thanks to a bureaucratic reorganization in 1908 which separated out the offices of DPP and Solicitor to the Treasury once more, though not repeating the mistake of 1879 when the advisory and prosecuting functions were kept apart: both responsibilities remained with the DPP.[77] While private fraud prosecutions endured up to and beyond the Wright case, the number of state prosecutions continued to dwarf them, as had been the case since the 1890s.[78]

The major reconfiguration of company law in 1928–29 formalized and amplified the procedures for triggering prosecutions which had been developed after the 1890 Winding-up Act. If it appeared to the court that any past or present director or officer was guilty of any criminal offence, it could direct the liquidator either to prosecute, or to refer the matter to the DPP (or the Lord Advocate in the case of Scottish companies).[79] This power extended even to voluntarily liquidations, and

[73] 11 & 12 Geo. VI c. 38, s. 332; Companies Act 1985, c. 6, s. 458, schedule 24. The penalty was further increased to ten years in 2006: Fraud Act 2006, c. 35, s. 10.1.

[74] Ben Summers, 'The Fraud Act 2006: Has it had any Impact?' *Amicus Curiae*, 75 (Autumn 2008), 10–18; David Ormerod, *Smith and Hogan's Criminal Law* (13th edn, Oxford, 2011), ch. 23.

[75] For more on the Attorney General's powers, see J. Ll. J. Edwards, *The Law Officers of the Crown* (London, 1964), 389.

[76] He had been involved in the English Bank of the River Plate, Portsea Island Building Society, Balfour Group, and Millwall Dock prosecutions, among others.

[77] Edwards, *Law Officers*, 388.

[78] The decline of the private prosecution in the period up to 1940 is charted in Barry Godfrey, 'Changing Prosecution Practices and their Impact on Crime Figures, 1857–1940', *British Journal of Criminology*, 48 (2008), 171–89.

[79] Scotland was included in the liquidation procedures for the rest of the country from 1908, having been exempt from the original 1890 act.

the Board of Trade was authorized to cover the costs incurred by liquidators in proceeding against delinquent directors.[80] Private prosecutions were no longer envisaged at all by the 1948 act, which amended the clause to eliminate any mention of prosecution by the liquidator: all cases of fraud would be referred to the DPP or Lord Advocate.[81] In 1928–29, machinery for initiating criminal prosecutions *before* a company had begun winding up was also established, by means of an amendment to the provision for the appointment of Board of Trade inspectors on a shareholder vote at a general meeting, which had first appeared in the Companies Act of 1856. If after the inspection it appeared to the Board of Trade that anyone had committed criminal acts, it was authorized to refer the case to the DPP or the Lord Advocate.[82] The DPP retained chief authority for fraud prosecutions outside Scotland until the 1980s when a series of breakdowns of high-profile fraud trials prompted the formation in 1988 of the Serious Fraud Office (SFO), tasked with investigating and prosecuting the biggest and most complex financial crimes.[83]

Underpinning this twentieth-century widening of the reach of the criminal law was a set of beliefs which had emerged and solidified into consensus in the nineteenth century. As well as reducing fraud and its associated costs, the SFO's other two stated objectives are 'delivering justice and the rule of law', and 'maintaining confidence in the UK's business and financial institutions'.[84] These objectives are what had persuaded nineteenth-century governments to begin prosecuting company frauds.

THE DECRIMINALIZATION OF FRAUD?

The run on Northern Rock's branches in high streets across Britain in September 2007 recalled scenes not seen since 1911.[85] The run was only halted when Chancellor Alistair Darling announced a full guarantee of the bank's deposits, a prelude to its full, if temporary, nationalization. The disaster at Northern Rock presaged a wider crisis in the global banking system triggered by the collapse of the US sub-prime mortgage market and the pricking of the housing price bubble in the major economies. Further runs and collapses involving larger banks, including the gigantic Royal Bank of Scotland (RBS), were only prevented by vast emergency rescue packages sanctioned by the government. As Chancellor Darling subsequently

[80] 19 & 20 Geo. V c. 23, s. 277.

[81] 11 & 12 Geo. VI c. 38, s. 334.

[82] 19 & 20 Geo. V c. 23, s. 136.

[83] Though its remit excluded Scotland. Criminal Justice Act 1987, c. 38.

[84] SFO, 'What we do and who we work with' <http://www.sfo.gov.uk/about-us/what-we-do-and-who-we-work-with.aspx>.

[85] After a run on the Birkbeck Bank in November 1910 which hastened its demise the following year, November 1911 saw a run on the National Penny Bank, which it weathered, only to collapse in 1914 at the start of the Great War: *The Times*, 7, 8, 9, 10 November 1911, 2 August 1914. The run on Northern Rock was widely and erroneously hailed as the first since 1866, 1878, or 'since Victorian times'. For an example, see 'The Run on the Rock', House of Commons Treasury Committee, January 2008, 3.

explained, without immediate government action, RBS's 'doors would close, cash machines would be switched off, cheques would not be honoured, people would not be paid'.[86] This pattern of crash and bailout, played out in other western economies, raised a host of serious questions concerning the structure of the financial sector, particularly the wisdom of permitting banks to become 'too big to fail', the internal and external causes of the crisis, such as perverse incentive structures and the policy of deregulation pursued by governments since the 1980s, and whether and how those responsible for the crisis could be punished.

'Incompetent' and 'reckless' were words easily and freely used to describe the behaviour of the boards of the banks brought to ruin. But were they criminal? After a century of refinements and supplements to the law, it seemed there were a number of avenues for prosecutors to explore. Did the April 2008 prospectus issued by RBS in support of a £12 billion share issue misrepresent the bank's finances in a way that left its directors liable to prosecution under the Fraud Act? Or perhaps the same act could cover the 'allegedly fraudulent misrepresentation, packaging and bundling' of sub-prime mortgage securities, for which RBS was being sued in the US. A third possibility was that the company had incurred criminal liability under the 2006 Companies Act for failing to keep 'adequate accounting records' disclosing 'with reasonable accuracy, at any time, the financial position of the company'.[87] However, a Financial Services Authority (FSA) investigation found no evidence of 'fraud or dishonest activity' at the bank and therefore no grounds for 'enforcement action', either criminal or civil. The bank had been brought down, the FSA concluded, by 'a series of bad decisions'.[88] The sentiment echoed *The Times*'s 1880 judgement that '[m]en must not be sent to prison because they are not good bankers'.[89] Though the authorities resisted calls for prosecution, the former CEO of RBS Sir Fred Goodwin was belatedly stripped of his knighthood by the Honours Forfeiture Committee in January 2012, in a move which bore a passing resemblance to eighteenth-century methods of dealing with fraud by public degradation.

What this book has shown is that to secure the proper punishment of company directors, the existence of laws was not sufficient; what was also needed was the political will to enforce them. This will was lacking in the aftermath of the 2008 crisis. Popular demand for retribution, though present, was blunted by government policies which insulated the public from the direct economic consequences of bank failures. The nationalizations, part-nationalizations, and guarantees which rescued the banks, together with the Financial Services Compensation Scheme which indemnified savers against losses, had the side-effect of insulating bankers from the consequences of failures by dampening popular outrage. Moreover, in the

[86] Alistair Darling, *Back from the Brink: 1,000 Days at Number 11* (London, 2011), 154.

[87] Ian Fraser, 'Looks Like Fred Goodwin May Face Criminal Charges After All', *Huffington Post*, 14 December 2011 <http://www.huffingtonpost.co.uk/ian-fraser/looks-like-fred-goodwin-might-face-criminal-charges_b_1148201.html>.

[88] Financial Services Authority Board Report, 'The Failure of the Royal Bank of Scotland' (2011), 354 <http://www.fsa.gov.uk/pubs/other/rbs.pdf>.

[89] *The Times*, 6 May 1880.

years preceding the crisis, there had been signs of a retreat by the political class from using criminal sanctions as a regulatory tool, for a mixture of ideological and economic reasons. Government-commissioned reviews explored alternatives to criminal prosecutions such as administrative penalties—levied by regulators without the intervention of a court—which had the virtue of being 'quicker and simpler than court proceedings'.[90] It was an agenda which shaped practice across Whitehall, and which ironically gained further purchase as the devastating impact of the crisis on the public finances became clear, and the need for reining in budgets became pressing. The SFO was no exception, and began showing 'a marked enthusiasm' for alternatives to the criminal trial such as plea bargaining and fines in order to reduce the length and cost of investigations.[91] A longer-term trend contributing to reluctance to prosecute was the squeeze placed on the SFO's access to police resources since the 1990s caused by the Labour government's creation of a 'target culture' to improve public services. With fraud not on the list of police performance indicators, police commanders became unwilling to devote personnel to SFO investigations because, in the words of one City of London detective sergeant, 'they want them to stay at home and deal with performance indicators'. The result, claimed a 2008 report on the SFO by a former senior prosecutor for New York City, was 'the decriminalisation of fraud', which undermined public confidence in the criminal justice system and the state.[92] Such criticisms were echoed in popular perceptions of the SFO. The organization regularly appears in satirical magazine *Private Eye* as the 'Serious Farce Office', while it is dismissed by political journalist Peter Oborne as a 'bunch of clowns'.[93]

Experience in the late nineteenth century showed that bureaucratic innovations raised public expectations to unrealistic levels, and no matter how active prosecutors were, they faced a difficult job satisfying public opinion. Successful prosecutions then, as now, were often taken for granted and quickly forgotten, whereas cases which failed, or were not prosecuted at all, were seized upon as emblematic of the failings of the system, with little allowance made for the inevitable difficulties and complexities involved in such prosecutions. Recent criticisms of the SFO derive in part from the failure of a small number of high-profile trials, and are not entirely borne out by the bigger picture.[94] The SFO's annual reports show a continuing stream of criminal prosecutions for fraud. For 2010–11, for example, the

[90] Philip Hampton, 'Reducing Administrative Burdens: Effective Inspection and Enforcement' (2005), s. 2.82 <http://www.hm-treasury.gov.uk/hampton>. See also Richard Macrory, 'Regulatory Justice: Making Sanctions Effective', Final Report (2006) <http://www.bis.gov.uk/files/file44593.pdf>.

[91] Fraud Advisory Panel, '11th Annual Review: 2008–9', 15. <http://www.fraudadvisorypanel.org/new/pdf_show.php?id=122&PHPSESSID=bc518baff3366c7d95fd87e46db07073>; Fraud Advisory Panel, 'Roskill Revisited: Is there a Case for a Unified Fraud Prosecution Office?' (2010), ss. 69–70 <http://www.fraudadvisorypanel.org/new/pdf_show.php?id=124&PHPSESSID=4a52a94920e121c09ea35bb6504c9c0a>.

[92] Jessica de Grazia, 'Review of the Serious Fraud Office: Final Report' (2008), 113–14 <http://www.sfo.gov.uk/media/34318/de%20grazia%20review%20of%20sfo.pdf>.

[93] *Private Eye*, 24 February 2012; Peter Oborne, 'The Lesson David Cameron Can Learn from Margaret Thatcher', *Daily Mail*, 16 September 2010.

[94] Fraud Advisory Panel, 'Roskill Revisited', s. 72.

SFO tried thirty-one defendants in seventeen cases, twenty-six of whom were found guilty, a conviction rate of 84 per cent.[95] Big cases involving established City firms are sometimes taken on and brought to a successful conclusion, at great public expense, such as the prosecution of the chief executive and two directors of the Independent Insurance Group, Britain's ninth-largest insurer, which collapsed in 2001. In 2007 they received sentences of between three and seven years.[96]

Nevertheless, the absence of prosecutions for recent misdeeds in the banking sector has created a sense of resentment, both in Britain and in the US, which seems to be growing rather than dissipating. While government reports repeat the line that executives did not behave dishonestly and were simply caught out by a bolt from the blue, the question 'Why have no bankers been arrested?' does not go away.[97] When Charles Ferguson, US director of *Inside Job*, a 2010 documentary on the crisis, received his Oscar, he began his speech by pointing out 'that three years after our horrific financial crisis caused by financial fraud, not a single financial executive has gone to jail, and that's wrong'.[98] Serious banking reforms for the UK are in the pipeline, the centrepiece of which promises to be the separation of banks' retail and investment arms, recommended by the Independent Commission on Banking in September 2011.[99] These aim to stabilize High Street banking, safeguarding depositors and taxpayers against future crises. But structural reforms do not address the moral component of the catastrophe. History shows that fraud trials have been an effective means of reasserting moral standards and restoring trust in times of crisis. It remains to be seen what the effects of dispensing with them will be.

[95] Serious Fraud Office, 'Annual Report and Accounts, 2010–11', 8 <http://www.sfo.gov.uk/media/175084/resource-accounts-2010-11.pdf>.

[96] *Reg. v. Bright* (2007): see Serious Fraud Office, 'Annual Report, 2007/08', 11–24 <http://www.sfo.gov.uk/media/30954/sfo%20annual%20report%202007-2008.pdf>.

[97] Jon Snow, 'Why Have No Bankers Been Arrested?' 13 September 2011 <http://blogs.channel4.com/snowblog/bankers-arrested/16148>.

[98] Quoted in Jonathan Fisher et al., 'Economic Crime and the Global Financial Crisis', *Law and Financial Markets Review* (July 2011), 276.

[99] Independent Commission on Banking, Final Report Recommendations (2011) <http://bankingcommission.s3.amazonaws.com/wp-content/uploads/2010/07/ICB-Final-Report.pdf>.

Bibliography

PRIMARY WORKS

Unpublished

British Library

Peel Papers, Add.40385, 40390.

Cross Papers, Add.51265.

East Dunbartonshire Archives

Letter from Fox Maule to Peter Mackenzie, 1 July 1839, GD185/3/3.

Letter from Fox Maule to Peter Mackenzie, 18 March 1841, GD185/3/8.

London Metropolitan Archives

Mansion House Justice Room, Court Register, November 1868–November 1869, f. 44 (26 January 1869), CLA/004/04/030.

The National Archives

Oxford Circuit: Crown Minute Books, 1833 Lent–1842 Summer, ASSI 2/32.

Oxford Circuit: Indictment Files, Oxon, 1838 Lent, ASSI 5/158/11.

Oxford Circuit: Criminal Depositions and Case Papers, 1836–40, ASSI 6/4.

Memorandum from Francis Whitmarsh to Board of Trade (7 February 1850), BT 1/477/431/50.

Indictment Nos 105–6, William White (11 July 1870), CRIM 4/779.

Indictment No 81, Thomas Wood (27 May 1878), CRIM 4/889.

Oxfordshire History Centre

Calendar of Prisoners for Michaelmas Sessions 1837 and Lent Assizes 1838, QS1837/4/A7/1.

Published

Government Reports and Parliamentary Papers.

Hansard's Parliamentary Debates, series two, three, and four.

Journals of the House of Commons.

Report from the Select Committee on the Arigna Mining Company, PP 1826–27 III.

Report from the Secret Committee on Joint Stock Banks, PP 1836 IX.

A Return of Joint Stock Banks in Ireland, PP 1836 XXXVII.

Report from the Secret Committee on Joint Stock Banks, PP 1837 XIV.

Report on the Law of Partnership, PP 1837 XLIV.

Report from the Secret Committee on Joint Stock Banks, PP 1837–38 VII.

First Report of the Select Committee on Joint Stock Companies, PP 1844 VII.

Report by the Registrar of Joint-Stock Companies to the Committee of Privy Council for Trade, for the year 1845, PP 1846 XLIII.

Report by the Registrar of Joint-Stock Companies to the Committee of Privy Council for Trade, for the year 1846, PP 1847 LIX.

Accounts of the Number of Depositors in Savings Banks, Money Received, Interest Credited, &c, PP 1847 XXXIV.
Abstract of Report by the Registrar of Joint Stock Companies to the Committee of Privy Council for Trade, for the year 1847, PP 1847–48 LI.
Select Committee on Savings Banks (Ireland), PP 1849 XIV.
Report from the Select Committee on Investments for the Savings of the Middle and Working Classes, PP 1850 XIX.
Report from the Select Committee on the Law of Partnership, PP 1851 XVIII.
Report from the Select Committee on Assurance Associations, PP 1852–53 XXI.
Select Committee on Assurance Associations; First Report of the Commissioners appointed to Inquire and Ascertain how far the Mercantile Laws in the Different Parts of the United Kingdom of Great Britain and Ireland may be Advantageously Assimilated, PP 1854 XXVII.
A Bill to Amend the Law Relating to the Criminal Appropriation of Property held by Persons as Trustees or Bailees, PP 1856 II.
Report from the Select Committee on the Bank Acts, PP 1857–8 V.
Returns from the Official Managers and Liquidators of every Joint Stock Company Wound-up or Winding-up under the Joint Stock Companies Winding-Up Acts, PP 1861 XXXIV.
Copy of all Correspondence between the Secretary of State for the Home Department and Messrs. Lewis and Lewis, on behalf of persons interested in the affairs of the Unity Bank, respecting the Prosecution of Messrs. Terry and Burch, PP 1865 XXX.
Report from the Select Committee on Limited Liability Acts, PP 1867 X.
Judicature Commission: Fifth and Final Report of the Commissioners, PP 1874 XXIV.
Report from the Select Committee on Loans to Foreign States, PP 1875 XI.
Report from the Select Committee on the Companies Acts, 1862 and 1867, PP 1877 VIII.
An Estimate of the Sums Required to be Voted for the Service of the Year Ending 31st March 1879, in Addition to the Sums Already Provided in the Estimates Presented in the Session of 1878, PP 1878–79 XLVIII.
Return of all Prosecutions and other Proceedings in the Nature of Prosecutions Conducted by the Solicitor to the Treasury during the last Three Years, 1877–80, PP 1881 LXXVI.
Copy of Correspondence between the Director of Public Prosecutions and Mr. George Lewis in reference to the case of the Queen v. Taylor and Boynes, PP 1883 LV.
Return of the Proceedings of the Director of Public Prosecutions, PP 1883 LV.
Report of the Committee Appointed to Inquire into the Office of Public Prosecutor, PP 1884 XXIII.
Draft of Regulations Framed under the Prosecution of Offences Acts, 1879 and 1884, PP 1886 LIII.
Final Report of the Royal Commission Appointed to Inquire into the Depression of Trade and Industry, PP 1886 XXIII.
Copy of Return Showing the Working of the Regulations made in 1886 for Carrying out the Prosecution of Offences Acts, 1879 and 1884, PP 1887 LXVII.
A Bill to Consolidate and Amend the Companies' Acts, PP 1888 II.
Report of Committee Appointed by the Treasury to Inquire into the System of Conducting the Legal Business of the Government, PP 1888 LXXX.
Return of all Companies which have been Ordered to be wound up, under the Provisions of the Companies Acts, Compulsorily or under the Supervision of the Court, since the Commencement of the Companies Act, 1862, PP 1888 LXXX.
Reports from Her Majesty's Representatives Abroad respecting the Formation, Regulation, and Dissolution of Public Companies in Foreign Countries, PP 1889 LXXVII.

Returns of the Names, Objects or Business, Places where Business is or was Conducted, Date of Registration, &c, and the Total Amount of Calls Received of all Joint Stock Companies Formed since the 1st day of January 1889 to the 31st day of December 1889, and also the Number of Shareholders in Each of the said Companies at the Date of the Last Return, PP 1890 LXVIII.

Return Showing the Working of the Regulations made in 1886 for Carrying out the Prosecution of Offences Acts, 1879 and 1884, PP 1892 LXV.

Report of the Inter-Departmental Committee Appointed to Inquire into the Limits of the Action of the Board of Trade as Regards the Liquidation of Companies under the Companies (Winding-up) Act, 1890, PP 1893–94 LXXXI.

First Report by the Board of Trade under Section 29 of the Companies (Winding-up) Act, 1890, PP 1893–94 LXXXI.

Second General Annual Report by the Board of Trade under section 29 of the Companies (Winding-up) Act, 1890, PP 1893–94 LXXXI.

Return Showing the Working of the Regulations made in 1886 for Carrying out the Prosecution of Offences Acts, 1879 and 1884, PP 1894 LXXI.

Third General Annual Report by the Board of Trade under section 29 of the Companies (Winding-up) Act, 1890, PP 1894 LXXVII.

Fourth General Annual Report by the Board of Trade under section 29 of the Companies (Winding-up) Act, 1890, PP 1895 LXXXVIII.

Report of the Departmental Committee Appointed by the Board of Trade to Inquire what Amendments are necessary in the Acts relating to Joint Stock Companies Incorporated with Limited Liability under the Companies Acts, 1862 to 1890, PP 1895 LXXXVIII.

Return Showing the Working of the Regulations made in 1886 for Carrying out the Prosecution of Offences Acts, 1879 and 1884, PP 1896 LXIX.

Fifth General Annual Report by the Board of Trade under section 29 of the Companies (Winding-up) Act, 1890, PP 1896 LXXVI.

Return Showing the Working of the Regulations made in 1886 for Carrying out the Prosecution of Offences Acts, 1879 and 1884, PP 1897 LXXIII.

Sixth General Annual Report by the Board of Trade under section 29 of the Companies (Winding-up) Act, 1890, PP 1897 LXXX.

Return Showing the Working of the Regulations made in 1886 for Carrying out the Prosecution of Offences Acts, 1879 and 1884, PP 1898 LXXIII.

Seventh General Annual Report by the Board of Trade under section 29 of the Companies (Winding-up) Act, 1890, PP 1898 LXXXIV.

Return Showing the Working of the Regulations made in 1886 for Carrying out the Prosecution of Offences Acts, 1879 and 1884, PP 1899 LXXIX.

Ninth General Annual Report by the Board of Trade under section 29 of the Companies (Winding-up) Act, 1890, PP 1900 LXXVIII.

Tenth General Annual Report by the Board of Trade under section 29 of the Companies (Winding-up) Act, 1890, PP 1901 LXIX.

Eleventh General Annual Report by the Board of Trade, PP 1902 XCIII.

Report of the Committee on Company Law Amendment [Cmd. 6659], PP 1944–45 IV.

Fraud. Report on a Reference under section 3(1)(e) of the Law Commissions Act 1965, PP 2001–02 Cm 5560.

Other Official Publications

Hampton, Philip, 'Reducing Administrative Burdens: Effective Inspection and Enforcement' (2005) <http://www.hm-treasury.gov.uk/hampton>.

Macrory, Richard, 'Regulatory Justice: Making Sanctions Effective', Final Report (2006) <http://www.bis.gov.uk/files/file44593.pdf>.

Serious Fraud Office, 'Annual Report, 2007/08' <http://www.sfo.gov.uk/media/30954/sfo%20annual%20report%202007–2008.pdf>.

de Grazia, Jessica, 'Review of the Serious Fraud Office: Final Report' (2008), 113–14 <http://www.sfo.gov.uk/media/34318/de%20grazia%20review%20of%20sfo.pdf>.

Serious Fraud Office, 'Annual Report and Accounts, 2010–11' <http://www.sfo.gov.uk/media/175084/resource-accounts-2010-11.pdf>.

Financial Services Authority Board Report, 'The Failure of the Royal Bank of Scotland' (2011) <http://www.fsa.gov.uk/pubs/other/rbs.pdf>.

Independent Commission on Banking, Final Report Recommendations (2011) <http://bankingcommission.s3.amazonaws.com/wp-content/uploads/2010/07/ICB-Final-Report.pdf>.

Law Reports
Cox's Criminal Cases
English Reports
Old Bailey Proceedings Online <http://www.oldbaileyonline.org> version 6.0.

Newspapers and Periodicals
Aberdeen (Weekly) Journal
Age
Bankers' Circular
Belfast News-Letter
Bell's Life in London and Sporting Chronicle
Berrow's Worcester Journal
Birmingham Daily Post
Blackburn Standard
Bradford Observer
Bristol Mercury (and Daily Post)
Bury and Norwich Post
Caledonian Mercury
Cheshire Observer
Daily Express
Daily Gazette
Daily Mail
Daily News
Daily Telegraph
Derby Mercury
Dundee Courier and Daily Argus
Economist
Era
Examiner
Financial News
Freeman's Journal
Fun
Funny Folks
Gentleman's Magazine

Glasgow Herald
Graphic
Hampshire Advertiser
Hampshire Telegraph and Sussex Chronicle
Huddersfield (Daily) Chronicle
Huffington Post
Hull Packet
Illustrated London News
Illustrated Police News
Ipswich Journal
Jackson's Oxford Journal
John Bull
Joint Stock Companies Journal
Judy
Lancaster Gazette
Law Times
Leeds Mercury
Leicester Chronicle and Leicestershire Mercury
Liverpool Mercury
Lloyd's Weekly Newspaper
London Dispatch and People's Political and Social Reformer
London Review
Manchester Guardian
Manchester Times
Money Market Review
Monthly Magazine, or, British Register
Monthly Repository
Morning Advertiser
Morning Chronicle
Morning Post
Musical Standard
New Monthly Magazine and Literary Journal
New York Times
Newcastle (Weekly) Courant
News of the World
North-Eastern Daily Gazette
Northern Echo
Northern Star
Nottinghamshire Guardian
Observer
Pall Mall Gazette
Penny Illustrated Paper
People's Paper
Preston Guardian
Private Eye
Punch
Puppet-Show
Review of Reviews

Reynolds's Newspaper
Royal Cornwall Gazette
St James's Gazette
Satirist
Saturday Review of Politics, Literature, Science and Art
Scotch Reformers' Gazette
Scotsman
Sheffield and Rotherham Independent
Standard
Star
Statist
The Times
Tinsley's Magazine
Trewman's Exeter Flying Post
Truth
Weekly Dispatch
Western Mail
Westminster Review
Wrexham Advertiser
York(shire) Herald

Contemporary Books and Articles

Anon., *Remarks on Joint Stock Companies by an Old Merchant* (London, 1825).
——'The Legislation of 1844', *Westminster Review*, 42 (December 1844), 318–62.
——*A Record of the Proceedings of the Committee of Deputies from the Joint Stock Banks of England, Wales, and Ireland* (London, 1845).
——*The Great Trial of the Seven City of Glasgow Bank Directors for Using and Uttering False Balance Sheets* (London, 1879).
——*Report of the Trial of the Directors of the City of Glasgow Bank* (Edinburgh, 1879).
——'The Story of the Liberator Crash: With some Account of the Life and Character of Jabez Spencer Balfour', *Westminster Gazette* Popular No. 5 (November 1893).
Bamford, Francis, and the Duke of Wellington (eds), *The Journal of Mrs Arbuthnot, 1820–1832*, 2 vols (London, 1950).
Beaumont, John Augustus, *Thoughts and Details on Life Insurance Offices, in a Letter to the Shareholders and Insured in the Provident Life Office* (London, 1842).
Bell, Robert, *The Ladder of Gold: An English Story*, 3 vols (London, 1850).
Belloc, Hilaire, *Emmanuel Burden, Merchant* (New York, 1904).
Bottomley, Horatio, *Horatio Bottomley: Hys Booke* (London, 1892).
Boult, Swinton, *The Law and Practice relating to the Constitution and Management of Assurance, Banking, and other Joint Stock Companies* (London, 1841).
Bourne, Kenneth (ed.), *The Letters of the Third Viscount Palmerston to Laurence and Elizabeth Sulivan, 1804–1863* (London, 1979).
Bowen-Rowlands, Ernest, *Seventy-Two Years at the Bar: A Memoir* (London, 1924).
Bowring, John (ed.), *The Works of Jeremy Bentham*, 11 vols (Edinburgh, 1843).
Brooks, Collin (ed.), *The Royal Mail Case* (1933; repr. New York, 1980).
Burchell, James, *The Joint Stock Companies Registration Act* (London, 1844).
Carlyle, Thomas, *Latter-Day Pamphlets* (London, 1850).
Clarke, Edward, *The Story of My Life* (New York, 1919).

Clay, William, *Speech of William Clay, Esq., MP, on Moving for the Appointment of a Committee to Inquire into the Operation of the Act Permitting the Establishment of Joint-Stock Banks* (London, 1837).

Cockton, Henry, *George St. George Julian, the Prince* (London, 1841).

Colchester, Charles, Lord (ed.), *The Diary and Correspondence of Charles Abbot, Lord Colchester*, 3 vols (London, 1861).

Costello, Dudley, 'The Joint-Stock Banker', *Bentley's Miscellany*, 39 (April 1856), 346–65.

Cox, Edward W., *The New Law and Practice of Joint Stock Companies, with and without Limited Liability* (4th edn, London, 1857).

Darling, Alistair, *Back from the Brink: 1,000 Days at Number 11* (London, 2011).

Dickens, Charles, *Little Dorrit*, 2 vols (London, 1857; repr. 1891).

—— *Martin Chuzzlewit* (London, 1844; repr. Ware, 1994).

English, Henry, *A General Guide to the Companies Formed for Working Foreign Mines* (London, 1825).

Evans, D. Morier, *Facts, Failures and Frauds: Revelations Financial Mercantile Criminal* (1859; repr. New York, 1968).

—— *Speculative Notes and Notes on Speculation, Ideal and Real* (1864; repr. New York, 1969).

Farrer, Frederick Edward, *The Law Relating to Prospectuses Simply and Exhaustively Stated for Lawyers and Laymen* (London, 1913).

Finlason, W. F., *A Report of the Case of the Queen v. Gurney and others, in the Court of Queen's Bench* (London, 1870).

Foot, M. R. D., and H. C. G. Matthew (eds), *The Gladstone Diaries*, 14 vols (Oxford, 1968–94).

Fraser, Ian, 'Looks Like Fred Goodwin May Face Criminal Charges After All', *Huffington Post*, 14 December 2011 <http://www.huffingtonpost.co.uk/ian-fraser/looks-like-fred-goodwin-might-face-criminal-charges_b_1148201.html>.

Fraud Advisory Panel, '11th Annual Review: 2008–9' <http://www.fraudadvisorypanel.org/new/pdf_show.php?id=122&PHPSESSID=bc518baff3366c7d95fd87e46db07073>.

—— 'Roskill Revisited: Is there a Case for a Unified Fraud Prosecution Office?' (2010) <http://www.fraudadvisorypanel.org/new/pdf_show.php?id=124&PHPSESSID=4a52a94920e121c09ea35bb6504c9c0a>.

Gilbart, James William, *The History and Principles of Banking* (London, 1834).

—— *The Letters of Nehemiah: Relating to the Laws Affecting Joint Stock Banks, and the Effects Likely to be Produced, by the Measures of Sir Robert Peel, upon the System of Banking in London, and Throughout the Country* (London, 1845).

—— *The Moral and Religious Duties of Public Companies* (2nd edn, London, 1856).

Hardcastle, Mrs. (ed.), *Life of John, Lord Campbell*, 2 vols (London, 1881).

Harris, Frank, *My Life and Loves*, 4 vols (n.p., 1922).

Hemyng, Bracebridge, *'The Stockbroker's Wife' and other Sensational Tales of the Stock Exchange* (London, 1885).

Hill, Headon, *The One Who Saw* (London, 1905).

Hopkins, John Baker, 'Catch 'Em Alive, Oh!', *Tinsley's Magazine*, 40 (January 1887), 63–72.

Hurrell, Henry, and Clarendon G. Hyde, *The Law of Directors and Officers of Joint Stock Companies* (London, 1884).

—— *The Law of Directors and Officers of Joint Stock Companies* (3rd edn, London, 1896).

—— *The Law of Directors and Officers of Joint Stock Companies* (4th edn, London, 1905).

Kelley, Philip, and Ronald Hudson (eds), *The Brownings' Correspondence*, 18 vols (Winfield, KS, 1984–).

Lever, Charles, *Davenport Dunn; or a Man of our Day* (London, 1859).
Lewins, William, *Her Majesty's Mails: An Historical and Descriptive Account of the British Post-Office* (London, 1864).
Lewis, George Henry, *The Liabilities Incurred by the Projectors, Managers and Shareholders of Railway and other Joint-Stock Companies Considered: and also the Rights and Liabilities arising from Transfers of Shares* (London, 1845).
Lewis, Gilbert Frankland (ed.), *Letters of the Right Hon. Sir George Cornewall Lewis, Bart. to various Friends* (London, 1870).
Ludlow, John Malcolm, *The Joint-Stock Companies Winding-up Act, 1848* (London, 1850).
—— *The Autobiography of a Christian Socialist* (London, 1981).
Macdonald, J. H. A., *Life Jottings of an Old Edinburgh Citizen* (London, 1915).
Mackenzie, Peter, *Reminiscences of Glasgow and the West of Scotland*, 3 vols (Glasgow, 1866).
[Mallalieu, Alfred], 'Whig-Radical Prosperity', *Blackwood's Edinburgh Magazine*, 41 (February 1837), 147–62.
Manson, Edward, *The Builders of our Law during the Reign of Queen Victoria* (London, 1895).
Marx, Karl, and Frederick Engels, *Collected Works*, 50 vols (London, 1975–2004).
Meek, Andrew, *Observations on the Government of Joint Stock Banks in England* (London, 1841).
Morgan, Henry Lloyd, *Personal Liabilities of Directors of Joint Stock Companies under the Fraudulent Trustees' Act* (3rd edn, London, 1858).
O'Brien, D. P. O. (ed.), *The Correspondence of Lord Overstone*, 3 vols (Cambridge, 1971).
Purcell, Edmund D., *Forty Years at the Criminal Bar* (London, 1916).
Rawson, William, *The Present Operations and Future Prospects of the Mexican Mine Associations* (London, 1825).
Russell, William Oldnall, and Charles Sprengel Greaves, *A Treatise on Crimes and Misdemeanors*, 2 vols (8th American edn, Philadelphia, PA, 1857).
Scratchley, Arthur, *A Practical Treatise on Savings Banks, Containing a Review of their Past History and Present Condition, and of Legislation on the Subject* (London, 1860).
Shepherd, Elizabeth (ed.), *Journal of Sir Peter Laurie* (Tunbridge Wells, 1985).
[Spencer, Herbert], 'Railway Morals and Railway Policy', *Edinburgh Review*, 100 (October 1854), 420–61.
Thom, Adam, *Overend and Gurney Prosecution: in its Relation to the Public as Distinguished from the Defendants* (London, 1869).
Thomas, William (ed.), *The Journals of Thomas Babington Macaulay*, 5 vols (London, 2008).
Thomson, Basil, *The Story of Scotland Yard* (London, 1935).
Trollope, Anthony, *The Way We Live Now* (London, 1876).
—— *An Autobiography* (Oxford, 1950; repr. 1980).
Vincent, John (ed.), *A Selection from the Diaries of Edward Henry Stanley, 15th Earl of Derby (1826–93)* (London, 1994).
Wade, John, *The Black Book: Or, Corruption Unmasked!* (London, 1820).
Wallace, William (ed.), *Trial of the City of Glasgow Bank Directors* (London, 1905).
[Warren, Samuel], 'Ten Thousand a-Year', *Blackwood's Edinburgh Magazine*, 49 (March 1841), 379–405.
Watkin, A. E. (ed.), *Absalom Watkin: Extracts from his Journal, 1814–1856* (London, 1920).
Watts, J. Stockwell, *The Truth about the 'Liberator' Building Society: Respectfully Addressed to the Thirty Thousand Shareholders and Depositors* (2nd edn, London, 1892).

Wells, H. G., *Tono-Bungay: A Novel* (1909; repr. New York, 1916).
Williams, Montagu, *Later Leaves: Being the Further Reminiscences of Montagu Williams, QC* (London, 1891).

Films and Television Programmes
Inside Job, Charles Ferguson, dir. (Sony Pictures Classics, 2010) [documentary].
Little Dorrit (BBC1, 2008) [drama].
The Way We Live Now (BBC1, 2001) [drama].

SECONDARY WORKS

Acheson, Graeme G., and John D. Turner, 'The Death Blow to Unlimited Liability in Victorian Britain: The City of Glasgow Failure', *Explorations in Economic History*, 45 (2008), 235–53.
Alborn, Timothy L., 'The Moral of the Failed Bank: Professional Plots in the Victorian Money Market', *Victorian Studies*, 38 (1995), 199–226.
—— *Conceiving Companies: Joint-Stock Politics in Victorian England* (London, 1998).
—— 'The First Fund Managers: Life Insurance Bonuses in Victorian Britain', in Nancy Henry and Cannon Schmitt (eds), *Victorian Investments: New Perspectives on Finance and Culture* (Bloomington, IN, 2009), 58–78.
—— *Regulated Lives: Life Insurance and British Society, 1800–1914* (Toronto, 2009).
Anderson, Gregory, *Victorian Clerks* (Manchester, 1976).
Ardern, Dean, and Maxwell Aiken, 'An Accounting History of Capital Maintenance: Legal Precedents for Managerial Autonomy in the United Kingdom', *Accounting Historians Journal*, 32 (2005), 23–60.
Arnold, A. J., '"Publishing Your Private Affairs to the World": Corporate Financial Disclosures in the UK, 1900–24', *Accounting, Business and Financial History*, 7 (1997), 143–73.
—— and S. McCartney, *George Hudson: The Rise and Fall of the Railway King: A Study in Victorian Entrepreneurship* (London, 2004).
Atiyah, P. S., *The Rise and Fall of Freedom of Contract* (Oxford, 1979).
Bain, Wilson Harvey, 'The Life and Achievements of James, First Baron Moncreiff, 1811 to 1895', MLitt thesis, University of Glasgow, 1977.
Banner, Stuart, *Anglo-American Securities Regulation: Cultural and Political Roots, 1690–1860* (Cambridge, 2002).
Barker, Hannah, *Newspapers, Politics, and Public Opinion in Late Eighteenth-Century England* (Oxford, 1998).
Barnes, Paul, 'A Victorian Financial Crisis: The Scandalous Implications of the Case of Overend Gurney', in Judith Rowbotham and Kim Stevenson (eds), *Criminal Conversations: Victorian Crimes, Social Panic, and Moral Outrage* (Columbus, OH, 2005), 55–69.
Barrow, G. L., 'Justice for Thomas Mooney', *Dublin Historical Record*, 24 (1970), 173–88.
Batzel, Victor M., '"The General Scope of the Act": A Study of Law, Moralism, and Administration in England, 1844–1910', *Canadian Journal of History*, 22 (1987), 349–66.
Beaven, Alfred P., 'Notes on the Aldermen, 1701–1838', in The Aldermen of the City of London: Temp. Henry III—1912 (1908), 195–211 <http://www.british-history.ac.uk/report.aspx?compid=67248>.
Bentley, David, *English Criminal Justice in the Nineteenth Century* (London, 1998).

Bodenhorn, Howard, 'Free Banking in Ireland', in Kevin Dowd (ed.), *The Experience of Free Banking* (London, 1992), 137–56.
Bowen, H. V., '"The Pests of Human Society": Stockbrokers, Jobbers and Speculators in Mid-Eighteenth-Century Britain', *History*, 78 (1993), 38–53.
Brake, Laurel, and Marysa Demoor (eds), *Dictionary of Nineteenth-Century Journalism in Great Britain and Ireland* (London, 2009).
Brooke, Justin, 'Thomas Saunders Cave, Speculator Extraordinary', *British Mining*, 43 (1991), 9–34.
Brown, Callum, *The Social History of Religion in Scotland since 1730* (London, 1987).
Bulwer, Henry Lytton, *The Life of Henry John Temple, Viscount Palmerston, with Selections from his Diaries and Correspondence*, 3 vols (London, 1871–4).
Burt, Roger, and Norikazu Kudo, 'The Adaptability of the Cornish Cost Book System', *Business History*, 25 (1983), 30–41.
Chandler, Roy, John Richard Edwards, and Malcolm Anderson, 'Disciplinary Action against Members of the Founding Bodies of the ICAEW', *Accounting, Auditing & Accountability Journal*, 21 (2008), 827–49.
Checkland, S. G., *Scottish Banking: A History, 1695–1973* (Glasgow, 1975).
Clark, Anna, *Scandal: The Sexual Politics of the British Constitution* (Princeton, NJ, 2004).
Cocks, R., 'Victorian Barristers, Judges and Taxation: A Study in the Expansion of Legal Work', in G. R. Rubin and D. Sugarman (eds), *Law, Economy and Society, 1750–1914: Essays in the History of English Law* (Abingdon, 1984), 445–69.
Colaiaco, James A., *James Fitzjames Stephen and the Crisis of Victorian Thought* (London, 1983).
Collins, Michael, 'The Banking Crisis of 1878', *Economic History Review*, 42 (1989), 504–27.
Cook, Chris, *Britain in the Nineteenth Century, 1815–1914* (London, 1999).
Cornish, W. R., and G. de N. Clark, *Law and Society in England, 1750–1950* (London, 1989).
——S. Anderson, R. Cocks, et al., *The Oxford History of the Laws of England*, 13 vols (Oxford, 2003–), xi–xiii.
Cottrell, P. L., *Industrial Finance, 1830–1914* (London, 1980).
——and Lucy Newton, 'Banking Liberalization in England and Wales, 1826–1844', in Richard Sylla, Richard Tilly, and Gabriel Casares (eds), *The State, the Financial System, and Economic Modernization* (Cambridge, 1999), 75–117.
Cowles, Virginia, *The Great Swindle: The Story of the South Sea Bubble* (London, 1960).
Curthoys, Mark C., *Governments, Labour, and the Law in Mid-Victorian Britain: The Trade Union Legislation of the 1870s* (Oxford, 2004).
Daunton, Martin, *Trusting Leviathan: The Politics of Taxation in Britain, 1799–1914* (Cambridge, 2001).
Davis, Jennifer S., 'Prosecutions and their Context: The Use of the Criminal Law in Later Nineteenth-Century London', in D. Hay and F. Snyder (eds), *Policing and Prosecution in Britain, 1750–1850* (Oxford, 1989), 397–426.
Dawson, Frank Griffith, *The First Latin American Debt Crisis: The City of London and the 1822–25 Loan Bubble* (Yale, 1990).
Duman, Daniel, *The Judicial Bench in England, 1727–1875: The Reshaping of a Professional Elite* (London, 1982).
Edwards, J. Ll. J., *The Law Officers of the Crown* (London, 1964).
Edwards, John Richard, *A History of Financial Accounting* (London, 1989).

Elliott, Geoffrey, *The Mystery of Overend and Gurney: A Financial Scandal in Victorian London* (London, 2006).
Emsley, Clive, *Crime and Society in England, 1750–1900* (2nd edn, Harlow, 1996).
Fay, C. R., *Huskisson and his Age* (London, 1951).
Feldman, David, and M. Page Baldwin, 'Emigration and the British State, ca. 1815–1925', in Nancy L. Green and Francois Weil (eds), *Citizenship and Those Who Leave: The Politics of Emigration and Expatriation* (Urbana, IL, 2007), 135–55.
Felstead, Sidney Theodore, *Sir Richard Muir: A Memoir of a Public Prosecutor* (London, 1927).
Ferguson, R. B., 'Commercial Expectations and the Guarantee of the Law: Sales Transactions in Mid-Nineteenth Century England', in G. R. Rubin and D. Sugarman (eds), *Law, Economy and Society, 1750–1914: Essays in the History of English Law* (Abingdon, 1984), 192–208.
——and A. C. Page, 'The Development of Investor Protection in Britain', *International Journal of the Sociology of Law*, 12 (1984), 287–305.
Ferris, Graham, 'Larceny: Debating the "Boundless Region of Dishonesty"', in Judith Rowbotham and Kim Stevenson (eds), *Criminal Conversations: Victorian Crimes, Social Panic, and Moral Outrage* (Columbus, OH, 2005), 70–86.
Fifoot, C. H. S., *Judge and Jurist in the Reign of Victoria* (London, 1959).
Fisher, D. R. (ed.), *History of Parliament: The House of Commons, 1820–1832*, 7 vols (Cambridge, 2009).
Fisher, Jonathan, et al., 'Economic Crime and the Global Financial Crisis', *Law and Financial Markets Review* (July 2011), 276–89.
Freedeman, Charles E., *Joint-Stock Enterprise in France, 1807–1867: From Privileged Company to Modern Corporation* (Chapel Hill, NC, 1979).
Freeman, Mark, Robin Pearson, and James Taylor, *Shareholder Democracies? Corporate Governance in Britain and Ireland before 1850* (Chicago, IL, 2012).
French, E. A., *Unlimited Liability: The Case of the City of Glasgow Bank* (London, 1985).
Garnett, Jane, 'Commercial Ethics: A Victorian Perspective on the Practice of Theory', in Christopher Cowton and Roger Crisp (eds), *Business Ethics: Perspectives on the Practice of Theory* (Oxford, 1998), 117–38.
Gatrell, V. A. C., 'Crime, Authority and the Policeman-State', in F. M. L. Thompson (ed.), *The Cambridge Social History of Britain, 1750–1950*, 3 vols (Cambridge, 1990).
Getzler, Joshua, *A History of Water Rights at Common Law* (Oxford, 2004), 243–310.
Godfrey, Barry, 'Changing Prosecution Practices and their Impact on Crime Figures, 1857–1940', *British Journal of Criminology*, 48 (2008), 171–89.
——and John P. Locker, 'The Nineteenth-Century Decline of Custom, and its Impact on Theories of "Workplace Theft" and "White Collar" Crime', *Northern History*, 38 (2001), 261–73.
Griffiths, Dennis, *Plant Here the Standard* (London, 1996).
Guinnane, Timothy, et al., 'Putting the Corporation in its Place', *Enterprise and Society*, 8 (2007), 687–729.
Handler, Phil, 'Forgery and the End of the "Bloody Code" in Early Nineteenth-Century England', *Historical Journal*, 48 (2005), 683–702.
Hannah, Leslie, 'Pioneering Modern Corporate Governance: A View from London in 1900', *Enterprise & Society*, 8 (2007), 642–86.
Hansen, Per H., 'Introduction: Special Issue on Scandals and Panics', *Business History Review*, 83 (2009), 1–7.

Harling, Philip, *The Waning of Old Corruption: The Politics of Economical Reform in Britain, 1779–1846* (Oxford, 1996).

Harris, Ron, 'The Bubble Act: Its Passage and Its Effects on Business Organization', *Journal of Economic History*, 54 (1994), 610–27.

—— 'Political Economy, Interest Groups, Legal Institutions, and the Repeal of the Bubble Act in 1825', *Economic History Review*, 50 (1997), 675–96.

—— *Industrializing English Law: Entrepreneurship and Business Organization, 1720–1844* (Cambridge, 2000).

Hay, Douglas, et al., *Albion's Fatal Tree: Crime and Society in Eighteenth-Century England* (London, 1976).

—— 'Prosecution and Power: Malicious Prosecution in the English Courts, 1750–1850', in D. Hay and F. Snyder (eds), *Policing and Prosecution in Britain, 1750–1850* (Oxford, 1989), 343–95.

——, and Francis Synder 'Using the Criminal Law, 1750–1850: Policing, Private Prosecution, and the State', in D. Hay and F. Snyder (eds), *Policing and Prosecution in Britain, 1750–1850* (Oxford, 1989), 3–52.

—— (eds), *Policing and Prosecution in Britain, 1750–1850* (Oxford, 1989).

Hickson, Charles R., and John D. Turner, 'The Genesis of Corporate Governance: Nineteenth-Century Irish Joint-Stock Banks', *Business History*, 47 (2005), 174–89.

Hilt, Eric, 'Wall Street's First Corporate Governance Crisis: The Panic of 1826', Working Paper 14892, National Bureau of Economic Research (2009).

Hilton, Boyd, *The Age of Atonement: The Influence of Evangelicalism on Social and Economic Thought, 1785–1865* (Oxford, 1988; repr. 2001).

Holdsworth, William, *A History of English Law*, 17 vols (London, 1922–66).

Hopkins, Eric, *Working-Class Self-Help in Nineteenth-Century England* (London, 1995).

Hoppit, Julian, 'Financial Crises in Eighteenth-Century England', *Economic History Review*, 39 (1986), 39–58.

—— *A Land of Liberty? England, 1689–1727* (Oxford, 2000).

Horne, H. Oliver, *A History of Savings Banks* (London, 1947).

Hunt, Bishop Carleton, *The Development of the Business Corporation in England, 1800–1867* (Cambridge, MA, 1936).

Hyman, Alan, *The Rise and Fall of Horatio Bottomley* (London, 1972).

Innes, Joanna, and John Styles, 'The Crime Wave: Recent Writing on Crime and Criminal Justice in Eighteenth-Century England', in Adrian Wilson (ed.), *Rethinking Social History: English Society 1570–1920 and its Interpretation* (Manchester, 1993), 201–65.

Ireland, Paddy, 'Capitalism without the Capitalist: The Joint Stock Company Share and the Emergence of the Modern Doctrine of Separate Corporate Personality', *Legal History*, 17 (1996), 40–72.

Ireland, Richard W., 'Sanctity, Superstition and the Death of Sarah Jacob', in A. Musson and C. Stebbings (eds), *Making Legal History: Approaches and Methodology* (Cambridge, 2012), 284–302.

Itzkowitz, David C., 'Fair Enterprise or Extravagant Speculation: Investment, Speculation, and Gambling in Victorian England', *Victorian Studies*, 45 (2002), 121–47.

Jack, Sybil, and Adrian Jack, 'Nineteenth-Century Lawyers and Railway Capitalism: Historians and the Use of Legal Cases', *Legal History*, 24 (2003), 59–85.

Jefferys, J. B., 'Trends in Business Organisation in Great Britain since 1856', PhD thesis, London University, 1938.

—— 'The Denomination and Character of Shares, 1855–1885', *Economic History Review*, 16 (1946), 45–55.

Jeremy, David J. (ed.), *Dictionary of Business Biography*, 5 vols (London, 1984–6).

Johnson, Paul, 'Civilizing Mammon: Laws, Morals and the City in Nineteenth-Century England', in Peter Burke, Brian Harrison, and Paul Slack (eds), *Civil Histories: Essays Presented to Sir Keith Thomas* (Oxford, 2000), 301–19.

——*Making the Market: Victorian Origins of Corporate Capitalism* (Cambridge, 2010).

Johnstone, Peter, 'Serious White Collar Fraud: Historical and Contemporary Perspectives', *Crime, Law & Social Change*, 30 (1999), 107–30.

Juxon, John, *Lewis and Lewis* (London, 1983).

Keymer, Thomas, 'Parliamentary Printing, Paper Credit, and Corporate Fraud: A New Episode in Richardson's Early Career', *Eighteenth-Century Fiction*, 17 (2005), 183–206.

King, Peter, *Crime, Justice, and Discretion in England, 1740–1820* (Oxford, 2000).

Kostal, R. W., *Law and English Railway Capitalism, 1825–1875* (rev. repr., Oxford, 1997).

Kynaston, David, *The City of London: Volume 1, A World of Its Own, 1815–1890* (London, 1994).

Lee, T. A., F. Clarke, and G. Dean, 'The Dominant Senior Manager and the Reasonably Careful, Skilful, and Cautious Auditor', *Critical Perspectives on Accounting*, 19 (2008), 677–711.

Lemire, Beverly, *The Business of Everyday Life: Gender, Practice and Social Politics in England, c. 1600–1900* (Manchester, 2005).

Lester, V. Markham, *Victorian Insolvency: Bankruptcy, Imprisonment for Debt, and Company Winding-up in Nineteenth-Century England* (Oxford, 1995).

Levi, Michael, *The Phantom Capitalists: The Organization and Control of Long-Firm Fraud* (London, 1981).

Lobban, Michael, *The Common Law and English Jurisprudence, 1760–1850* (Oxford, 1991).

——'Nineteenth Century Frauds in Company Formation: *Derry v. Peek* in Context', *Law Quarterly Review*, 112 (1996), 287–334.

——'Misrepresentation', in *Oxford History of the Laws of England*, xii. (Oxford, 2003–), 400–32.

——'Joint Stock Companies', in *Oxford History of the Laws of England*, xii. (Oxford, 2003–), 613–73.

——'Commercial Morality and the Common Law: or, Paying the Price of Fraud in the Later Nineteenth Century', in Margot Finn, Michael Lobban, and Jenny Bourne Taylor (eds), *Legitimacy and Illegitimacy in Nineteenth-Century Law, Literature, and History* (Basingstoke, 2010), 119–47.

——'The Politics of English Law in the Nineteenth Century', in Paul Brand and Joshua Getzler (eds), *Judges and Judging in the History of the Common Law and Civil Law: From Antiquity to Modern Times* (Cambridge, 2012), 102–37.

Locker, John P., and Barry Godfrey, 'Ontological Boundaries and Temporal Watersheds in the Development of White-Collar Crime', *British Journal of Criminology*, 46 (2006), 976–92.

MacCulloch, Diarmaid, *Reformation: Europe's House Divided, 1490–1700* (London, 2003).

McEldowney, John, 'Crown Prosecutions in Nineteenth-Century Ireland', in D. Hay and F. Snyder (eds), *Policing and Prosecution in Britain, 1750–1850*, (Oxford, 1989), 427–56.

McGowen, Randall, 'From Pillory to Gallows: The Punishment of Forgery in the Age of the Financial Revolution', *Past & Present*, 165 (1999), 107–40.

——'Making the "Bloody Code"? Forgery Legislation in Eighteenth-Century England', in Norma Landau (ed.), *Law, Crime and English Society, 1660–1830* (Cambridge, 2004), 117–38.

——'Managing the Gallows: The Bank of England and the Death Penalty, 1797–1821', *Law and History Review*, 25 (2007), 241–82.

McKie, David, *Jabez: The Rise and Fall of a Victorian Rogue* (rev. repr., London, 2005).

McLynn, Frank, *Crime and Punishment in Eighteenth-Century England* (1989; repr. London, 2002).

McQueen, Rob, *A Social History of Company Law: Great Britain and the Australian Colonies, 1854–1920* (Farnham, 2009).

Madge, Nic, 'Summing Up: A Judge's Perspective', *Criminal Law Review* (September, 2006), 817–27.

Manley, P. S., 'Gerard Lee Bevan and the City Equitable Companies', *Abacus*, 9 (1973), 107–15.

Mannheim, Hermann, *Criminal Justice and Social Reconstruction* (1946; repr. London, 2001).

Matthews, Derek, *A History of Auditing: The Changing Audit Process in Britain from the Nineteenth Century to the Present Day* (London, 2006).

Michie, Ranald, *The London Stock Exchange: A History* (Oxford, 2001).

——*Guilty Money: The City of London in Victorian and Edwardian Culture, 1815–1914* (London, 2009).

Mitchell, Dennis J., *Cross and Tory Democracy: A Political Biography of Richard Assheton Cross* (New York, 1991).

Morgan, Edward Victor, *The Theory and Practice of Central Banking, 1797–1913* (Cambridge, 1943).

Morrah, Dermot, *A History of Industrial Life Assurance* (Abingdon, 2006).

Moss, David, 'Business and Banking: Ethics and White-Collar Crime in Norwich, 1825–1831', *Albion*, 29 (1997), 373–98.

Mouat, Jeremy, 'Whitaker Wright, Speculative Finance, and the London Mining Boom of the 1890s', in Raymond E. Dumett (ed.), *Mining Tycoons in the Age of Empire, 1870–1945: Entrepreneurship, High Finance, Politics and Territorial Expansion* (Farnham, 2009), 127–50.

Musson, Anthony, and Chantal Stebbings (eds), *Making Legal History: Approaches and Methodology* (Cambridge, 2012).

Mutch, Alistair, 'Theology, Accountability and Management: Exploring the Contributions of Scottish Presbyterianism', *Organization*, 19 (2012), 363–79.

Nash, Thomas Arthur, *The Life of Richard Lord Westbury*, 2 vols (London, 1888).

Ó Gráda, Cormac, 'The Early History of Irish Savings Banks', Working Paper WP08/04, University College Dublin Centre for Economic Research (2008).

——'Savings Banks, Famine and Financial Contagion: Ireland in the 1840s and 1850s', *Irish Economic and Social History*, 36 (2009), 21–36.

O'Shea, James, *Prince of Swindlers: John Sadleir M.P. 1813–1856* (Dublin, 1999).

Oldham, James, 'Special Juries in England: Nineteenth-Century Usage and Reform', *Journal of Legal History*, 8 (1987), 148–66.

Ollerenshaw, Philip, *Banking in Nineteenth-Century Ireland: The Belfast Banks, 1925–1914* (Manchester, 1987).

Ormerod, David, *Smith and Hogan's Criminal Law* (13th edn, Oxford, 2011).

Oxford Dictionary of National Biography [online] <http://www.oxforddnb.com>.

Paul, Helen Julia, 'Politicians and Public Reaction to the South Sea Bubble: Preaching to the Converted?', *Discussion Papers in Economics and Econometrics, no. 923*, School of Social Sciences, University of Southampton, 2009.

Pearson, Robin, 'Shareholder Democracies? English Stock Companies and the Politics of Corporate Governance during the Industrial Revolution', *English Historical Review*, 117 (2002), 840–66.

Pitt-Lewis, G., *Commissioner Kerr: An Individuality* (London, 1903).

Porter, Dilwyn, 'City Editors and the Modern Investing Public: Establishing the Integrity of the New Financial Journalism in Late Nineteenth-Century London', *Media History*, 4 (1998), 49–60.

—— '"Speciousness is the Bucketeer's Watchword and Outrageous Effrontery his Capital": Financial Bucket Shops in the City of London, *c.* 1880–1939', in John Benson and Laura Ugolini (eds), *Cultures of Selling: Perspectives on Consumption and Society since 1700* (Aldershot, 2006), 103–26.

Preda, Alex, *Framing Finance: The Boundaries of Markets and Modern Capitalism* (Chicago, IL, 2009).

Reed, John R., 'A Friend to Mammon: Speculation in Victorian Literature', *Victorian Studies*, 27 (1984), 179–202.

Reid, Jean Margo, 'Judicial Intervention in Accounting Behavior: A Reevaluation of the Nineteenth-Century Experience', *Journal of Accounting and Public Policy*, 6 (1987), 9–34.

Robb, George, *White-Collar Crime in Modern England: Financial Fraud and Business Morality, 1845–1929* (Cambridge, 1992).

Rock, David, 'Victorian Globalization in Microcosm: The Rise and Fall of Jabez Spencer Balfour', in Fernando López-Alves and Diane E. Johnson (eds), *Globalization and Uncertainty in Latin America* (New York, 2007), 27–46.

Rock, Paul, 'Victims, Prosecutors and the State in Nineteenth Century England and Wales', *Criminal Justice*, 4 (2004), 331–54.

Rosenblum, Leo, 'The Failure of the City of Glasgow Bank', *Accounting Review*, 8 (1933), 285–91.

Rowbotham, Judith, and Kim Stevenson (eds), *Criminal Conversations: Victorian Crimes, Social Panic, and Moral Outrage* (Columbus, OH, 2005).

Rozenberg, Joshua, *The Case for the Crown: The Inside Story of the Director of Public Prosecutions* (Wellingborough, 1987).

Rubin, G. R., and David Sugarman (eds), *Law, Economy and Society, 1750–1914: Essays in the History of English Law* (Abingdon, 1984).

Rutterford, Janette, 'The Shareholder Voice: British and American Accents, 1890–1965', *Enterprise and Society*, 13 (2012), 120–53.

Ryan, Roger, 'Banking and Insurance', in Carole Rawcliffe and Richard Wilson (eds), *Norwich since 1550* (London, 2004), 361–84.

Safley, Thomas Max, 'Business Failure and Civil Scandal in Early Modern Europe', *Business History Review*, 83 (2009), 35–60.

Saville, Richard, *Bank of Scotland: A History, 1695–1995* (Edinburgh, 1996).

Seaman, L. C. B., *Victorian England: Aspects of English and Imperial History, 1837–1901* (London, 1973).

Searle, G. R., *Morality and the Market in Victorian Britain* (Oxford, 1998).

Shannon, H. A., 'The First Five Thousand Limited Companies and their Duration', *Economic History*, 3 (1932), 396–424.

—— 'The Limited Companies of 1866–1883', *Economic History Review*, 4 (1933), 290–316.

Simpson, A. W. Brian, *Leading Cases in the Common Law* (Oxford, 1995).

—— *Victorian Law and the Industrial Spirit* (London, 1995).

Sindall, Rob, 'Middle-Class Crime in Nineteenth-Century England', *Criminal Justice History*, 4 (1983), 23–40.

Smith, Keith, 'The Trial: Adversarial Characteristics and Responsibilities; Pre-trial and Trial Procedures', in *Oxford History of the Laws of England*, xiii (Oxford, 2003–), 58–121.

Snow, Jon, 'Why Have No Bankers Been Arrested?' 13 September 2011 <http://blogs.channel4.com/snowblog/bankers-arrested/16148>.

Stebbings, Chantal, *The Private Trustee in Victorian England* (Cambridge, 2002).

—— 'Benefits and Barriers: The Making of Victorian Legal History', in A. Musson and C. Stebbings (eds), *Making Legal History: Approaches and Methodology* (Cambridge, 2012), 72–87.

Stephen, James Fitzjames, *A History of the Criminal Law of England*, 3 vols (1883; repr. Abingdon, 1996).

Sugarman, David, and G. R. Rubin, 'Towards a New History of Law and Material Society in England, 1750–1914', in G. R. Rubin and D. Sugarman (eds), *Law, Economy and Society, 1750–1914: Essays in the History of English Law* (Abingdon, 1984), 1–123.

Summers, Ben, 'The Fraud Act 2006: Has It Had Any Impact?', *Amicus Curiae*, 75 (Autumn 2008), 10–18.

Sutherland, John, *The Stanford Companion to Victorian Fiction* (Stanford, CA, 1989).

Symons, Julian, *Horatio Bottomley* (London, 1955).

Taggart, Michael, *Private Property and Abuse of Rights in Victorian England: The Story of Edward Pickles and the Bradford Water Supply* (Oxford, 2002).

Tarn, John Nelson, *Five Per Cent Philanthropy: An Account of Housing in Urban Areas between 1840 and 1914* (Cambridge, 1973).

Taylor, James, 'Commercial Fraud and Public Men in Victorian Britain', *Historical Research*, 78 (2005), 230–52.

—— 'Business in Pictures: Representations of Railway Enterprise in the Satirical Press in Britain, 1845–1870', *Past & Present*, 189 (2005), 111–45.

—— *Creating Capitalism: Joint-Stock Enterprise in British Politics and Culture, 1800–1870* (Woodbridge, 2006).

—— 'Company Fraud in Victorian Britain: The Royal British Bank Scandal of 1856', *English Historical Review*, 122 (2007), 700–24.

—— 'Numbers, Character and Trust in Early Victorian Britain: The Independent West Middlesex Fire and Life Assurance Company Fraud', in Tom Crook and Glen O'Hara (eds), *Statistics and the Public Sphere: Numbers and the People in Modern Britain, c. 1800–2000* (New York, 2011), 185–202.

—— 'Watchdogs or Apologists? Financial Journalism and Company Fraud in Early Victorian Britain', *Historical Research*, 85 (2012), 632–50.

Thomas, S. Evelyn, *The Rise and Growth of Joint Stock Banking* (London, 1934).

Thomas, W. A., *The Provincial Stock Exchanges* (London, 1973).

Thompson, E. P., *Whigs and Hunters: The Origin of the Black Act* (London, 1975).

Thorne, Roland G. (ed.), *History of Parliament: The House of Commons 1790–1820*, 5 vols (London, 1986).

Tolmie, Fiona M., *Corporate and Personal Insolvency Law* (2nd edn, London, 2003).

Turner, John D., '"The Last Acre and Sixpence": Views on Bank Liability Regimes in Nineteenth-Century Britain', *Financial History Review*, 16 (2009), 111–27.

Vander Weyer, Martin, *Fortune's Spear: The Story of the Blue-Blooded Rogue Behind the Most Notorious City Scandal of the 1920s* (London, 2011).

Vincent, David, *The Culture of Secrecy: Britain, 1832–1998* (Oxford, 1998).

Walker, Stephen P., 'More Sherry and Sandwiches? Incrementalism and the Regulation of Late Victorian Bank Auditing', *Accounting History* 3 (1998), 33–54.
Weiss, Barbara, *The Hell of the English: Bankruptcy and the Victorian Novel* (Cranbury, NJ, 1986).
White, Lawrence H., 'Free Banking in Scotland before 1844', in Kevin Dowd (ed.), *The Experience of Free Banking* (London, 1992), 157–86.
Wiener, Martin J., *Reconstructing the Criminal: Culture, Law, and Policy in England, 1830–1914* (Cambridge, 1990).
Wilson, Sarah, 'In Defence of Respectability: Financial Crime, the "High Art" Criminal and the Language of the Courtroom, 1850–1880', in Ian Inkster (ed.), *The Golden Age: Essays in British Social and Economic History, 1850–1870* (Aldershot, 2000), 199–215.
—— 'Law, Morality and Regulation: Victorian Experiences of Financial Crime', *British Journal of Criminology*, 46 (2006), 1073–90.
—— 'Fraud and White-Collar Crime: 1850 to the Present', in Anne-Marie Kilday and David Nash (eds), *Histories of Crime: Britain, 1600–2000* (London, 2010), 141–59.
Zedner, Lucia, *Criminal Justice* (Oxford, 2004).

Index